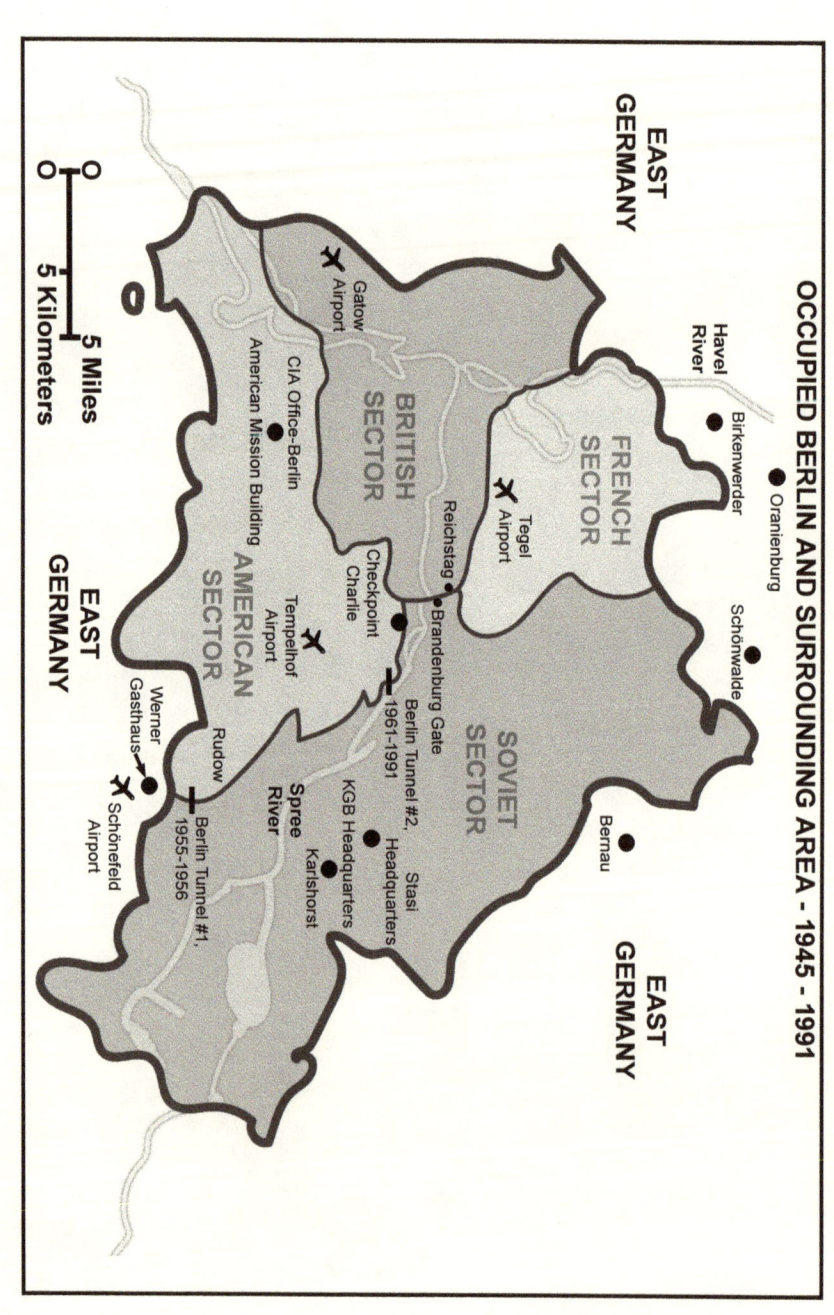

THE COLD WAR BEGINS

SECOND VOLUME OF THE
THE BERLIN TUNNEL TRILOGY

ROGER L. LILES

First Edition
Copyright © 2019 Roger Liles
San Diego, California

FBI Anti-Piracy Warning:

The unauthorized reproduction or distribution of a copyrighted work is illegal. Criminal copyright infringement, including infringement without monetary gain, is investigated by the FBI and is punishable by up to five years in federal prison and a fine of $ 250,000. Advertencia Antipirateria del FBI: La reproducción o distribución no autorizada de una obra protegida por derechos de autor es ilegal. La infracción criminal de los derechos de autor, incluyendo la infracción sin lucro monetario, es investigada por el FBI y es castigable con pena de hasta cinco años en prisión federal y una multa de $ 250,000.

The Cold War Begins
Second Volume of the Berlin Tunnel Trilogy

First Edition
Copyright © 2019 Roger Liles

All rights reserved. No part of this book may be used or reproduced in any manner whatsoever, including Internet usage, without written permission from the author.

This story is a work of fiction. References to real people, events, establishments, organizations, or locales are intended only to provide a sense of authenticity and are used fictitiously. All other characters, and all incidents and dialogue are drawn from the author's imagination and are not to be construed as real.

Library of Congress Cataloging-in-Publication Data
LCCN: 202090402

Paperback ISBN: 978-0-9724449-5-8
Hardcover ISBN: 978-0-9724449-6-5

DEDICATION

This book is dedicated to the American, British, and French military forces who were stationed in Berlin, right on the front lines of the Cold War from 1945 through 1994. If a war had started in Europe, Berlin would have fallen in hours; they and their families would have been immediately captured or killed. Today, many of the buildings they lived and worked in have been abandoned and are now weed-infested ruins. Others, perhaps most of those structures they knew have been torn down and replaced with something that the new vibrant city of Berlin needed. Tempelhof Airport has been turned into a park commemorating those who resupplied the city by air in 1948-1949.

The book is also dedicated to the numerous CIA agents who risked their lives in Berlin and Germany trying to counter communist plans to conquer the world. Hundreds of nonfiction books and millions of newly released documents reveal the extent of their activities. I have used a small bit of that information to generate this work of fiction; I can only hope that it has the ring of truth.

Lastly, I would like to dedicate this book to the thousands of Germans and other nationalities including a few Russians who risked their freedom and lives as well as that of their relatives and friends to spy on the communists in the Soviet Union, Warsaw Pact countries, and East Germany. The information they provided ultimately helped destroy communism in Europe.

"From Stettin on the Baltic to Trieste on the Adriatic an Iron Curtain has descended across the Continent. Behind that line lie all the capitals of the ancient states of Central and Eastern Europe. Warsaw, Berlin, Prague, Vienna, Budapest, Belgrade, Bucharest, and Sofia; all these famous cities and the populations around them lie in what I must call the Soviet sphere."

Winston Churchill in his famous Iron Curtain Speech, 5 March 1946

AUTHOR'S NOTES

Almost one hundred years of relative world peace was shattered in 1914 and again in 1939 with two devastating world wars. Tens of millions of military personnel and civilians on both sides were killed. By 1945, most of the world's population was exhausted by war and craved peace. Over 11 million displaced survivors roamed Europe in search of a meal and shelter.

Because Germany was viewed as being directly responsible for both conflicts, the Allies demanded it surrender unconditionally. In May 1945, the Four Powers—the French, British, Americans, and Russians—began to take over their agreed-to areas of occupation in that country.

Joseph Stalin, the leader of the Soviet Union, decided to take advantage of the instability caused by the second war to further the communist goal of world domination. When hostilities ended, Soviet troops occupied most of central Europe. Using rigged elections, palace coups, outright force, and even murder, the Soviets began imposing communist regimes on Poland, Czechoslovakia, Romania, Bulgaria, Hungary, and of course, East Germany.

In his Iron Curtain Speech, Winston Churchill noted that a new era had started less than a year after World War II hostilities ended. This new era would last for the next forty-three years. It is best characterized as a confrontation between two radically different political, social, and economic ideologies for control of the world—America and the Free World versus Russia and the Communist World. This conflict is known in history as THE COLD WAR.

It was given this name, because with few exceptions—Korea and

Vietnam—this was not a shooting war. America and her allies sought to contain communist expansion using every means short of war. In addition to a massive arms buildup, this is the era of spy versus spy. Much like a chess match, one side would seek an advantage and the other would attempt to counter that move with one of its own.

*

Conversations between characters in this novel are in both English and German. In English, contractions are used for informal conversations and there are no familiar verb forms. In German, there are no contractions and the familiar form is used in everyday conversations with close business associates, friends, and relatives. The main characters in this novel speak both English and German fluently and switch from one to the other. Thus, if a conversation appears stiff and formal, it is in German. The presence of contractions in a sentence means that they are conversing in English.

FOREWORD

Late in 1944, troops of the Soviet Union began arriving in territory which had been part of Germany for thousands of years. Russian generals ordered their men to "rape every German female from seven years of age to seventy as revenge for what they did to us." These troops did just that as they also murdered and pillaged their way through cities, towns, and villages on their way to their ultimate target—Berlin. Ahead of the Russians, a huge wave of refugees fled west. Millions of other residents of the East stayed in their homes, waiting for the inevitable end of hostilities, dreaming of peace. Little did they realize that they would soon be living in a communist state.

As the Cold War between East and West commences, so does our story. The setting is war-ravaged Berlin in late 1946. From that devastated and divided city, spies from both sides began to move with relative ease throughout occupied Germany. America and its allies needed to determine the composition and deployment locations of the military forces Russia had moved into the very heart of Western Europe. The Russians worked diligently to deny the Western Powers knowledge of their intentions and strategies while consolidating their position in their new vassal state—East Germany. The communist satellites in Eastern Europe served as a buffer from future invasions and a springboard for communist expansion into the rest of Europe.

Recently declassified documents have revealed the true nature and extent of the spy versus spy conflict that occurred from the mid-1940s through the early-1990s between the American CIA and British MI6 on one side and the Russian KGB and GRU (plus eventually the East German Stasi) on the other.

This work of fiction is based on real people and events, which reveal how

Berlin was at the very center of a huge game with global consequences. My first novel in this series, *The Berlin Tunnel—A Cold War Thriller,* describes spy versus spy interactions in Berlin in 1960 and 1961; the period before, during and after the closing of the Berlin Wall and the Berlin Crisis. In this prequel, Kurt Altschuler, who was a supporting character in the original novel, takes center stage as the main protagonist.

*

In the years immediately after World War II, many people living in East Germany became disaffected with the controlled economy, suspension of personal liberties, and arbitrary government intrusion into all aspects of life imposed on them by communist Russia. Each year, between 100,000 and 300,000 East Germans rejected that system by emigrating to West Germany through a simple route; they bought a train ticket to East Berlin and took the subway train to West Berlin. At most, they managed to take one or two suitcases with them—but they were free. Good, high-paying jobs were readily available for them in the West.

Most people stayed in East Germany. Some were dedicated communists determined to make that system work. Others, certainly the majority, decided to live within this new system because home, family, and other ties made them reluctant to leave. A few heroes among them determined at some point that they would help undermine the communists, providing western intelligence agencies a ready cadre of informants and operatives throughout Berlin and East Germany.

Too little is remembered of the contribution these men and women made to world peace and the ultimate downfall of communism in Europe. Newly released, once highly-classified documents provide limited information about what they did and who they were. Details of their motivations and their successes or failures have been lost in time. Many were arrested by communist counter-spy agencies—the Stasi, KGB, or GRU and summarily executed. The survivors grew old, waiting for the communist domination of Eastern Europe and East Germany to end. This novel is to a great extent their story—they are now very old or have passed from the scene. But they made a very substantial contribution to the formation of a reunited Germany, prosperous united Europe, and the relative peace we all enjoy today.

PART 1

1946-1950

"A tough struggle is going on in back alleys all over the world in which no quarter is asked and none given."

— Dean Rusk, U.S. Secretary of State, 1961-1969, speaking on the important role espionage and counter-espionage played in the Cold War.

CHAPTER 1

Kurt
Sunday, November 19, 1961

I HAVE BEEN in Berlin on the front lines of the Cold War almost continuously for the last 15 years. Earlier today, I had an armed confrontation with the East German Secret Police (Stasi) in an abandoned warehouse in East Berlin and was severely wounded. Now, I'm the only person involved in the shootout who is still alive. I'm slowly dying, but if somehow I survive, my superiors in the American Central Intelligence Agency (CIA) will demand that I tell them how the shoot-out occurred and why Thomas Lane, my fellow CIA agent, was killed. By the way, my name is Kurt Altschuler.

Is the story I'm going to tell them entirely true? No! But I hope it is close enough to the facts revealed by the physical evidence around me to hide what happened. If my version is not believed, my close friends and I might be tried in a court of law and sent to prison.

As I tell my version of what happened to my superiors, I will be interrupted with an almost constant barrage of questions. That will mean that my story must be consistent and believable.

My story would start something like this; "We were preparing to reseal the tunnel after the extraction of the husband and wife double agents and their family. You all have the required security clearance to know the why of the tunnel—it was built into East Berlin so that American intelligence agencies could tap into the communications between communist East

Germany, Warsaw Pact, and Russian military and political leaders. During the tunnel's construction, the top of an East Berlin storm drain was severed and resealed. By reopening that portal, we had unfettered access to that area of abandoned factories and warehouses in southeastern Berlin. We had brought our double agents to the West via that route earlier in the day.

"Thomas Lane, my boss returned to the building where the tunnel entrance was located and requested that I take him through the entire extraction process. I objected, explaining that it would be best to just reseal the tunnel—a process that would take several hours. He insisted and I eventually relented and took him down through the tunnel which runs under the River Spree. We used a hole in the tunnel floor to enter the storm drain. After a quarter of a mile walk, I pushed up a manhole cover. We entered the courtyard of a derelict factory.

"We walked several blocks to a ramshackle vehicle-tire warehouse that had been abandoned since the end of World War II. This is where I had met the double agents earlier that day. During this needless excursion, I figured out what Thomas Lane was doing—he wanted these details to claim that he had personally conducted the harrowing extraction of the eight people in the double agent's group. This might help him get the promotion I knew he craved.

This assertion would certainly get the attention of my superiors. Perhaps this would divert them from asking questions I did not want to answer.

"As I was showing him the exact spot where I met that group, three Stasi Agents, guns drawn, entered the driveway that led to the loading dock we were standing on. They must have seen us as we walked into this building. Perhaps they had been following our double agents earlier, had lost them, but had not given up their search.

"We ignored their orders to stop, entered the loading dock door to the warehouse, and drew our weapons. I took a position behind a steel pillar. Agent Lane crawled over and eventually took cover behind a low wall on the loading dock itself. He took the firing stance we had been taught in CIA weapons training; he knelt on his right knee and took his weapon in both hands. We both tensed, feeling the adrenalin rush that always occurs before an impending encounter with the enemy.

"Both of us were armed with the standard CIA-issued weapon—

the Browning Special semi-automatic pistol. It's an exceptional weapon because the energy of each fired cartridge automatically advances the next available cartridge into position for firing.

Here I was currying my superior's favor by bragging about CIA agents' training and weapons.

"The Stasi spread out and took turns scrambling from the protection of one piece of discarded junk to the next. Soon they were halfway across the loading dock's broad driveway. Following standard CIA tactics, we waited until we could pin all three of them down before we fired our first shot. The sun was just setting. Their vehicle was undoubtedly equipped with a two-way radio and they could have retreated and called for help. Their leader had decided that he'd best conclude the confrontation quickly. Darkness might give us a chance to escape.

"Eventually, Thomas pointed and gestured for me to cover the two Stasi on the left. He took aim where he expected the man on our right to expose himself on his next move forward. I heard Thomas fire his weapon twice. A deafening BANG-BANG occurred and out of the corner of my eye, I saw the barrel of his weapon jerk up slightly each time. Someone cried out the word '*Scheisse*' ('*shit!*'), followed by an almost imperceptible thud as he hit the ground. The smell of cordite filled the air and my ears rang.

"I remember thinking at the time, *one down, two to go*. I was both surprised and amazed that Lane who has no field experience was performing well.

"Both of us now turned our weapons toward the surviving two Stasi Agents. Through hand signals the two of us agreed that I would cover the Stasi agent on our left; he the one on the right.

"Unfortunately, the Stasi agents used the muzzle flashes from Thomas' weapon to determine where he was. Using hand signals, they both fired several rounds at us. One hit my metal post with a reverberating thud; another hit the metal door frame next to me, glanced off and continued to ricochet off surfaces in the warehouse itself. Thomas stayed behind the low wall. I used a slot in my post to observe and report their movements to him. When one exposed himself, I fired three rounds at him. He quickly scrambled back to his original position.

"At this point, I whispered loud enough for Thomas to hear—'We've got them pinned down.' He gave me a thumbs up. We both realized that if they tried to advance or retreat, they would have to expose themselves; thus, we just needed to wait for them to take action because we had the tactical advantage of looking down on them from an elevated platform."

"For a few minutes, neither side did anything. Then suddenly, one Stasi agent fired a whole clip of bullets from what was probably the Stasi standard arm—the Walther PPK Pistole-38nl. The other Stasi waited for us to expose ourselves, hoping he could take one of us out. Then the other fired his clip, still trying to get a reaction. They repeated this tactic. We held our fire—primarily because we each only had a single spare clip and were safe behind our barriers.

"In the silence that followed this failed tactic, Thomas deliberately took aim and fired two more shots at the man he had taken down earlier, I was surprised; the man had been lying motionless on the ground for some time. Then I remembered our training—'Make sure a dead man is dead—if you don't you'll be the dead man.'

"The Walther PPK has a magazine which holds only 10 rounds. Our Stasi friends had obviously brought several extra clips with them but were now apparently conserving their ammunition. At this point, I was certain we were winning; we just had to be patient. We needed to get back to the tunnel so it could be sealed, but had to be exceedingly careful not to expose its existence to the Stasi. The intercept site that was associated with the tunnel had been described by Secretary of Defense McNamara as 'A national treasure of inestimable value.'

"It was a good thing that the two in front of us were pinned down; otherwise, they would have radioed for help. Then I realized that if they did not check in soon, help would probably be dispatched to determine what had happened to them. Also, there was a possibility—although the immediate area seemed to be deserted—someone might hear the gunfire and telephone the East German Peoples Police (VoPos).

"Fortunately, at this point, the two Stasi Agents decided to extract themselves from their tenuous position. They fired numerous rounds at us and began to retreat, seeking shelter in the process. Eventually, we were able to hit them both. Thomas advanced, intending to ensure that they were both dead. One of the men was still alive, managed to raise his weapon quickly, and shot Thomas at close range. I was so intent on taking the surviving Stasi agent out, I foolishly exposed myself. Just as I fired, so did he. I was shot in the abdomen. The throbbing, searing pain surprised me.

"Nauseated, I fell back onto a nearby bench. Focusing through the pain, I realized I had to stop the blood flow. The bullet had made a small hole in my abdomen, which was hardly bleeding. But my back was soaked around the exit wound. I removed my overcoat and tied my suit coat tightly around my mid-section, almost fainting from the pain and exertion. That seemed to have stopped the bleeding; now I needed to start the ten-minute walk back to my friends and the safety of the storm drain and tunnel. Lane was beyond help. I could see from where I was that the bullet had taken off part of his head.

"Sensing moisture again, I put my hand in the small of my back and thought to myself, *I'm still losing a lot of blood. Calm yourself…calm down…you've got to reduce blood loss…but how? Maybe if I get on my back, my overcoat and body weight can stanch the flow.*

"After several futile attempts to stand-up, I managed a painful and uncoordinated lurch to my knees and then the floor. I struggled but finally succeeded in getting my bunched-up overcoat beneath me. The bleeding seemed to lessen. I tried to relax—conserve my energy and think of a way out of this mess.

"Even though it was a cold night, I started sweating; my throat went dry, and I became thirsty…so thirsty. Recognizing the signs, I knew what was happening. In the war, I'd seen several people die from stomach wounds.

"Looking at my watch, I said aloud to myself, 'You've just three minutes to get to the tunnel.' Earlier I had told my Air Force friends, 'You must seal the tunnel by 17:00. Don't risk compromising its existence. If I'm not there, I'll find another way to get to West Berlin.'

"It's strange how time passes very slowly when you're dying. I began worrying that the Stasi would show up and capture me. If I don't talk, they will turn me over to the KGB for their 'advanced methods.' Eventually everyone talks.

"I decided that death was preferable to torture. Damn, the pain was excruciating as I searched for my Browning Special. Eventually, I found it under my back. Fumbling and then finally picking it up, I put the barrel in my mouth, and with a great effort pulled the trigger. All I heard was a loud CLICK! It was empty. I asked myself how I could have fired thirteen times and tried to count them.

"At this juncture, I remembered I had put an extra clip in my overcoat pocket, but that was wadded up underneath me. I knew that I'd never get to it. I should have brought the cyanide capsule from my desk drawer—that would have been easier and fast.

Barely able to move my arm into view, I checked my watch—17:16. As the pain diminished, I became strangely calm. The blood flow had slowed. That was good; it meant the end was near. I could die knowing the Stasi wouldn't get me, plus my daughter and her mother had escaped.

As I peacefully drifted off, I recalled what someone had once told me, *"Your life flashes before your eyes just before you die."* Smiling, I remembered another person had added, *"So make sure it's worth watching."* In my mind's eye, I could see Ben, the AP photographer, greeting me at the bottom of the metal stairs when I arrived in Berlin in November of 1946—almost exactly fifteen years ago.

CHAPTER 2

Wednesday, November 13, 1946

FOUR HOURS AFTER my propeller-driven, British Overseas Airlines DC-3 left Heathrow, it descended into Gatow Airport in the British Zone of Occupation. The cloud cover cleared as the aircraft passed over the familiar sights of the River Havel and the Wannsee.

The AP's Berlin photographer, Ben Stevens, greeted me at the bottom of the metal stairs, "You must be Kurt Altschuler—Welcome to Berlin."

"Thanks. I don't know if they told you but I was born and raised here in Berlin. I'm anxious to see the city."

"You'll be disappointed. Central Berlin is still a mess. I've reserved a room for you in a pensione in Charlottenburg. Owners of those larger houses and mansions have been forced to take in boarders or divide them into small apartments. The furnished apartments I checked out for you were expensive and fairly shabby."

After we retrieved my luggage, Ben hailed a taxi. Soon he and the driver were negotiating the fare. The driver said, "Elf zigaretten— Eleven cigarettes."

They finally settled on eight as a fair price.

"I've read that the Reichsmarks are essentially worthless and everyone demands American cigarettes as a medium of exchange."

"American-made Chesterfields, Lucky Strikes, and Camels are worth the most," Ben replied. "British Players are a close second. The current going rate is seven Reichsmarks per cigarette. So, we're giving the taxi driver the equivalent of 77 marks for the 20-mile ride into central Berlin. As you can tell, each mark isn't worth much."

"How did cigarettes become the medium of exchange?"

"A significant part of the German population smokes and they are only allowed to purchase forty cigarettes a month at the rationed price—so cigarettes are in significant demand on the black market."

"How did the Reichsmark become so valueless?" I asked.

"At the Potsdam conference, the four victorious powers agreed to use the old Reichsmark as the medium of exchange in all of occupied Germany. In a gesture of goodwill, some American idiot gave the Russians a set of Reichsmark printing plates. They have been using the money they print to pay for everything—tens of billions are now in circulation and no government is guaranteeing its value—as a result, Marks are almost worthless.

Berliners in our zone are allowed to purchase 800 calories worth of near-starvation rations at low fixed prices, but they must barter for enough food to survive. So, they trade antiques, cameras, watches, jewelry, silver, and fine china for cigarettes, the de facto local currency."

"And the cigarettes are straight from the American Post Exchange?"

"Yeah. One of our soldiers can buy a carton of 200 cigarettes for a dollar at the PX and sell it for around 1,000 marks. He can then take the marks and exchange them at the American Express Bank on their bases for $100, which he can ship back to the States in a good old American Postal Money Order. Every month, three times the monthly pay of all of the American military personnel in the occupation forces are being shipped back to the States."

"So, the black market is where everything is bartered or traded for the lowly cigarette?"

"That's correct."

"I don't smoke and didn't think about bringing any with me."

"Don't worry. I have a friend who'll supply both of us," Ben offered.

Our taxi sped into central Berlin on one of the autobahns Hitler had built ten years earlier for the 1936 Olympics. Occasionally, we would have to avoid debris from a destroyed overpass or slow for a hastily repaired section of the road, but otherwise, traffic was light and our trip into the city was quick.

I thought back over the events of the last month and how I'd ended up with a cover as an Associated Press (AP) reporter. My German language skills and a CIA generated resume recounting my exploits as a U.S. Army Information Officer on the front lines in Europe got me the job in Berlin. Only two people in the States knew I worked for the CIA. For my protection, I never went near CIA Headquarters in Washington.

On successive days, I had meetings in New York with a senior CIA agent in a Roosevelt Hotel room, and the AP's European News Chief at their office in Rockefeller Plaza. They both gave me essentially the same instruction—"find out what is going on over there and report it back to us." I had to find out what the Russian military, civilian authorities, and spies were doing, as well as cover the political and economic news in central Europe. Sources and documentation were paramount for both.

Ben interrupted my reverie by pointing out, "As you can see, the west side of Berlin suffered little damage; the bombing and shelling focused on the government and industrial facilities in the central and eastern parts of the city."

Once we left the autobahn, I began to recognize streets and eventually asked the driver, "Please turn right at the next corner and drive slowly down this street."

As we neared my old home, the neighborhood looked the same. Relieved, memories came flooding back—learning to ride a bicycle down the sidewalk along here and playing soccer with my buddy, Jacob, on his front lawn over there.

A minute later, I asked the driver to stop. It was almost surreal—except for the façade, my home was just a pile of burned-out rubble, while the houses on either side were fine.

For years, I'd yearned to return to the vibrant city I'd known in my youth. Now I sat in stunned silence while the taxi drove us to my nearby pensione. Thomas Wolfe's rumination was correct; there is an end to all things, no matter how much we want to hold on to them, "You Can't Go Home Again".

CHAPTER 3

Wednesday, November 13, 1946

AFTER DROPPING MY luggage at the pension, Ben and I walked some distance to a gasthaus, the German equivalent of a tavern or pub. On the way, he handed me a ration card, "You'll need this until you can register at the American Mission. American military and civilian employees eat primarily at government facilities or at home with food they get from the commissary. Those of us who work for American companies get special ration cards allowing us to purchase food in German stores and restaurants at fixed low prices. You present your card and the merchant cuts off a tab, which represents what he's selling to you. He then keeps the tab to prove he legally sold whatever it was."

"Interesting."

"Meat is heavily rationed and most eating establishments scrimp on what and how much they add to your order. They'll serve you, say a quarter pound, about 100 grams of meat, and demand a 200- or 300-gram coupon—so be careful. In any event, what most places serve is an old dairy cow or a hen on its last legs, usually tough as an old boot."

"What would you recommend at the restaurant we're going to?"

"Order the goulash. It'll have some identifiable meat and will be spiced to perfection. You'll also have to give them a tab for 200 grams of noodles, but you'll be surprised how little the meal and a beer will cost. Perhaps nine American cents."

On the way, we passed two attractively-dressed women who gave us the come-hither eye.

"As you would expect, the oldest profession flourishes here," Ben observed. "Most of an entire generation of men are dead, crippled, or in POW camps in Russia. Women need to survive and provide for their families. The Provost Marshall estimates there are almost 200,000 women here in Berlin who prostitute themselves. Some are full time, but most only sell themselves when they need money for necessities. If you're interested, the going price is five cigarettes. A few more, if she's young and attractive."

"Not interested at any price," I said.

"That's probably best, all kinds of venereal diseases are prevalent, and black-market penicillin costs almost $100 per vial," Ben said, as we walked down four steps from street level into the restaurant. It was furnished with a mismatched hodge-podge of chairs and tables. The bar and a few booths at one end of the room were the only original furnishings in what had once been an elegant eating establishment. The host immediately discerned that we were Americans, and courteously led us to the only vacant booth.

"So, how did you end up here?" I asked Ben after we were seated.

"I was a combat photographer in the army. When the chief photographer for *Life* Magazine in Paris offered me a job, I took an overseas discharge. Turns out he didn't have the authority to make the offer."

"But you're here," I exclaimed.

Ben shrugged and smirked. "I went to the AP office in Paris, showed them a few of the photos I'd taken on the front lines. They offered me this job. I arrived here in early July of last year in a convoy with the first Americans to enter Berlin. Several of the photographs I took at that time made the front pages of most daily newspapers back home."

"So, our arrival here was delayed until almost two months after the war ended?"

"Yeah, the Russians intentionally delayed the other occupying forces' move to Berlin."

"Why?"

"They wanted to establish communist control of the whole city. First, they claimed the city was still unsafe, and then they found out we planned to parade our troops under the Brandenburg Gate on July 4th. They had conquered Berlin and didn't want to share the glory with anyone."

"That's almost understandable. As I recall, the Russians suffered 100,000 casualties taking Berlin and over 20 million died during the war."

"That delay was the first of hundreds of examples of them being obstructive over matters large and small," Ben said. "You remember after the war the vision for the future was that the victorious allies would work together in harmony to establish a new world order to prevent future wars and ensure peace."

"Of course."

"Working relationships between the four powers have deteriorated dramatically in the last year and a half," Ben said. "A control commission for Berlin and another for the whole country were supposed to establish policies for governing the Germans until democratic institutions were established. The Russians routinely veto any measure that would interfere with their establishment of a dictatorship in their zone of occupation."

"This is the story we'll need to pursue," I replied. "The political struggle between democracy and communism for control of the hearts and minds of the people of Central Europe including, of course, Berlin and Germany."

"My thoughts exactly. Tell me a little about yourself. Why did your family leave Germany?"

"My father was the leader of one of the larger political parties in Germany. I was only fourteen at the time, but still recall the crucial election of 1932. The communist party received more votes than the Nazis did. Hitler was asked to form a coalition government with the parties in the center to prevent the communists from being part of the government. Soon after taking power, his henchmen burned down the Reichstag, blamed the communists, and outlawed them. Over 4,000 prominent communist politicians were arrested in a single night."

"I thought that most dedicated German communist party members fled to Russia and sat out the war in Moscow," Ben said. "Now, they've returned and for the last eighteen months have worked feverishly to ensure communist candidates were elected in recent provincial and municipal elections throughout Eastern Germany. In the Russian sector of Berlin, the communist party received less than twenty percent of the vote. They're also a minority party in the four provincial assemblies in eastern Germany."

"Just as in 1918, being in the minority will probably not prevent the communists from taking power in the Russian Zone of Occupation," I observed.

"You're right, Kurt. I recently heard that liberal and social democratic candidates in those areas have been arrested as Nazis or subversives. That's another story we need to pursue together."

"I thought I was the reporter here," I laughed.

"You are, but together we can do great things. For example, two weeks after the first Americans arrived here, the Big three—Stalin, Churchill, and Truman—met in Potsdam. I took several photographs of them, which appeared in almost every newspaper in America. If you'd written the story to go with my photos, coverage of that momentous event would have been far better."

"As I understand it, an AP reporter arrived here a short time after you did. What happened to him?" I asked.

"They fired him for cause. He would rather chase skirts than a story and was often drunk when the deadline for the morning dailies back home came around. His successor got promoted to the Rome bureau. But, I'm still here."

"I'd think there were a lot of opportunities to move around within the AP," I observed.

"I've been offered other assignments as a photographer, but I turned them down. I have a German girlfriend and it's pretty serious. We live together with her two small sons. Her husband was killed in early 1944 during a nighttime bombing raid. She's had a pretty rough time. You'll have to meet her, she's a super girl."

"I look forward to meeting her. Now, tell me a little more about the black market."

"It's the wild west—'buyer beware' prevails. Often what you get in trade is underweight or inferior. Even some shop owners will deliver defective or inferior goods unless they get something beyond the ration card."

"Isn't that illegal?"

"Of course, it is. It's also illegal to sell most commodities without a ration card. Both occur every day on every street in Berlin. The price of black-market goods is usually about thirty times the rationed price for a food or clothing item. And probably most telling, here in Berlin there are over 250 break-ins of grocery stores and food distribution centers a day!"

"Really! How widespread is the black market?" I asked.

"Ubiquitous! Everyone in Berlin participates at some level, including most of the occupying forces and their civilian employees. All the occupying powers claim to be trying to control it, but the truth is their half-assed efforts are having little success. Our military men's commercial activities aren't restricted to cigarettes; they include selling and trading high-value items such as coffee, gum, chocolate, alcohol, and stockings. Even the lowest-ranking soldiers are living like kings here."

I shook my head surprised and somewhat disappointed that our forces would engage in such activities, and their leaders would condone them.

During the meal, we discussed Berlin's unique position in occupied Germany. "The city is an island located 110 miles east of the British Zone of occupation in northern Germany, and 145 miles northeast from the American Zone in southeastern Germany," Ben said. "All rail, road, air, and barge access to the city is controlled by the Russians."

"Sounds precarious to me. How's it working out so far?"

"Food and other goods currently pass freely from one zone to another, and people within the four sectors of Berlin and Germany can move about with relative ease. The Russians recently turned policing the citizens of their zone over to the Peoples Police, the Volkspolizei, which is known universally as the VoPos. The Russians still man all interzonal crossing points. The VoPos monitor the movements of individuals into and out of the Russian sector at a few points in the city, such as the Brandenburg Gate and Potsdamer Platz, but nearby side streets are usually open. Just go to one of them if you don't want to pass through a checkpoint. The VoPos, who also patrol the streets, can ask for your identification at any time."

"How would they single me out for questioning?"

"Believe me, Kurt, you may have been born here, but you look, dress, and act like an American. You'll stand out in any crowd. Most of the subway lines and stations you knew are open and you can still travel anywhere within the confines of Berlin. Checkpoints have also been established at some of the major subway transit points."

"I'll get a subway map tomorrow and study it before I venture away from the areas I know."

"Be especially careful of the Interurban lines, designated with an S. Many of those trains go into eastern Germany—if you take one of them, you'll be stopped and questioned. I don't want to have to get you out of jail."

"I'll be careful," I said.

We paid our check and walked out. As we shook hands before parting, Ben added, "One of your first stops needs to be the American Mission Building. The basement and lower floors are open to the public including Germans, who perform most of the routine tasks. Get your press pass at the American Information Office. They'll tell you how to get to the office where you get your ration card and an ID card; it'll allow you to enter US government facilities."

CHAPTER 4

Friday, November 15, 1946

THE NEXT MORNING, I went to the American Mission Building press office and obtained my press pass. A clerk typed my information on a card stock form, took a photo of me, and laminated both into a card. She handed it to me, and said, "You will be asked to show this when you enter or leave this building."

Following the instructions I'd received before leaving New York, I headed down to room B327 in a secluded area of the basement. My new boss, Brandon Williams, Chief of CIA Station Berlin, opened the door to my knock. He matched the description I'd been given in my briefing—early-forties, tall, broad-shouldered, an imposing figure dressed in an expensive suit. His pencil-thin mustache, full head of hair, and handsome good looks reminded me of Clark Gable.

As we shook hands, Brandon said, "Welcome aboard. We are in desperate need of experienced agents."

Pointing me to a seat, he continued, "This building survived the bombing and shelling unscathed despite the fact it was German Luftwaffe Headquarters during the entire war."

"That's amazing, given the destruction elsewhere in Berlin."

"This area is away from central Berlin and the building was covered with camouflage netting; it looked just like trees from the air. Toward the end of the war, it was spared because we knew we'd need space for our occupation forces."

After pausing, he continued, "I had them install that heavily insulated door and I'm sure this room is secure. You'll notice there are no telephone lines."

The room was a painted concrete rectangle with a blue vinyl tile floor. Its sparse furnishings included a conference table and six chairs; a small table to one side held coffee service. Acoustic tiles and fluorescent light fixtures were attached to the ceiling. A large two-drawer safe with a built-in combination lock sat in one corner of the room. Whoever designs government offices must take pride in drab and dismal.

"Is this our meeting place?" I asked.

"For now. The combination for the lock on the door is 47-28-75. Memorize it and don't write it down. In your guise of an AP reporter, you'll be expected to enter this building to receive the daily press releases generated by the American Military Government of Berlin. Have you picked up your press pass?"

"Yes, on my way here."

"That'll allow you to also get a press pass for the Russian, British, and French sectors at their press offices. Here's a list of their locations. The commanding general in each of the zones of occupation here in Berlin is the ultimate authority on all matters in his zone."

"You're saying anything I generate will be given to you in this room?"

"Correct," Brandon replied. "Call my office anytime you have something for me or when we need to meet. Place whatever you have in the safe over there in the corner and lock it. The combination to it is 27-85-43. When we need to meet, ask my secretary to connect us and we'll arrange a time. For those telephone contacts, your name is James Forrester with two Rs. For as long as possible, we are going to hide the fact you're a CIA agent from everyone in Berlin, including my entire staff."

"What can I do to support you?" I asked.

"I cleared my calendar and we're going to spend the day discussing exactly that. First, let's talk about your job as a reporter. According to the records in the American Mission Press office, two AP reporters arrived in Berlin two days ago—you and George Stevens. Anytime you have something negative to report about the Russians or their zone, you'll use the George Stevens byline. In your name, you'll only report the good things occurring over there. You'll go to the Russian press office often, attend trade fairs in the East, interview their leaders, and report nothing they can object to strongly. It'll give you more freedom to move around over there and you are more likely to learn what is going on if they trust you'll give it a good spin."

"Makes sense," I said.

"Hectic is the way I'd describe my year here. You're now on the front lines of a battle of wills with the Russians—a battle whose outcome is far from certain. Every time I think we've finally got a leg up, the bastards over there spring something new on us."

"I'm here to help. What's my CIA assignment?"

With a serious look on his face, Brandon said, "What I'm about to tell you is highly classified. In March of 1945, General Patton's frontline forces in central Germany encountered a heavily armed German convoy of trucks. They all displayed the white flags of surrender from their front fender stanchions. Fortunately, our troops hesitated to open fire. Once the Germans realized they had reached American lines, they stopped their vehicles and held their hands up in surrender.

"The convoy was escorted to a rear echelon headquarters, where Wehrmacht General Reinhardt Gantz convinced his counterparts in the American military that he was a virulent anti-communist, declaring, "I have both the men and information that, together, will help us win the inevitable next war against the Russians."

I stared in wonder at what Brandon was saying and stammered, "You mean…"

"General Gantz, the group's leader, was the Chief of Military Intelligence for the entire Eastern Front. He transferred his complete files on the Russians and their civilian and military intelligence gathering apparatus. He also offered his services and that of his staff. At first, we accepted his support with a great deal of trepidation; now, his help is universally viewed as essential for our intelligence collection activities to be successful."

"So, his information has proven to be authentic and valuable?"

"Yes, everything the general provides substantiates Russian intention to conquer the world. You and I have been tasked with countering their efforts. General Gantz and his associates are essential to our success."

"Isn't the current stated American policy for us to cooperate with the Russians?"

"Yes and no. The Russians recently moved eight additional divisions of troops and their best aircraft into Germany. This is being viewed by Washington as the possible prelude to hostilities. Our job is to determine what the Russians' short- and long-term intentions are."

"How does General Gantz's information involve us?" I asked.

"How much do you know about the conditions in Europe since hostilities ended?"

"Very little. I've been immersed in a Russian language course for the last twelve months."

"Over the last 18 months, one-by-one the countries behind the Iron Curtain have fallen via coups or election fraud into the political and economic sphere of Russia. Only Czechoslovakia has managed to maintain some democratic institutions. When the war ended, millions of people were homeless. Many had been in Nazi concentration camps or employed in forced-labor factories, and still more fled the advancing Russians. Another huge number were forced to leave their homes in the eastern part of what had been Germany; they were from the territories which had been ceded to Poland and Czechoslovakia when the German border was moved hundreds of miles to the west."

"I've read that almost six million displaced persons are still living in camps the United Nations established throughout Europe."

"In the last eighteen months, perhaps 2 million people have been resettled, but the millions you mentioned are still homeless. The Soviets decided this was a perfect opportunity for them to introduce a whole cadre of spies into every country in Western Europe. General Gantz's files helped the US Army Counter Intelligence Corps (CIC) to identify and arrest 385 potential spies just in the American Occupation Zone. As you probably know, the CIC performs intelligence collection overtly and leaves covert intelligence to us.

"When interrogated by CIC officers, communist spies revealed the existence of hundreds of additional communist agents. Our allies were apprised of those residing in their areas of responsibility and they have made similar arrests. It appears that over two thousand highly trained

Soviet agents have been sent to spy on us and our allies. And remember, those are only the ones we know about."

"We're lucky such a valuable resource became available when it did," I said. "How does this affect us?"

"Gantz has also provided us a list of prospective operatives his organization left behind in the Soviet-controlled zone. In the spy trade, these individuals are called sleepers, and you're going to wake them up. This will allow us to determine what is going on in Eastern Germany. Your task is to enter the Russian Zone, contact those individuals, make sure they still want to support us, and give them assignments. You will also establish a means for us to retrieve the information they generate and report your findings back. My staff will use the information to generate reports, which will be sent to the decision-makers in Washington."

Brandon paused, awaiting my reaction. My first thought was, *I've successfully operated behind enemy lines for months surrounded by friendly forces—this time distinguishing friend from foe will be much more difficult and dangerous.*

"If I'm understanding you correctly, my job is going to be setting up a spy network of former Wehrmacht soldiers in Russian-occupied Germany. Sounds like a real challenge, and perhaps even risky. Why me?"

"None of our agents have your qualifications—fluent in German and Russian, extensive time behind enemy lines, able to think on your feet, and perhaps most importantly, you're here now. We've no idea where the Russian military forces in Germany are located. Your task is to find out."

I smiled as my mind raced. *A year and a half of inaction is over—time to return to the front lines!*

Then, someone knocked on the door. "Lunch has arrived," Brandon said. "Time for a break."

CHAPTER 5

Friday, November 15, 1946

BRANDON ENSURED HIS secretary had left the area before he retrieved our lunches from outside the door. "It's best that none of the rest of the CIA staff, even my secretary, know you're in Berlin or what you're doing."

"I agree, sir."

"Kurt, it's important we get to know each other. I have the advantage of having read your dossier. As you probably know, shortly after the Pearl Harbor attack, Winston Churchill had offered to help us establish a secret intelligence agency similar to the British Secret Service, which as you know they call MI6. It's widely recognized as the best spy agency in the world. Roosevelt accepted this offer and the Office of Strategic Services was born; it became known to the world by the abbreviation OSS."

"I remember that from my training in 1942."

"President Roosevelt appointed William Donovan to lead the OSS. I was working in his law office and he tapped me to help him get the group organized. During the early part of the war, I was stuck in Washington and pulled strings to get out into the field and fight. The best I managed to do was trade my desk in Washington for one in London. You, on the other hand, were right in the thick of things in France before, during and after the invasion.'

"That's true. My group of OSS Agents and the French resistance fighters in our area were able to give a good account of themselves..."

"—And toward the end, you decided to stay in the OSS. Is that right?"

"Yes, I did. After recuperating from a wound, I was told to report to OSS Headquarters in Washington. Mister Donovan himself welcomed me, thanked me for my service, and concluding said, 'I have a job if you want it.'"

"When I asked him what he had in mind, he told me the OSS is going to need trained agents to counter the threat of communism worldwide. One of the primary skills that will be essential is reading and writing the Russian language. 'People tell me you have an exceptional faculty for languages,' he said to me. 'Spend the next year learning Russian until you can speak it like a native.'

"I accepted General Donovan's offer but did not share one of the main reasons I did so with him. I already knew a Slavic language—Czech. My grandparents owned a large house on a lake in the Usti region of the Sudetenland which became a part of Czechoslovakia after World War I. My family had owned the mansion for over a hundred years. I spent a month to six weeks there every summer from the time I was three or four years old. Virtually all of the children in the area were Czech and I soon picked up the language. I was able to converse freely with them and even able to read their books. During my visit in 1932, I met a Czech girl. We had an intense romance via letters which gave me an added incentive to study that language to become entirely proficient. We agreed to eventually marry during my visit there in 1933. She married someone else in 1938, a long time after I immigrated to the States."

"Do you think that a native Russian would accept that you were also born in the Soviet Union?"

"For months, four other students and I studied under recent emigres from Russia. Only Russian was spoken in a complete immersion program. The curriculum included Russian language skills, culture, history, and political/military organization. We learned by hearing and speaking. Soon, I was thinking in Russian. Czech and Russian are closely related—same grammar and sentence formation, just somewhat different vocabulary and intonation. When I graduated in early October of this year, two of the teachers told me I'd even developed an authentic accent—I sounded like someone who had been born and raised in Minsk, the capital of Byelorussia. So, in the future when the necessity arises, I'll be from that area of the USSR."

Brandon returned after setting our dishes outside. "I need to give you a bit more background before we discuss the details of your assignment. During hostilities, we frequently shared the locations of our troops with the British and Russians. After the fighting stopped, we and the British supplied the Soviets with two lists—current troop deployment and intended future deployment at facilities throughout our zones of Germany. This time, the Russians didn't reciprocate. We currently have no idea what forces they have in East Germany, their locations, or capabilities. We're completely blind."

"If hostilities commence, they would have a tremendous advantage," I observed.

"Exactly, so here is a list of five categories of information we need immediately," Brandon said, handing me a sheet of typewritten paper with TOP SECRET- U.S. EYES ONLY- LIMITED DISTRIBUTION rubber-stamped top and bottom. It read:

1. Determine current unit locations and strengths, with particular attention to division titles, numerical composition, zone of deployment, armaments, and the quality of their munitions (new or old).
2. Determine the size of munitions stockpiles and transport routes for redeployment.
3. Monitor the construction of new bases, particularly new airfields or the provisioning of supply depots, or any form of military construction.
4. Gather details on uranium mining near Chemnitz, especially the amounts of the processed ore shipped to the Soviet Union.
5. Immediately communicate any information regarding Soviet mobilization for war.

I said nothing because the sheer magnitude of the tasks on this list was overwhelming.

With a smile, Brandon handed me a second similarly classified document and said, "The first sheet is a list of the names of 163 former

Wehrmacht soldiers who the General says are willing to support our efforts. Their location in southeastern Germany and last known occupations are listed after each name. These individuals have been vetted using all-source information. Other pages contain the locations and descriptions of former German military bases we believe the Russians have probably occupied and a map that shows their locations."

I spread the eight sheets of paper out on to the conference table beside the map. "I'll need some time to study this?"

"I have an important meeting now and will be back in about an hour,' Brandon said as he stood and exited the room.

It was almost two hours before he returned. Once he was seated, I pointed at the map and said, "Our area of responsibility in the Russian sector is almost 200 miles wide by 150 miles long. A huge area, but most of the installations are concentrated in the southern part of this region, which simplifies our task."

"Go on."

"The gasthaus proprietor near this military installation will know if the base is occupied, and if it is, can gather the information on it. The farmer near this airfield will know if aircraft are operating from it. The train conductor on this line will probably know if the eight divisions arriving in Germany by train last month went north or south…"

In a few minutes, I identified the people I should approach in a limited area of the map and said, "I can see how people in different, contiguous locations can be contacted in a limited time. I just have one question. How the hell am I going to get into and back out of the Russian Zone of Occupation?"

"Like this." Brandon handed me an American passport without a photograph that identified the bearer as Hanz Zimmerman. Birthplace: Frankfort-am-Main, Germany; 1916. Naturalized American Citizen. Occupation: Purchasing agent for Bausch and Lomb Optics Company.

"The Russians and their East German communist toadies are desperate for hard currency. The Germans make the best optical devices in the world. Their prewar laboratories and factories are in Eastern Germany—in the state of Saxony and cities of Jana, Dresden, and Leipzig. Coincidently, the area where most of your objectives are located. You'll actually purchase perhaps as much as $100,000 worth of cameras, binoculars, telescopes, and theodolites for resale to retailers and industrial users throughout the States. Here's a book on optics and cameras."

"The guise you've selected for me is perfect. But as a purchasing agent, I should have intimate knowledge of optics from years in the business."

"Study the book. After you're familiar with the subject, you'll spend several days with an optics buyer in Britain before your mission; that'll make it easier for you to pull this guise off."

"Mitigating one of my concerns. But I have others."

"Enlighten me."

"In France, friendly partisan forces and usually other OSS agents were always involved in our operations. We took risks as a group in operations lasting only a few hours—a day at the most and there was always a haven nearby."

"There'll be no place to retreat on this mission," Brandon stated. "Plus, what you need to keep in mind is that even though these people have been vetted, no one has contacted them for a year and a half, perhaps even longer. We have no way of knowing how much they can be trusted. Be wary, very wary."

"Approaching a stranger to ask them to become a spy can be very tricky. Why don't we let General Gantz organize and run the spy network and then give us the results of their efforts?"

"A spy organization works best if the people who need and collect the information are citizens whose loyalty can be verified. There's no way we can train and send Americans to live and work anywhere in the Soviet Bloc for any length of time. We want to have direct control over these new operatives. That way we can task them, determine what they are doing, and evaluate what they provide objectively. One of us must enlist them, and then control them after they're recruited."

"That makes sense. Tell me the whole plan. Perhaps together we can find some way to mitigate some of the inherent risks."

"We found and purchased a car for you—a 1937 Wander W24 coupe. It's mechanically in top shape and has a new paint job. You'll drive it to your various destinations. If you get lost along the way, ask for directions from a nearby farmer or barman who just happens to be on your list. We'll know when you leave and when you expect to be back. If you don't return by the scheduled date, we'll have the cavalry in the form of the State Department and military authorities raise hell with the Russians until you're returned to us—hopefully none the worse for wear. One of the advantages you have is you're new here and know nothing about CIA or Army CIC operations in Germany, so you can't tell them anything of real value."

"That doesn't prevent them from beating the hell out of me for information I don't have."

"Unfortunately, true."

"How long do you anticipate I'll be over there?"

"Ten days to two weeks. Using your company's letterhead, we applied for the permits requesting you to visit several cities in Saxony. The bureaucracy in the Soviet Zone is slow and very cumbersome, but within a few weeks, we should have all of the paperwork required for you to travel there. Few private individuals have cars, so gas stations are few and far between—that'll give you another reason to be some distance away from your most direct route or stated destination."

"When would I leave and how many stops do you expect me to make?"

"You would go sometime in January and would enlist perhaps thirty operatives and drive past almost the same number of military installations."

"On the surface that would appear to take me more than a couple of weeks!"

"It's up to you—plan the entire trip in detail and we'll discuss it."

"So, you don't expect me to be followed or harassed while over there?"

"No American has ever tried such a mission. The British have been successful, but many of their people are old hands at this kind of thing. If you become concerned about the level of danger, you can return to West Berlin from anywhere on your route in a few hours."

"Let's explore what bothers me the most."

"Shoot."

"The initial contact with the operatives—it will be fraught with danger. Say I decide a gasthaus proprietor is the ideal operative for a given area and I enter his premises and ask for him. He's not there or is no longer the owner—I've just raised the suspicions of whomever I talked to. Do we have photographs and descriptions of these individuals?"

"Yes, for most, but not all of them. Unfortunately, those photos and that information was generated years ago when these men first entered the German military."

"I have a thought," I said. "You're telling me that the entire American intelligence community trusts the General."

"Wholeheartedly."

"What if one of the General's men he trusts as implicitly knew all these people and had worked with them in the war. One gets to know and trust people he lives and serves with in such dire circumstances. That individual could make the initial contact with each operative, saving me the risk of blowing the whole mission because I contacted the wrong person or somehow inadvertently gave the game away."

"That's a great idea. Germans think all Americans and their corporations are immensely wealthy. This individual could act as your chauffeur, make the initial contact with the prospective operatives. If he grew up in what is today the Soviet Zone of occupation, especially Saxony, he might know people you two could trust, places for you to hold up in, or the best way out of a tight situation, even an escape route."

"Actually, you've listed a lot more advantages than I'd thought of," I said.

"I'll fly to Munich early next week and talk to the General about your idea. In the interim, you need to plan the trip and study the optics manual."

"My AP photographer friend indicates I need to get a press pass at Soviet Occupation Headquarters. In light of my mission, should I register with the Russians? As I understand it, they're going to take my picture and thumbprint and attach it to the identity card they give me."

"And they'll retain a copy for their files. You'll fly to Britain a few weeks before your mission begins. Once there, you'll devise a disguise which you'll wear when you return to Berlin. The picture of you taken just before you leave will be attached to Hanz Zimmerman's passport. Go ahead and register with the Russians and start issuing stories—establish your cover here as soon as possible."

"I'll start on Monday."

"We'll meet several times before you leave on your first trip," Brandon said, standing and shaking my hand. "It'll take a while for you to absorb and memorize all of the information in these documents. Lock them and any notes you make in the safe every time you leave the room."

"I take it this is where I'll spend most of my time over the next few weeks."

"Perhaps not all, but much of your time should be devoted to planning this mission. You must also please your AP bosses or your cover will cease to exist. Let's plan on meeting here next Friday to determine how things are going on both fronts."

CHAPTER 6

Monday, November 18, 1946

YESTERDAY, I RENTED an overpriced but large one-bedroom apartment near a subway stop, and within walking distance of the American Mission Building. It wasn't available until the first of December, so I was stuck in the pensione until then.

Both of my jobs required I become intimately familiar with all four occupation zones of Berlin, especially the Russian one. So, after a modest continental breakfast, I decided to walk all the way to the old administrative center of Berlin and the capital of Germany, which was called "Mitte"—middle of the city, now inside the Russian Zone of occupation. This would be an excellent way for me to get an idea of what was really going on in my old hometown. Once there, I'd apply for my Russian Occupation Zone press pass.

The temperature was crisp and the sky was overcast, so I donned a suit, overcoat, homburg hat, and set out using my large umbrella as a walking stick. I headed northeast toward a nearby familiar landmark, the Charlottenburg Palace. Once there, I was shocked to see the extent of damage to this magnificent Baroque and Rococo structure. Through a chain-link fence designed to keep visitors out, I could see the part of the roof that was still intact was being used to protect architectural elements that had been salvaged from the more heavily-damaged part of the structure. The magnificent gardens that once surrounded the palace were now muddy fields.

Moving east, I took an oblique right turn down Berliner Strasse. The street itself was free of debris, although structures on both sides of it were either partially or totally destroyed. Only a few small shops on the lower floor of a few buildings were undamaged. I entered a bakery; it revealed only a few loaves of freshly baked bread on its shelves. The price was marked—eighty marks and a 400-gram ration stub. A small handwritten sign below read, "Zehn Zigaretten" (ten cigarettes).

A little further on, a mostly female work crew was engaged in clearing a construction site. Most were dressed in what looked like men's wool army pants cinched tightly around their waists with wide belts. All wore loose-fitting ex-military jackets around their emaciated frames, and handkerchiefs of many different colors tied around their heads. Their boots were also military issue. Some were cleaning bricks and stacking them in neat rows. Others were shoveling debris into trucks. In German, I asked one woman, "Where do they take the debris?"

Her eyes twinkled. "Berlin has always been so flat, now in the south, we are building mountains—perhaps in the winter we can even ski on those peaks."

"How much do you earn for a day's work?"

"Acht zigaretten (eight cigarettes)," she replied.

I shook my head and walked away. The preponderance of female labor in the construction crews was necessitated by the death, disability, or imprisonment of most of the younger men. At the end of the war, Hitler even used old men and young boys in a vain attempt to stop Allied armies from destroying the Third Reich. Now the surviving women were reduced to whatever work they could find to survive.

Further down the street, a lopsided bell tower came into view and I instantly recognized the severely damaged Charlottenburg Town Hall. As I drew closer, I was amazed that the building was still standing. Rubble filled it and the surrounding area. It was closed, so I moved on to the east.

A construction crew was standing outside a building in the middle of the next long block, and the road was cordoned off. At the corner, I was warned, "Please stand back, we are going to implode this building." Nearby a workman began operating a hand-cranked warning klaxon; it sounded for almost a minute. Then another man pushed down a plunger on a small box and a deafening explosion followed. The building shuddered for a moment before suddenly falling into itself, spewing dust and debris in every direction. A crew spent a few minutes cleaning the rubble that had flowed out into the street and then reopened the thoroughfare.

Further down the street, I was struck by the sight of a south-facing building missing its entire front. It was four floors tall and, in each of the upstairs rooms, a woman was tending a garden. On the first floor, a woman was using a watering can to cultivate her crops. I walked over and shouted up, "What are you growing?"

"Winter crops—parsley roots, turnips, and cabbage."

"How did the soil get into this building?"

"I carried it into the building and up the stairs in a bucket. These vegetables will ensure that my family survives this winter. The Russians have stopped the importation of fruit and vegetables from the East into the three Western Zones of Occupation. My family lives in the room behind here—this is what is left of our living room. I tried growing my crops in the garden out back, but there is little sunshine and what grew there was stolen before it even matured."

Last week, Ben had told me, "bands of feral orphaned children still live in the ruins of Berlin. Efforts to capture and get them into orphanages have been only partially successful."

On the next block, I saw several ragged and disheveled urchins scramble over the rubble of a destroyed building. I approached as close as possible and shouted in German, "I have chocolate for you," but they just scampered away.

In my heart, I loved Germany, my home for my first fifteen years. But I've yet to come to terms with how a virtually uneducated Austrian corporal had led a once proud and mighty nation with so many Nobel Prize winners to its destruction. My job was to report the current state of the world—not determine what caused the last war. Or, what led most Germans to loyally and blindly follow Hitler right up to the bitter end.

Later in my journey, I entered what used to be the most beautiful park in Germany—the Tiergarten. A large group of women, also dressed in hand-me-down military trousers and jackets, was harvesting potatoes from fields that covered almost every inch of the park. Buckets of potatoes were being dumped into the back of a truck.

"How do you decide who gets the potatoes?" I asked them.

"The town council gets half and we get the other half," a woman down on her hands and knees in the muck looked up and replied. "Our families would starve if it was not for this supplement to what the occupying powers allow us to purchase."

"The town council distributes the other half to the truly needy widows with children and severely wounded veterans with families," claimed another worker. "We are all suffering through these hard times and so must share."

Another woman dumped a pail of potatoes in the truck. "You're an American, right?" she asked me.

"I was born and lived here until I was fifteen."

"All of the soldiers and bureaucrats in your occupying forces are eating and drinking their fill each day while we starve. Some of us opposed Hitler from the start—we should be allowed to live like real people, not suffer with Nazi supporters."

"If few people supported Hitler," I started to retort, "how had he been able to conquer most of Europe?" but it was a rhetorical question no one could answer.

The first woman now stood, joined the group, and said, "We plant and water the potatoes. We guard them at night to ensure no one steals them. We dig them up. Yet this and our meager rations are barely enough to keep us and our families alive. When will there be enough food?"

I shrugged my shoulders and held my hands out. I wasn't emotionally or intellectually prepared to address the woes of this defeated nation.

Turning away from their haunting eyes, I walked toward the eastern edge of the park. There the Russians had recently built an ugly war memorial to their soldiers who had died while taking Berlin. A squad of Soviet soldiers stood guard over it. The park was in the British sector. Ben had told me that 'most Germans hate the Russians.' The soldiers were obviously stationed to prevent the monument from being defaced.

Ahead I could see the Brandenburg Gate. This neoclassical structure had been built in 1791 to celebrate peace. A few years later Napoleon, having defeated Prussia, rode in triumph beneath it, and then took the Victory Quadrille from its top back to Paris. The gate was now the dividing point between the British and Russian Zones of Occupation.

CHAPTER 7

Monday, November 18, 1946

THE BRANDENBURG GATE still stood despite numerous bullet and shell holes. Several thousand people mingled about the huge open plaza in what seemed to be an aimless shuffle on both sides of the invisible line between the two zones—Germans dressed in everything from workman's clothes to suits and fashionable dresses with hats, mixed with obviously displaced persons from Eastern and Central Europe dressed in rags. Everyone lugged a package or two, a knapsack, or a cardboard suitcase.

Standing to one side, I watched, finally figuring out what the people were doing. A person having several things to trade or sell would stand in a fixed location. People would walk by them and hear a low voice say something like, "400 grams of sugar for 5 cigarettes," or "100 Reichsmarks for a dressed chicken" or perhaps "300 grams of bread flour for a bottle of milk." It was unclear how they reached an agreement, but frequent furtive exchanges took place. The British soldiers, VoPos, and on-duty Russian soldiers ignored what was going on, perhaps receiving some consideration for allowing such an obvious violation of the spirit, if not the letter of the law against black-marketing.

The middle of the Brandenburg Gate had once been reserved for royalty. I intentionally walked through it, coming eye-to-eye with a machine-gun-toting Russian soldier. Neither of us spoke as I passed him into the steady gaze of two VoPos. The one with stripes on his sleeve stepped in my way. "Papers, please," he said in heavily accented Saxon German.

I looked them both in the eye, smiled, and politely said in English, "I'm an American." Ben had told me everyone could travel freely throughout the city—time to find out if this was true.

"You must show your papers!" the sergeant said in German.

"Everyone has free access to all of Berlin—this is an occupied city," I said in English, and moved aside to walk around them.

The junior VoPo stepped in my way as his superior asked in German, "Are you a soldier or officer in the American military?"

I held out my hands with my palms raised, touching my right ear indicating I didn't understand.

I was merely having fun with these petty functionaries, which abruptly ended when the senior officer took his pistol out of his holster and pointed it in my face. I needed to do something to defuse what was turning into an explosive situation. In the High German of a highly educated individual, I said, "I am a senior member of the American Occupation Force and take issue at being stopped."

The senior man immediately holstered his pistol and they both became contrite. I breathed a sigh of relief, and without hesitation walked around them, my identity papers snugly tucked in my coat pocket. While I had the right under the Four Powers Agreement to enter the communist-controlled sector, I had to avoid being dead right. This little incident proved the VoPos had their instructions and would follow them unquestioningly.

The huge red Soviet hammer and sickle flag atop the Brandenburg Gate made a rustling noise as it fluttered in the breeze. It left little doubt about who was ultimately in charge of this sector of defeated Germany.

Unter den Linden, the street on the other side of the Brandenburg Gate, was the cultural and government center of pre-war Berlin. It was now lined with ruins as far as the eye could see. Many of the buildings I had known in my youth, including the magnificent Hotel Adlon and numerous government buildings, were now just damaged walls jutting out of piles of rubble. A few others were occupied after being hastily repaired. The neoclassical façade of the opera house was destroyed in 1945, but from the sidewalk I could see efforts were being made to preserve the magnificent interior of the auditorium.

Following this wide boulevard east, I recalled that the final and fiercest battles in Berlin had taken place in this area. The still-standing walls reflected the damage the intense shelling and hand-to-hand combat had caused here eighteen months earlier.

The old library I remembered from my youth had been repaired and was open, so I entered. Inside, I could see the shelves were only partially full of books, but the tables were filled with people intently reading or taking notes from the books in front of them. The building was unheated and everyone was wearing outdoor clothing. When I came out of the library, I passed a short, ferret-faced individual leaning up against a wall. He began following me. My counter-surveillance training kicked in. Since I had no reason to lose him, I decided to see how he would react when I eventually entered the Russian Occupation Force Headquarters.

Further down the street, a large brass plaque read: "University of Berlin." The occupied buildings had been hastily repaired—bullet and shell holes were filled with cement and different colored tiles had been used to repair the roof.

A group of students was entering and I asked a young female student if the Russians were interfering with the curriculum.

"In September, they tried to make the Russian language and literature required classes, but the professors resisted and won. We currently have full academic freedom. How long will that last?' she asked rhetorically, hunching her shoulders. "One hears all kinds of rumors since the communists lost the recent elections badly. But who knows?" She paused. "Could you tell me the time?"

When I responded, she excused herself. "I now have a class."

Looking back, I saw that my follower had stopped and was sitting atop a short retaining wall. Sensing no real danger, I walked on.

I passed the Protestant Berlin Cathedral called the Domo, where my parents had worshiped. Most of the walls that had supported its exceptional dome still stood, but the dome itself was missing and the doors to the church were closed.

As I neared the Alexander Platz, I looked for a restaurant in what had once been the entertainment center of Berlin. The front door of a gasthaus on the far side of the River Spree was open; a fare board in front offered a variety of German meals.

Once seated, I ordered a dark beer, bratwurst, and potato salad, then went to the restroom to check on my tail. He was seated at the bar facing my table, sipping a beer. My pistol-packing VoPo wanted to make it clear he didn't appreciate the attitude I'd displayed.

I still had several American coins in my pocket, so I placed a silver dime on the table and asked the waiter, "Will this be enough for my meal?"

"Very generous of you," he said, looking around before putting it in his pocket. He brought me a second beer with my meal and refused any other compensation.

*

The Red Town Hall, named for the color of the bricks used in its construction, had housed Berlin's central government until 1945. It was also damaged and closed. I asked a passerby where the city government meets. He pointed to a nearby undamaged building, "That defunct insurance company headquarters—the building to its right contains the Russian Occupation Forces Offices—everyone calls it 'Russia House.'"

A Russian soldier guard lugging a submachine gun slung over his shoulder escorted me to a desk in the lobby of Russia House. I showed the young Russian officer behind the desk my American Zone press pass. "Can you direct me to your press office?" I asked in German.

I'd heard that Russian bureaucracy was the most draconian in the world and after my first encounter with it, I can add two additional modifiers—slow and inefficient. After delays at each office, the third individual I met was wearing the uniform of a captain and said in halting German, "We demand...a letter...from your employing agency...until then no pass." I handed him a letter from the AP office in New York. I waited for over thirty minutes for his return. He stayed with me to serve as a translator as I visited three more increasingly senior officials' offices. Since I spoke Russian, I knew that all of them refused to take responsibility for granting me a press pass. In the American Information Agency Office, this process had taken fifteen minutes, most of that time devoted to filling out a form.

At a little after 15:30, the translator and I entered a Colonel's office. "Please let us see your passport, letter from your news agency, and American press pass," he said in Russian which was then repeated by my ineffective translator.

After I handed the requested items to the Colonel, he looked at them and said in Russian, "Tell him we must keep these documents for one week. He can return then."

I replied in German, "I must have my American passport and press pass to continue with my duties. Apparently, you do not want me to present your side to my readers in America. I'm told your press releases and briefings are usually ignored by my American and British colleagues here in Berlin. This lack of cooperation and deliberate delays may be the reason. If you give me my press pass today, I'll give you favorable coverage whenever I can. Otherwise, forget my cooperation."

In the next forty-five minutes I was handed my press pass, taken on a tour of the office spaces non-Russian reporters were allowed to use, given a glass of vodka, and introduced to the Russian Military Press Liaison officer, Lt. Colonel Daniil Kuznetsov. He spoke passable German, and we exchanged our backgrounds during a cordial if brief conversation.

As I exited the building my watch indicated it was 16:25. The sun was setting, but it would not be dark for another hour. I still had one more stop I wanted to make. My tail was waiting outside of Russia House. Ignoring him, I hailed a cab and within five minutes was standing in front of the roofless, burned-out, pockmarked shell of the Reichstag. Appropriately, it started to drizzle and I turned up my overcoat collar and moved my hat forward to shelter my eyes, but did not open my umbrella.

I'd been fifteen years old when this building burned. The Nazis blamed the communists for a fire they set themselves. They used it as justification for suspending the provisions in the constitution which guaranteed German citizen's civil liberties. Suspension of these rights inevitably led to their takeover of Germany, then to World War II and the destruction of this glorious city.

Once on the north side of the building, I entered what a sign indicated was the British Sector. I shook my head, thinking of what might have been, trying to forget what had happened to the country of my birth. The Germany I knew and loved died the night of February 27, 1933, when this building burned. America must win the inevitable next war with Russia before Germany could again become a united, prosperous, and respected member of the world community.

There was just enough light remaining for me to see a path into the building. Following it I took damaged stairs to a second-floor landing. There a large windowless opening allowed me to view a silhouette of my severely damaged home town. Street lights soon illuminated the route that several major thoroughfares took through the city. I stood there for some time—turning over in my mind the fact I had been given an important task which would hopefully help America win the next war.

Hearing a noise, I turned just in time to see two small figures rush toward me. They hit me, and soon I was falling through space. I hit the ground hard and was momentarily stunned. My umbrella flew out of my hand. Almost immediately a large number of tiny to medium-sized forms surrounded me. I could see that they had rocks in their hands. One of the largest, a teenager and their obvious leader said, "We must finish him."

I gathered up my umbrella and quickly got to my feet; my back was against a solid wall. The first rocks were aimed at my head with deadly accuracy. I ducked and moved to avoid them, but one grazed my forehead and a second hit my right shoulder with surprising force. I realized that this was no child's game, I was in serious danger. My assailants had an endless supply of ammunition lying at their feet; I was unarmed and there were perhaps as many as twenty of them.

I decided my only hope was to rush the leader. Using my substantial umbrella as a bludgeon I hit him twice—first knocking a large rock out of his hand, and then hitting him in the head. He went down and I jumped over him in a headlong rush to escape.

Soon I entered a large paved plaza; my pack of foes was in hot pursuit. One rock hit me in the back and a second knocked my hat off. I just kept running as fast as I could. Knowing my longer strides would eventually propel me out of the range of their missiles, I fled toward a lighted major street; a few automobiles with their headlights on were traversing that avenue. If I could reach there, I might be safe. As I approached it, a rock hit me in the left calf. I fell to my knees, knowing that now they would get me. I turned and watched them approach and opened my umbrella as if that might somehow protect me from the inevitable hail of rocks when they came to finish me. A well-aimed missile from the side hit me in the left temple; soon blood dripped from the wound. I was certain I would be overwhelmed.

First, my pursuers hesitated, then turned, and scampered from view. Surprised, I turned around and look at the street. Two armed British Royal Military Policemen passing by in a jeep had seen my plight, stopped, and come to my aid. They assisted me as I hobbled into the jeep's front passenger seat. Using a first aid kit, they stopped the bleeding and then offered to take me to a nearby hospital, but I declined. They then transported me to my pensione which was in the British sector. On the way, the senior man leaned over from the back seat and said, "Perhaps as many as fifty bands of orphaned urchins still occupy the ruins of Berlin. Most are harmless, but a few are real savages. Those usually manage to bag one or two unsuspecting individuals a week. Once they are incapacitated, they are stripped of their clothing and valuables; then left for dead. You're one of the lucky ones—they won't get much for your hat."

I learned my lesson—a hungry city can be a very dangerous place for an overconfident individual, even a trained combat veteran.

CHAPTER 8

Friday, November 22, 1946

IN MY SECOND meeting with Brandon, he informed me that General Gantz had identified the perfect companion for my excursion into the Russian Zone. "Andreas Lehman was the General's driver and aide-de-camp during most of the war. Hence, he knows virtually all of the people on the General's list. He was born and raised in Saxony and worked as a truck driver, so he also knows our area of interest. He's going to be here in two weeks and together, you and he will finalize the plan."

"That's great news," I said smiling, shaking Brandon's hand. "Having someone familiar with the area and the people we'll be contacting will be a big help in developing and completing a successful mission."

We reviewed my preliminary plan for setting up spy cells in Russian-controlled Germany. "The main problem I see is it's a little too ambitious," Brandon said. "You've crammed too many tasks into the two weeks we agreed should be the maximum time you stay in harm's way. Focus on the areas around Dresden; that's where your cover story indicates you should be. On a second trip, you can hit the sites nearer Berlin. We'll fabricate a different cover story and different guise for that later mission."

Our discussions were interrupted a few minutes later by the familiar knock on the door signaling lunchtime. "So, what brought you into the spy game?" Brandon asked me while chomping on a piece of rare roast beef.

"I was born in Berlin and lived here until I was 15. My father was a prominent member of the Reichstag who had to leave Germany in 1933, shortly after the Nazis came to power. His outspoken criticism of Hitler almost cost him his life. We emigrated to America and settled in Manhattan, becoming U.S. citizens. I went to Groton and graduated from Yale in June of 1940. What about you?"

"I grew up in Connecticut, went to public schools, and did well enough to get into Brown, took business management, and moved to New York City because my girlfriend at the time was living there. That relationship didn't last long, but I found I liked the city. I didn't like selling insurance and eventually landed the office manager's job in General Donovan's law firm. I'd still be there if it hadn't been for the war. What did you do after Yale?"

"My father's business in Manhattan flourished as a result of the rearmament, which occurred in the late 1930s. Reluctantly, I agreed to join him. We bought and sold industrial diamonds—those small or defective jewels used in numerous industrial and manufacturing processes—they're essential for the cutting and abrasion tasks required to build machines of all forms."

"The armaments build-up also stimulated the stock market and I managed to make a lot of money during those years," Brandon said. "But you still haven't told me how you got into this business."

"Before America got into the war, the State Department was responsible for foreign intelligence collection. Two of their people contacted my father and me at our office and told us, 'The Germans have no domestic source of diamonds, which are essential for their war production. They have been able to capture a sizeable quantity of jewelry-quality gems. A dedicated Nazi who now lives in Zurich has been tasked with offering neutral countries like ours those diamonds in exchange for industrial diamonds.' They told us they wanted us to facilitate the trade."

"So, you were in the game early. Did you manage to meet with him?"

"Yes. I flew to Zurich via Lisbon. By simply calling his office, I was able to contact him. After several days of negotiations, we agreed to an exchange rate and that the exchange would take place in a neutral site, Lisbon. My father and I prepared several boxes filled with crushed anthracite coal covered with a thin layer of industrial diamonds. I was there for the exchange. Herr Gruber beamed when the first carton was opened and the exchange paperwork was signed. Our State Department ensured that before either consignment could be forwarded out of the country, Portugal would seize the diamonds as contraband. Soon Pearl Harbor was attacked. Before I could join the military, one of my contacts at State asked me to join the OSS, and by then, I was hooked on the spy game."

"I'm hooked too. Your successes against the bad guys create unbelievable highs," Brandon stated, raising his hands, "and your defeats only cause you to want to work harder and smarter. My wife wants to go back to the states and lead a normal life. I'm not sure I'll ever be happy working in a law office again."

"Living in a city devastated by war and populated by desperately hungry people certainly isn't pleasant or appealing to most of us."

"She's pregnant and would like to be near her family in Philadelphia when the baby is born, and then never come back. It's something we'll have to work out soon. It would help if we could get out of the small apartment we're living in and into government housing near the commissary and clubs. The CIA hasn't managed to get any priority with the military."

I hated the thought of losing him as a boss but said nothing when he looked at his watch and stood. I joined him and we exchanged a warm and lasting handshake—spies addicted to the adrenaline rush that those engaged in a normal office routine cannot envision.

CHAPTER 9

Friday, November 29, 1946

THE FOLLOWING WEEK, Brandon arranged for us to meet for three hours around lunchtime. When he arrived late, he apologized, then reminded me that Andreas would arrive on Monday. "I needed to see you so we can go over some details. First, he has agreed to a large one-time fee for this excursion to the East, so there's no need for you to discuss his compensation with him. Part of his pay is the title to the car and a chauffeuring business we've established here in West Berlin."

"Great plan," I said. "That's the perfect cover for him to assume while taking me into the Russian-occupied zone."

"Second and most importantly, Andreas is only to be informed about this mission and its objectives. Nothing more. It's almost lunchtime now, we'll have time after we eat to remove all the material not directly related to this mission from the safe; I'll store it in my office upstairs for now."

"Makes sense; if we're caught, the less both of us know, the better."

My last statement was made just as we heard the usual knock on the door.

Over lunch, we again exchanged OSS war stories—mine in France and Germany—his in London.

"You young guys had all of the fun," Brandon stated. "I was stuck behind a desk in London shuffling paper. I was forced to share an office on the floor we rented at Claridge's Hotel with two other paper pushers. One was an attractive female agent. She and the buzz bombs were the most dangerous things I faced. The bombs all missed me, but she didn't; we were married in late 1944. That's what bothers me about her pushing to return to the States; she understands the excitement of this job—she's done it."

Brandon looked down and shook his head, then straightened his back and smiled. "Tell me how it was in the field."

"I parachuted into France in late November of 1943. Everyone knew the Allied cross-channel invasion would occur in mid-1944, but only a few knew exactly when or where. There were only two viable options from England—south to Normandy, or East and South somewhere along the Pas-de-Calais. The latter was the closest to Britain—just across the English Channel from Dover, but it was also the most heavily defended."

"My main task was to work with MI6 to ensure that all allied efforts to confuse the Germans about the site of the invasion were consistent and believable. Go on, Kurt."

"My team of American OSS agents and French resistance fighters was located just south of the Seine River, which was the dividing line between the German forces assigned to defend Normandy and those who defended the southern part of the Pas-de-Calais. German reserve forces were stationed nearby—they would move either north or south depending on which area we invaded…"

"—Stopping their movement was a vital task," Brandon interjected.

"By May of 1944, American and British bombers and fighter aircraft had forced the once-vaunted Luftwaffe to surrender the skies over France to the allies. This meant the supplies we needed to perform our sabotage against the Germans could be parachuted into us at night in relative safety. It also meant light aircraft could land at improvised airfields to provide additional personnel and direction for our efforts. Our primary mission was to disrupt all rail and road traffic between the two potential invasion areas and isolate German troop concentrations wherever possible."

"How'd that work out?"

"Won a few, lost a few. In April 1944, one of my French resistance associates reported that sixty new German Tiger tanks were located at a base south of Rouen. Because these were heavier, larger, and more capable than anything the allies had at this time, they were a significant threat on the battlefield. These tanks, however, were gas guzzlers and their treads wore out quickly, so the Germans always moved them by rail. Flatbed rail cars hidden under trees on a remote siding near the German base were being held in reserve to move those sixty tanks. The base was heavily guarded, but no one was protecting the rail cars. London was apprised of that fact and told us that rendering the rail cars inoperative was my group's highest priority task."

"How'd you manage that—explosives?"

"A civil engineer French partisan suggested a solution, which London loved," I replied.

"How's that?"

"For several weeks in early May, we siphoned axle oil out of the flat car wheels and replaced it with an abrasive compound parachuted in expressly for that purpose. When the Germans tried to transport the tanks toward the invasion beaches of Normandy on June 8, 1944, the train's wheels seized up a short distance from where they started. Those tanks were now out in the open and sitting ducks for allied aircraft who bombed and strafed them repeatedly. Later we learned it took a week for the few surviving tanks to arrive at the front lines."

"That was a fabulous plan," Brandon said. "After the war, I read a report about those Tiger tanks. They were easily capable of destroying our tanks and were almost impervious to our bazookas. Those sixty tanks might have made a difference in the Normandy battle. Isn't it amazing what a little individual initiative can accomplish? Man, I would have loved to have been doing what you did. Being in the action, *wow*, nothing like it."

"Yeah, it went remarkably well," I added. "In late April 1944, a light aircraft landed with instructions for us to monitor the 20:00 BBC radio broadcasts on the first and second as well as the fifteenth and sixteenth day of each coming month. We guessed that was when the tides and moonlight would be favorable for the invasion. We were told that we'd receive instructions in a subsequent broadcast forty-eight hours after hearing the message, 'Your Aunt Ellen sends her regards,' We were given codes associated with a list of potential targets. For the next two months, my OSS area commander and I avoided being directly involved in our unit's sabotage operations. We had a good idea when the invasion would occur and couldn't risk capture.

"On June second, we heard the requisite preparatory message and two days later our assigned targets were identified. That's when we divided into fighting units and began using the explosives that we had been stockpiling to sabotage the train engines, rail and road bridges in our assigned area. After the war, I was told we helped prevent reinforcement from the north deploying to Normandy in time to push us back into the sea."

"What happened to your group after the Normandy breakout in mid-July?" Brandon asked.

"Many of the French partisans were locals who stayed behind at their homes. My group of OSS officers combined with some French ex-military men to move east behind enemy lines; there we inflicted whatever damage we could on German forces. Sometimes we were successful and sometimes we were not, but the enemy always had to look over its shoulders to ensure we wouldn't come at them from behind."

"Impressive. Most OSS agents who had been in the field as long as you were brought back to England in mid to late 1944 for a well-deserved rest, but you weren't?" Brandon asked.

"They extracted me, but after three months in England, I was climbing the walls to get back into action," I replied. "In February, a group of experienced OSS agents who could speak German and I were among the first Americans parachuted into Germany. We were tasked with reporting Wehrmacht troop movements. Our orders were to observe, but not engage them unless we could do so without risking discovery..."

"—That sounds like a difficult task," Brandon interjected.

"It was, but we managed. In March 1945, German armies were ordered to retreat to the East bank of the Rhine River. We were tasked to let the Wehrmacht pass by us and then conduct a last-minute attack to prevent German sappers—explosive experts—from destroying a bridge that crossed the Rhine north of Koblenz."

"That sounds dangerous."

"We intentionally waited to approach the bridge until the sappers were setting their charges. As soon as we began firing on them, gunfire erupted behind us. Unfortunately, some retreating German troops were still on the west side of the river. During an intense running gun battle, I took a serious hit to my abdomen. A couple of my guys dragged me along and we managed to retreat a safe distance. Although my wound hurt like hell, I was still conscious and watched as the bridge we'd been assigned to save exploded and fell into the Rhine. A month of hardship and a shot in the gut for nothing. Several hours later, one of my buddies managed to commandeer an Army Jeep and took me to an American field hospital. I survived, but my war was over."

"Fascinating. I wish my war experiences were filled with as much excitement and bravery," Brandon said. "You'll certainly have a great story to tell your grandchildren."

"For that, I'd need children, and for that, I'd need a wife," I replied. "Neither is on the horizon. I need to get through this mission before I can consider having a personal life."

"You're right. We'd better get back to planning your mission to the East."

CHAPTER 10

Monday-Monday, December 2-16, 1946

ON MY SECOND visit to the Russian Press Office, Colonel Kuznetsov greeted me by name and invited me to join him in his office for a drink. I let him know I wanted to present his country in a positive light—he understood what that meant. After that, he often provided information I used in my stories. Most of it was used by my alter-ego, George, to expose the negative side of communist control of Eastern Germany and Europe.

Andreas Lehman had arrived in Berlin on the scheduled date. I picked him up at his pension and brought him to the small room in the basement of the American Mission Building. The room was unchanged except that I'd added detailed maps of all of East Germany and its major cities to assist us in our mission-planning efforts.

"I'm twenty-nine and unmarried," Andreas informed me brushing back his military-trimmed, sandy-blonde hair with his hand. "I was born and raised on a farm in central Saxony near Meissen. I drove a truck, before joining the military in 1939. General Gantz first promoted me from private to Technical Sergeant, and then in 1943, after he claimed I saved his life during a major retreat on the Eastern Front, made me a Lieutenant. I was his driver and aide for the last two years of the war. In 1945, I went back to the Technical University in Munich to finish my studies. I was looking for a job when the General indicated I might be able to help you."

As we stood looking over the maps on the wall, I noted that he was a few inches taller than me and I'm six feet tall–both of us were much taller than most Germans. I found that I liked him because of his infectious smile and can-do attitude. During a discussion of how we might accomplish an especially difficult objective, I said, "You know we could both end up being tortured in a KGB prison, sent to Russia, or even shot."

He smiled confidently. "Kurt, I live under a lucky star. I was in the war almost continuously for five years in Belgium, France, and then Russia and never even once was I concerned about my safety. The only wound I received was this," he said, pulling at his right ear. The tip of his earlobe was missing in a clean circle made by a passing bullet. "At the end of next month, you'll tell me 'job well done' and perhaps give me a full-time job as a spy. I hate the Russians and would do anything to deal them some serious shit."

His air of confidence made me sure our mission would be a success. He didn't know English, and it took me a while to get used to his High Saxon accent. Most of his consonants were pronounced differently, giving common words a unique intonation. That, combined with his tendency to talk fast, meant that I had to listen carefully to understand him.

We spent hours memorizing our objectives, the route, and the roads surrounding the operations area, since our escape from a tight situation might depend on our knowledge.

Early in our discussions, I asked Andreas if he thought the weather was likely to cause us any major problems since we'd be traveling in January.

"A little rain, perhaps some light snow. Cold, but not too cold. No problem," was his response.

Still concerned, I went to the library and checked. According to the records from past years, four to eight rainstorms and a little snow were usual for January. The temperature was seldom above 5 degrees Celsius (42 degrees Fahrenheit) or below 1 degree Celsius (29 degrees), and sunlight showed only once or twice a week. Not ideal conditions, but I was satisfied that the weather shouldn't interfere with our mission and might even hamper enemy surveillance of us.

The English-language optics book Brandon had given me was filled with technical terms. Using books acquired from the public library in West Berlin, I memorized the German names for those terms.

In our third meeting with Andreas, Brandon informed us that our travel permit had been approved. "Your amended permit states that a chauffeur-driven automobile is approved for this trip."

The three of us reviewed the details of the fifty-one objectives of our ten-day trip. After Brandon approved our plan and a date in mid-January for our departure, he stood, extended his hand, and said, "You're ready to go. I have every confidence in your ability. Don't forget, just before you depart, call that special number from the hotel in East Berlin. Tell my secretary, 'Mr. Forrester will visit today.' Oh, and I'll reserve a whole day for your debriefing when you two return."

CHAPTER 11

Monday-Tuesday January 13-14, 1947

IN LATE DECEMBER, I flew to London, grew a mustache, acquired some horned-rimmed glasses, had a brown double-breasted suit made on Savile Row, and bought a lined, tan Banbury weather-proof trench coat and a matching fedora. I almost didn't recognize myself in the mirror in my dapper American businessman's garb.

I adopted the debonair, carefree persona I intended to use on this mission. I tried it out on a salesgirl while buying gloves at Selfridges toward the end of my stay. We had a lovely evening—supper at the Ritz restaurant and dancing on the rooftop bar to the music of Jimmy O'Toole and his band. At the door to her flat, she made it clear she'd like to see me again. I promised to write but knew I wouldn't—the complications of a long-distance romance were difficult; for a spy, they were impossible.

The flight from Heathrow to Tempelhof aboard a Pan Am DC-3 was uneventful. A taxi dropped me at the entrance of an upscale hotel near the Alexander Platz in the Russian Zone. The next morning, Andreas showed up at the appointed time in a crisp new chauffeur's uniform. He helped the bellhop load my bags in our car and held the door for me. The weather was gray and overcast, but dry up to this point. I'd remember to tell Brandon that Mr. Forrester was going to visit.

We entered the Berlin-Dresden autobahn and, as expected, encountered a Russian checkpoint where the road left Berlin. A soldier approached our car and in response to a request in broken German, Andreas presented our travel and identity papers.

After a delay of almost an hour, which involved some hasty phone calls to their superiors from a nearby shack, we were signaled to proceed. We were immediately followed by a very old, pre-war Russian-produced GAZ; attached to its rear fender was a long radio aerial indicating a capability for two-way communications with other watchers.

When a thick fog followed a quick rain, Andreas increased his speed. "I think we lost them," he told me. "With so few cars on the road, I should be able to spot a tail from this point on."

To ensure we lost an unseen tail, we pulled off the autobahn and stopped for lunch. From there, we took a back road which went by a former German army base, Luckau Kaserne. "It is deserted," Andreas said as we drove by. We did not slow down or indicate in any way we were interested in the former army base, but I noticed the impression of the Nazi swastika over the main gate.

Both of us mentally crossed off the first objective on our list. We had memorized our objectives and would avoid preparing any incriminating notes while on the road.

Our first planned overnight stop was at a combined gasthaus and hotel about 120 kilometers south of Berlin. My actual training as a spy had been all too brief. In France, the population hated the occupying Germans and would help us in any way they could—or remain silent about anything that might compromise us. I was again behind enemy lines, but this time many of the locals supported the communist cause and felt compelled to report anything suspicious to the authorities. We'd know soon enough if all of our planning would pay off. Perhaps our luck would run out and we'd disappear into communist hell like so many millions before us.

We pulled into the car park of the Jagerhof gasthaus just after 15:30. I remained in the car. The plan called for Andreas to determine the proprietor's willingness to become one of our operatives while the establishment was deserted mid-day.

Ten minutes after he entered, Andreas gave me the thumbs-up signal—our contact was successful. He then removed our bags and escorted me into the gasthaus.

One end of the polished wood bar served as the hotel's front desk. A burly, balding man with ruddy complexion rushed forward, vigorously shaking my hand. "I will help you any way I can, Herr American director!"

I looked around; no one else was in the hotel bar/lobby. Afterward, Andreas agreed to warn the individuals we contacted to be more circumspect. The proprietor's face matched the military photo and description we'd been given, including the missing two little fingertips on his right hand. "Herr Otto Hoersch?"

"Yes?" he responded.

"Something I ate in Berlin disagreed with me and I must recover before I can continue my journey. Do you perhaps have two rooms available for the night?" I slid a fifty-mark note across the counter with the words, 'Albrecht the Bear Lives' written across it in bold letters. Albrecht was king of Germany in the 11th century and a national hero.

The man put the money in his pocket. "You are fortunate, I have two rooms left. I also have a special dark beer that always helps me with digestive problems. Let me get my wife to take over here and the three of us can get that bottle from my cellar."

As soon as we were seated opposite each other in one corner of his cellar, I relaxed a little. "I assume it is safe for us to talk here."

"This building is two-hundred years old and the beams and flooring are massive. No one will know what goes on down here," Hoersch said. "How is General Gantz?"

"He sends his regards. Now, from what I can tell as we drove by, the Russians have taken over the Wehrmacht base just outside of town."

"Yes, that is correct," Hoersch confirmed. "From the patches on their uniforms, there appear to be two different paratroop divisions stationed there."

"Your task, if you agree to work for us, is to determine the size of the force, unit designations, and equipment positioned at that facility. This request is urgent."

"That should not be too hard. On weekend nights, the Russian troops outnumber the locals here and they talk fairly freely. A local lad I trust implicitly recently returned from three years in a Russian POW camp.

He hates the Russians but speaks the language. He'll be glad to inform on them. Perhaps he can even get a job on their base."

"Good. You understand exactly what is required. Also, you are in a central location here, so we will need you to serve as a cell leader. You will recruit a cadre of people who live in the right location to collect information on other nearby Russian military units. This will require you to travel to Berlin frequently with the information your cell produces. Is that feasible?"

"Well, I am seeing a physician in Berlin for ulcers. Will that do?"

"Perfect," I replied, impressed with our first recruit—he seemed smart and quick to understand the situation. I felt comfortable he would be loyal to us. The three of us spent several hours using a map of the local area to determine the Russian military facilities his network of operatives would collect information on.

CHAPTER 12

Friday-Saturday, January 17-18, 1947

THE LAST TWO days were similar: we enlisted an agricultural supply company manager, a Lutheran Minister who had been a military chaplain, a small-appliance repair shop owner, a farmer, and another gasthaus owner to serve as operatives for the organization I was building. People gathering information for these operatives would have legitimate reasons to maintain close and frequent contact with them. Most days, we also reconnoitered some of the sites on our list.

From the start, we knew that everything would not go exactly according to plan. Mid-morning on the 17th, the butcher we wanted to recruit no longer managed the shop. Andreas extricated himself by indicating that he "wanted to buy a fellow veteran and war buddy a beer." Two hours later, a builder he contacted refused telling Andreas, "I have a wife, three children and another on the way. The risk is just too great. My brother and boss are both decided communists—if people came to see me, they would get suspicious. I'll keep your secret Andreas, old friend, but must say no to helping you."

While Andreas approached those two individuals, I was safely ensconced in our car which was parked in a side street several blocks away.

On January 18th we were in Dresden; I ordered some optical equipment from Welta, and then later in the day Andreas and I contacted a newly-elected member of the provincial assembly. Virtually everyone we contacted agreed to become an operative. "I have been expecting contact from you for eighteen months now," one man told us. "I am ready to help in any way I can."

All of our successful contacts voiced a common theme: "These bloody Russians and their German communist hangers-on are the scum of the earth. They raped and pillaged their way through our country and now expect us to love them."

"I will not rest until they are gone from the face of the earth," said our newly enlisted farmer; to emphasize his disgust he spat on the ground.

Each new operative was given some money so they could make a trip to Berlin. Once there, the plan was to give these former soldiers some training in spy-craft and instructions on how to get the information to us in either East or West Berlin.

We spent Friday evening at a gasthaus in a village outside of Freiberg. In the middle of the night, Hans Gruber, the proprietor, awakened me. He indicated three men wanted to see me.

Andreas joined me as Hans brought the men into my room. "They do not want me to tell you their names, but I can verify that these men work in middle-level management jobs in the nearby headquarters of the Wismut Mining Company," Hans said.

A tall man, who appeared to be the spokesman for the group began, "Last year, the Directorate of Soviet Property in Germany confiscated all of the uranium mining and refining facilities in southern Germany. The Russians have no uranium mines of their own and are relying on these facilities to support their atomic-bomb development program."

One of the other men handed me a document. "These are the monthly uranium production and shipment figures for our group of mines since the Russians arrived here in February 1945," he said, pointing to the numbers. "We can provide monthly production figures from this point on. Would this be of interest to you?"

Finding out about uranium production in East Germany was one of my top priorities. "This information is very valuable," I said. "I'll ensure it gets to the proper authorities."

"There's another paper in there that lists the equipment and supplies we are unable to purchase from anywhere but the West," another of the group stated. "The most important item on the list is distilled calcium.

Without that chemical and some of the other components on that list our production rate of refined uranium would be dramatically reduced."

The third man, who had been silent to this point, reiterated, "We know about the bomb and are worried about what it means for the future of our country and the world."

I spent time the next morning using an alphanumeric simple substitution code to transfer their information onto several of my purchase order forms. I was the only one who knew the subject, the key to the code, and how it was formatted; now I could safely transport this exceedingly valuable information back to West Berlin. I burned the pieces of paper my visitors had given me and pulverized the ashes before leaving my room.

Later that day, Andreas made the initial contact with a restaurant owner in the city of Gera; he had been on the General's staff. When Andreas came rushing to the car, he voiced concern; "Helmut is very nervous, never looked me directly in the eye, and only gave me furtive glances. I recommend that we leave immediately. He may not be trustworthy. I saw him pick up the telephone receiver as I walked out the door!"

"Let's get out of here quick!" I said as Andreas put the car in gear.

CHAPTER 13

Wednesday, January, 29-Friday March 17, 1947

YESTERDAY, I PLACED a large optical device order with Zeiss Jena. After ten days, we were heading back to West Berlin and I was ecstatic—our trip had been a huge success. I'd almost gloated when the new operative I'd enlisted this morning informed me that, "A large number of propeller-driven fighter aircraft is operating out of an old German airfield near here; ten big transport aircraft also fly in and out frequently." I told him that when he came to Berlin for training, we would show him photographs so he could identify the make and model of those aircraft.

Forty-five of our fifty-one objectives had been completed. At this point, I was contemplating a second trip in the same guise to cover the areas nearer Berlin.

We had lunch at a gasthaus just off the autobahn and were less than two hours from the safety of the American Sector when we passed two cars parked alongside the road. I thought nothing of them, but after looking in the rear-view mirror, Andreas glanced back at me, "We have picked up a tail—two cars." Soon we were forced over to a narrow parking apron. Four men approached. Andreas rolled down his window. Before he could say anything, he was dragged out of the car and forcefully hurled into the back seat of one of their autos. Others demanded I unlock the back door. I complied and was allowed to exit the car before my arms were grasped by two men who lifted me off the ground and bodily carried me to the second car. Soon a convoy of three cars including ours went to a nearby Russian military base.

Andreas was force-marched through a door at the far end of an immense, sparsely-furnished warehouse. I expected to be interrogated, but instead was chained to a metal chair and told in German, "Watch us find the evidence."

Our car was then driven through a roll-up door. Men in civilian clothes practically tore it apart. Even the rubber floor mats and side panels in the doors were removed; the spare tire was deflated in an attempt to find out what we were doing in the Soviet Zone of Germany.

They found nothing except my briefcase and our luggage. They opened our bags and spread the contents across three large tables. They examined everything, even slicing open the lining of the suitcases as well as the toothpaste and hair-cream tubes.

Next, the papers of my briefcase were placed neatly on another large table. Each sheet was arranged so it was visible. Two individuals picked up the chair I was sitting in and placed me in front of the table. "What are these pieces of paper?" I was asked by the German translator.

"Purchase orders for German optical devices of various forms from several firms. Your occupation zone will receive over 100,000 American dollars in recompense." Soon we were going over each purchase order. Then we covered the same questions again and I gave the same answers. Then they questioned me again about various purchase orders, this time at random. They hoped I would give different answers, but by focusing my mind and going slowly, I managed to smoothly give them the same answers.

They didn't believe me. "Where have you been and what have you done," they began screaming in my face, flailing their arms around my body. I answered each question and went over the route we had taken over the last ten days.

When they started to go over the same ground for the tenth time, I decided that a real purchasing agent would have had enough by this point, so I said in German, "You have the original of a permit issued by your Russian Ministry of Commerce for me to visit these firms. Your leaders want American companies to purchase optical equipment to help the economy in this area. Since you treat me so badly, I am tempted to cancel all of these orders immediately and never return to this area of Germany. You need me. I do not need you. It is your choice."

A bit to my surprise, the main interrogator began apologizing obsequiously. Then, one of his associates who to this point had stood quietly in one corner walked up beside me. "I will beat the truth out of him," he said in Russian, raising a metal baton over my head. I tried not to react because I should not have been able to understand him but flinched when I heard and felt the swish of air as the baton barely missed the top of my head.

Concern that I had revealed something to my captors was abated when a man whom the others had deferred to for hours shouted in Russian, "Stop right now! My superiors in Berlin will raise holy hell if this guy is really a merchant. Let him go immediately!"

My shackles were removed and soon Andreas was escorted into the room. Judging from his appearance, they had roughed him up; a bruise on his right cheek and a small cut over his left eye were visible. By his smile, I knew they had gotten nothing out of him.

Trying to appear calm and composed for the hour it took them to put our car and possessions back together was difficult. I was both seething at being stopped and concerned they still might change their minds about letting us go. Once everything was reassembled, they allowed us to go to a bathroom together. Once there I warned Andreas to say nothing by putting my index finger to my lips. "After this, I need a beer," I said grinning. "Perhaps we can stop at that bar near my hotel you were telling me about."

"Sounds great, sir. I may even have a Schnapps or two."

We were driven back to the front gate by the German interrogator in the group, who kept apologizing for any inconvenience our "brief" detention had caused. A car followed us to the autobahn, made sure we turned north, and then appeared to have broken off contact. However, it had a whip antenna attached to the back fender.

Andreas sped up and then slowed down to determine if they were again tailing us. Using a raised hand, he indicated that he could not see anything. My first encounter with the Russian KGB confirmed they were an intimidating group.

After driving for almost an hour, we approached the checkpoint on the Berlin border. I hoped the delay and hassle would be brief. As it turned out, we would again be tormented by another lengthy delay. The guards compared our travel documents with a list on a clipboard and ordered us to pull into a parking area. Two cars I recognized soon pulled in behind us, blocking our way, and our tormentors from the Russian base again surrounded us. I cringed at the thought that our detention and interrogation might have just begun.

They demanded we get out of the car. Once we did, one of the KGB guys opened the passenger side door and removed a microphone and tape recorder they had hidden under the front seat. Most of the Russians went into the guard shack after ordering the border guards to handcuff us. We stood in the late afternoon cold as the sun went down, once again waiting for our fate to be decided.

Over an hour later, the German interpreter came out of the shack and told the guards, "Let them go." Luckily Andreas and I had agreed we would minimize discussion while in the car, on the off-chance we were bugged along the way. The KGB was expecting us to congratulate each other and say something incriminating once we were released from the base.

Andreas drove the car to where the autobahn ended in East Berlin and then via surface streets to a nearby checkpoint. Once in the American Zone, I relaxed. Andreas parked the car on the street near my apartment.

I patted Andreas on the back and shook his hand. "We did it. We survived. Let's hit the pub in the next block."

"For several hours I was sure we were goners," Andreas replied. "I think I felt more in danger on this trip than I did the entire war, but, hey, it gets my juices flowing."

"I agree. Those KGB guys are truly frightening."

At the pub, Andreas and I sipped beer and schnapps at a secluded table in the back. Despite being safe, one thought gnawed at me, so I asked, "How did they know where we were?"

Andreas grinned confidently. "They had instructions to follow us on the first day but lost us during the rainstorm and fog. Someone has probably been raising hell with his subordinates since then. They may have just missed us several times, but they knew our approximate route and some of the companies we would be contacting. Perhaps they picked us up again when you visited that big Zeiss factory in Jena yesterday. They may have been following us since then."

"You are probably right."

After that, we sat in silence nursing our drinks; each thinking of what might have happened. As I walked back to my apartment, I briefly thought, *Papa's import/export business is looking more attractive as a long-term career choice.*

"You're hooked and you know it," I told myself aloud. "This is the life you'd select no matter what else was offered—you're a CIA agent, a spy, and love the life. Admit it."

CHAPTER 14

Friday, January 24, 1947

"YOU WILL NEED many more operatives," Andreas suggested after our detailed debriefing to Brandon on our recent mission. "So far you have only covered the area around Dresden. I would say we need thirty, perhaps even forty additional cells, each with a senior operative if you plan on covering all of the southern half of Russian-controlled territory."

When neither of us responded, Andreas continued. "I could make excursions of limited duration. Some of my trips to the areas around Berlin could start early in the morning and end the same evening. Most others would involve only a one- or two-night stay over there."

"Give us a few minutes to discuss this, please. Can you wait outside?" Brandon asked, opening the door to Room B327 for Andreas.

"I have no idea how he figured this out on his own," I said holding my hands up, palms extended defensively, once he left the room. "He demonstrated superb capability on our trip and understands our objectives."

"Plus, he wants a job and is capable of recruiting people he knows and worked with in the Wehrmacht," Brandon observed. "His idea for short-duration excursions makes sense."

"If I train all the new recruits and do my job as a reporter, I could easily be overwhelmed," I admitted. "It'll certainly be difficult for me to plan and execute another extended recruiting trip. I could direct his efforts. This looks like a win-win solution to me."

When Brandon invited Andreas back into the room, he offered his congratulations. "Kurt and I agree with your proposal."

Andreas grinned from ear to ear. "Thank you."

"Be here on Wednesday morning at 09:30. We will plan your first mission. See you then," I said and both of us shook Andreas' hand.

Once he left, Brandon said, "Wait here—you're going to need help."

Brandon returned with two other individuals he introduced as Jerry Henderson and John Robinson. "The three of you speak and read German fluently," Brandon told the group. "Kurt here is one of us and has recruited many German nationals who live in the Soviet area of occupation. They'll form the basis of a spy network which will eventually cover all of that area. You three will instruct these recruits on what information to collect and how, and also provide survival training. Kurt has overall responsibility for this effort."

After some discussion on the details of these tasks, Brandon said, "As far as the rest of the world knows, Kurt is a newspaper reporter. Both of you must remember to help him maintain that cover. It's an important and dangerous role he's playing. Let's help him in every way we can."

Brandon excused himself and left; the three of us then spent the rest of the afternoon planning how we would accomplish the training and direct the operatives during these two-day training sessions.

CHAPTER 15

Wednesday, January, 29-Friday March 17, 1947

A CIA SAFE house was typically a furnished two- or three-bedroom, one-bath apartment in a Berlin residential area. The only unusual accessories were a moveable chalkboard and a large map of Eastern Germany.

Otto Hoersch, the first operative Andreas and I had recruited, arrived at the safehouse on-time, a little before eight. "Are you sure you were not followed?" I asked as I let the smiling, jovial man in after checking the hall outside the door.

"Once I got off of the subway in the American Sector, I implemented your instructions to get lost in the crowd of commuters, take a circuitous route, pausing every once-in-a-while to observe those around me, and trying to spot a tail. I am sure I was not followed here."

"Good. From what we can determine at least 2000 KGB agents and their trained operatives come over to the Western Sectors every day by foot or subway. Those are in addition to the tens of thousands who live over here, and report anything of interest to their KGB handlers in the East. Typically, they monitor our military and civilian forces; and, identify and eliminate those Germans that are supporting us—especially those living in the Russian sector like you."

"As I told you when we met, I'm willing to help in any way possible. I have determined that the two rifle divisions that are stationed at the Kaserne near my pub are the 260th and 328th."

After a lengthy discussion on his sources for this information, I said,

"Good work. As we stated during our first meeting, your job and that of your subordinates are to determine how those units are equipped and report activity indicating they are preparing for war. Your responsibility is to correlate your subordinates' information and transport it here."

"I understand. Remember I worked three and a half years for General Gantz as an intelligence officer on the Eastern Front against the Russians."

"Ah. That experience will help you, but in a way, this task is different than anything you have ever done. You will be operating behind enemy lines. During these two days, we will cover numerous topics, but will concentrate on covert surveillance and countersurveillance techniques, and how we make contact with each other."

"You are correct. Much of this will be new and different, Herr Director. Let's get started." The short, rather rotund man saluted me with his maimed hand.

"When you need to pass information to us or we need to give you something including your pay and that of your subordinates, one of two methods will be used. The first is a dead drop. This is a secret hiding place where information can be left or exchanged between us in an agreed-to location. The second is a brush pass. Two individuals near each other, usually in a public place, surreptitiously pass something between themselves. Before you leave, we will practice both methods."

"Can we not meet here for these interchanges?" Otto asked.

"Face-to-face contact will be minimized. That is safer for both of us."

"You are probably right," he conceded.

"What time is your doctor's appointment that we requested you make for today?"

"15:00."

"Okay. You will leave here and again look for a tail. Go to the appointment. After you leave the doctor's office, you will find the back stairs which are on the left as you exit his door. You will go down to the basement and through a door marked 'utilities.' Here are three photos of the dead drop, which will be used exclusively by you. It is the large tube hidden behind the cabinet in the back corner of that room. Open the lid, remove the money that you will use to pay you and your sub-operatives, then place your reports in the tube and close it.

The dead drop must only be visited after a pre-agreed signal is given to the receiving party. Your signal will be a purple chalk mark on the far-left column of the bakery building across the street from your doctor's office entrance. After the dead drop has been emptied, you must erase the signal."

"How do I do that without being observed?"

"If you are under surveillance, the game is already up. Usually, one will stop, rest one's hand over the chalk mark, and do something normal like checking his shoe for foreign matter or cough and act ill. In the process, you will erase the mark using a simple swipe of your wrist."

"So, what you are telling me is that I will practice going to the dead drop this afternoon."

"Correct. Practice makes perfect," I observed. "You will see, it is easy. We will probably not have to make brush passes with you, but you need to understand what they are."

"I am interested. Go ahead," Otto said.

"One person is given something by a second individual as they pass each other on the street. Or, the one with information leaves something behind, say a newspaper on a park bench, just as the other sits down to retrieve this otherwise seemingly valueless object. The dead drop is the safest, thus the preferred method. You will also be given a phone number to call in the event of an emergency."

"Will we ever meet?" Otto asked.

"Face-to-face meetings of any duration are kept to an absolute minimum, and always occur in safe houses like this. If required, you will request a meeting or brush pass via the dead drop."

We spent several hours going over his assigned area of responsibility, the operatives he anticipated recruiting, and spycraft techniques.

As his doctor's appointment approached, I said, "Being an operative involves constant vigilance. Know what is going on around you at all times. If you suspect you are being followed, leave the area immediately—do not try to complete your objective. When possible, conceal your identity in some way. Hide your presence or intentions whenever possible. And perhaps most importantly, trust only those who know what you are doing—everyone else is a potential threat."

*

Working in several different safe houses for two months, Jerry Henderson, John Robinson, and I provided our new operatives a two-day training session in spycraft. Only one operative was trained at a time. We did not want them to know anything about each other—total isolation of each cell was critical for good security.

Once the training was complete, Jerry and John were assigned to service the dead drops or make the brush passes with all of our new operatives. Andreas began his recruiting trips, while my main function was to supervise all of the activities of this new spy network. This and my AP reporter duties kept me extremely busy.

Shortly after I published the findings of my excursion into Soviet-controlled territory, several items the Russians needed to process uranium were added to the list of goods that could no longer be shipped to the East.

The motor compartment of a new refrigerator delivered to Hans Gerber's hotel contained a kit that allowed his sub-operatives in the uranium manufacturing facility to generate microdots. From then on, the uranium production reports or other important information were photographed, reduced to microdots, and affixed to letters or postcards which the Bundespost faithfully delivered to a safe house in West Berlin. Those microdots were only slightly larger than the period on a page and were virtually undetectable. Mail from the East was heavily censored by the Russian authorities, but these innocuous epistles were delivered within a day or two. I suspect that interested people in Washington received those uranium mining reports almost as quickly as Moscow did.

Ben and I worked closely together, but he also supported another AP reporter who had recently joined us. As AP station manager, I assigned the new guy to write the daily news while I concentrated on the feature stories that appeared in the Sunday supplement of most newspapers back in the States. This gave me time to concentrate on my CIA administrative duties.

CHAPTER 16

Natalie
Saturday, April 26, 1947

Our last letter from Papa had arrived just after Christmas 1944, several weeks after it had been mailed. German forces on the Eastern Front were now in almost constant retreat. Mama had managed to keep our gasthaus open; one of my jobs, when I got home from school, was to clean the glasses and dishes from the noon meal she had prepared and served.

My name is Natalie Warner. When Papa came home in Early February of 1945, I was eleven years old and in my second year at the nearby secondary school.

Although it was midafternoon, the bell attached to the door rang indicating that a customer had arrived. I walked out of the kitchen into the bar, asked "May I serve you?" before I recognized the haggard, bearded man in civilian clothes.

I shouted so Mama and Ernst could hear, "Papa's home," and rushed around the tables that filled the large room toward him. He staggered back and held his hands out to protect himself. His limp was worse than before and his milky white eye was watery. Slowly, I put my arms around this thin, weak figure's waist and gave him a welcoming hug.

Mama hurriedly descended the stairs from our living quarters and tenderly enfolded both of us. My older brother, Ernst who had been in the basement installing a fresh keg of beer soon joined us in a group hug which lasted several minutes in tear-filled silence.

"Are you okay?" Mama finally asked after kissing Papa tenderly.

"No additional injuries. The rations at the front are sparse and I have been on the road for over a week, but I am fine now that I am home with my family."

Mama asked me to hang the 'closed' sign outside. This was not unusual; we had been forced to close several days a week because our supply of alcohol of all forms and meat had been limited for the last several weeks.

"It has been two weeks since I had a bath, shave, and change of clothes," Papa said.

"I will heat the water for your bath on the stove. Ernst, bring the tub up from the basement." Mama said.

At dinner, Papa finally told us of his past year and why he was home. "My General, who was responsible for intelligence collection on the entire Eastern Front, called those of us whom he knew hated the communists together and simply told us to go home. 'Our fight with the Russians and their henchmen has just begun. Someday, someone will contact you. When that happens—I expect each of you to support our cause by working toward a free, united, and democratic Germany," he told us. "My discharge papers show I was sent home as unfit for duty on November 20, 1944, and never fought on the Russian front. Remember that in case anyone asks."

*

Now, more than two years since he returned home, Papa was standing behind the bar. The black eye patch he wore over his right eye made him look like the pirates I had read about in novels. He still limped from the shrapnel wound to his left leg. Mama and I were in the kitchen preparing the evening meal for our anticipated customers. A bent-over man in soiled workman's clothes came in, ordered a beer, and handed Papa a Reichsmark banknote with the long-awaited four words written on it—'Albrecht the Bear lives.' Papa took the man into an alcove near the kitchen, and at Papa's instructions, Mama left to tend the bar while I watched the pots on the stove.

When I first saw the man, he seemed to be stooped over like a farmer who had labored in fields all his life. After he bowed to Mama and me, he assumed his full height and was younger than I first thought. When he removed his slouch hat, I could see he was handsome with well-groomed hair and mustache. *He is no day laborer*, I thought.

While I stirred the simmering pots, he and Papa talked; I was close enough to hear what they said. "Well, Willie, you are looking fit. General Gantz sends his regards. You were one of his best men." The stranger looked around and lowered his voice, "He is supporting the Americans against the Russians. They have a special assignment for you if you are still willing to help." I nonchalantly cupped one hand around my left ear, trying to hear and understand the stranger's High Saxon accent.

"I will help in any way I can," Papa replied. "And my wife and children, too. We all want to help. You can speak freely around my family."

"That's great news. But, of course, they must recognize the danger and be very careful. Your gasthaus is located just outside the Berlin boundary line and on the main road that runs through the Russian zone of occupation into the middle of the city."

"As you probably saw, the main bus stops going both ways are just on the corner. We get a lot of Russian military men who stop in here for a beer on their way to and from the city," Papa said.

"Help us by generating a spy cell here that will report directly to you. Your cell will consist of as many people as you need to do the following tasks—oh, you and they will be paid generously," the stranger smiled. "Schönefeld Airport, the primary Russian civilian and military airfield in Berlin, is less than half a kilometer from here. First, monitor the fighter aircraft regiment that operates out of there. How many aircraft of what type? Two, monitor the military transport aircraft that arrive and leave that same airport—which generals and senior colonels by rank and name come and go, plus their destinations. Third, keep track of the civilian airport for the arrival and departure of Russian, East European and East German communist officials." Then, turning toward me and smiling, he added, "Looks like you've already found your first three recruits," pointing at me. This was when I noticed a tiny part of his lower right earlobe was missing.

Papa nodded, returning the smile. He seemed to relax. "Yes, they are willing to help me. As General Gantz probably told you, I was responsible for several operatives on the Eastern Front during the war. So, I understand what you are asking. How do I contact you?"

"To start, you will travel to the Sophie-Charlottenburg subway station in the British Sector of Occupation. Perhaps you seek medical care there for your war injuries? There are several doctors' offices near there. What is the best day for us to meet?"

"I usually take Wednesday off."

"Okay. Next Wednesday and Thursday, you will meet a German-speaking American in a safe house near that subway stop—the address is 143 Schillerstrasse, Apartment 19. Arrive early. Your training will last until at least noon of the second day."

"I know a number of my neighbors who work in various positions at both the airport's military and civilian facilities. I also know their political leanings. It will not be difficult to satisfy your requests. Many of them would spy on the Russians without remuneration, but with current economic conditions being what they are, that added incentive will help these people to put food on the table for their children and clothes on their backs. I even need a little financial boost myself. Last year, the communists confiscated this gasthaus and made me an employee of one of their state-run distribution collectives. Recently, they fixed all my prices unreasonably low and forced me to purchase all of my supplies from them at higher prices than I had paid previously. That made it difficult for me to make a profit beyond my tiny salary."

"I am glad we can help you out financially, old friend."

Papa made sure the Gasthaus was still deserted before turning to me, "Natalie, could you prepare a couple of plates for me and our guest? He needs nourishment. Helga, two beers, please." Papa and the man took seats at a table near the bar and, from what I could hear sounded like two old friends sharing war stories.

After shaking Papa's hand and thanking me and Mama for the food and drink, the tall man returned to his former bent-over guise and left.

CHAPTER 17

Thursday, September 17, 1947

A GASTHAUS WAS the perfect cover for a spymaster. People freely enter from the time it opened at eleven in the morning until we closed twelve hours later. Despite his apparent disability, Papa was capable of performing any task; however, he frequently asked one of his sub-operatives with information to impart to help him in the basement. No one ever questioned Papa's frequent contact with many of the same individuals.

A heavy door with an inside bolt and outside lock was installed over an unused, otherwise inaccessible area of the basement. Only the four of us knew where the key was hidden. There Papa collected the information, correlated it, and encrypted the most sensitive and detailed information using a one-time code based on the first letter at the top of each succeeding page in the Luther Bible. Only the people at the other end knew each week's key; only they could decrypt the message.

Papa could have his pick of recruits among the people of the village; most hated the Russians, but never openly expressed their opinions because the communist sympathizers relished reporting their neighbors to the authorities. Papa only contacted people he knew and trusted.

Most of those operatives were men. Fewer women worked on the base but were still recruited in significant numbers. "These women want revenge for the rape and pillage that occurred at the end of the war," Papa told me once while looking out onto the street from the gasthaus. "Many have loved ones who died or are still being held as POWs." I knew exactly what Papa's women spies did, but he insisted on characterizing their activities to me as "working in ways only a female can effect."

Ernst was admitted to a prestigious gymnasium located in the Russian sector of central Berlin; this provided an excellent opportunity for him to service a dead drop near his school. The only things coming our way were infrequent requests for specific information and money to pay us and the operatives.

Finally, Papa capitulated to my constant pleading and allowed me to help. I picked up messages from Papa's subordinate operatives and brought them to the gasthaus. No one paid any attention to a twelve-year-old girl who was small for her age as I made my way around our village and the two neighboring hamlets.

CHAPTER 18

Kurt
Wednesday, November 5, 1947

GENERAL LUCIUS D. Clay, the Commander-in-Chief of all American forces in Germany, requested that one of his senior civilian advisors, Lewis H. Brown, prepare what was called *A Report on Germany*. It was soon published in book form, and I, as the 'AP's Expert on Germany,' was asked to prepare a Sunday Supplement Review of the book. Below are excerpts from what I wrote:

> Mr. Brown spends most of his book describing the causes of the present conditions in Germany. At the close of World War Two, the eastern border of Germany was moved several hundred miles to the West. Millions of Germans were forced to leave the areas which are now part of Czechoslovakia and Poland. Those areas and the Russian-controlled portions of Germany were the breadbasket of pre-war Germany. Millions of additional Germans moved west because they did not want to live in the areas that communist Russia controlled.
>
> Farms located in the American, French, and British Zones of Occupation can only feed 20 million of the 48 million people that now live there. The Russians have intentionally limited the export of foodstuffs from the areas they control. The people of most of western Ger-

many and West Berlin are now quite literally starving.
The terrible weather of the past winter exacerbated
this problem.

The Potsdam Agreement limited the amount of industry Germany was allowed to keep after reparations.
Germany has always manufactured export goods to pay for
imports. Now massive amounts of food must be imported,
but exports have been reduced to a trickle. Germany
cannot afford to feed itself

At the end of his book, Mr. Brown recommends aid in the form of food be supplied to Germany immediately. Other recommendations include that reparations cease and denazification regulations should be modified so industrial technicians, managers, and skilled workers can return to work until their cases can be heard in the appropriate courts. To put Germany back on her economic feet, he recommends the infusion of massive amounts of capital and the establishment of a stable currency. Finally, he urges that a national democratic government be established as soon as possible.

CHAPTER 19

Kurt
Thursday, April 1, 1948

A YEAR AGO, Brandon gave in to pressure from his wife and was subsequently reassigned to CIA headquarters in Washington, D.C. His replacement lasted less than a year. Today I met my subsequent new boss for the first time. His name was Martin Lowell. He'd spent the last fifteen years in the FBI and, most recently, successfully pursued Nazis and their sympathizers in the States. He had been readily welcomed into the senior ranks of the CIA because of his proven spy-catching record. But as far as I was concerned, he was an unknown entity. Physically he was unimpressive—short, plump, and red-faced, but I decided to reserve judgment on his abilities to do his job—someone thought he was capable or he wouldn't be here. Soon I heard that he had proven his claim to be capable of drinking everyone else under the table.

I still had never entered the CIA offices on the third floor of the American Mission building. I met Martin in good-old basement Room B327—the place I'd used as a CIA office since arriving in Berlin. It was unchanged, except for detailed maps of Berlin and Eastern Germany I'd acquired, which now adorned all four walls.

After I introduced Martin to Jerry and John, my two CIA subordinates, I began describing the spy network the three of us had established. "Our 76 senior operatives and their 300 plus subordinates are actively collecting intelligence on all of the Russian military facilities of any size in the southern part of their zone of occupation. British MI6 have their operatives scattered throughout the northern part of the Russian controlled area. Last August, together we achieved our assigned goal of developing a complete picture of the disposition and movements of Russian military forces in Eastern Germany."

"Very impressive!" Martin commented, hooking his thumbs inside of the bright colored suspenders he seemed to always wear. "Have the KGB and GRU been able to penetrate any of these operating entities?"

"Our operatives are organized into cells with specific responsibilities," I added. "No cell has any knowledge about any other cell. In the two years since we started, the Russian security forces managed to penetrate seven of those cells, but since they were isolated, this caused little damage to our overall information collection efforts. Whenever a cell was compromised, a new one was quickly established to take over its area of responsibility."

"Since we're engaged in a war—in every sense of the word—one must expect casualties from time to time," Martin observed. "At this time, it appears our losses have been small and successes great."

"The most important thing is, I can assure you and our leaders in Washington that if Russian forces begin mobilizing for war, we would know about it soon after the first orders are given," I said.

"Hope you're right in that assessment—everyone back home is counting on you," Martin replied with the first half-grin I'd seen on his face.

Over the next two months, our complacency was shattered when the Russians decided to test our will to stay in Berlin in a big way.

CHAPTER 20

Wednesday, April 7, 1948

DURING LATE 1947 and early 1948, the Cold War deepened when the Soviets refused to assent to any proposals put forth by the other three occupying powers in the Control Commission; the Western Allies plans were designed to promote an economically viable democracy in Germany. The Soviets made it clear that their only interest was an impoverished, starving, and divided Germany that was as defenseless and communistic as possible.

On April 3, 1948, President Truman signed bipartisan legislation establishing the Marshall Plan. It implemented the recommendations in *A Report on Germany* and extended the aid to all of destitute Europe; this aid amounted to $12 billion—almost 4.5% of the estimated entire US gross national product for 1948. This action amazed everyone on both sides of the Iron Curtain.

For the last two days, I'd made my way to the press office in the Russian sector in an attempt to find out what the communists thought of the Marshall Plan. The Kremlin had been slow to react to the news of this threatening action. Perhaps something would happen today. As I walked through West Berlin, I stopped passersby, identifying myself as an American reporter. "Have you heard about the Marshall Plan?" I asked them.

Once I'd explained to several who hadn't heard of it and those who had, they all gave positive responses:

"Wonderful news—America is finally going to help us."

"Perhaps we will now be able to end rationing and eat our fill."

"I can finally get a job to support my family—I am a trained machinist."

I wasn't certain exactly how to weave this into a story, but took down the comments from the happy, smiling people who now appeared more confident about the future.

The Russian Information office still didn't have any official reaction from Moscow, so I asked for Colonel Kuznetsov. Once he heard I was waiting for him, he took me to his office and poured me a glass of vodka. The CIA had a file on him which indicated he was a member of Soviet Military Intelligence, the GRU. He had training in spycraft and would only provide me with the communist party line; however, I was itching to get a story out of him anyway.

"Forgive me for disturbing you, but I was hoping to get your government's official reaction to the enactment of the Marshall Plan."

"Today, Marshal Sokolovsky, Head of the Group of Soviet Forces in Germany, will deliver a strong letter of protest to the Control Commission for all of Germany on the provocation represented by this legislative act of your government. Here is a copy of his protest—you can take it with you. This American legislation is unacceptable. It gives the aid to those who participate, but also has provisions for countries like the Soviet Union to help support nations such as Great Britain and France; these two countries have constantly shown hostility to my homeland."

"Almost every country in Europe, including yours, needs aid of some form—this is a generous gift of the American people to ensure the ultimate economic recovery of this continent."

"No!...No!...No!..." He yelled, turning red and slamming his fist on his desk. "It is a blatant attempt on the part of the United States to make all of the countries of Europe into economic and political colonies!"

I couldn't believe his childish response. "It is a magnanimous gesture of assistance with few strings attached..." I tried to reply.

"—These actions are in direct violation of all of the agreements made by the victorious allies after the last war," he interrupted me. "Plus, I have heard that plans are underway for the replacement of the Reichsmark with a new currency called the Deutsche mark. These provocative actions will be answered by the Soviet Union swiftly and forcefully. Mark my words—your country will regret this course of action!"

"Something must be done. Almost three years after the war ended, Germans in western Berlin and Germany are still suffering from malnutrition and even death from starvation."

"So what?" He asked, obviously unconcerned about anything but the communist party line.

"I guess your leaders and I must differ on this issue, Daniil, my friend!"

Genuinely disturbed at what I was hearing, I stood up quickly, leaving my vodka glass half full. I extended my hand but he refused to shake it. I turned and walked out of his office with a copy of the Russian declaration firmly in my hand. My alter ego, George Stevens, had a hot story; I could make amends with Daniil later.

CHAPTER 21

Friday, June 11, 1948

FOR ALMOST FOUR weeks now, our operatives had been reporting preparations by Russian forces for deployment into positions around Berlin. My CIA team and I worked tirelessly to generate reports as enemy forces were moved into new positions. It appeared to everyone in the know that war was inevitable.

At about the same time, a reliable source in our military revealed in confidence that fewer than 100,000 American servicemen were stationed in our zone of occupation in Germany and Berlin; of those, only about 30,000 were classified as combat-ready. The British and French had far smaller forces in their occupation zones. Estimates my group had generated for reports to Washington indicated the Russians had over 200,000 combat-ready troops stationed in their occupation zone, and trained reinforcements were close at hand in Poland and Czechoslovakia.

The situation in Berlin was revealed to be even worse. The French, British, and Americans combined had less than 21,000 military men stationed there; few of those were first-line fighting men and those who were had few of the tanks or the other heavy weapons required to resist a well-equipped enemy.

Recently, the Russians had occupied several abandoned or little-used Wehrmacht bases immediately north of Berlin. The British had no assets near many of those "new" locations. During a meeting with his counterparts at MI6, Martin had "volunteered my team to establish spy cells near those bases." When he ordered me to make it happen, I replied, "The German national, Andreas Lehman, will be perfect for this assignment. He's managed to make the initial contact with most of our senior operatives and has successfully serviced all of the dead drops in the Russian zone of Berlin for several months now."

"Good. Make it happen ASAP."

*

In late May, we planned Andreas' mission together. A map of the area north of Berlin was laid out before us.

"I will start here with the postmaster in Schönwalde," Andreas said, pointing to the map. "Then I'll spend a night in the gasthaus at Oranieburg enlisting its proprietor, and then contact the butcher in Brinkenwalder on my way back to West Berlin. One night and only forty-hours."

"How are you going to get back?"

"I intend to take the Interurban train from Stope into the French Zone."

"Good luck," I said, shaking his hand.

Andreas called our office asking for Herr Reinhardt, indicating he was on his way. We didn't hear from him for two weeks and feared he'd been captured by the KGB or GRU. Yet on Wednesday, June 3, the postmaster in Schönwalde showed up right on schedule for his orientation briefing. This meant Andreas had gotten that far. We kept watch outside of the safe house where Agent Robinson was supposed to meet the gasthaus proprietor from Oranieburg, but no one ever appeared. We waited for a week hoping Andreas had survived—when he didn't reappear, we were forced to use alternate means to establish spy cells in those areas.

Our operatives arrested by the Russian security organizations always just disappeared. American military authorities couldn't ask about German citizens under Russian control and even if they did, it's highly unlikely they'd be told anything. They'd just vanish as if they no longer existed. The likelihood we would ever know what had happened to Andreas was slight.

However, knowing what happened to him was important—if captured, we had to assume he'd told his captors everything he knew. I shuddered because he knew everything about our spy network in Russian-occupied Germany.

I had trouble sleeping and drank more than usual, assuming I'd lost another comrade in arms. We had shared so many dangers and celebrated so many successes that we'd become good friends. His infectious certainty that he lived under a favorable star had proven true so many times. But I'd sent him to certain death, and at this very moment, he might be suffering torture to tell everything he knew. Something had gone wrong, very wrong. But what?

Martin and I met to figure out our next steps. "We could notify our numerous operatives of potential danger, but have no way to protect them except to have them all defect," I observed. "It's probably best we just wait until something untoward happens."

"I concur," Martin said. "No sense dismantling a huge, functioning spy organization in anticipation of one man's compromise. He may be dead or in hiding."

CHAPTER 22

Natalie
Friday, June 11, 1948

ON MY WAY home from school that Friday afternoon, the tall man with the bottom of his earlobe missing called my name in a low voice, "Natalie—Natalie Werner." I turned in his direction and he showed himself briefly.

I sat down on a low wall near the clump of bushes he was hiding in. "Tell your father I need his help," I heard through the shrub. "What time does the gasthaus close?"

"23:00," I replied.

"I will be hiding in the clump of trees adjacent to the doors which cover the stairs down into the cellar of the gasthaus. Ask your father to wait at least an hour after he closes. When he opens one of those doors, this will signal it is safe for me to join him."

At a little after midnight, I snuck downstairs and waited out of sight until Papa opened the door and the tall man scrambled into the basement. Once he caught his breath, the man grabbed Papa, gave him a heartfelt hug, and blurted, "I have been running for my life for thirteen days now. I must get back to West Berlin as soon as possible."

"Tuesday is the day my son usually carries my weekly report into East Berlin. I will let them know you are safe."

"I will hopefully be out of here by then. Will you hide me for a few days and help me determine the best route from here to there?"

"Sure. It is the least I can do for you," Papa said, showing him the room at the back of the cellar with the heavy, lockable door. "Will this do? You'll have to sleep on the pallet we will prepare and use a chamber pot."

"It's perfect."

"Then you are welcome to stay as long as it takes. So, what happened to you?" Papa asked.

"Before I tell you details, I need something to eat and a strong drink."

Mama warmed up some pork with potatoes and Papa served him a half-liter of beer and a glass of Schnapps. Though I was supposed to be asleep, I heard the whole story from my hiding place in the nearby pantry.

"I was on another recruitment trip into the area north of Berlin. I went through the usual recruitment routine with Gunther Fisher, asking him to be our cell leader in his hometown of Oranieburg."

"I remember Gunther, he always vociferously claimed he was a dedicated anti-communist."

"He accepted my offer. I had supper, retired to my room and was just going to sleep when I heard a sound and looked out the window. Cars and trucks began arriving from all directions. I dressed, raised the window, and managed to get out onto the second-story roof. Several pistol shots barely missed me as I hurriedly climbed down a tree whose foliage hid my position. Running as fast as I could, I managed to elude capture that evening. When it rained later, I slept under a tree. It took me a whole day to walk to Stope via back lanes and across farmers' fields."

"The two towns you mentioned are northwest of Berlin, but we are southeast of Berlin. How did you get here?"

"Well, on the third day, I cautiously approached the train station in Stope just before the last train for East Berlin was scheduled to leave. From my vantage point behind a small building, I could see that everyone who approached the ticket window was being scrutinized closely and their papers were being examined thoroughly by both VoPos and Russian soldiers. I decided to sneak onto the train and hide in one of the bathrooms until the train was over the border, which was only eighteen minutes away. The train arrived at the station. I snuck near the train opposite the platform, but suddenly heard dogs barking and someone shouting, 'Halten Sie.'

"The VoPos and the dogs chased me into nearby woods. They would have caught me, but I happened upon a small stream, which I moved down slowly, hiding in the dense foliage. After moving through deeper water became difficult, I swam. In my headlong flight, I somehow managed to lose them.

"For the two days it took me to get to the train station in Bernau, I mostly walked at night and slept during the day. That station was packed with Russian soldiers and everyone's identity was again being checked. Even if I managed to get on that train, I would have had to change trains at Alexanderplatz. As you can see, I was filthy, my clothes were torn, and I would quickly be questioned there for sure. The next evening, I managed to climb into the back of a half-empty truck that was heading south. That is when I decided to head here. You were the closest to Berlin of the people I recruited, and I trust you."

That evening, the tall man took a bath and was given some of Papa's clothes. He stayed in our basement for three nights. I never learned how he managed to get back to West Berlin. He just disappeared while I was at school.

CHAPTER 23

Kurt
Monday, June 21, 1948

I WAS WORKING on a report in my basement office when there was a knock on the door. I opened it, expecting that either Jerry or John needed something. To my complete surprise, there was Andreas wearing tight-fitting clothes and a bit hollow-eyed. I embraced him like a long-lost brother. "Where the hell have you been, you blaggard?"

"That bastard Gunther Fisher betrayed me. When I knew him in the Wehrmacht, he was always spouting anti-communist slurs. I should have been suspicious."

"How did you survive?"

For the next few minutes, Andreas described his harrowing experience and several hundred-kilometer route around Berlin to Warner's gasthaus near Schönefeld Airport in the south.

"Willie helped me cobble together a disguise—wig to cover my ear, and his old army summer uniform coat, clean clothes underneath. As you can see, I am a little bigger than he is. Looking just like hundreds of other down-on-their-luck Berliners, I caught a bus at the stop in front of his gasthaus. It took me directly to a subway station in the Russian Zone, where I left the coat in a restroom and joined the commuters coming over to West Berlin—no problem. I'm ready to go back to work. Is tomorrow soon enough?"

"They may still be looking for you. So, I think we will let Jerry service the dead drops in East Berlin and you can do the same here in West Berlin. Plus, we can probably find other ways to use your unique talents. The first thing we need to do is have a plastic surgeon make your earlobe look normal. As it is, you are very recognizable, even in a VoPo's casual glance."

"That is probably wise."

"Welcome back, old buddy."

CHAPTER 24

Wednesday, June 30, 1948

IN MID-MAY, DESPITE strong and persistent Russian protests and the threat of military action, the British, French, and Americans finalized plans for the establishment of a tri-zonal economic entity where the new Deutsche mark would be a single currency. The new currency became official in western Germany on June 20, 1948. The next day, after lodging another protest and threatening immediate military action, the Soviets walked out of the four-power council in protest. The communist press declared that "the four-power agreements are now null and void as a result of the provocative and illegal action of the Western Powers."

Three days later, the Russians banned the importation of all food and fuel to West Berlin. A few days after that, all rail, road, and barge access to Berlin was severed. The Berlin Blockade had begun.

The western powers were in a quandary; they contemplated but soon rejected the idea of using force to open a way into Berlin. They just weren't militarily strong enough. Instead, they started airlifting everything the citizens of that city needed into the two airports in their sectors.

Today, Ben and I met with three new reporters—Harold Elkins, Gary Hamilton, and Jimmy Jones, plus another photographer, Abe Lyman. The AP had dispatched them all to Berlin to help us cover the story of the blockade. Over beers, I got us organized. "The stories and photos we generate for the foreseeable future will be front-page news around the world. We mustn't miss anything of significance. American aircraft will all land at Tempelhof and British aircraft will land at Gatow. Jimmy, you and Ben will go over to Gatow and cover the story from there."

"Kurt, as you know, British Military Headquarters is in the 1936 Olympic Stadium Building near Gatow," Ben said. "Jimmy and I'll also cover the press releases they generate and talk to the people involved in planning from their end."

"Great, Ben. That's important."

"Harold, Abe, and I'll work on the American side. I've reserved rooms for you two at a small hotel near Tempelhof. I'll direct your efforts and cover the American Mission building."

"Dramatic photographs of aircraft taking off and landing should be accompanied by stories of how the freight is being unloaded and the aircraft is being made ready for another mission," Ben said. "Our deadline is 18:00 today and every day from now on."

"We should also include photos and interviews of the aircraft crews if we can," I said.

"The people back home always want to know what our guys in uniform are doing," Abe added.

"We'll meet here at 17:00 each day to finalize what we send out," I said. "Ben, another aspect you need to cover is the British flying boats that are landing on the Wannsee. Some of those aircraft can transport a lot of freight."

"I'll take that," Ben said. "Someone also needs to cover a rumor that the three Western powers are going to build a runway in the French Zone."

"Do you have any details?" I asked.

"What I heard is a scheme to use bricks salvaged from buildings destroyed in the war to quickly make a runway near Tegel," Ben said.

"I'll ask around the American Mission Building and you need to ask the British authorities. That would make another dramatic story for our readers on how the Western Allies are countering the Russian Blockade. Also, if the Russians invade Berlin, we'll meet here to decide who covers what. It's a story none of us wants to cover, but we may have to address eventually."

I looked around at my colleagues—from their faces, I could tell no one wanted to contemplate that prospect.

CHAPTER 25

Sunday, July 11-Sunday, August 8, 1948

MY OFFICE IN Room B327 of the American Mission Building became the war room for America's effort to determine the number and disposition of the Russian forces surrounding the city. This wasn't my idea and caused me to think less of my new boss. Twice I'd reminded him that knowledge I was a CIA agent must be limited to as few people as possible. There was a knock on my door and since I was expecting Andreas, I opened it. Martin was standing there next to a man in an Army Major's uniform. "This is Major Fred Jacobs."

To avoid a passerby from viewing me and the room, I said, "Come in. What's this about, Martin?'

"Major Jacobs here is from army CIC. The guys upstairs have directed that we jointly develop a clear idea of where Russian forces are located and their intentions. This secluded room is the best place for you two to make that happen."

"Mr. Altschuler, we each have only half of the picture," Fred said before I could reply. "You have spies on the ground. My group has side-looking airborne camera images, signals, and electronic intelligence, as well as debriefings from people who have recently left the Russian Zone of Occupation. We will bring our summary information to this room and our teams will generate an answer for the generals and guys in Washington."

"Major, my cover story is that I'm a newspaper reporter who comes into this building only to pick up news releases," I informed him. "The more people who know my true identity, the more likely someone will slip up and ruin what has proven to be a very effective guise."

"Could just you and I work together here for a few hours a day?" Fred asked. "We could use the maps you have on the walls. I could have MPs posted outside to protect the information when we aren't here—that way we could leave everything up until this crisis is over."

"Correlating all the sources of information makes sense. Let's start at 08:00 tomorrow morning and work until noon each day. Then we'll only have to make updates when new information is available."

"Sounds like a plan. See you in the morning," he said, as I motioned my two visitors toward the door.

*

The next morning, I suggested, "Aircraft deployment information is probably most important. My operatives have determined that one squadron of 32 aircraft has moved. It's a group of MiG-15 jets from a base near Halle, which flew to Schönefeld Airport just south of Berlin."

After shuffling through a stack of papers, the Major said, "Our information agrees. All other fighter and bomber aircraft remain at their home bases. Transport aircraft have moved all over the place and I don't see how or why we'd want to keep track of them."

"Let's discuss tank movements next," I said. "My operatives report that the entire 2nd Guards Tank Army moved *en masse* from bases around Fürstenberg to the following bases—Altlandsburg, Rendersdorf, and Koperlick."

"My data indicates that tanks from that army also went to two other locations. Let's review my data and see…"

It took us four days to make a complete list of where all the Russian military were located. In the end, there was an overall agreement. We generated a report that was widely distributed here and at home.

*

Several times, photos my AP team took and stories we wrote made the front page, above the fold, of virtually every newspaper in the United

States. Some of the most interesting news stories we covered included the continued flow of people between all zones of occupation. Checkpoints manned by both Russian soldiers and VoPos were established all around West Berlin. Their main function was to control the flow of food or other commodities into the West; people were still allowed to move freely into Eastern Berlin, including going out for a good meal. Those who decided to sneak a few small sausages or a wedge of cheese across the border were usually not stopped or searched.

My news team documented the scene on July 25, when half a million West Berliners assembled in the plaza in front of the Brandenburg Gate to rally in support of the Western Allies efforts to deliver supplies by air. In retaliation, the Soviets used their extensive propaganda apparatus to offer free food to anyone from West Berlin who would register with them; so far, there were few takers. Last week, the Soviets introduced a new East German mark, valued on par with the Deutsche mark. It was declared the only legal tender in Russian-occupied Germany.

CHAPTER 26

Saturday, August 21, 1948

YESTERDAY MORNING, MAJOR Jacobs and I met in my basement office to prepare another assessment of the military situation in Berlin. After two hours, I stated, "Our conclusions must be that there's no longer a threat of immediate invasion of West Berlin."

Fred concurred. "Too many first-line units have returned to their home bases for us to arrive at any other conclusion."

In the AP bureau office later that day I realized I had nothing scheduled for the upcoming weekend. The airlift was now keeping up with the needs of the local populous, and the next big difficulty wasn't anticipated until fall and winter when coal for heat and electricity generation would be needed in huge amounts.

I decided to spend a couple of days going through the exhibits on Museum Island in the East. At the end of the war, the magnificent collections of those museums had been divided between East and West Berlin. I'd visited the museums in the West, but I hadn't been to those in the East yet.

Another reason for going East was to eat lunch at a restaurant near the island; it served wonderful sauerbraten and spaetzle. Since the blockade had started, food of this quality was difficult to find in the West. Only canned meat was being brought in by air.

What sounded like a perfectly relaxing but inconsequential day would change my life forever.

Saturday was one of those balmy days of late summer. In Berlin, the sun gets up before you do and stays up until well past 20:00. My mood matched the weather. I decided to start with the Pergamon Museum, which I knew housed a magnificent collection of antiquities.

When I ventured East, I always wore the attire of an American. It was safer as far as the authorities were concerned, but tended to attract panhandlers who seemed to be everywhere. Today, I wore pleated tan slacks and a short-sleeved white shirt with a brown tie and a tan fedora, no coat or jacket. After I purchased my entry ticket, an attractive young woman in a stylish dress approached me, and in somewhat halting, but perfectly enunciated British English asked, "Would you like a guide to this exhibit?"

Since the study of ancient civilizations was one of my favorite pastimes, I almost refused; but then she flashed a quirky grin and glanced away, slyly tilting her head to one side as if unsure she wanted to lead a single man on a tour. After that momentary sign of hesitation, she turned her head back toward me and smiled charmingly; her large, bright hazel eyes sparkled. That's when she won me over. "Yes, that would be nice," I said willingly.

"My name is Erica Hoffmann," she said, holding out her hand. I glanced down at her elegant, very long fingers.

"My name is Kurt Altschuler. I am a reporter for the American news service, the Associated Press, stationed here in Berlin."

When I didn't immediately release her hand, she withdrew it gently, smiling that crooked smile again. I noticed her dimples as she directed me toward the entrance. Following behind, I couldn't help but notice her nice trim waist and the enticing way her body moved when she walked. Once inside, she told me the history of the building. As we went around to each exhibit, she explained where it was from, when it had been acquired, and spent time pointing out other details of interest.

I was fascinated as much by her as what she was saying and the artifacts themselves. She had pale white skin, no makeup, except for perhaps a little lipstick. The green, gold and blue colors of her large, hazel eyes were luminous, like the depths of the sea. I had seldom seen any like them. Overall, she was breathtaking; the epitome of the word fetching.

As we walked past each exhibit, she would get caught up in what she was saying and walk a few steps ahead, then gesture and turn back; her light brown hair, permed to stay behind her ears, danced with each movement. Her blue full-skirted, print dress, which extended below her knees, had white piping around the collar and sleeves.

Occasionally, she would pause as if trying to think of the words she wanted to say in English. The third or fourth time this happened, I smiled while lightly touching her hand. "Miss Hoffmann," I said in German, "I was born here in Berlin and lived here for the first fifteen years of my life. If we converse in German, it will be easier for both of us."

"I thought I detected a slight accent in your speech but did not think it was German," she said, surprised. "Your English sounds like British English with an American lilt, which is very pleasing."

"Thank you. It's now 12:30. Would you like to join me for lunch? I know of a nearby, very nice restaurant."

She hesitated, reddened in embarrassment, then looking down quietly explained, "I had hoped to lead another group or two of people on tours today. I—my family—we need the money I earn in tips from my tours."

"Miss Hoffmann, how much had you hoped to earn today?"

She blushed, pausing. "Fifteen West marks."

That was about five dollars at the current mark/dollar exchange rate—a modest sum for me. "Fine," I said, pulling out my billfold, and handing her the requested amount. "You can now spend the day as my guide, and it is time for us to have lunch. Shall we go?" I asked, gesturing with my arm.

Looking down at my arm and then up into my eyes, she seemed to be evaluating me and my motives. She then gave that quirky smile again, looked down at my arm and took it in her hand. I smiled, having been found to be an acceptable companion.

CHAPTER 27

Saturday, August 21, 1948

IN GERMANY, A restaurant is an upscale eating establishment which usually costs more than a gasthaus or café, and typically has more ambiance and better food. I led the way to the Bauhof Restaurant, which was just across a nearby bridge. On the way, I said, "I have eaten here twice and think it is one of the best restaurants in Berlin. Their sauerbraten and spaetzle are exceptional—just like my mother used to make."

"I hope it is not too expensive," Erica said apprehensively.

"This will be my treat—you have made the morning special for me."

"If you insist, I will let you pay, but don't get any…funny ideas."

Taken aback for a minute, I understood her meaning and said, "I can assure you I intend to have a nice lunch with a lovely lady and nothing else."

"It is I who must apologize," she said, blushing. "I have heard that many American men feel everything in Germany is for sale. And you all seem to have so much money."

"Have you ever encountered such Americans?"

"Only once and it was not very pleasant," she said with a frown.

She didn't go into more detail, so I didn't ask.

"Your German indicates you are well educated," I said after we ordered our meal.

"Thank you, I am in my second year studying the classics at Berlin University, just down the street from here. A subject I love."

"So, you do know about the ancient world and about the cities and palaces where the artifacts we saw today come from. I envy you being able to pursue a subject you care about. I was forced by my family to study business; it was boring. You make your subject come alive and obviously care about the past."

She blushed again and her rose-colored cheeks indicated that she was not used to being the center of attention. "Thank you," she said, demurely looking down.

"Do you live in East Berlin?"

"No, outside of the city. My parents' farm is on an Interurban route northeast of the city, near the village of Bernau. I live with them in a farmhouse my family has owned for over 200 years. It is very old, but we do have electricity and running water, so it is not so bad."

"One of my jobs as a reporter is to find out the conditions in the East. I understand that the farmers around Berlin did well after the war."

"For a time, the people of Berlin were hungry and traded valuables to us for our products; we acquired many valuable Persian rugs, cameras, watches, rings, and silverware—even furniture. One can use only so many of them, but we have kept them as a form of financial security. When the Russians allowed it, we took our produce to a farmer's market in West Berlin and traded them for American cigarettes, which we used to buy things we needed. But now with the closing of the access routes to Berlin, and the surprise introduction of new currencies in both West Berlin and East Germany, our large hoard of cigarettes became almost worthless. And, we can only sell our products in East Berlin—too many farmers must also sell there, so the prices don't even cover the cost of production and transportation." Hesitating, she finally blurted, "So, I must earn money to pay for my university expenses and help my parents out."

"I see. I thought tuition was free for students who qualify for university education in Germany."

"It is, but I must pay for books, tickets on the U-Bahn, meals in the city, clothes—it adds up."

"Miss Hoffmann. Do you mind, if I address you by your given name?"

After a long hesitation, she blushed and then said, "Yes. You can call me Erica."

"And how old are you?"

"I am 23. My education was interrupted for a while during the war. But I hope to take advanced studies after my undergraduate classes are completed next year. Now you know everything about me and I know almost nothing about you. It is your turn."

Just then, our meal arrived. While we ate, I intentionally made small talk—all the time contemplating what I could tell her about myself. The truth about my war service might end any chance of a relationship with this gorgeous young woman. I was forbidden to tell anyone about my duties in the CIA. So, I decided to skirt around the truth and hope she would understand later, when and if my life story came out.

We lingered over a dessert of funnel cake and espresso. "This strauben is delicious and the coffee has a nice pungent, nutty flavor. Thank you for such a nice meal—this is a real treat for me," Erica said.

Then looking down at her watch, she jumped up, took my hand and said, "I am cheating you, Kurt. Now we must continue our tour."

She released my hand almost immediately, but had given me a melt-your-heart smile and called me by my first name.

Once back in the museum, she showed me around the remaining exhibits. When we came to an empty display case, she asked me to join her on a nearby museum bench. "This is perhaps the saddest exhibit in the museum. Before the war, the gold objects Heinrich Schliemann found in the ancient city of Troy, which he called 'Priam's Treasure,' were displayed in this case. In 1943, when British and American aircraft began their carpet bombing of Berlin, these treasures were moved to a safe in a deep bunker beneath the Berlin Zoo for safekeeping. In 1945, the Russian military opened the safe and took the treasure back to Moscow."

"I know the story. The Russians deny that they have Priam's Treasure."

"That is true, but one of my professors at the university was in the bunker when a Russian General said, "This will help make up for all the art treasures of the Soviet Union you Germans took from us or destroyed during your evil invasion of my homeland."

Just before the museum was scheduled to close, we completed our tour. "Thank you for lunch and the generous tip," Erica beamed. "I hope you have enjoyed my tour around this museum." She held out her hand and I took it.

"Miss Hoffmann—Erica, it has been a pleasure to meet you. I have tomorrow off work and was planning to tour the other museums on the island. When I was last here, it was with my father before we were forced to leave Germany for America."

I took it as a good sign that she hadn't taken her hand away. "I need to come back tomorrow to again lead tours," she said quickly. "I know little about the objects in those other museums."

"Accompany me! We will view the objects together, have lunch, and I will tell you about my life—oh! And of course, I will pay you for your time." She looked doubtful, so I added, "Please, I work hard and have few non-work friends…so perhaps you would like to be my friend."

She smiled. "All right. Meet me in front of the Old Gallery tomorrow at 10:00."

I gently squeezed her hand, then released it. We chatted about which train lines would take us to our respective destinations as we walked side-by-side the several blocks to the subway station in Alexanderplatz. She turned and waved as she descended the stairs to her interurban platform.

CHAPTER 28

Sunday, August 22, 1948

I'D HAD SEVERAL brief wartime flings in Washington, England, and France, but had never found the right one. The war, Russian language school, and now my job had made long-term relationships almost impossible. I was ready for some female companionship. Erica could be the one, but unfortunately, everything I knew about her indicated I should avoid a relationship with her.

The CIA might send me back to Washington when they found I was dating an East German resident—too much of a chance she was a KGB operative. Positioning a beautiful, English-speaking woman at a popular tourist site would be a perfect way for her to identify and compromise unsuspecting American and British military and civilian personnel. Although enamored with Erica, I was superbly confident I was too smart to fall for what was known in the spy trade as a 'honeypot sting.'

When she finally arrived twenty minutes late, she explained she had missed a connecting train. While waiting for her, I became very concerned that she had decided not to make the commitment that a second meeting entailed.

After purchasing two tickets, I took her hand and led her into the museum bookstore. Two guides for the museum were prominently displayed near the front desk. One was a small pamphlet; the other, a hardback book that had black-and-white photographs of a few of the most important holdings and descriptions of other objects on display. I purchased it and then handed her an envelope which contained the agreed-to guide's fee; she blushed and then, obviously a little unsure if she wanted to take the money, put it in her purse.

We took turns reading the descriptions to each other in German and then discussed what we knew about the artist or what we thought about the piece of art—mostly paintings. We had fun amazing each other with facts we remembered from art-appreciation classes we had each taken years earlier.

When lunchtime arrived, she said, "There is a gasthaus near the university campus which serves inexpensive meals—the specialty is breaded veal and potato salad. You will like it."

"Is it quiet? I promised to tell you about my life."

"It is a bright and sunny Sunday so most of the students will be down at the river soaking up the warmth of the sun."

We took a secluded table near the back, ordered beers and the special. Erica looked at me, held her hands out palms up, waiting, before finally brushing my hand with the tip of her index finger. "I am anxious to hear about your life," she said,

Something about her made me lose all inhibition, and I decided to stick as close to the truth as possible. "My father was a senior member of the German Center Party. In the early 1930s, he often made speeches against both the Nazis and the communists, pleading for the retention of established democratic institutions. After Hitler took power, he was arrested, tortured, and told he had two choices—either leave the country or 'be taken care of permanently.' We sailed out of Hamburg in August of 1933."

"How old were you?"

"Fifteen."

"So, you are now thirty or thirty-one years old."

"Yes, thirty-one on my last birthday, in June. My family owned an import/export business with an office in New York City. We got an apartment in the city and I completed my education. I managed to get into Yale University and stayed there, eventually getting a business management degree in 1940."

"What did you do then?"

"I went to work for my father in his business for a while. In 1940, my entire family became American citizens, and I had to register for the American military draft. I volunteered to serve and spent the first half of the war in training. When they found out I could speak both French and German, I was tasked with gathering information to help the Americans with the invasion in France. Later I went to France and even into Germany serving as a translator. Late in the war, I got in the way of some retreating German troops and was shot."

"Are you all right now?"

"My recovery was slow. In the process, I decided I did not want to work for my father. So, I became a reporter and eventually landed this job in Berlin in late 1946. The Associated Press is a news agency that collects information from all around the world and sends it to subscribing newspapers throughout America. It is a well-respected news organization, and I am privileged to be the Bureau Chief here in Berlin. Our responsibilities include providing coverage for all of north-central Europe—Eastern Germany and Berlin, Poland and Czechoslovakia."

"I'm impressed. That is much responsibility for one so young. Have you been to those countries that have communist governments?"

"I have been to both of them twice. I like Berlin and will probably stay here in this job for several more years."

"What then?"

"Who knows. I will have to see what fate brings."

After I paid for our meal, she took my hand and silently led me to a shaded park bench situated on the paved verge of the Kupfergraben Canal. Erica looked around to ensure we were alone and began. "I must tell you my story and it is neither pleasant nor happy like yours. Before the war, my mother, father, younger brother, and I lived with my father's parents in the large farmhouse I told you about. My parents had separate living room and bedrooms but shared the kitchen and we ate communally; it was all under one roof. In the mid-to-late 1930s, my father's three younger brothers decided to leave the farm for jobs in the city. The farm was not large enough to support more than two families."

"Your home is on the land your family farms, not in a nearby village?"

"That is correct, but the village is close by…less than a kilometer away. By 1940, two of my uncles were married and had families. One-by-one, they were drafted into the Wehrmacht or Kriegsmarine. They were given training and eventually each was sent to fight. In 1942, one of uncle Fredrich's fellow soldiers sent a letter informing us he had been killed in Russia and buried in a mass grave. Uncle Karl was then killed in Italy in 1943. He was buried there. A year later, we received an official notification that Uncle Otto's submarine never returned to its port in France and he was presumed dead."

Her chin quivered, so I put my arm around her. "If you can go on, it is probably best to get it out all at one time."

"…Because he was a farmer who supplied food for the soldiers, my father was exempt from military service until the end. My brother Peter was only fifteen, and thus also exempt. When our defenses crumbled on the Eastern Front in April 1945, my father and brother were given guns and forced into the trenches for the last-ditch defense of Berlin and that awful person Hitler. They were given little training and could not stand for long against the battle-hardened Russian hoards…just cannon fodder…that is what they were…they did not stand a chance!"

After a brief pause to wipe her eyes with the handkerchief I'd handed to her, she said in a quivering voice, "Peter was uninjured, but soon captured. He was sent to Russia to repair the damage the Wehrmacht had inflicted on that country. In 1946, we were notified he had died in one of those awful POW camps. Men who have returned from those camps have recounted unimaginable horrors—starvation, beatings, unheated and overcrowded shacks in winter, and brainwashing in an attempt to turn them into dutiful communists. They were told that if they espoused communism, they would be sent back to Germany ahead of everyone else."

"But your father is still alive?"

"Yes, the trench he was assigned to was nearby. He suffered a severe wound to his left leg during the battle. A medic stopped the bleeding and applied a pressure bandage to the wound. He could not stand. But by lying on his good right side, he could use his uninjured leg to push himself forward a few inches at a time. Because he had to avoid the Russians who seemed to be everywhere, it took him five days to move himself the perhaps 12 kilometers from the battlefield to the outskirts of our village."

As she talked, I kept hoping that each revelation of tragedy would be the last, but then she grasped my hand tightly and said, "While he was making his way home, the Russians arrived at our farm in several trucks. Because we knew they had been ordered by their superiors to rape every German female they saw 'between seven and seventy,' my grandmother, mother, and I hid in a well-concealed root cellar. My grandfather went out to meet the foraging Russians. He was an old man and unarmed, and we could hear him protesting when they began rounding up our livestock and hitching our plow horse to our wagon. Then we heard shots.

"For a while, all we could hear were faint voices. Then, more shots rang out mixed with the bellowing of cattle and the squealing of pigs. Hours passed; eventually, I volunteered to see what had happened. My mother and grandmother responded to my screams when I discovered my grandfather's mutilated body. Parts of butchered animals and blood-soaked soil covered the pens around the barn. The heads and feathers of our chickens had blown up against their wire fence.

"Weeping all the while, the three of us took turns digging a grave with a broken shovel; it was the only tool the Russians left behind. As we covered grandfather's body with dirt, a young man from the village came with the news that my father was seriously injured, but still alive. We left the half-filled grave and rushed to the village. With the help of others, we found a handcart and transported him back to the farm. Eventually, my father recovered. He still walks with a slight limp, but is able to work the farm."

I sat there in stunned silence uncertain what I could or should say. So, I just put my arms around her and waited for her to cry herself out. Finally, she looked up with tear-reddened eyes. "There is one more thing," she said while wiping at her cheek with my tear-soaked handkerchief, "the trauma of all of that loss has affected my grandmother's mental health. She is only happy when she is knitting or crocheting. We used to sell what she made at our stand at the farmer's market in the West and use the money to buy more material for her to make new creations. She can take care of herself to a limited extent, but will never be the same."

We didn't return to the museum that afternoon. Instead, we just sat on the bench, holding each other in a vain attempt to keep the real world at bay. When the sun began to set, we walked arm-in-arm in silence to the subway station and exchanged a single, tender kiss at the top of the stairs leading to her interurban train.

CHAPTER 29

Natalie
Tuesday, September 21, 1948

OCCASIONALLY, PAPA WOULD meet the Americans in Berlin. He reported that they always praised the result of our spy activities. Recently a variety of older World War II fighter aircraft were replaced with jets. Those airplanes made an awful noise when they took off and landed near our gasthaus. Often, I had to cover my ears with my hands.

As soon as the Deutsche Mark became the stable currency in the West, Papa asked the Americans if he could be paid in that currency. He then arranged for the expenses for Ernst and me to attend a school in West Berlin be paid out of those funds. The rest was put into a savings account in a West Berlin bank. "We are all saving for our future," Papa told us. "No one knows what tomorrow will hold."

Ernst and I never told any of our friends anything except that we were going to school in Berlin. By taking the early train and staying late studying at the school, we prevented others from knowing that our school was in the West. If our neighbors who supported the communists found out, they would have made trouble for my family.

Everything about our spy activities was the same, except now our dead drop was in West Berlin, inside a dark opening on the stairs which led to the basement of an apartment house near our school. We were given a key to the lock on the front door of the building. A chalk mark on a post outside an adjacent restaurant indicated whether anything was in the dead drop.

Neither Ernst or I ever saw or talked to people who serviced the dead drop we used. It was rather dull just being a courier, but schoolwork and helping out in the gasthaus kept me very busy.

CHAPTER 30

Kurt
Friday-Sunday, October 15-17, 1948

AS THE THREAT of invasion diminished and the blockade continued, our stories no longer made the front page of the dailies. My boss requested I send a reporter and photographer back to him for reassignment. I decided to keep Gary and Jimmy—they were the most capable and versatile. Yesterday, I got my smaller reporting staff together and told them, "I wanted you three to work as a team covering daily events, and I'll write all of the feature stories and the articles for the Sunday supplements." They were young and anxious to prove themselves on what they called the "real, breaking news stories."

"We'll meet at this gasthaus on Monday, Wednesday, and Friday for lunch to review what we're working on. I'll make adjustments as required to ensure we keep the editors and readers back home satisfied."

This additional staff gave me sufficient time to perform all of my CIA duties and keep my AP boss satisfied.

For the past two months, Erica and I saw each other once or twice a week. I always gave her a tip, because she and her family needed the money, and I was monopolizing the time she could have been earning tips leading tours. She used the money to explain what she was doing away from home most weekends. We went to museums, ate out, took in a movie, or went dancing at venues in both the American and Russian zones. I looked forward to our time together; after we parted, I could still see her beautiful hazel eyes sparkle with delight as she bit into a delicate morsel, or the disarming smile she made after some quirky remark like, "Do you think it is going to rain?" when it was pouring.

Every time we appeared in public together, I worried that someone from the CIA would see us. It would be just as bad if some Russian or East German agent or operative became curious about what an American was doing with an East Berlin girl. They could use threats against Erica and her family as leverage against me.

When I first arrived, the CIA Berlin Station was much smaller and only the Station Chief knew who I was and what I was doing. Over the last three years, the office had almost tripled in size and now eight people knew who I was and about my activities, including my newspaper reporter guise. Under my supervision, five junior agents now managed the ever-expanding cadre of German operatives who were supporting us.

Knowing I had to take action to avoid the discovery of my association with Erica, I gave notice to the landlord of my flat near the American Mission Building. Eventually, I found a nice, recently redecorated and furnished apartment located in the British Sector. Perhaps it was a strange phenomenon, but few of the Americans living in Berlin ever left their zone—same with the British. Now I could take Erica to my new apartment and we could visit nearby entertainment venues and restaurants without any real danger. Fortunately, I didn't have to worry about the added expense of this new, larger apartment—as they say, I'd been "born into money."

When I told Erica, I wanted to show her my new apartment, she said, "I will tell my parents I am visiting a friend next weekend," with a sly smile and wink.

I hoped that meant what I thought it did—but decided not to ask for clarification.

Time passed slowly for the next five days. Was she ready to take our relationship to the next level—perhaps the ultimate plateau so soon? I wanted to please her in every way, but also had to remember a slow seduction was always best.

The Blockade of Berlin was in its fourth month and many of the best cuts of meat, certain spices, as well as fresh fruits and vegetables were in short supply or unavailable. I went out on the black market to stock up my refrigerator and pantry. I also purchased a portable combination radio-record player and many 78 rpm long-playing records of classical, jazz, and popular music from an American who was rotating back to the States.

Mid-afternoon, hours after the appointed time, Erica finally arrived at the apartment. I had been worried that something had happened to her, including that perhaps she had gotten cold feet. In explanation, she said, "My father contracted with a Russian purchasing agent to sell a large portion of our cabbage and turnip crop to them. I was at the university most of the week, and had to spend this morning helping my family load that produce into a hired truck so it could be transported to the Russian base today."

We kissed and she brushed my cheek lightly with the tips of her fingers. Then she began rummaging through my cupboards until she found a large bowl, filling it with water. "My hands are a mess. Those rough gloves have chapped my skin. I will spend some time making my hands nice for you again."

I watched as she removed a rough stone, a pair of scissors, a nail file, and some lotion from the small suitcase she had brought with her. A few minutes later, she joined me on the couch, put her now 'soft' hands on my face and snuggled up close. We began fondling and kissing each other.

Soon, I could hear the soft hum of the record player ceasing; an album by Louis Armstrong and his Jazz All-Stars just finished. I replaced it with one of Rachmaninoff's romantic piano concertos and joined Erica back on the couch. Except for a brief breather, while I changed the record three times, we caressed and embraced each other for the next two hours. I could feel her heartbeat growing faster as I used my index finger to circle the apex of her breast or trace the line of her jaw while nibbling her ear. The fourth record ended and started making that obnoxious noise as the disc continued to go around and around. I stood, turned off the record player, took her hand, and pulled her to her feet. She hesitated briefly before allowing me to lead her into the bedroom.

She laid down on the bed, and I began undressing her. She helped me by lifting her hips and sitting up as required. I admired her wonderfully firm breasts with my hands and mouth. When she finally sat before me completely naked, I took a moment to take her all in. "You are so beautiful," I said as she beamed. "Would you like to undress *me* now?"

Erica hesitated, as if unsure what to say or do. The puzzled look stayed on her face so long I struggled to determine what to say when she finally revealed, "I've never undressed a man. In fact, I've never been with a man before."

I stared at her in astonishment. "You mean you are a *virgin*?"

"Yes, I am afraid so."

"Do you know about…"

"—Of course, silly. I grew up on a farm and had girlfriends who told me everything years ago, I was just never ready."

"Would you like to get dressed and we can go out for a meal at a restaurant instead? I only want to do what you're comfortable with."

"No—we are here and now is the time for you to prove you want me. You've never told me you truly care," she said with a confident smile.

I was a bit taken aback by her request for such a declaration. I had never seen a woman so confident. It made her even more radiant. Raising her to a sitting position, I bent to kiss her and said, "Erica Hoffmann, you are everything I have been searching for."

"Then, I will accept your invitation." First, she took my shirt and undershirt off and ran her fingers across my nipples through my chest hairs, exploring an unfamiliar landscape. Next, she undid my belt and unbuttoned my trousers, and let them fall to the floor. I removed my underwear myself. I took her in my arms, but she turned to avoid touching my penis with her body.

Suddenly she shuddered. "Are you cold?" I asked her.

"Yes. Perhaps. Also, maybe a bit frightened," she said hesitantly.

Winter was approaching, and the radiators in the apartment had been turned back on two weeks ago. I liked to sleep in a cold room under blankets, so I hadn't turned on the heat in the bedroom. "Join me under the covers and we'll keep each other warm," I said. My slow seduction took over an hour. Erica showed she appreciated how my experience and gentleness helped her enter a new phase of her life—our lives together.

Our post-coital cuddling lasted until sunlight ceased to penetrate the curtains. Finally, I broke the silence, checked my watch and said, "It is after 19:00. Are you hungry?"

"Famished."

"Would you like to join me in the shower?"

Erica blushed, "Well…I guess…"

"—You will see—it will be fun."

After we had slowly lathered and rinsed each other, Erica said, "I am now comfortable with my body and know yours."

After the shower, we dressed, prepared and ate a wonderful meal, and drank a bottle of wine as we frequently touched and caressed each other. Erica got a mischievous look on her face and said, "The shower cap you thoughtfully provided indicates that you frequently seduce women in this manner and also shower with them."

Flustered, I finally blurted the truth, "My experience with other women is very limited, and I can assure you that in the past they are all physical. With you, I feel a spiritual bond."

The urge returned almost immediately. We made love once more and again the next morning, both of us climaxing each time. I was in love—and was sure she felt the same way.

Late Sunday afternoon, she packed her overnight case and we spent a lingering few minutes in a fond embrace at the door. I had the envelope with two twenty-mark notes in a nearby drawer. Before I opened the front door, I said, "Oh. I almost forgot…"

"—You no longer need to give me money. My father is a good farmer. He figured out what the Russians want—cabbages, turnips, and potatoes. He has received a good price for his newest crops. Plus, he recently sold a large Persian rug and pre-war German camera to a Russian Officer for Deutsche marks. Now, we have sufficient money for me to go to school and for my family to live until next spring. Plus, Papa hopes to sell the crops that are left to East Berliners."

Uncertain how to react, I fumbled for words until I finally blurted, "I did not want to indicate…"

"—Now that we are lovers, I am no longer comfortable taking your money. I want to be with you because of how I feel about you."

She pecked me on the cheek and grabbed her bag. "I will see you next Saturday, liebchen."

"I know Berlin is a very safe city, but I must escort you to the nearest subway stop," I said. We walked hand in hand, staring into each other's eyes, paying little attention to our surroundings.

CHAPTER 31

Friday, December 17, 1948

ERICA HAD COMPLETED her coursework and was scheduled to graduate with honors in January from Berlin University (renamed Humboldt University later that year). She was awarded an assistantship, which meant she conducted research and graded papers for her major professor, a world-famous archeologist.

We spent much of every weekend together in bed. Erica went to a doctor, was fitted for a diaphragm, and used it when she thought she might become pregnant. She seemed happy with our current life, but I knew she assumed we would eventually marry.

CIA security regulations stated that agents must not have a close relationship with foreign nationals—I had been flagrantly ignoring this dictum for months now. Erica wasn't just a foreign national, she resided in an area controlled by the Russians. I knew Erica was not a KGB or GRU operative, but convincing my superiors of that was probably impossible. My love for Erica made me take a sobering look into my future—our future. I'd been fresh out of college when world events propelled me into the spy game. I'd just floated along—taking life as it came—with no plan for the future—but, now Erica was my future.

I vacillated with indecision. I wanted to marry Erica, quit the CIA, and settle somewhere to raise a family. My father wanted me to take over his firm so he could retire. But, whenever a new critical piece of information was provided by one of my sources in the East, I decided I loved everything about my current situation. I could have both Erica and the CIA—the best of all worlds.

Disillusion occurred again when one of our best operatives, Manfred Mittag, the postmaster in a small town near a major Russian fighter base, failed to make contact with us. Andreas and I had recruited him on our first mission into the Russian Zone. I provided his two days of spy training when he came to Berlin two years ago. I had genuine respect, and perhaps even affection, for this older, portly, affable man. He had a wife and three teenage children, and he was risking everything to help his country—a country which was now merely a geographical area controlled by four foreign powers. I had to find out what had happened and, if necessary, establish a new cell to cover that area. I dispatched Andreas to find out about Herr Mittag.

Swiss plastic surgeons had repaired Andreas' earlobe and, at his request, modified his nose and chin enough that even his own family might not recognize him. He assumed the identity of a dead man from Dresden and with his usual cocky self-assurance, headed south. He claimed he had never had his fingerprints taken, so as far as the Russians and their sympathizers would know, he was a citizen who had every right to move around the Soviet zone of occupation.

He'd been gone for several days, and late last night had called my AP answering service to let me know he had returned safely. We met today in my basement office. "The news is not good, boss. They appear to have rolled up Manfred's entire cell. Seven people. They also took his wife and children into custody."

"They have probably threatened his family to get him to tell them everything," I observed. "We can assume he told them all about us and anyone else he came into contact with. I'll inform Jerry to close down the dead drops and safe houses we used with Manfred."

Eventually, our discussions ended and Andreas left. Glumly, I sat staring at one of the maps of Saxony. Manfred had undoubtedly been subjected to unimaginable mental and physical torture. Soon, he would be shot and dismembered. An ignominious end for a true patriot. After deciding this spy stuff was a young man's game, I prepared a letter of resignation—mind you, I wasn't even thirty-two yet. Vacillating with indecision, I locked the letter in my desk drawer.

Mine was an important task, which I was infinitely well qualified to do. If I left now, who would take my place?

CHAPTER 32

Saturday, December 18, 1948

LAST WEEKEND, ERICA asked me if I'd like to meet her parents and spend several days on their farm at Christmas time.

I hesitated. Several days in East Germany couldn't possibly be a good idea. Since Erica came to West Berlin every weekend, I seldom went East and felt a lot safer, so I replied, "I will have to see what is happening at work and let you know early next week."

When Erica brought the subject up again today, I replied in English, "Why don't we have your family here for Christmas Eve and I can make a day trip over to the farm on Christmas day?"

"That might suffice, but I definitely want you to meet them and to see where I've lived all of my life."

When Erica didn't arrive in time for lunch that Saturday, I began to worry. Unfortunately, I had no way to find out what had happened to her. Her family didn't have a telephone and I didn't know how to get to the farm.

Minutes ticked by slowly as I listened to the phonograph and tried to read a book. I was constantly bothered by one thought, *Could the KGB have some way found out about us and be holding her captive? No, that's impossible! Right? Well!*

I needed something to concentrate on and to distract myself. I sat down at my desk to again review my story, "Christmas in Blockaded

Berlin," for the Sunday supplements back in the States. It would be put on the wire on Monday.

Eventually, I made supper for the two of us—spaghetti and meat sauce. I wanted to have food ready for her when—if—she came back. I ate a little myself, the silence heavy in my apartment.

Finally, I heard a key in the door. My heart leapt as I jumped up and rushed over. There she was, my love. "Are you all right?" I asked Erica, holding her tightly in my arms. "I was so worried something had happened to you."

"Only something good!" She hugged me back excitedly. "My brother Peter is alive! All this time he has been in a POW camp in Far Eastern Russia. They let him go at Christmas time as a goodwill gesture towards the people of Germany. Apparently, a POW with the same or a similar name died and they accidentally notified us of his death."

I picked her up in the air and swung her around with joy. "That is wonderful! Is he okay?"

"Yes. He seems to be just fine—much like he always was—perhaps a little thinner and much taller, a little withdrawn into himself—but happy to be home. Now you'll have to come over to the farm next week for Christmas."

"Because of my schedule, I'd prefer to stick to the original plan—next Friday here and a Saturday excursion out to the farm. I have two special features to complete and two members of my staff have gone back to the States on vacation."

She pondered for a moment, obviously wanting to change my mind. Then she shook her head and smiled. "Yes, that is a good plan. Peter will be interested in seeing the western sectors of Berlin anyway."

CHAPTER 33

Tuesday-Saturday, December 21-25 1948

A FRIEND TOLD me about a black-market site in the French sector where delicacies from the nearby French commissary could be purchased for exorbitant prices. On Monday, I went there and purchased chocolate truffles, marinated mushrooms, pickled herring, stuffed peppers, several kinds of olives, mustard, a few bottles of Bordeaux wine, a standing rib roast, a half kilogram of smoked salmon, and gherkin pickles. This lot cost me almost five hundred Deutsche marks—one-third of my current CIA agent's monthly salary. Luckily, I wasn't forced to live on my salary.

Erica didn't have school this week, so she arrived on Wednesday to help me prepare the Christmas Eve feast for her family. She marveled over my purchases, holding up the truffles as if she had never seen chocolate in her life.

"You are going to spend the next three nights with me here," I stated. "What have you told your family about our relationship? And, more importantly, about me?"

As we embraced, she replied, "The truth—we love each other and are sleeping together; also, you are a wonderful man who treats me right," running her index finger down my nose before pecking me on the cheek.

I smiled at her response; we were as happy as birds in spring together.

*

Erica made spätzle and cabbage salad while I put the standing rib roast in the oven. Her family was scheduled to arrive just before noon.

Erica's father was the first one I could see when she opened the door; his constant exposure to the sun had darkened and wrinkled his skin, which contrasted with his starched white shirt, solid black suit, and tie. Once the rest of our guests entered the apartment, he handed his daughter a bouquet.

Erica closed the door, walked around her family, and took my hand squeezing it, "Kurt…Kurt Altschuler. This is my family."

She went over to and hugged a short, gray-haired woman dressed all in black. "This is my grandmother, Hannah." Her frail frame and stooped posture made her appear much older than she probably was.

"Glad to meet you. Erica has told me so much about you," I said, careful not to hold her fragile-looking hands too tightly.

"And this is my mother, Lena," Erica said, putting her arm around an attractive, dark-haired woman in a nice print dress and cloche hat. Her face was unwrinkled except for small crow's feet at the eyes. She stood up straight and showed few signs of aging except for a scattering of gray hairs. Her face echoed that of Erica. I stared at her a moment longer, knowing that, without a doubt, Erica would age wonderfully.

"You look so youthful. You and Erica could be sisters."

In response, Lena said, "Thank you for the compliment; you are too kind."

"And this is Papa. His given name is Hans—Hans Hoffmann." His firm handshake and broad smile won my admiration immediately, but he looked uncomfortable in what was probably his best suit. I had seen German farmers in their fields, and I was sure he would be more comfortable in his usual dark long-sleeved shirt with the cuffs rolled up around his elbows, a pair of rough wool trousers being held up with suspenders, and a hat capable of shading his eyes in sun and shedding water when it rained.

"You are the only thing Erica ever talks about," Hans said in a firm voice with the standard German common in Brandenburg. "A German who fought against Hitler because of what was done to his father—that is a man I can like."

"I only did what I thought was right," I said in reply.

"And finally, this is my now-nineteen-year-old younger brother, Peter; although as you can see, he is now a grown man," Erica said. Peter was handsome and broad-shouldered, about my height—so just under six feet. His dark blonde hair, suntanned face, and rough hands indicated he had worked long hours out in the sun.

"Glad to meet you, sir," Peter said as we politely shook hands. I noticed how his sleeve did not cover his wrist as he shook my hand; his ill-fitting suit and shirt were obvious hand-me-downs from his father.

"I understand you have recently returned from the dead. That must have been a shock to all of you," I said.

They all nodded in agreement and Lena's chin even quivered.

"Please everyone, find a seat" pointing "while I put these flowers in water and we will talk," Erica said. "Dinner will not be ready for a couple of hours. I will set out some snacks soon, but first Kurt, you must get our guests something to drink. We have gluewein (a non-alcoholic drink made of apple juice, black tea, orange juice, lemon, and sugar), beer and Mosel Wine."

After I served everyone, I sat on a dining room chair I'd pulled up, and asked, "Peter, have you decided what you are going to do with the rest of your life?"

"Before I can go to university, I have to go back to the gymnasium and complete my studies there. I'm now three and a half years behind my friends. That is a problem I will have to face after the new year. I could work with father and eventually take over the farm. I just do not know which way to go."

When the meal was served, Lena said, "I have not seen a standing rib roast since before the war and everything looks so delicious—Kurt and Erica, you have done yourselves proud."

As we ate, most of the conversation happened between Erica, her parents, and me. Hannah gave only hesitant, one-word responses to the questions or comments directed at her.

It bothered me that Peter was also mostly silent. It was as if in his mind he was somewhere else. So, in an attempt to include him in the conversation, I asked, "Do you know where your POW camp was located?"

He paused for a long time as if he were evaluating a group of possible answers. "They moved us around a lot, but always further to the East; the last place was near Irkutsk on Lake Baikal in Siberia," he replied quietly.

We all waited, expecting him to say more. When it was clear he was not going to add anything, I asked, "What did you do all of that time?"

He took another long pause. "Construction of all forms—mostly manual labor, but I did learn to lay bricks and became a very good plumber."

I pressed him. "Did you learn some Russian?"

This time he quickly replied, "Yes, I learned to read, write, and speak Russian and am fluent." Quickly, without thinking, he added, "Another thing I could do is go to work for the Russian occupation forces in some capacity. They might pay well for someone who can speak and read their language."

Hans reacted immediately, raising his voice. "Peter, you and I have not had a chance to talk since you returned. The communists in our Volkskammer (parliament) are pushing for the collectivization of all farms in the Russian sector. If this happens, you and Erica will lose your birthright. Hoffmanns have farmed there for over two hundred years!"

Lena took Hans's hand. "Please lower your voice, we can all hear you. The boy has just returned, he did not know that two of the large estates near our farm had been turned into collective farms. Those very productive places are now being run into the ground by the lazy peasants who now control everything there."

Peter visibly cowered as a result of his father's verbal barrage but said nothing. Hans took a deep sigh of relief, "Why do you think the Russians had to buy produce from me this year? Because those collective farms are very inefficient—why work hard from sunup to sundown to support those who contribute little or nothing. On those collectives, everyone does just enough to get by—the communists' ideal of 'from each according to his ability and to each according to his need' is against human nature."

Everyone exchanged furtive glances until Erica deftly changed the subject, but the light-hearted, celebratory atmosphere never fully returned. Later, we opened presents. Erica spent days selecting a variety of small items that were difficult, if not impossible, to find in the East. There were so many, she announced, "Each of you needs to take something with you today. Then I'll carry a few of these presents home each week."

"Also, today you need to take home some of the food from today's dinner—Erica and I could not eat it all before it spoils," I added. They agreed and everyone laughed when I remarked, "there are no restrictions on taking food out of West Berlin."

With hugs and kisses, the family left soon after dark. This would ensure they could make their connections before the last holiday-schedule train left Alexanderplatz.

After the door closed, Erica and I embraced and kissed. Then I said, "I think they liked me; they are such lovely people. I know we will get along. I just wish they were not stuck behind the Iron Curtain. Do you think, it would be possible for us to get them to immigrate to the West?

"Not a chance. Papa, mama, and grandma are tied firmly to the farm you will see tomorrow. We can only pray that nothing untoward happens with it or them."

*

Our visit to East Berlin and into Eastern Germany the next day went without incident. I saw only a few VoPos at one train station and otherwise, the trip was very pleasant. Virtually every German seemed to be celebrating this blatantly non-communist holiday.

On a tour, Hans showed me how the original, small stone farmhouse had been enclosed in a large three-story wooden frame structure with modern windows. Most of the newer section was a massive room that contained the living area, kitchen and dining area. He then led me outside for a tour of the barn, adjacent farm buildings, and livestock.

Lena showed me the Christmas goose that was cooked in a massive wood-burning stove. I was amazed when Hans showed me how that stove was also used to heat the water that circulated through the house as well as the huge structure itself through gravity air vents.

After the tour, the five of us settled in the conversation area situated around a massive fireplace. Obviously, the house had been built to accommodate a large family. Erica's father dominated the conversation with a description of the history of his family, the house and farm, what was grown there, and the economic hardship caused by not allowing them to sell their crops in West Berlin.

Over a delicious meal, the harsh words of yesterday seemed to have been forgotten. There were also no more questions about Peter's years of captivity. He had suffered many traumas no teenager should be forced to endure. He wasn't ready to talk about it. I decided to find some way to help him.

Erica's family was wonderful; they were friendly people who cared deeply about each other and made me feel welcome.

CHAPTER 34

Saturday, January 1, 1949

DURING THE BERLIN Blockade, most Americans were interested in events in Berlin. Hence, the New Year's feature article I wrote and Ben took photos for, appeared in most American newspapers. Below are some extracts from a much longer article:

THE BERLIN BLOCKADE PASSES THE SIX-MONTH MARK

Christmas Eve marked the end of sixth months since the Berlin Blockade and the Berlin Airlift began. The blatant attempt by the Russians to force the Western Allies out of Berlin appears to have failed, at least for now. They expected the Western Allies to surrender and leave the city without firing a shot. This effort was unsuccessful due to the tireless efforts of the Allied airmen and the thousands of freight handlers at both ends who work tirelessly to provide the food and coal required to sustain western Berlin's two and a half million people. The newly built airfield at Tegel in the French sector has allowed a dramatic increase in tons delivered daily. This runway was built in less than 90 days by the West

Berliners themselves out of bricks previously salvaged from buildings destroyed in the war.

The Allied Control Commission, which was set up by the four powers to jointly control everything in Berlin, still exists but is no longer a functioning body. Its infrequent meetings are devoted to the exchange of letters of protest between the West and Russia.

In all but name, Berlin is no longer one city; it is two. Following a recent election which the communists lost badly, they attempted to seize the governing legislative body and appoint a communist mayor. Most of the elected officials moved to West Berlin and set up a government in buildings there. The communists were left in possession of the old Berlin government buildings, which are located in the Russian Zone.

There are now two administrative centers, two mayors, two police forces and two currencies in Berlin. It is only one city in that even with the blockade, people move freely over the line separating the two. Numerous subway lines go back and forth frequently. Control of what one carries onto a train bound for the West is the responsibility of the People's Police (VoPos) at each station. West Berliners go East, and while there, they can eat a meal and also purchase food and other commodities to take home if they are small, compact and inconspicuous.

It is worth again repeating the open cable General Lucian Clay sent to President Truman at the start of this crisis: "I feel that the world is now facing the most vital issue that has developed since Hitler placed his political aggression underway. In fact, the Soviet Government has greater strength under its immediate control than Hitler had to carry out his purpose. Under the circumstances which exist today, only we can assert world leadership. Only we have the strength to halt this aggressive policy here and now. It may be too late the next time."

CHAPTER 35

Monday, April 4, 1949

ERICA SPENT ALMOST an hour getting back to the farm each evening. She had a heavy academic load and her teacher's assistant job required her to stay late a couple of days a week. In February she asked if she could stay with me most nights. "That way we could see more of each other," she said, her eyelashes batting flirtatiously at me.

"Nothing would make me happier."

Having her in my apartment was a constant joy. This almost-normal home life made me feel like a real human being for the first time in my life. Yet I still fretted about the ramifications of making this arrangement permanent. No matter how I looked at the problem, if I married Erica, I would have to quit my job at the CIA; they might even insist we leave Berlin.

I was constantly receiving updates about Peter following Erica's frequent visits to the East:

"Peter is eligible for a special program of accelerated classes and a comprehensive knowledge test. If he passes, then he could enter the university in September."

"He has started dating a girl he knew from school."

"Good news. Peter passed the test that allows him to enter the University next term."

My first effort to help Peter was to write a feature story about the returning German POWs. I learned that over 3 million German men were estimated to have been in Russian custody when the war ended. Most were released in 1946 and 1947, but at least half a million weren't repatriated until 1948. This meant Peter's story wasn't unique. I was troubled by reports that a significant percentage of these prisoners opted to embrace communism in return for favorable treatment, including early release. Peter would appear to be one of the last ones released if that meant anything.

One of our best operatives was assigned to monitor the activities at a Russian base several kilometers north of the Hoffmann farm. I decided to use this individual to surreptitiously determine if Peter had been brainwashed while in Russian captivity. The operative eventually found out which gasthaus Peter frequented, made his acquaintance, and tried to determine his political leaning.

When the operative's report arrived on my desk, I read it in haste: Peter Hoffmann neither hates nor loves the Russians and communism. He expressed only one strong opinion—Germany should be reunited as soon as possible. He said he is not informed enough to say what form of government the reunited nation should have. I pressed him hard, but that is all I was able to get out of him.

The interview was inconclusive, but I still decided to have our cell leader offer Peter a position as a paid CIA operative. There was no reason he or any of his family had to ever know I was involved.

He would transport reports from a dead drop in northeast Berlin to another dead drop in the city's center. For that, he would be paid a generous 200 Deutsche marks a month. This would mean Peter wouldn't be a burden on Erica's family, and hopefully, it could increase his sense of self-worth. He would be relatively safe because he wouldn't interact directly with other operatives. However, in the spy business, there was always some risk.

CHAPTER 36

Monday, May 30, 1949

FOR THE LAST month, I had been swamped generating reports for both of my employers. Among the stories I covered were the following:

BERLIN BLOCKADE OVER!

May 12, 1949. The Soviets abandoned the blockade as the first British and American convoys drove through 110 miles of Soviet-controlled Germany to reach West Berlin. Crowds gathered in West Berlin as the first trucks carrying supplies reached the beleaguered city.

Western Allies flew over 275,000 relief missions, delivering over 2.3 million tons of supplies in just eleven months.

My covert sources confirmed CIA estimates that the economy in the Russian sector of Germany shrank about 20% during these eleven months; this contraction resulted from a lack of commodities and spare parts from the West, plus the dramatic reduction in sales of consumables including food to western Berlin and western Germany. The Kremlin had failed to realize how interdependent the economies of the two parts of Germany still were. Sources close to the Kremlin revealed that once they were committed to the blockade, Stalin and his cronies were afraid of losing face by backing down...

The German Federal Republic Formed

May 23, 1949. The 11 states controlled by the Western Allies have formed a new central government in Germany. The draft constitution generated by representatives of the legislative bodies in those 11 states was approved and went into effect immediately. Konrad Adenauer, leader of the Council that drafted the constitution, will lead the country until a new chancellor can be selected in elections that are scheduled for the fall.

The Grundgesetz (Basic Law), as the constitution is called to emphasize the provisional nature of the new republic, states it is designed for temporary use until a new permanent constitution can be freely adopted by the German people as a whole. Bonn, a small university town on the Rhine River, will serve as an interim capital.

The four states in the Russian Zone of Occupation have refused to join this federation.

West Berlin has applied to be the 12th state in the federation. Speculation is rampant on what, if anything, Russia may do to prevent it from joining.

CHAPTER 37

Friday, June 3, 1949

TODAY ERICA RETURNED home with a sheepish smile on her face. I'd seen this look before—she had something to tell me. After an unusually long, passionate kiss, she retreated into the bedroom, leaving me in the hall. I followed her and said, "Do you have something you want to tell me?"

"Yes. We must celebrate—make a reservation at a restaurant and I'll tell you of my surprise."

"Where do you want to go?"

"Someplace nice. You pick." A call to the Alter Keller secured us a table.

I went back to my typewriter on the dining room table and the news story I was working on—"Will West Berlin become part of the new Federation?" Soon I heard the bathtub being filled. She usually bathed in the morning, so something was definitely up.

Then it struck me, and my heart sank. Her monthly cycle was as regular as clockwork, yet we had made love every day since…I paused…I couldn't remember for sure, but for much longer than usual. I panicked, walking around the small apartment in circles to let off steam. *What are you going to say when she tells you she's pregnant?* My heart was racing; I knew it was true. This would change everything—we would soon have to get married and be forced to leave Berlin.

Erica exited the bathroom wearing only a towel, and glanced at me standing there with a glum look on my face. In reaction, she moved her head slowly side to side, started to say something, but instead retreated into the bedroom. A few minutes later, she came out all dolled-up—she cautioned me against mussing her up when I tried to give her a fervent kiss and embrace—this was my effort to muster the courage to face the dramatic change to our lives. Neither of us wanted to be the first to initiate the inevitable conversation.

A few minutes later, the maître d' at the Alter Keller restaurant seated us at the secluded table I'd requested over the phone. This restaurant was situated in the basement of a building that survived the war unscathed. Its interior included marbled columns, mosaic walls, and patterned floors from the late 19th century. The French provincial tables were covered with starched linen, a lovely flower arrangement, and candles. Several huge chandeliers and wall sconces provided sparkling, diffuse light. *If one is going to be executed, he might as well go in style*, I decided.

We engaged in small talk while we ordered wine and the meal. We talked about our day as we ate our first dish—she had a salad and I, French onion soup. Finally, I couldn't take it any longer. "Erica dear, you're dying to tell me something. What is it?"

She leaned forward, took my hand, and with a twinkle in her eyes said in English, "I got a grant and will be able to accompany my major professor on an archeological dig in Greece this summer. Isn't that exceptional news?"

"That's wonderful," I said with pure excitement—and relief. I hadn't even given myself the option that her secret could be something else besides pregnancy. "You're intelligent and have worked hard, so you deserve this recognition. Plus, you're now using English contractions correctly. When do you leave?"

"Two weeks."

"How long will you be gone?"

"Two and a half months."

"Erica, dearest, I'm not sure I can survive being separated from you that long. Now that I've found you, I want to be with you every minute of the day and especially the nights. I thought you felt the same way."

"My career as a classical studies scholar is important to me; if I miss this opportunity, I'll regret it forever," Erica said, moving toward me, tilting her head inviting a kiss. "Perhaps you can join me after the dig is over. A vacation together in Greece—warm sand and sun in the day and warmer me at night."

I kissed her and then stroked her neck lovingly. My heart skipped a beat as I took a deep breath and without any real thought blurted out, "Having a nice vacation with you sounds wonderful, but I'm still concerned that we are going to be separated for such a long period."

"Our time apart will pass quickly. Just wait and see."

"I am a bit relieved, I thought you were going to tell me you were pregnant."

"Oh…That…Yes, I am pregnant and unmarried," she said, smiling as she leaned over for another kiss. She put her head on my shoulder, obviously expecting the second prolonged kiss that she received. "Are you willing to solve that little problem for me?"

I sputtered, then said, "Of course, I'll marry you—I love you. But you cannot marry me and then just run off to Greece. What about your health and that of our child? Here you can get the proper care. What if something happens?"

"I am just pregnant, not ill. The doctor says I am healthy and if I take care of myself, I should be able to go on the dig. There are trained doctors in Greece. My next appointment isn't until after I return. I really…"

"—Erica, be reasonable. You ask me to marry you, and if we do marry, you cannot then run away for several months!" I blurted in an attempt to gain control over my emotions and, if possible, the situation.

She seemed annoyed, a rapid change from her previous excitement. "I didn't ask you to marry me. I guess I was stupid to think you wanted to marry me and would ask as soon as you knew I was carrying your child."

I felt my face become flushed and my thoughts became confused. This conversation had turned in a way I wasn't prepared for. Without thinking of the ramifications or its exact meaning, I retorted, "Did you get pregnant intentionally so I would have to marry you…" I stopped, realizing I'd gone too far—but it was too late.

Erica stood and threw down her napkin. "What kind of woman do you think I am?!" Her voice was deathly calm and cold. She glared at me as if my face had transformed into something frightening. She grabbed her purse and ran out of the restaurant.

I waved the waiter over, quickly paying the bill and caught a taxi. When I entered our apartment, she was already packing.

"I'm a blockhead. Can you forgive me? Everything I said in the restaurant was wrong. I didn't mean any of it. Please marry me immediately. I've accrued several weeks of vacation. We can honeymoon in Greece. Warm seas and lazy days in the sun." At this, she seemed to soften, dropping a blouse on the bed next to her suitcase and finally looking up at me.

I should have kissed and held her, and said nothing, then perhaps everything would have been all right. Instead, I said, "I'd hoped we could continue as we were for a year or two longer. You just caught me off guard. I thought you would complete your education and I'd finish my assignment here. The baby complicates our lives—now and in the future. You were being so careful. It honestly never crossed my mind you might become pregnant."

"No! And I'm still angry you would even for a second entertain the idea that I'd get pregnant intentionally."

"It happens all the time, it's called the 'tender trap' in English," I said thoughtlessly. At this, she gasped, recoiled in revulsion, and then slapped me. I almost lost my temper and feared an accelerating physical altercation, so I left, hoping that after we both cooled down, I could make amends. When I returned an hour later, she was gone. The rest of her things disappeared the next day while I was at work.

With just a few words, I had ruined a night that should have been the happiest of our lives. I still resolved to make amends.

CHAPTER 38

Tuesday, June 7-Friday, June 17, 1949

FOR THREE LONELY days and nights, I kept hoping that Erica would return to our apartment. I worked at home as much as possible fearing if she returned, I'd miss her. Finally, I went to the university campus and found her small office. She was there with a student. I knocked on the glass door that was slightly ajar. "Can we talk?" I asked, pushing the door open a bit more.

"I'm with someone now, but we'll be finished soon. Meet me at the café down on the next floor—Room 312."

I waited for twenty minutes, but she never came. I went back to her office but it was locked.

The next Sunday, I went out to the farm. Erica wasn't there but her father, Hans, was. "Kurt, I think you should let her go to Greece. Perhaps when she returns, you and she will mend your relationship." Dejected, I returned to the West and wandered around Berlin in a daze, somehow arriving home at just before midnight.

Another fruitless visit to the university did allow me to determine her departure date. Today, I called the university and pretended to be her father. "Erica has left behind some medications she needs. Please give me the airport, time, and airline she will be departing from and I will take them to her."

"Mr. Hoffmann, she is leaving from Gatow on BOAC flight 229 for Athens at 12:45 today. You have only three hours to get there."

I arrived at the gate a little before noon and could see her standing in the middle of a group of obviously happy people. I hesitated to interrupt them and just stood there frozen, staring at her. How could I have been such a fool—I longed for her touch, laugh, and funny, crooked smile. The stewardess announced the flight and the passengers lined up to board. I went around several people and lightly touched the sleeve of her jacket. She looked at me, frowned, then turned away without saying a word. I whispered loud enough for her to hear, "Erica, please say something to me."

She turned and said only one word—in English. "Goodbye."

Heartbroken, I watched through the waiting room window as she ascended the metal stairs and disappeared into the plane without even a glance back.

CHAPTER 39

Sunday, August 21, 1949

ANTICIPATING ERICA'S RETURN, I went to the farm to talk to her parents two weeks ago.

"Hans and Lena, I love your daughter and want to marry her. I know I made a huge mistake and hurt Erica badly."

After we discussed the situation briefly, Hans revealed, "She returns on 17 August."

"I want to make amends and give our baby a father."

"Erica is pregnant?!" They both exclaimed, almost in unison.

"Yes, she did not inform you of the fact before she left?"

"No. We did not realize that…" Lena said.

"—she must marry soon. What will our friends and neighbors think?" Hans said raising his voice—revealing his tradition-bound conservatism.

"On the Sunday after she returns, you will come for dinner and we will help you two to work out your differences," Lena said patting me on the shoulder. "You just wait and see."

*

When the appointed Sunday arrived, I boarded the train confident that, with her parent's help, the difficulties between Erica and me would be resolved. I walked the kilometer to the farm toting two relatively expensive bottles of Mosel white wine and two large bouquets—one was multicolored with a mixture of blooms for my hostess—Lena; the second was two dozen long-stemmed pink roses for Erica—in Germany pink flowers are an expression of love and admiration.

Erica, who obviously knew I was coming, greeted me with a perfunctory hug and kiss on the cheek. It was more like the greeting for an old friend, not a sign of true, lasting affection. I could detect a small bulge in Erica's stomach, so she was still pregnant.

Peter was there and over a meal of baked chicken and noodles, we engaged in a lively conversation centered around the archeological dig and Erica's first visit to a foreign country. I couldn't take my eyes off Erica, but every time she noticed me staring, she quickly turned her head away.

After coffee and some sweets, without smiling or even showing any emotion, Erica asked me in a quiet tone of voice, "Would you please join me for a walk?"

As we went down a narrow path, she tried to make small talk by asking how I'd been and what I'd been doing. When I tried to take her hand at one point, she intentionally moved it away from my grasp. At the end of the path, there was a grove of trees around a pond where farm animals drank. She sat down on a log and patted a spot next to her. "Please join me."

I sat beside her—the closest we'd been in months, "Kurt, I want you to know that I appreciate everything you have done for me. But I…"

"—Erica, I want to apologize again for the pig-headed way I treated you that evening and ask your forgiveness. You wanted a memorable night where we would plan our lives together, and I ruined it. Can you forgive me?"

"I loved you—very much and you hurt me deeply. I was still aching when I went to Greece on my dig."

"Please, Erica dear, I…"

"—Kurt, things have changed for me since that night. I went to Greece with four other students, including a man I've known for a long time named Stephen…Stephen Schäfer. We were together almost every hour. Early on, he recognized my pain, tried to comfort me, and then declared his love for me. I told him that I was carrying another man's child; a man I still cared about. Stephen responded with gentleness, understanding, and respect. Gradually, I fell in love with him—he's a good man who has asked me to marry him, and wants to take responsibility for my child. I've accepted his proposal."

I stared at her in disbelief. I couldn't think of anything to say. I physically wilted from the weariness of spirit and hopelessness. My dreams for the future were crushed. I took her hand in mine, but she quickly removed it. Then I said, "Erica, dear one. You are my first and will be my only love—it hurts to be rejected by the only person in the world I truly care about. You've broken my heart."

When Erica did not respond for a long time, I hoped she would relent. That hope was dashed when she eventually looked me in the eye and said, "Kurt. I did love you once, but now I love another—it's settled; you must accept that fact."

After staring at her for what seemed like an eternity, I decided to change my plea by calmly saying, "Erica, I am our child's father, and I want my name on the birth certificate. My family is financially comfortable, I only work because I want to and enjoy what I'm doing. Although I've considered going elsewhere, I've stayed in Berlin because of you, and I waited here because you're having our child—my child. I can give you and our child all of the advantages. We could live anywhere you like and you could sponsor an archeological dig every year in any country in the world, attend any university in the world, and live with me in any city in the world. We could hire a nanny to care for the child—you wouldn't be tethered by the baby."

"Thank you. Your offer is very generous, but I've decided to marry Stephen, be a mother, and a student, studying under my current professor until I receive my doctorate. I know it'll not be easy, but I welcome the challenge. Stephen is a wonderful man and will be there to help us. And, since he and I'll be married, I think it would be better for the child to be given his last name."

"Your praise for Stephen hurts me. The baby is ours, not his."

When Erica failed to respond, I gave up saying, "I'd like to at least help you financially by paying for *my* child's expenses." I'd intentionally emphasized the word 'my.'

"I thought you'd like not having to take responsibility for our child."

I cringed as I said, "No, it's exactly the opposite. I want him or her to know I am their father and will gladly help you and Stephen achieve your dreams—whatever they are.

"What do you have in mind?"

"You'll need a place to live near the campus and someone to care for our baby while you are in school during the day. I could pay those expenses. All I'd ask is my name be put on the child's birth certificate. Then he or she would be an American citizen and my heir. Think of it as a nice insurance policy against whatever the future holds for the two of you. All I'd ask in return is to be a part of his or her life. If I could spend a day a week with the child that would be enough."

Erica looked at me in disbelief. "You would do all of that for so little in return?"

"I will be a part of our baby's life." *And, it will allow me to be a part of your life as well.*

"Your offer would solve many problems we would have to face as a very young married couple with a newborn baby. His parents can provide us no financial assistance. I'll talk to Stephen and let you know." She stood and I followed as we made our way back to her parents' house in silence. I took my leave of the family and cried for almost the first time in my adult life as I walked stoop-shouldered back to the train station and then to my cold, empty apartment.

CHAPTER 40

Natalie
Friday, September 9, 1949

TODAY, MY FAMILY went to Tempelhof airport in West Berlin. Ernst, my brother, had finished the gymnasium (high school) and been admitted to the Technical University in Munich. He would become a West German citizen and probably live there permanently. Mama, of course, cried, and I had to fight back tears. Even Papa's lip quivered as he hugged Ernst. It was as if we would never see him again.

Ernst had saved all he had earned as a spy; this gave him sufficient money to complete his three years at the university without financial worries. Recently Papa talked about us all going West, but he decided to continue his spying efforts, hoping what we were doing would help ensure that the Russians left Germany so our country could be reunited again. With difficulty, he avoided conducting a celebration in the gasthaus when the new country of West Germany was established.

Now that Ernst was no longer involved in spying on the Russians, I took over all of his duties, including being my father's courier. Each of the fighter aircraft stationed at Schönefeld Airport had a unique tail number; one of my new jobs was to find out how many MiG-15 aircraft were assigned to the base by observing those jets take off and land; I was also tasked to report if any of the newer MiG-17 aircraft were observed there. At the age of fifteen, I was a real spy.

CHAPTER 41

Kurt
Tuesday, January 17-Sunday, February 5, 1950

SINCE THAT DAY at her parent's house, I'd only seen Erica once. Three months later, she called to ask if we could meet for lunch near her university. Now very pregnant, she gave me a peck on the cheek in greeting. I immediately noticed the gold band on her right ring finger. Most of our time together was spent exchanging pleasantries about her life and family. I waited, assuming Erica would tell me why she wanted to see me. After a long silence, she took my right hand in hers and in a caring voice said, "Kurt, have you found someone new?"

"No, I haven't even tried."

"You must move on. Stephen and I are exceptionally happy together. You're a good man and need to find someone to love as much as I once loved you and now love him. It is a wonderful feeling. It's like the quote: 'Love is like water…We can fall in it…We can drown in it… but we cannot live without it.' Please try to find someone—for your own sake."

"I'll try."

"Promise."

"Yes, I promise," I said.

After we separated, I thought about what she had said but concluded that I might never love again.

*

Our baby daughter was born on January 15, 1950. Two days later, Erica called and asked me to visit her in the hospital. She was in bed and the baby was asleep in her arms. After a peck on the cheek—our new routine—she said, "We must decide on a name for the baby."

"You're asking me to help you name our baby?!"

"We need a name for the birth certificate. I'm using my married name as mother. I think Gretchen would be a nice name. It is an old family name."

"If that is the name you want for her, then I concur. Have you also decided on a middle name?"

"No. What is your mother's name?"

"Marie."

"Gretchen Marie Schäfer. I like that. Is it acceptable?"

"Schafer?" This conversation wasn't going as I expected.

Before I could object further, she added, "And we want you to be Gretchen's godfather. By tradition, one of the godfather's main responsibilities is to help select the child's name. Also, I want you to have a legal document generated which makes you her legal guardian, should something happen to Stephen and me."

"But…"

"—Kurt, dear friend, please try to see this situation from our viewpoint. Stephen and I have decided we don't want to have our daughter identified on her birth certificate as illegitimate. She was born after we were married, and hence, she is legally Stephen's daughter."

"I thought…"

"—Little changes, you'll see her once a week. When she's of an age to understand, the three of us will tell her that you're her biological father, but Stephen will play the role of the father while she's young. You'll play the role of godfather and best friend to her parents."

I was astonished they had made this decision without allowing me to have any input. "Erica, if Gretchen's recognized on the birth certificate as my daughter, she'll automatically be an American citizen and could have dual citizenship. At present, the situation in Germany is unstable, to say the least. And you, as the mother of an American citizen, could immigrate there with her. Someday that might save your lives."

"We intend to raise our daughter in Germany. Once we complete our education, we can emigrate to West Germany, which should be safe for all of us," she said quietly, but very resolutely. "We might also stay here…the Russians won't always be here."

Given what I knew, I could tell her several valid reasons why her naïve plans might end in disaster, but it was clear she wouldn't accept my warning. "I understand your concerns," I said defeated. "You and Stephen are correct— a birth certificate is an important document—which could be used against Gretchen later in life."

I rose from my chair. I didn't even know how to say goodbye. "Kurt, one more thing. Gretchen will be christened on Sunday, February first, in the Marien Kirche (Saint Mary's Church) near the Alexanderplatz," Erica said as I quietly made my way to the door. "You, as the godfather, will have an important role in the ceremony. Please be there at 10:45."

"I will," I said, turning quickly to look at Erica. It felt like I was losing her all over again. In an audible whisper, I then said, "As I've said from the beginning, I want to be a part of my daughter's life."

*

I asked a family lawyer to draw up a document that stated I was the biological father of Gretchen. It also stated that in the event of the death of both her parents, I would be her only legal guardian. In addition, that firm also drafted a will that named Gretchen as my sole heir, should I die without further issue. If other children were born to me, they would each have an equal share of my estate.

The document signing was two days before the christening. Erica introduced Stephen to me; it was the first time we had met. I hated him for stealing my family, but grudgingly admitted to myself that he was a decent if very reserved young man. The documents were signed and notarized in both East and West Berlin to ensure they would be legally binding irrespective of future circumstances.

This last step was necessary because, in October of 1949, the Russians had allowed the German communists, in their zone of occupation, to organize a new country which was called the German Democratic Republic. Few countries outside the communist block officially recognized their existence, but the Russians had given them legal and administrative control of the eastern part of Germany.

While they were in West Berlin to sign the papers, Gretchen and Stephen opened a bank account at my request. Each month I deposited sufficient Deutsche Marks into that account to cover most of their expenses. We never again discussed the monetary aspects of our unique arrangement.

*

The christening took place in the small 13th-century church—the oldest in Berlin. The parents, their families, and I gathered around the magnificent Baptismal Font, which church records show was fabricated and installed in its current location in 1437. It was supported by three dragons and decorated with the figures of Jesus, Mary, and the Apostles. The Lutheran priest reminded everyone present of their duty to raise the child within the church. I held Gretchen for the first time as I was reminded of the special role the godfather plays in a child's life. Then I handed her to Lena, who became her godmother.

After the ceremony was over, the family gathered for a special meal in a small, cozy private room at a nearby restaurant. Peter sat next to me and we talked about how his university education was progressing, and his plans for the future. "I'll finish my education in two more years and might have to move to the West. I'm taking business and accounting—there is much demand for those skills over there."

Peter had no idea I was the one who had given him the opportunity to become a CIA operative, and I intended to keep him in the dark. Him knowing my position wouldn't be helpful for either of us.

PART 2

1950-1957

"The East German Secret Police, known to the world as the Stasi, are far worse than the Gestapo."

Simon Wiesenthal, Nazi Hunter, 1985

CHAPTER 42

Kurt
Tuesday, October 24, 1950

TODAY, I DISPATCHED the seventh of a series of CIA memorandum for the record on Russian/East German spy activities in Germany that I'd written since arriving in Berlin.

TOP SECRET/US/UK EYES ONLY

In 1933, Hitler outlawed the communist party. At that time, it was the largest single political party in Germany. Tens of thousands of German communists fled to Russia to avoid imprisonment. There, they received training of various forms with one central objective—the establishment of a Soviet-style dictatorship in Germany. The brightest and best received training from the KGB to perform covert spy operations, and provide internal security in protection of a communist state.

Previous reports (reference items 1 through 6 in Appendix A) have detailed how these dedicated communists followed the Soviet Army into Germany and how for over five years, they helped them maintain a firm grip over the civilian population in the Russian Zone of Occupation.

This report contains a summary of what is known about the recently established East German Ministry of State Security and its role in the new communist state. This organization is known under the cognomen "Stasi." Its headquarters is in a prewar industrial complex located in the Lichtenberg Section of Southeastern Berlin. Eight subordinate regional headquarters have been established. (See Appendix B for a list of these locations, areas of responsibility and the approximate number of people assigned to each of these units.)

Without exception, the leaders of this new organization have been approved for their positions by the KGB, and high-level agents from that organization are collocated with and oversee the daily operations of all Stasi units. (Organization charts of the Stasi Headquarters and 6 of the 8 subordinate units are contained in Appendix C).

Although the KGB has been a worthy opponent of the CIA in Western Europe, the Russians have failed to win the hearts and minds of the average East German citizen. The rape of German women in 1945, the wanton confiscation and destruction of factories and private property, plus perhaps most importantly, the blatant seizure of the reins of government from democratically elected officials have turned most people who live in the East against them.

The Stasi was established to address this problem. Our best estimate is the organization has 17,600 full-time employees and almost 30,000 individuals who support their efforts part-time in return for some remuneration. They continue to recruit employees and supporters at the rate of around a thousand a month.

The Stasi have been tasked with ensuring that every East German citizen conforms to the communist ideal of being an eager participant in the goal of world domination. Stasi agents have been assigned to factories, businesses, schools, universities, collective farms, military units, and hospitals to ensure conformity with established communist norms of thought and behavior. One individual in each apartment house has been assigned the task of monitoring the activities of everyone else who lives there or visits. Individuals have been prosecuted if they don't report a friend or neighbor who said something negative about communism and the current regime . . .

TOP SECRET/US/UK EYES ONLY

Reports of this type check off a box in some bosses' list of required activities but provide little detailed information about the real spy war on the ground.

Since the loss of Manfred Mittag and his six operatives months ago, I'd worried about the vulnerability of my ever-expanding spy network. None of our operatives had more than two days of training in spycraft. Despite this, they had functioned remarkably well. When the KGB managed to interrupt our operations in one limited area, we recovered the lost capability quickly. Now the Stasi enlisted a cadre of dedicated communists who were trained by the KGB and had the big advantages of being German, speaking German, and perhaps most importantly, having the backing of a German government.

Recently, several operatives had aborted an assigned surveillance task due to fear of being discovered, and surveillance chains were broken when operatives just disappeared. We rarely knew how they had been compromised, what happened to them, or exactly what they revealed under almost certain torture. All at once, Stasi agents seemed to be everywhere and began winning the behind-the-scenes war.

In reaction, with CIA headquarters concurrence and assistance, I implemented a spycraft training program. Our operatives would take a week off work/school in the East and go to one of ten safehouses in West Berlin. There a German-speaking CIA agent would give one-on-one operative surveillance/countersurveillance training. We couldn't risk training them as a group because if captured, they might reveal the identity of others they met.

We taught them how to create disguises, conduct surveillance, use concealment, procure information, and exchange secure messages. This program lasted for eleven weeks, and over a hundred senior operatives received this training. The program was successful and our losses decreased. I made sure that Peter Hoffman was one of the individuals who received this training.

For months, I'd called Erica to arrange to pick up my daughter for the day. Then I traveled East, picked Gretchen up, and usually brought her back to the West. Knowing that our agents and operatives watched the border, I decided to inform the CIA of my relationship with Erica and that I had a daughter named Gretchen with her. I even named Gretchen as my official beneficiary and dependent. My new station chief, James Wilson, seemed unconcerned by this revelation.

CHAPTER 43

Friday, April 3, 1953

LATE IN 1951, I decided to personally make contact with a male, East Berlin resident who had volunteered to work for us. He was recommended by an operative who had been working for us since 1947. I entered East Berlin in my usual AP reporter's garb—briefcase, dark blue, pin-striped, three-piece suit, white shirt, tie, and fedora hat. I went into a gasthaus bathroom but exited as a slightly stooped older man after donning a heavy sweater, a gray wig, thick glasses, no hat, and a large knapsack.

We met in a park a few blocks away. I introduced myself as Walter Schultz and took him to a safe house the CIA maintained in East Berlin. Both he and his friend were communist party members; this affiliation had helped his friend to avoid detection all these years. He reported a job offer with the Economic and Scientific Research Institute, which was a front organization for the Stasi. People from that organization regularly defected to the West, bringing information of little real value with them. After the first few defections, we realized that these individuals had been tasked with becoming part of a new, well-organized Stasi-controlled spy network in West Germany.

Initial contact with a new operative was always risky. They might be a Stasi agent or operative. One of my first questions was always, "Why do you want to help us?"

"Life in the East just keeps getting worse," he stated. "My wife and I must share a tiny one-bedroom apartment with two children. We share a bathroom with two other apartments. There are rats and filth. Food is cheap, health care is free, but the nice things one sees in West Berlin are unavailable. My friend Karl indicates you will pay for my help. I want you to keep the money I earn until I defect. That will help Irma and I start a new life over there."

Because of who had recommended him and his motives, I decided to take a chance on him. I then explained how a dead drop worked and showed him diagrams of one I'd established between the place he worked and his home. In reaction, he said, "Can we continue to meet here? I feel safe with you—the wrong people could see me enter that building, and challenge my reason for being there. Not so here."

We were anxious to get someone inside of this organization; so, after trying to apprise him of the inherent dangers of face-to-face meetings, I agreed our next meeting could be in the same place.

The next time we met, he gave me two different Stasi spy-training manuals. As I leafed through them, I asked, "How did you get these?"

"I knew where they were kept and broke into an office to acquire them."

"Did you leave any marks on the door?"

"Maybe."

"Are they going to know these are missing? They don't seem to be numbered."

"Perhaps," he replied sheepishly.

"Please be more selective in the information you provide," I demanded. "Focus on your primary task. We want the names of the Stasi agents operating in West Germany. Become a sleeper operative until you can provide that list."

At our next two meetings, he provided the names of the other students in his class and his instructor's name. But he still refused to use a dead drop or brush pass. Each time we met, he was more and more nervous. If he was acting jumpy around me, how was he acting around his training officers and fellow spy trainees?

Uncomfortable with this arrangement, I had Andreas follow him after each meeting; he reported this young operative wasn't being followed by anyone else.

I arrived early for each meeting to conduct surveillance of the safe house before entering it. From my vantage point on a nearby bus bench, I determined that two individuals were surveilling the building—one was leaning against a wall and the other seated at a nearby outdoor cafe. My operative was scheduled to arrive soon.

The whole operation had to be aborted. Following established procedure, using chalk I put an X on a column in the next block. This told this young operative that his cover was blown and he must defect immediately. I hoped he would see it before he blundered into the Stasi trap.

Fortunately, later that day, he, his wife, and children managed to board a subway in East Berlin and defect to the West. He called a phone number I'd given him for emergencies and told the CIA operator, "I have defected. Have Herr Schultz come to take a large briefcase of valuable information from me."

The case and information he provided revealed the names of 37 Stasi spies located in West Germany. Alan Dulles, director of the CIA, decided to give this information to the newly established West German Office for the Protection of the Constitution. The early morning arrest of all but two of the Stasi moles made headlines around the world. It became famous as Operation Vulkan (Volcano). The agents were convicted of espionage, sentenced to 12 to 15 years in prison, and would be expelled to the East after serving their sentence.

For now, it would appear that we were still on top of the spy game in Berlin.

CHAPTER 44

Monday-Tuesday, June 15-16, 1953

FOR THE LAST three years, my life had a dull sameness: write feature stories for the AP and direct the effort of my AP staff; occasionally cover a trade fair or other special event in either East Berlin, Leipzig, Dresden, Warsaw, or Prague, where I would pick up information from one of our operatives. Usually, I would spend one or two days a week in the CIA office in the American Mission so I could maintain cognizance of the activities of the spy network I'd established, but no longer directly controlled.

On either Saturday or Sunday of most weeks, I'd pick up Gretchen in East Berlin and take her West. Once there, I'd put her in her perambulator and later pushcart for hours-long jaunts through the streets and parks of West Berlin. I was virtually the only male caring for a young child, but I wanted her to know I loved her and couldn't care less what others thought of me. Often, I related to Gretchen the wonderful times I'd had with her mother. To the amazement and amusement of others, I changed her diapers, fed her, and burped her. My cleaning bill increased dramatically until I mastered the care and feeding of a young child while wearing a three-piece suit.

For the last year, one of Gretchen's favorite activities was for me to read her one of the myriad books I kept in her room at my apartment. If the weather was warm enough and dry, we ate lunch on a park bench, then she would play with other children.

Recently I purchased a membership to a swim club with an indoor heated pool. On weekend afternoons, children were allowed in the pool. We swam together for an hour or so; she was like a lithe fish in the water. After the swim, we'd visit an ice cream or chocolate shop. Now that she was three and a half, she was capable of carrying on a conversation about things she was interested in, such as her dolls and make-believe.

By agreement, she was told to call me Uncle (Onkel in German) Kurt. At first, I was haltingly called…"Okl" or "Kur." As her language skills improved, she would hug and kiss me and say, "I love you, Onki." My heart always melted.

Occasionally, I had lunch with Erica and Gretchen; those days, though snippets in time, were the happiest of my entire year. Sometimes I had supper with them and Stephen—that was always pure torture. Seeing how happy Erica and Stephen were together, and how much they cared for each other and Gretchen, gave me a deep heartache. Around Gretchen, we three adults assiduously played our assigned roles—happy couple and best friend.

I still longed to touch and hold Erica. Nothing had changed. I forced myself to be satisfied with the little time we spent together. I had no other choice.

Occasionally, I dated. Once we became intimate, it seemed they always wanted a commitment, one which I wasn't prepared to make. So far, no one had managed to get inside of the shell I'd constructed after Erica left me. I tried but failed, to fulfill my promise to her to fall in love again.

*

The Berlin CIA office's mandate included the collection of military, political, and economic intelligence on the communist bloc of East European nations. The East German five-year plan for growth in their economy continuously fell far behind the arbitrary goals that Ulbricht and his henchmen set in 1951. Those figures were a commitment to the Kremlin to end the subsidies East Germany had been receiving from Russia since 1945.

Last week, one of our operatives in the East German government informed us of the East German government's solution. On Monday morning, June 15, arriving workers would be handed leaflets informing them that each of them must produce a minimum of ten percent more for the same pay. If they failed to meet these new goals, their pay would be docked by the same percentage.

In my guise as an AP reporter, I met some of my East German (non-spy) friends for lunch that same day. They reported widespread unrest in Berlin, including a great number of workers who had already walked off the job. One individual passed around a pamphlet he'd been given; it declared a nationwide worker's strike for the next day. Late that afternoon, I generated a CIA report describing these events. I then called Ben Stevens, the AP photographer, and asked, "Have you heard about the strike over in the East tomorrow?"

"No? What's happening?"

I told him what I knew.

"No wonder their economy is a mess," Ben said. "They're spending most of their budget building a huge army and air force, constructing fences along their border with West Germany and around West Berlin."

"Don't forget the Stasi," I added. "They have hired tens of thousands of people and given them unlimited resources to spy on the West and to make all East Germans into model communists. Anyway, the workers have declared a strike for tomorrow. Word has spread throughout East Germany; the strike will be a news story that we must cover."

"I agree. Where will they gather in East Berlin?"

"From what I can tell, they're going to start in Alexanderplatz early tomorrow morning and march to Unter den Linden and on to nearby government offices."

"I'll meet you beneath the big clock in the Alexanderplatz Train Station at 07:00," Ben said, concluding the conversation.

My press pass allowed me to move freely between East and West Berlin; gathering information about the East in this guise had been one of my primary CIA tasks for the past several years. The Berlin uprising proved to be another opportunity for me to satisfy both bosses.

*

The train station was crowded, but Ben and I managed to make our way through the masses and ascend the stairs into the huge open space above.

The square was packed with people who were milling about aimlessly. No one appeared to be in charge of the strike effort.

Just before 08:00, a truck with a flatbed moved slowly through the crowd toward its center. An individual with a megaphone clambered up onto the truck's bed and tried to get everyone's attention. He repositioned himself several times and made the same announcement, "This strike is no longer just about increased work for the same wages. It is about the kind of government the Russians have imposed on us."

Ben and I moved through the masses toward the truck. I gave ten Deutsche Marks to two men so we could take their place standing on a park bench. From there, Ben could photograph the scene and I could see what was happening.

Six others joined the man with the bullhorn on the bed of the truck. They carried placards which read: "Down with the Government; Down with Ulbricht (The East German government leader); We Want to Be Free People; Ivan Go Home; Reunite Germany; and, The SED (East German Communist Party) has Brought Only Hardship." As each placard was paraded around the truck bed, the man with the megaphone led the crowd in chanting that message for a few minutes.

From my vantage point, I could see vehicles on side streets disbursing uniformed Peoples Police (VoPos). A group of men in the leather trench coats of the Stasi were directing their efforts.

Soon the leader with the megaphone said, "Follow me to Ulbricht's office so we can present our grievances." With that, he and the sign carriers descended into the crowd. The protest signs were moving up and down as the strike leaders passed through the crowd toward East German government buildings.

At this point, a large group of truncheon-wielding VoPos charged through the crowd, trying to reach the placard carriers, whose position was visible. They intended to break the assembly up and arrest those who had taken a leadership position. Instead of separating for the police, the protesters began pummeling them with their fists and taking their batons. Those at the forefront of the charge were soon on the ground, being kicked and beaten with their own billy clubs.

Some of the VoPos drew their handguns in a vain attempt to save themselves. The crowd gasped in unison after one of them fired his weapon into the air. This appeared to infuriate the crowd, who grabbed him and other officers, disarming them. Another weapon discharge was followed by a scream, "Gunther's been shot."

Instead of cowering, the onslaught against the police became more intense, forcing them to withdraw. Those officers who were injured were soon helped by other VoPos back to the relative safety of their trucks and vans.

The few policemen who had been assigned the dubious task of stopping the crowd's movement westward were rapidly swept aside. Ben and I had little choice but to join this mass movement down Karl Liebknecht Strasse. In the article I wrote for the American newspapers that evening, I observed: "Ironically, the crowd of East Germans who were marching to demand freedom from their communist government was going down a boulevard named for the founder of the German Communist Party."

To our right, a police car was overturned and on fire. Then I saw that a small community police station on the ground floor of a large building was also on fire.

At the next intersection, we passed a detachment of VoPos marching toward us. Police radios had been used to summon help.

Unter den Linden was a very broad boulevard with equally wide sidewalks, and could, therefore, hold a huge crowd. Ben and I slowly made our way around the masses and under a construction barrier up onto the ruined portico of the Kaiser's Old Palace. From this elevated position, I could see that the street was full of people; protestors were still entering to my right. The placard carriers were to my left but were not moving. Looking straight ahead, I saw the front of Humboldt University. Erica and Stephen worked in that building. I hoped they had the good sense to go home and ensure Gretchen was safe.

Near my vantage point, I could see new groups of VoPos arriving; they were blocking off nearby streets. The self-appointed leader of the protesters scrambled atop the nearby ruins of the Deutsche Bank building. He turned his megaphone from side-to-side, shouting slogans such as: "Workers join us!" "Unity is Strength!" "We want free elections!" "We want to be free, not slaves." Each of these enjoiners received loud applause of approval from the masses assembled before us.

Out of the corner of my eye, I caught movement at the edge of the crowd and heard the unmistakable metallic clanking as distant shapes moved toward the mass of people. Then hollow metal tubes became visible. The people scattered as the *rat-a-tat-tat* of machine guns were added to the metal clanking of tank treads. Even though the tank's machine guns appeared to be firing over people's heads, my war experience took over as I grabbed Ben's neck and pushed him onto the ground beside me.

People were screaming, rushing around every which way. Many were trampled in the process. The tank's treads were destroying the surface of the road by churning-up the cobblestones beneath. The defenseless crowd was seeking a way to fight back. Soon a cadre of young individuals was pelting the tanks with cobblestones. The lumbering beasts moved slowly as agile youths moved out of their way.

The Russians inside the tanks heard the stones strike the metal tanks, and reacted by trundling in the direction of the stone-throwers. Soon, machine guns fired from the tanks, killing and injuring several young protestors. One stumbled and was crushed beneath a tank's treads.

It was pure chaos. Ben and I crawled away and eventually found shelter behind a concrete barrier. He stood up to take a photograph of the action, but soon screamed and fell to the ground clutching his arm. The wound was bleeding profusely. I took my belt off and used it as a tourniquet, which managed to stop the bleeding. We retreated behind the old palace and moved up a side street.

At a VoPo-guarded barrier, we showed our press passes. They confiscated Ben's camera but assured us we could collect it the next day at the Mitte police station. We let them have it; three rolls of exposed film were securely hidden in my jockey shorts. I knew enough to loosen Ben's tourniquet every few minutes to allow blood to circulate through the injured arm. Eventually, we walked into West Berlin and took a taxi to the nearest hospital.

In less than an hour, Ben was stable and on the way to surgery. I could do little for him. I called his wife, then left the hospital. I needed to file my story for the AP and report what I'd seen to the CIA. The latter had priority, but first I met with my AP associate Gary Hamilton and handed him the film with instructions on how to get the images back to the States expeditiously.

James Wilson and I were in a conference room with most of the CIA station personnel. An analyst whose job was to integrate the information we'd received was providing a summary. "We have phone reports from operatives all over East Germany that strikers and their supporters have taken to the streets in all of the major cities, and many of the smaller towns and villages. At least half a million people were involved here in East Berlin. We stopped getting reports from some parts of the East an hour ago; now, virtually all telephone connections with the East have been severed."

"The entire VoPo force of East Berlin, which is thought to number around 5,000, has been employed in some capacity. At least 20,000 Russian soldiers and 36 of their tanks have been sent to suppress the strike and guard the dividing line from Westerners sympathetic to the protestors' cause. The official East German radio station reported only 19 people were killed, and several hundred were injured when trampled by their fellow rioters. The real toll of dead and injured is unknown, but it's likely much higher."

"And interestingly, a very reliable source indicates that around 11:40, a heavily armed convoy transported Walter Ulbricht and his senior staff to the Russian military base in Karlshorst. Also, the subway system has stopped running into the East and most services in the West have also been severely curtailed."

The station chief had just completed information collection and report writing assignments when my assistant came to get me. When I stepped out of the room, she said, "An Erica Schäfer is on your line and needs to speak to you urgently." I'd given Erica this number and told her only to call it in the event of a dire emergency.

My heart sank. Had something happened to her or Gretchen? When I picked up the receiver, Erica was sobbing and eventually composed herself enough to blurt out, "Stephen has been killed. I need you to come here and help me. Now!" She then hung up the phone before I could even ask where she was.

CHAPTER 45

Tuesday-Saturday, June 16-20, 1953

AFTER HAILING A taxi, I handed the driver a 50 Deutsche Mark note and told him where I wanted to go. As he drove east, we discussed the best route given what had happened in the center of Berlin. First, we tried the bridges over the River Spree to the south of what the driver called "the rioting." All three bridges over the River Spree were closed. Russian tanks were conspicuously positioned in the middle of each. We now turned around and drove through most of West Berlin to try to find a crossing point. Finally, we were successful. Far north in the French sector, a small group of VoPos at one checkpoint told us they had been ordered to close the border. I offered them a large bribe; they took it and directed us to a route around them.

All the way I worried about Erica and Gretchen's safety. In front of their apartment, I gave the driver another 50 Mark note and told him to go have a meal at a nearby gasthaus and then return and standby. "I must get back to West Berlin soon," I said.

"How long do you expect to be here?"

"Two hours at the most." I still had to write my story and get it on the wire machine before 20:00.

My first knock on Erica's front door went unanswered. After several more attempts, she came to the door. Her puffy, red eyes and fringe of wet hair told me she had washed her face before admitting me. She almost fell into my arms. I carried her to the couch and for a long time just held her. Finally, I used my free hand to raise her chin and asked if Gretchen was alright.

"She's asleep in her bedroom. I let the nanny go, once I had a shower...I just had to...get out of those blood-soaked clothes...Stephen's blood...I..."

I waited through a long silence. "You're unhurt?" I finally asked her. Even in this light, with her swollen eyes and reddened cheeks, she was glowing.

"Yes, I'm all right...but..." She broke down at this point, hiding her face in my shoulder and wailing. Eventually, she looked up at me and blubbered, "It...it was awful."

"I went East to get the story of the strike for the American papers. I was opposite your university when the Russians attacked the people on Unter den Linden."

"Oh...so you know...the shooting...the Russians unexpectedly firing their guns over the people's heads...to scare them."

"It worked. The crowd dispersed."

"A few minutes before that happened, Stephen came to my office...I accompanied him to a library on the upper floor of the main administration building...you know, the building that faces Unter den Linden...we had a good view of the people...all those people..."

Erica broke down again. She cried so hard she could barely breathe, and then slowly she calmed herself enough to speak. "Stephen pointed out the tanks and the crowds dispersing... suddenly the window glass in front of us burst...for a brief time, I thought the bullet had passed between us... then Stephen shuddered and crumpled to the floor...I cradled his head in my arms as he coughed...tried to say something...then went limp...I could tell he was dead...I stayed there without moving for an eternity."

Wrapping my arms around her body tighter, I hoped somehow my presence was a comfort. Although Stephen had taken my family away from me, he didn't deserve to die in such an awful way. Erica also did not deserve to have her life shattered so abruptly.

I lifted Erica's head and gave her my handkerchief. She dried her eyes and blew her nose delicately. She even smiled, but her pallor concerned me. "Are you hungry?" I asked her. "Perhaps we can eat something, it might make you feel better."

"There is sliced wurst, cheese, and bread."

"I'll make us sandwiches," I offered.

As we ate the sandwiches in silence, I could see the color starting to come back into her face; she would survive this latest trauma but was still emotionally fragile. She had called me for help. I couldn't just abandon her. If I did, she might never forgive me. But the AP would probably fire me if our rivals, the United Press, got the story of the June Uprising in Berlin and we did not. That would, in turn, mean that I could no longer use my guise as a reporter to cover my CIA activities and would be forced to leave Berlin. Either way, I would lose Erica and Gretchen.

Erica's parents didn't have a telephone and I had no idea how to get in touch with Peter. I surreptitiously checked my watch—half an hour until the taxi driver would expect me to meet him. Another half-hour after that it wouldn't make any difference if I left or not—I'd miss the deadline. Time was running out.

Alternately, Erica and I passed the time discussing anything except today and Stephen's death, when suddenly she would begin crying and needed to be held. It was less than twenty minutes before I had to leave when someone knocked. Erica looked up and gestured for me to answer it. I opened the door. Peter stood there. Once inside, he rushed over to embrace her tenderly. "A few minutes ago, I ran into Hermann from your department; he told me what happened to Stephen. I'm so sorry, dear sister. How can I help you?" he asked while holding her tightly.

Her brother's presence seemed to calm Erica even further, so I said, "Peter, someone needs to stay with Erica and Gretchen tonight. Could you stay with her until I can return—it will probably be sometime tomorrow?"

"Certainly. I heard that classes at the university were canceled, so neither of us needs to leave here."

"Good," I said. "Erica, do you know where Stephen's remains are?"

"No…The VoPos came and took him…took him away…They would not let me go with him," she replied, again looking as if she might cry.

"Those dirty bastards will try to cover up the number of people they killed today by hiding his body and claiming they have no idea where he is or what happened to him!" Peter exclaimed. "They have done it before, and they will do it now for sure!"

"Okay. I'm going to leave now. I need to ensure that the truth about the atrocities committed by the communist authorities yesterday receives worldwide coverage. Then come morning, I'll check with my contacts in the Russian and East German press corps and stop by the Mitte Police Station. I know a high-ranking official there. After that, I will come here. Erica, you decide where you want Stephen to be buried—you might contact his parents if you do not want to make that decision alone. I will come back tomorrow as early as possible."

I went into Gretchen's bedroom to assure myself she was safe. I kissed her forehead and adjusted her covers, tucking her into the comforter. "Dearest daughter," I whispered, "you need me now more than ever."

Erica gave me a lingering hug as I turned to walk out the door. "Thank you for your help—I could not have managed without you. You are a good man, Kurt Altschuler."

During the taxi ride back to West Berlin, I began writing my story on the paper I always kept in my suit coat pocket. Although the taxi's overhead light was dim, I managed to compile a detailed description of the day's events as I knew them. The taxi driver dropped me off at the Western Union Office, where I filed my story just in time to meet the American morning daily deadline.

*

It took me most of the next day to locate Stephen's body. Someone high up in the East German government, probably at the urging of the Russian KGB, had decided "19 people had died in the 'minor disturbance' caused by a few dissidents under the direct control of the American CIA." The bodies of the rest had to just disappear. Fortunately, even a totalitarian regime has a hard time getting rid of a body. A few generous bribes and a lot of detective work took me to the medical school in St. Hedwig's Hospital in central Berlin. They had been instructed to dissect his body "and use it for medical training."

Several additional bribes were required before I could get the hospital staff to agree to embalm Stephen and provide a natural-cause death certificate; thus, allowing me to have the body transported to the nearby town of Hertzfeld for the funeral on Saturday.

Erica, her family, and I traveled to Hertzfeld in two cars I hired for the occasion. After a short Lutheran eulogy, Stephen was buried in a family plot adjacent to several generations of his ancestors.

Erica was inconsolable with grief. I vowed to be a close and supportive friend for her and Gretchen. If the time ever came that she wanted to be with me again, I'd be close at hand.

CHAPTER 46

Thursday, December 10, 1953

AS I WALKED between the row of massive columns up the front steps to the entrance of the red-brick, two-story CIA headquarters on E street in Washington, D.C., I speculated why I'd been summoned here. During my seven years in Berlin, I refused reassignment here three times; each time I was told, "You won't be promoted to a real management position in the CIA until you've completed a tour of duty in Washington." Now I'd been ordered to report to Conference Room 139 for a meeting. For the entire flight to New York and train trip down the East Coast, I wondered what was next for me. Events of the last several months made it imperative that I stay in Berlin.

After checking in at the front desk, I got a badge and was escorted to a nearby, tiny room. I refused the offer of a coffee but was immediately concerned; it was not room 139 and no one else was in the room. It contained only a table and two chairs. Soon a burly, red-faced man took a position at the desk across from me. After introducing himself, he told me I was being briefed on Operation Gold today. "Sign this paperwork that certifies you understand your obligations to protect all the information related to this project. You'll be prosecuted under the espionage laws if you reveal anything about this program to uncleared people." He used his plump finger to point out the signature line at the bottom of the paper, handing me a pen.

Once I'd signed, he put the paper in a manila folder with my name on the tab and showed me to conference room 139. Eventually, three individuals walked into the room, introduced themselves, and, without saying another word, took seats around the mahogany conference table. When two other men entered, everyone else rose to their feet; after a brief hesitation, I followed them. A balding, gray-haired man with a well-trimmed mustache moved forward and extended his hand. "Agent Altschuler," he said with a deep baritone voice. "I've heard a lot about your exploits in Berlin and East Germany. I'm Allan Dulles. We have a new assignment for you."

"It's a pleasure to meet you, sir." Although we'd never met, I knew he led our OSS team in Switzerland during the war. Now, he was the director of the CIA.

"Have a seat and we'll get started," Dulles said. I'd heard he was a conservative Republican; his black three-piece pin-striped suit, white dress shirt, and solid black tie meant his conservatism extended to his dress.

The other man who had entered with the director took over the meeting after introducing himself as James Lawrence. He was balding, slightly stooped, and wore a sport coat with a turtlenecked sweater. "As everyone here knows," he said while glancing around the table, "every year we become less sure of what happens behind the Iron Curtain. This is primarily because the Soviets have directed that as much of their communications as possible be routed through buried cables. This has caused the extensive network of signals-intelligence collection sites NSA has scattered around the edge of the communist world to become less effective.

"A year and a half ago, I was tasked by the director here," gesturing in his direction, "with finding a solution to this problem. What I'm about to say mustn't go out of this room. The East German Minister for Telecommunications and many of his subordinates are MI6 operatives. They have provided details of all underground communications links between Berlin, the rest of Central Europe, and the Soviet Union. We and the British have decided we will build a tunnel into East Berlin from a place called Rudow in the American Sector of Berlin."

This revelation surprised me. I immediately wondered why I'd been informed of this program and what my role might be.

Lawrence now spread a map out on the table. We all stood looking at it as he continued, "Although a part of the American Sector of Occupation, this area in southeast Berlin consists of small villages and farms. This is the path of the barbed wire fence, which separates our sector from that of the Russians," running his finger along the map. "This road, Schönefelder Chasse, is located just over 650 feet inside the Russian zone; it leads from the center of Berlin to the main East Berlin airfield here at Schönefeld.

"Our target is buried about eighteen inches beneath the road's center. Three buried cables come together near there and carry telephone and teletype communications to and from all of Central Europe. Importantly, one of those cables comes directly from Group of Soviet Forces Germany headquarters, thirty miles to the West at Wünsdorf," he said as his index finger pointed some way beyond the map.

"The tunnel will be constructed by a team from Army Corps of Engineers led by Captain Bradley Williams," pointing to an individual in uniform standing next to me. "He is a graduate of the Colorado School of Mines, has experience in such construction efforts, and will take over to impart details of our plan."

"I'm Bradley Williams," said a tall young man with a white sidewall haircut and the ramrod-straight posture of a military man. "Why don't you get some coffee and get comfortable? This will take a while."

Once we were all seated again, the Captain began. "A dedicated crew of men from various government agencies has been working on the design for this tunnel for over a year. This includes building a prototype at Sandia Laboratories in the sandy soil of New Mexico. This soil is thought to be similar to that which we will encounter in Berlin. We are in the process of gathering the supplies and men required to build the real thing."

"First, we'll fabricate what should be called 'the warehouse' to anyone who doesn't have the need to know. Its basement will contain the entrance to a tunnel which will ultimately extend underground about 1,450 feet and come up under the road. We'll tap into those communications lines and bring the tap lines back to 'the warehouse.' It'll also house the exploitation center, where the intercepted signals will be processed. Two other buildings will be built on the site; a motor pool and a barracks-mess hall. The complex will be surrounded by two razor wire-topped chain-link fences with guard posts at all the four corners of the outer fence. Any questions up to this point?"

The room was quiet, so the captain continued. "We have conducted a preliminary site survey. The water table in this area is at 32 feet. As a result, we plan to dig our tunnel with its top at eighteen feet and its bottom at twenty-six feet. This'll ensure that any noise we make while digging the tunnel won't be discernible on the surface. We've purchased the land on our side of the border, and will use a local German contractor to build what we'll tell him is a warehouse. It'll consist of a large two-story high building with a 12-foot-deep basement made of poured concrete. The building will have roll-up doors high enough to provide loaded trucks access to the basement via a ramp. Then…"

"—Excuse me," Lawrence interrupted. "We know the construction plans will be in the hands of the East German Stasi and Russian GRU within hours of their release to the German contractors being asked to bid on the contract. As soon as the building is finished, we'll install several ELINT (Electronic Intelligence) antennas on its roof.. That'll serve as a cover for our real purpose and the activities going on there," gesturing back to the captain.

"Seventeen hundred steel quarter-circle panels, 21 inches wide and 8 feet tall when placed on edge are being fabricated as we speak. They'll be used to line the tunnel. Once the construction of the 'warehouse' is complete, my Army Corps of Engineers troops will arrive in Berlin. They'll be housed in the barracks and fed in the mess hall. In the beginning, some of my men will work on installing electronic intelligence antennas on the roof. Most will make a hole in the concrete floor, dig a vertical shaft down to 26 feet of depth, and then start digging a horizontal tunnel aimed at Schönefelder Chasse. The initial horizontal shaft will be large enough so we can build a tunnel shield. This structure is solid on the top and sides; it's designed to support the soil surrounding the diggers and keep them safe from cave-ins. Similar devices have been used since the mid-16th century and always work. The tunnel shield will be moved forward manually using hydraulic jacks." As he talked, he handed around classified photographs of the prototype tunnel and various pieces of equipment.

"My men will be organized into four six-man teams and dig 24 hours-a-day, seven days a week until the tunnel is complete. All of these men have secret clearances and will be warned to never discuss what they're doing with anyone. The tunnel panels have plugs, which can be removed so that fine-grained concrete can be injected above the panels to prevent surface soil deformation."

"All digging will be done with short-handled shovels. Only two men can work on the face of the tunnel at one time. Others will be busy filling sandbags, installing tunnel sections, and transporting the sandbags away. Once the basement is full, the sandbags will be stacked along the sides of the tunnel. The electrical wires for the lights and tunnel equipment, the air handling pipes and ducts, as well as the wire bundles which carry the signals from the tapped lines will all be placed atop the sandbags. The men will push a wooden cart with rubber wheels down a wood-railed track to transport the sandbags, panels, and equipment through the tunnel; that'll help us minimize the sound of metal on metal of normal miner's carts, which might be discernible on the surface. We will…"

"—How do you know you've gotten to the right spot?" asked Director Dulles interrupting.

"I'll be in Berlin supervising the tunnel construction," the captain answered. "We'll use a theodolite to determine angles and keep the tunnel on a perfectly straight course. We'll also use it to measure the distance to the road, which is a very visible point. It's pretty rudimentary, sir."

The Captain fielded several other questions about construction details and when the Director looked around the room, I raised my hand in the air. "Mr. Dulles…why am I here?"

"I guess you haven't been told," he replied, smiling. "You'll be the tunnel-site CIA manager and report directly to Mr. Lawrence and me on your progress, and any problems Captain Williams and his team encounter. You're the on-site decision-maker, and one of your main responsibilities will be to work with him and your British counterparts to solve problems when they occur."

"Sir, as you may know, I have other responsibilities in Berlin including my cover job with the Associated Press."

"Not any longer. In the future, your cover story will be that you work for the American Information Service (AIS)—many ex-journalists work there," Lawrence retorted. "However, you will have no real duties at the AIS or in the CIA office in Berlin. You were selected for this job because of your knowledge of the local scene and enemy, as well as your demonstrated management ability."

They were allowing me to stay in Berlin and, perhaps, even providing a needed boost to my career. So, I nodded my head in assent.

Lawrence glanced over at the director and then back at me, "Kurt, you'll fly from Berlin to London for a meeting with the British on the 13th of January. At that meeting, Captain Williams will give this briefing to the British. In concert with them, you'll generate a detailed program schedule. We will pay for the building, tunnel, and most of the intercept equipment. The British will provide experienced men who know how to tap into those cables and exploit the intercepted information. We'll provide about half of the intercept operators and share the intelligence output. That concludes our prepared remarks. Are there any questions?"

After looking around the room, Mr. Dulles pointed his index finger at me and said, "I would like to emphasize to you, Mr. Altschuler, what your most important task is. Those who work for you must review all information derived from these tapped lines. Your objective is to determine as far ahead as possible if and when the Russians intend to attack Berlin or West Germany. I have personally assured President Eisenhower that the tunnel will provide the early warning that is essential for the defense of Europe." He looked at his wristwatch and rose from his seat, indicating the meeting was over. "Good luck, gentlemen," and walked out of the room.

CHAPTER 47

Saturday, December 26, 1953- Sunday, January 3, 1954

SEVERAL HIGH-RISE APARTMENTS had recently been built in Berlin; I decided to move into one so Erica and Gretchen could visit together. I found the perfect unit on the top floor of a 14-story building; it had three bedrooms, three baths, and a large living room with a 180-degree view of the city looking east toward the Tiergarten, River Spree, and Frits-Schloss Park. It was an extravagance I could easily afford.

After I returned from the States, I told Erica about my new apartment and explained that we would each have our own bedroom and private bath. She hesitated. Was she concerned I might make advances or that she might seek comfort from me? I wasn't sure. I tried to reassure her. "You'll have no classes over Christmas break and I can tell you need a vacation. I'll help take care of Gretchen and you can relax in luxury for a change. The apartment building has a heated swimming pool and sauna, plus my apartment has clothes washing-drying machines and a television set. We'll go out for most meals, so we don't have to worry about cleaning up."

On Saturday morning, I waited nervously. Erica and Gretchen were scheduled to arrive soon and would spend the Saturday and Sunday after Christmas here in my apartment. They continued to live in the small apartment she and Stephen had occupied since they were married; I took this as a sign she wasn't ready to move on with her life—after all, it had only been seven months since the trauma of Stephen's death. I'd have to be patient, but still hoped we could reestablish our old relationship.

In response to the buzzer, I went down to help them with their bags. On the sidewalk, Gretchen ran into my arms. "Onkel Kurt. How soon can we go swimming? Can we go now, please? Oh, please."

"You will have to ask your mother."

"We can go now, and again this afternoon after your nap," Erica said while smiling at her daughter, "but first we must take a tour of Uncle Kurt's new home and get settled."

"Do I have to take a nap? That is for babies and I am almost four."

"After a long swim, we will all need to rest," I said to support Erica. She smiled and touched my arm in thanks.

My immediate desire was to give them a vacation away from the cares and inconvenience of living in East Germany. Anytime Gretchen and I were together we talked in English, so she would be fluent when she grew up. At Gretchen's request we saw *Peter Pan* twice, once in German with English subtitles, and once in English with German subtitles. Later in the week, we saw another Disney movie called *Toot, Whistle, Plunk, and Boom*. Afterward, in a very serious and sophisticated manner, Gretchen exclaimed, "It was the very best movie ever."

There was little of interest on the TV, so it stayed off most of the time. I read to Gretchen, and the three of us played games together. They stayed with me for the whole week. We saw the Nutcracker Suite Ballet, built a snowman, and watched a puppet show. For the first time, it felt like we were a real—normal—family.

Each day brought joy to my otherwise dull routine; and, each day hope grew for a future with Erica. She loved the modern conveniences, and they both seemed to have a wonderful time. As they were leaving, Erica seemed to kiss my cheek longer and with more affection than usual. When the house was empty again, I decided I'd only imagined it.

CHAPTER 48

Monday-Friday, March 15-19, 1954

THE JANUARY MEETING in London with British MI6 gave me a much better idea of the magnitude and schedule for the building of the tunnel. Two months later, I prepared the following Eyes-Only Memorandum for my bosses in Washington:

TOP SECRET GOLD/STOPWATCH
US/UK EYES ONLY

TO: CIA Headquarters, Washington, D.C.
Eyes-Only Confidential for Director Allan Dulles and Mr. James Lawrence
CC: MI6 Program Lead, Matthew Brower

From: Kurt Altschuler

Sirs,
During the January 13, 1954 meeting with MI6, a firm schedule for construction of the "warehouse" building was generated. I forwarded you each a copy at that time. The schedule allowed eight weeks for us to get a German firm under contract, and gave them six months to complete its construction. We got the bids back this week. Captain Williams and I selected the firm of Mueller and Sons, GmbH, which the local procurement office indicates is their most reliable contractor. This firm was selected because they were 9% under the nearest

bidder and 21% under the allocated budget. The contract between them and the Army Central Procurement Office-Berlin was signed today.

My next problem was how to get the tunnel-lining sections to Berlin. They are too heavy and bulky to be brought to Berlin by air. East German Customs Officers' inspection of incoming surface freight was very rigorous. They open most boxcars, trucks, barges and wooden crates. Anything unusual is immediately referred to a large contingent from the Stasi and GRU officials who are located at each crossing point. If the tunnel sections are shipped in bulk, openly exposed for all to see, everyone will ask themselves, "What are those and what can they possibly be used for?"

A visit to one of the customs houses revealed that a large number of huge crates were atop many of the flatcars; they contained heating systems for under-construction apartment houses. Hence, my solution is to have the tunnel sections encased in huge wooden cartons and identified as boilers and/or water filtration systems. Twenty sections will be shipped in each carton. Berlin is connected to the West by two train routes, three autobahn routes, and two river/canal routes. Three cartons a week will be shipped via one of these routes; no route will be used more than twice a month. The tunnel sections will be stored in an Army facility until "warehouse" construction is complete; then, they will be moved to the tunnel site as needed.

The Associated Press has yet to identify and hire a replacement for me here in Berlin. My new job with the US Information Agency is a real job and I must spend several hours a day completing those tasks. As you may know, we are short-handed here in Berlin so James Wilson, the CIA Station Chief, has asked me to help him in my spare time. An individual in the Army subcontracts administration office and Captain Williams will be monitoring the German contractor's progress on the construction of the "warehouse." This means once I implement a plan for getting those tunnel sections into Berlin and it starts working smoothly, I should be able to satisfy all of my varied commitments.

This is the first of my bi-monthly status reports on this program.

With Best Regards,
Kurt Altschuler
Berlin Program Manager

TOP SECRET GOLD/STOPWATCH
US/UK EYES ONLY

CHAPTER 49

Wednesday-Tuesday, May 19-25, 1954

MY FINAL PLAN for shipment of the steel tunnel sections to Berlin called for the construction of one set of eight different sized and shaped wood cartons. Each had typical factory stencils in German on all four sides identifying the contents by a fictitious make and model number, and a functional name. Other stencils indicated the up-direction and that the contents were heavy; they also gave the weight of the carton when loaded with twenty tunnel sections. In every way, they looked like real heating and air handling equipment crates. Once the loaded carton arrived in Berlin, its contents were removed, it was disassembled, and then it was shipped back to West Germany by truck so it could be used again for a later shipment.

Almost twenty percent of the tunnel sections had safely arrived in Berlin when the inevitable happened. One of the customs inspectors asked for one of our cartons to be opened. Soon a group of German and Russian officials arrived to take a look, and the carton was impounded.

Two days ago, Mr. Brandt, the head of the freight-forwarding firm I'd hired, left an urgent message for me to call him as soon as possible. All of my contacts with his firm had been via telephone and he knew me as Hans Schneider, a manufacturer's representative. I called, identified myself using my pseudonym, and asked for him. He came on the line and in a concerned tone, said, "The carton you shipped contained twenty unusual curved, quarter sections of steel. The customs official's superiors (a common euphemism for the Stasi, KGB, GRU, or all three) have demanded to know what these items are going to be used for. You have one week to respond or the shipment will be confiscated, meaning you will never see these items again—they will be identified as contraband."

Extra tunnel sections were being manufactured, so the loss of this small number wasn't a major concern; however, if the East Germans or Russians studied those unique steel curved sections too long, they might figure out what they were used for. Swift action was required.

*

At 08:35 the next morning, I arrived at the European Headquarters of the CIA in Frankfort. I walked up the steps of the structure known as the I.G. Farben Building and boarded the paternoster (a unique revolving elevator), got off on the third floor, and was badged into our area.

Soon, graphic artist, Greg Cook rose from his drafting table, shook my hand, and said, "I understand this project has top priority. How can I help?"

I took a photo and line drawing of a single tunnel section out of my briefcase. "The Reds have confiscated twenty of them and I need to ship hundreds more into Berlin. The outside of the carton identifies them as water-filtration systems for apartment-house heating and ventilation. We need to make a commercial brochure that is good enough to fool anyone. Please don't ask any questions about these items' real use. Do you have any ideas?"

After studying what I handed him and doodling on a piece of paper for a few minutes, he said, "When twenty of these twenty-one-inch-wide, quarter section panels are assembled they easily form a cooling tower," showing me a sketch. "We just put an imaginary fan at the top of the tower. The drawing isn't a problem. I can even make it look like a photograph if you desire. To sell this as a commercial product in a brochure, you need a complete description, specification sheet, model numbers, manufacturers name, logo, phone numbers, and addresses. This information can be easily verified, so it needs to be real or as close to real as possible."

"How can that happen quickly?"

"In the past, we've used British, French, and Italian companies. How long do we have?"

"Five days!"

"I'll start on the drawing immediately and it'll be ready in two days. You get the information together and we can produce something in twenty hours using our on-site printing plant. You need to figure out where and how to get the other required information."

Uncertain what to do, I paced up and down the long broad halls of the building for a few minutes, scratching my head. Suddenly, it hit me and I went to the communications center, got on the KY-7 scrambler telephone, and called my counterpart at MI-6, Matthew Brower. "We have a huge problem," I said on the phone. "Do you have a commercial heating and cooling manufacturer who's willing to support our efforts?"

"I'm sure we do. I'll have to determine who and where they're located. Why don't you fly over? Call me with your arrival time and I'll pick you up at Heathrow."

*

The next afternoon, we were in the office of Philip Merriweather, the sales manager for Grayson Environmental Manufacturing, Limited. "Your firm's been supporting our efforts since the 1930s and we appreciate it," Matthew Brower told Mr. Merriweather. "This time we need you to establish a new product line and provide telephone confirmation of the availability and use of this product."

"It's the least I can do," Mr. Merriweather replied.

"Can we see some of your brochures?"

After reviewing the brochures, I handed him back a long, handwritten sheet and copies of the line drawings/photos of the tunnel sections. "Here's the information on the shipping container which has been questioned. We must make this new brochure consistent with what they now know."

The three of us worked together for a few hours, and I left with all the information I needed, along with Mr. Merriweather's commitment to support this ruse.

Matthew Brower agreed to have one of his men meet a flight from Frankfort on Monday and transport the new brochure to Mr. Merriweather.

The whole scheme worked smoothly from that point on.

On Tuesday, I sent three copies of the brochure by courier to Mr. Brandt's office. Once I knew he had received it, I phoned and got him to agree that this was a legitimate commercial product.

"This shipment is urgently needed for a building which is almost finished, I stated. "How much would it cost for you to expedite this shipment by sending someone to personally escort it through customs?"

He named an exorbitant amount, to which I readily agreed.

The next day a heavily accented individual called and talked to Mr. Merriweather, requesting details about the product described in the new brochure. GCHQ, the British equivalent of the American NSA, intercepted that phone conversation, which had originated from the Russian embassy in London.

Two days later, the latest shipment was delivered to us in West Berlin. I suspected some of the money paid to expedite the shipment went to bribe the East German customs officials and perhaps even their "superiors."

Next, I sent a message to those responsible for initiating shipment of the tunnel sections: "In the future, only use the number-three shaped cartons for shipments via the Marienborn/Helmstedt train route, and don't use it on any other route."

CHAPTER 50

Saturday, May 29, 1954

TODAY, ERICA AND Gretchen arrived to stay for the weekend. They were now spending one or two weekends a month with me. I enjoyed every moment of our time together. Several times over the months, I caught Erica crying. Stephen had only been dead for a year and I assiduously avoided actions or words indicating how much I longed to renew our relationship.

After Gretchen was in bed, Erica turned off the TV and joined me on the couch. "We need to talk about something important. This year my professor and I are taking nineteen students on a dig to the ancient city of Miletus on the West Coast of Turkey. We'll start on the dig site early in the morning, and work there until noon. In the heat of the afternoon, I give a lecture and help the students identify and record their daily finds."

"Sounds like fun, but challenging work."

"I'm in a quandary as to what to do with Gretchen. She's only four. The dig site is several kilometers away from where we'll be staying, which is apparently fairly primitive. The nearest city is Izmir; it's too far for a daily commute."

"Erica, dear, I'd love to take care of our daughter for the summer. I'll need to hire someone to be with her while I'm at work—a nanny or an au pair. But I'll manage. When do you leave?"

"I'll drop her by on the 17th of June. The dig ends on the 12th of August and my return flight is on the 14th."

"When do you start back to school?"

"Not until the 8th of September."

"Why don't Gretchen and I fly down to Athens? You can meet us there. I've always wanted to see the ruins and museums of Greece. I'll even arrange for us to spend some time at a beach resort somewhere in Greece. Would you like that?"

"I cannot afford such extravagance and…"

"—I can. I want to treat my daughter to time swimming in the warm, crystal-clear waters of the Aegean Sea. You must accompany us to ensure we have fun. Please, it won't be the same without you," I said, touching her nose with the tip of my index finger.

She laughed and formed the smile I'd grown to love. "It sounds lovely. A classics scholar should visit the ruins of Greece, and I haven't seen most of them. I'll be able to serve as a guide, just like in the old days. Except now, I'll know my subject."

We both laughed and hugged. Having her familiar shape in my arms was lovely, but I must have held her too long; she suddenly released me and moved away. I looked at her, smiled and, trying to end the awkward moment. "I'll get us separate rooms, each with a private bath. A room with two beds and a bath will ensure you and Gretchen rest comfortably and have your privacy. We'll meet you on the 14th of August in Athens and will return to Berlin when?"

We took a calendar off of the wall and agreed we would return home on September 3, 1954. I happily made all of the travel reservations the next week.

CHAPTER 51

Natalie
Saturday, July 19, 1954

TWO YEARS AGO, Papa decided that it would be best if one of his subordinates assumed the courier duties I'd performed for several years. So briefly, I got out of the spy business. Having now finished my second year at the Free University, I began a summer internship in a West German publisher's office. I continued to live at home and commuted to West Berlin most days. But on Friday and Saturday evenings, I usually stayed in West Berlin. My parents thought I was at a female friend's apartment, but my boyfriend Michael and I were usually together in a modest hotel in the British sector.

He was making an exceptional wage for an apprentice in his third year. His boss was a dedicated communist who had gotten a contract to help the Russian military build new facilities at Wünsdorf, which is located about 25 kilometers directly south of Berlin. He was getting a free meal in a Russian mess hall each day, and the wages of a master plumber.

Michael was willing to spend most of his newfound wealth entertaining me at movies, clubs, and nice restaurants.

Weeks ago, he told me almost in awe, "This base I am working on became a German Army facility in the late 19th century and was the command center for all Wehrmacht operations in Europe from 1940 until the end of the war. I got a chance to tour the steel-reinforced concrete bunkers where our generals directed the war. Some tattered maps were still attached to the walls. It was a look back in time."

"What do you do on that Russian base?"

"I am installing inlet pipes, drains, and fixtures of all forms."

"What kind of buildings are you working on?"

"Married people's housing and barracks now, but the boss says we will soon start working on a large office building. He says we will be working there for several years. If that is true, we could afford to be married."

"I am really glad you have such a responsible position. Do you know what the Russians do on that base?

"It is the headquarters for all of the Russian troops in Germany."

"Really." I hesitated because the people Papa was supporting needed the information Michael could provide and it would enable me to get back in the spy game in a big way. So, I encouraged him to tell me more about what he was doing.

Two weeks ago, he brought me a large map showing all of the buildings on that base. "This shows the organizations located in each building," Michael said pointing.

While he slept, I took the map into the bathroom. To ensure I captured all of the contents of the map, I took photographs of the various sections. All I had to do was point and click the small Minox camera Papa had gotten for me.

Last week, he brought a thick document written in Russian to our favorite hotel in West Berlin. He said it was a facility plan his boss had been given. "It describes what buildings on the base will be remodeled and when; it also details what new buildings and facilities were approved and which were proposed for the future." Hiding my excitement, I asked, "They just gave this to your boss?"

"The truth is I found it in an office and smuggled it off the base in my plumber's bag," he answered. "I wanted to show you I will have work for the next several years. So, we can afford to get married now."

I shook my head. "We must wait until I graduate and have a job. Then we can marry. If the VoPos at the border found this document in your possession when you return to the East, you would be in big trouble. I'll take it to my office and run it through a paper shredder."

Michael agreed, so I hid it in my desk at work until Papa could arrange a meeting with an American at an apartment in West Berlin. During our brief exchange, the individual I gave the document to indicated it was "pure gold."

Today, Michael showed me plans for the new headquarters building. While he slept, I took pictures of all 18 pages. During this process, I noticed the new structure was being built over a heavily steel-reinforced concrete Wehrmacht bunker, which was being reused for the same purpose.

CHAPTER 52

Kurt
Friday, July 30, 1954

WE WERE UNSURE how Gretchen would take the first separation from her mother. I was a trusted and familiar presence—but we were still concerned. Much to my surprise, she settled right into my apartment as if she had always lived there. That evening at bedtime she said, "Is Mommy okay?"

"Yes, her airplane arrived safely about two hours ago."

"She told me she would think about me every minute. Sometimes I think of other things. Is that bad?"

"No. Dear. What she was saying is you are so important to her that she is keeping the memory of you close to her heart. Understand."

"Sure… Good…Me too…Night," she said, giving me a sloppy kiss and turning over.

I tucked her in. "Sleep tight, dear," I said in English. I was desperate to call her "daughter" out loud, but I held back. I knew it wasn't my place—at least, not now.

Because I didn't know exactly what my schedule would be from day-to-day, I hired Nora, an au pair from Norway, to stay with us for the entire two months.

Nora was only eighteen years old, but she looked and acted much younger—the perfect companion for Gretchen. They immediately became inseparable.

It had been some time since I'd taken a leave of absence and I filled out the required paperwork several weeks earlier. Today, my CIA boss James Wilson entered my office and told me my vacation was approved and asked me to accompany him to his office.

Once the door was closed, he said, "I think you know Prince—Peter Hoffmann. You had him recruited several years ago."

If you're a CIA agent, you aren't allowed to have secrets from the agency. Because Erica lived in East Germany, I continued to report my interaction with her and Gretchen. "Yes, I was confident he would make a good operative when I had him recruited, and I believe he has served our side with distinction."

"That's correct. Well, he recently graduated from Humboldt University with a degree in accounting and business management. We assumed he would soon leave our service and move West."

"Makes sense; over 200,000 East Germans emigrate every year. Most of those who leave are young, have an education, and can easily get good, high-paying jobs."

"Well, we just got a message from Peter; he's been offered a position with the East German Ministry of the Interior. When he went for the interview someone let slip that he'd be working for the State Security Service in their central recordkeeping facility in East Berlin."

"Having someone in that area of Stasi Headquarters would be exceptionally valuable. But it also might be dangerous for him," I said.

"The handwritten cards generated there are arranged alphabetically and reflect everything they know about an individual of interest irrespective of whether he resides in the East or the West. Anyone who has come to their attention for whatever reason has a file. Each of those cards rates an individual's loyalty to the East German state and communism."

"For all we know, they have a card on you and me, James," I observed almost in jest.

"Me…no, probably not. I haven't been to East Berlin since I got here. You on the other hand. You've been here…what…eight years? And move back and forth across the border frequently…AP reporter… seen going in and out of the seats of government in both halves of this city innumerable times…making friends with East German and Russian reporters…a female friend who lives in the East and daughter...you've undoubtedly got a big file."

"Your point being?"

"If Peter could look through their files and take photographs of selected records, that would be a major coup for us. Perhaps they know you're a CIA agent and have been playing you or others of us. Or perhaps they have two files on you: one your public persona; another very closely held. Perhaps your file reveals the truth about your exploits in setting up and maintaining one of the most successful spy networks in history."

"So, we're going to accept his offer. Do you intend to tell Peter that the average operational life of a double agent is only two or three years?" I said, jabbing back in concern for his safety.

"You've been in this game long enough to know we're all expendable. If we could get him in place and run him for a while, it could be an information bonanza. We can hopefully extract him just before they nab him."

"Only if we know about it in advance. In any case, he'll need training, a lot of it, and if he disappears for a long period, the Stasi will get suspicious."

"Exactly, this is where you come in. Your posh apartment will be vacant for over three weeks. If you agree, you'll ask Peter to check on your house while you're gone. That'll give him an excuse for coming to the West on occasion. He's staying in his sister's apartment while she is away, and it is also available. By using those two residences, and a safe house in the East, we'll be able to spend full time training Peter in every aspect of spycraft."

"He doesn't know I work for the CIA or was instrumental in his recruitment."

"Give him a set of keys to your apartment and we'll take it from there. He'll jump at the opportunity to use your apartment on occasion. We'll tell him he has to receive some training over here during that period you're gone or we can't use him."

"And when I return, he'll go back to his drab apartment in East Berlin and begin working for the Stasi."

"That's the plan. What do you think?" James asked.

"Is three weeks enough time?"

"It'll have to be."

Later that day, I thought about this conversation and its ramifications. If something happened to Peter, and Erica found out that I'd be responsible for putting him in this situation, I'd lose her and probably Gretchen forever. Yet I couldn't think of a way out of this dilemma, so I accepted it.

CHAPTER 53

Saturday, August 14-Thursday, September 2, 1954

ERICA'S FLIGHT FROM Izmir landed in Athens two hours after ours did. A seemingly independent and confident four-year-old Gretchen ran to her mother and wanted to be hugged and held for a long time. Finally, Gretchen asked, "Please put me down," and took both our hands as we moved through immigration and customs. I'd worked with the American Express travel agent in Berlin to plan the trip. It called for us to spend a day at ruins or a museum, and the next day at a beach or other activity suitable for a four-year-old.

Day after day, Erica and I laughed and talked, enjoying each other's company. Our daily interactions were almost like when we lived together. She didn't invite advances and I assiduously made none for the entire vacation.

The last evening in Greece, after Gretchen was in bed, I finally got the courage to ask Erica what she planned to do once she got her doctorate. "Will you move West or stay in the East?"

"I'm afraid I may be stuck in the East. Many people in my field have left for the West. There are too many experienced professors of classics over there—most are forced to do something else. In the East, I have a chance to become a lecturing professor quickly and study under Dr. Richter, who is widely recognized as the best in all of Germany."

"How long do you think it'll take you to get your doctorate?"

"Humboldt is trying to maintain its academic standards in the eyes of the world including, and perhaps mostly, German educational institutions in the West. It'll probably take two more years. I'm making a decent salary as a teaching assistant. When we return, I must select my dissertation subject and begin my research. I may need to return here or to Italy or Turkey next year. Are you willing to take Gretchen again next summer?"

"I have a new job and increased responsibilities, so we'll have to see," I replied, satisfied that the three of us would be living in Berlin for the next few years. Staying in Erica and Gretchen's life was important to me—I had a family of sorts. I still had to wait patiently until Erica was ready for a closer relationship, but constantly worried that it might never happen.

CHAPTER 54

Thursday, September 2, 1954

TODAY AS THE taxi took me from Gatow to my apartment after a wonderful vacation, I marveled at the new West Berlin. At first, it had slowly rebuilt after the devastation of the Second World War. The economic miracle that had followed the establishment of the hard currency, Deutsche Mark, in 1948 and a democratically elected central government in 1949 surprised the world. Like a phoenix, West Germany and West Berlin arose from the ashes and began rebuilding, followed rapidly by full employment and prosperity.

Now West Berlin was block after block of rebuilt or remodeled apartment buildings, businesses, and public structures. West German businesses were intentionally moving part of their administrative staff into modern high-rise office buildings near the East-West dividing line, as visible proof of the superiority of democracy and free enterprise. Most West Berliners lived well, dressed in the latest fashions, drove new cars, and vacationed away from the city.

In East Berlin, only some public buildings were restored. Close by were ruins interspersed with hastily repaired buildings, and drab, new tenement apartments built in the austere Soviet style. After the war, most manufacturing equipment in the factories of southeast Berlin was shipped by train to Russia as a part of the reparations they demanded; empty, derelict shells were all that remained in most of that area. Over half a million people lived in apartments in East Berlin but worked either full-

or part-time in the West; East Germany depended on the hard currency they earned, but their neighbors severely criticized the economic advantage this gave those "damned border crossers." They received free medical care, subsidized housing and food, and had little incentive to move to the West—they had the best of both worlds. On the black market, one could often get 15 East Marks for one West Mark.

After dark, the West was aglow with lights of all forms; in the East, except for a few public buildings near the border, it was dark. It was almost as if East Berlin ceased to exist after dark. By this point in time, there were two Berlins—a free, prosperous Berlin and a shabby, grey, ugly one.

CHAPTER 55

Thursday-Monday, September 2-27, 1954

CAPTAIN WILLIAM'S MEN arrived in Berlin in late August. All of them had SECRET clearances. They were told that they were digging an important tunnel into East Berlin, but not given any further details. The four who had TOP SECRET clearances were fully briefed on every aspect of the tunnel construction, including its ultimate purpose.

The installation of the electronic intelligence antennas and jackhammering of the hole in the floor of the basement commenced on September 2, right on schedule.

Two days later, Captain Williams called me, "You better get over here. We have a huge problem." To maintain my new cover, I spent most mornings at my American Information Service office.

I arrived in an army staff car within the hour and went to Captain Williams' office. "This may be a show stopper," the Captain said as we shook hands. "We completed the hole in the concrete floor of the basement two days ago and started digging down. Last night the swing shift hit water and we've been pumping it out of the hole ever since."

"But I thought your site survey indicated that the water table was at a depth of 32 feet," I said.

"That's correct for one point in our building site, but apparently not for the place we selected to start tunneling."

"Captain, do you mind if in private we address each other by our first names?"

"Not at all; I'm Bradley, but everyone shortens it to Brad."

"Great, Brad. My given name is Kurt. Here's what I suggest, I'll go to the Tempelhof District Building Department and find out if they have any information about the water table in this area."

From the building department, I was directed to the office of the Chief Hydrologist for Berlin. It was halfway across the city in the dingy, poorly lit basement of a pre-war office complex. When I expressed interest in building an industrial plant in or near Rudow, he laughed and said, "All of south-central Berlin is very tricky, and near Rudow may be the worst. During the last glacial period, the clay soil in that area was compacted in some areas and not others. Water can soak into the ground to a depth of 10 meters (32 feet) in one place, and nearby hardpan will prevent the water from even penetrating to a depth of 5 meters (16 feet)."

"How does this affect construction there?"

"It limits the height of a building because it might become unstable, and usually we do not allow the construction of basements any deeper than 5 meters (16 feet) below ground level."

I asked, "Do you have any information on this phenomenon?"

"Yes," he said handing me a mimeographed pamphlet on the subject.

Once I was back at the site, I translated its German contents for Brad and we agreed this appeared to be a major setback. While brainstorming ideas, I suggested, "Let's move the tunnel so the bottom is much higher—say the bottom around 16 feet and top around 8 feet.

"Remember the reason we were going to have the bottom of the tunnel at 26 feet was so people on the surface could not hear the workers during construction."

"Brad, your men are going to be digging in relatively soft soil with shovels. The hydraulic jacks that push the tunnel shield forward are manual. What's making noise?"

"Two things. First, my guys need to communicate to coordinate their efforts. Second, they're going to be assembling steel plates which will clang loudly if they hit each other."

"The men can communicate primarily with hand signals and whispers," I observed. "You can invent procedures that minimize the noise when metal tunnel sections are being installed. Perhaps employing additional men to control the movement of each section would help them prevent noise. They have several hundred feet to practice before we near the East Berlin fence. Plus, those three diesel-electric generators located on the east side of the warehouse make an awful noise. We'll just keep all three of them running 24 hours a day."

"I understand what you're thinking and that should work," Brad concluded after much discussion including the decision that, "the tunnel entrance will have to be much larger."

*

Two days later, Brad informed me that our facility in Rudow had received the "attention of many individuals in German and Russian uniforms, and civilian clothes. They arrived in a convoy and spent some time walking along the fence, looking at us through binoculars."

"The primary civilian and military airport that serves East Berlin is only two miles away at Schönefeld," I observed. "This is probably just them trying to figure out why we built this facility in this particular location. When we finish installing the antennas on the roof and those antennas are repositioned frequently to collect radar and other signals from the equipment at the airfield, that should provide them with the answer they seek. Perhaps we need to keep an eye on both sides of the border. The tunnel runs just a few feet inside of the foundation on the south side of the warehouse. Let's convert the small corner room on the second floor into an observation post; it has a large window. It can be manned 24 hours a day. We can paint the room's walls black, install curtains to cover the windows when anyone enters or leaves the room. What do you think?"

"Consider it done," Brad said.

"To keep the observers alert—have them fill out a log and make sure to install a telephone so they can contact the site duty officer in the event of anything unusual happening during the night or on weekends. Also, let's run a wire from that post into the tunnel and have the surveillance team turn on a red light whenever anyone is near the tunnel or road who might hear the diggers working."

"Consider that done, Kurt."

Soon Brad was using the observation room and his theodolite to determine the distance to our target, the center of Schönefelder Chasse; using the same point 37 feet below, he could accurately determine the distance the tunnel had covered, using what he called 'simple math'.

CHAPTER 56

Wednesday, November 17-Friday, December 17, 1954

OCCASIONALLY OVER THE last two months, I had entered the tunnel and watched the men work. It was difficult staying out of their way because everyone moved constantly; they managed to work together with a few whispered words and sign language while making little noise.

First, they filled most of the basement with sandbags. Then we began putting the sandbags along the sides of the tunnel. Sandbags also filled space freed-up as the tunnel sections stored in the basement were used.

Because we were making almost 10 feet of tunnel per day, my progress reports indicated we would finish the tunnel ahead of schedule. Then, today, I got another dreaded phone call. Once I arrived in the warehouse, I could smell the problem. Brad came over to me and reported, "We hit an abandoned full septic tank and leach field. The effluence is over a foot deep near the tunnel face, and has run down the slope almost back here to the entrance."

"Have you any suggestions on how to solve this problem quickly?" I asked.

"What we need are several septic disposal trucks. There must be companies in Berlin providing that service."

"I'll find out," I said.

I immediately notified the NCO in charge of those manning the four guard posts along the fence and monitoring room on the second floor to be on the alert for the foreseeable future. We needed to know if the unique activities of the next few days would catch anyone's interest from the nearby border.

The next day, I accompanied two septic pump trucks and their crews to the 'warehouse.' The group of GIs, whose job was to empty the numerous septic tanks at American military installations in Berlin, had signed hastily prepared paperwork that they would never reveal any information about what they would see and do for the next week. I could tell by their demeanor they took this admonition seriously.

Together, that crew and the Army Corps of Engineers people worked tenaciously and had the tunnel fairly clean in three days. It still stank, and months later still had a discernable odor but was no longer a health hazard.

Although an unusual sight, the frequent arrival and departure of the septic trucks did not appear to receive any attention from the other side of the fence.

*

For weeks, the team in the observation room watched as a farmer planted an orchard in the field that was located between the East Berlin boundary fence and Schönefelder Chasse. Unfortunately, the field was centered over the path the tunnel would take. Once the tunnel passed under the fence, the team in the observation room was forced to turn on the red light frequently during the day; this notified the diggers that the farmer was working above them. As a result, our tunneling rate was reduced to 8 or 9 feet per day. Despite this, we managed to stay ahead of schedule.

CHAPTER 57

Friday-Saturday, December 24-25, 1954

GRETCHEN AND I continued our weekly day together and sometimes she spent the whole weekend with me. Erica stayed with us occasionally, but not as frequently as when I first got the apartment.

I purchased a child's slate-topped table with a built-in seat that had the alphabet and numbers across the top. Soon, Gretchen was using chalk to reproduce them. Seeing what she was doing I said, "Your letters and numbers are neatly written."

"These make up the words you read to me from books. Please teach me to read."

She was attending kindergarten, but the students weren't taught to read until they were a year older.

I scanned the bookshelf in her room and selected an illustrated book with only simple words. The title was *Ich Bin Ich* (I am me). With my help, soon she was able to recognize and pronounce words. Within a few months, she began to read to herself. All those hours I'd spent reading to her paid off handsomely.

I invited Erica's entire family over for a Christmas Eve party. I hadn't seen Erica's father for several years and was a bit shocked at how much he had aged.

"There is always too much to do," he replied to my query about the farm. "Hired help wants more than I can afford to pay—so Lena and I do what we can. The Minister of Agriculture sets the price we can sell our crops for—they do not care if we make money—they want the workers in the factories to eat well and cheaply…"

"—They no longer allow us to take our produce into West Berlin where we can get a decent price," Lena interrupted. "That is the real problem."

"There is always talk in the village that all of the farms in East Germany will be collectivized," Hans continued. "I caught a ne'er-do-well villager on my land. When I told him to leave, he said, 'Your farm is the largest and best in the area and will be collectivized first. When that happens individuals will be given small parcels to farm on their own. I am trying to decide which part of your farm I want.' When I threatened him, he shook his fist at me, and said, 'Your time of reckoning will come soon!"

I was speechless and didn't know how to respond to this revelation. Erica's parents stared down at their food, almost as if they could envision their farmless future. To break the silence, I turned to Peter, who sat next to me with his girlfriend, Inger, to his side.

"How is your new job going?" I asked him.

"I am just a junior clerk in the Ministry of the Interior, so I only have a few subordinates to supervise. As I become more familiar with the work, I am sure I will be promoted. For now, I am content."

Everything about Peter's efforts for the CIA was highly compartmentalized; I didn't have the need or desire to know. I just hoped nothing would happen to him.

The rest of the day went very smoothly. Erica and Gretchen were going to the farm with her parents for several days but agreed to spend four days around New Year's Eve in my apartment. I was pleased that even though Erica didn't want a relationship with me, she wasn't involved with another man.

Shortly after everyone left my apartment, it began to snow. Soon, a beautiful white blanket laid across the city. Just before midnight, the winter's beauty turned ugly when the warehouse duty officer called saying, "Please come in immediately." Once there, he said, "The guy in the surveillance room noticed the snow was melting when it hits the ground over our tunnel."

I knocked on the door to that room and could hear the sergeant on duty say "one moment please" as he closed the curtain. Once I was inside, he opened the curtain. It was dark and I could only see the lighted area beyond the perimeter fence. Once I donned night-vision goggles, the snowless path of the tunnel was easily visible to where it stopped a few hundred feet this side of Schönefelder Chasse. Come morning, the path of the tunnel would be visible to everyone including the VoPos, who constantly traipsed back and forth along the fence.

The facility manager wasn't in his room in the barracks and it took me twenty minutes to find bolt cutters to remove the padlock on the heating-unit door. Once inside, I determined the thermostat that controlled the flow of air throughout the tunnel was set at 70 degrees Fahrenheit. I shut the heat off, turned the air conditioning on, and set the temperature to 45 degrees. All through the night, I checked the tunnel temperature and snow level along its path.

Just before 05:00 on Christmas day, heavier snow began to fall and stick to the area above the tunnel. By the time the sun came up, the tunnel's course was barely discernable in the white wonderland.

After that night, people working in the tunnel had to wear coats and thermal underwear.

CHAPTER 58

Thursday, February 3-Thursday, May 12, 1955

IN EARLY FEBRUARY, the tunneling phase of construction was complete, and most of the U.S. Army Corps of Engineers group who had dug the tunnel left Berlin without ever being told the why of it. A small cadre of four enlisted men who "had the right clearances" remained behind to assist Brad and me in the next phase of the program.

One of the things we did at this point was to install plastic explosives in a forty-foot long section of the tunnel just on our side of the border. The key-locked detonation switch was located in the duty officer's room. The key was kept in a safe; only Brad and I knew its combination.

Brad was sure we were "right on target at 1,476 feet," but there was no way of knowing for sure until the first of two British teams completed their job by uncovering and tapping the cables. One night in early March, that team, including their leader Major Raymond Wycliffe, arrived. They were picked up at Gatow Airfield by two U.S. Army trucks and transported to the barracks in the tunnel compound. Their leader turned out to be a friendly, good-natured veteran of many clandestine operations during World War II and since. Several years earlier, he and some members of this team had tapped into Russian General Staff Headquarters in Vienna as a part of Operation Silver.

The fact that this group of well-known communications experts was even in Berlin was a closely guarded secret. Fear that one or more of them might be recognized meant they were not allowed outside of the warehouse complex. After arriving, they changed into American Army uniforms and got GI haircuts. For the next four weeks, they lived in the barracks, ate in the mess hall, and played in the recreation center. They drank American beer which was provided free of charge to everyone; they characterized it as 'bland bilge water, unfit for purpose!'"

The day after their arrival, Raymond showed Brad and me a copy of what he called, 'German telecommunications drawings generated in the late 1920s when the cables were laid.' These records indicated that, in this area, our target was located 27 inches beneath the surface of the road and just east of its centerline. The thickness of the roadbed itself in 1928 was, however, not recorded. For several months, my team has been preparing for the task of finding and uncovering the cables located over there," pointing east. "Cables buried in similar locations have been utilized in our training exercises."

At this point, I told him about our surveillance room and the red light. In response, he said, "That's brilliant. Keeping us informed of potential threats of discovery by someone above us will ensure we can operate with impunity. Some of what we do may make enough noise to be heard on the surface."

The British began work at the far end of the tunnel. First, they and our men disassembled the tunnel shield in stages replacing it with a watertight, steel-reinforced concrete, rectangular structure they called the 'base chamber.' All of the concrete this team used for their many construction efforts was mixed in the basement and hauled a quarter-of-a-mile to the end of the tunnel using the wooden mining cart. The large hole they left in the roof of that chamber was centered over the assumed position of the three cables.

This team had designed a rectangular metal box they called 'the mole,' which they brought with them. Brad and I stood in the base chamber beside it as Raymond provided a whispered explanation of its function. "Note that the mole is positioned two feet to the side of where Captain Williams, here, expects the cables to be located—that's intentional. This wooden scaffolding currently supporting the earth above the mole will be removed. Concurrently, the mole will be extended upward using these eight car jacks," pointing. "Once it is in place, slats in the mole's top will be opened in turn, and small amounts of sandy Berlin soil from above will be scraped away. Once most of the soil immediately above the entire mole has been extracted, it will be moved up an inch or so, and the process will be repeated until the mole is about 8 feet above the base chamber. This delicate work will be performed by my people—two in the mole, and two standing by to assist as required. They will change positions every hour or so."

It took them six days to extend the mole up to the desired level. During that time, I got two reports from the British team. Over beers at the end of the second day, one of them reported, "We can hear traffic on the road and are sure it's immediately above us." Then early on the sixth day, Raymond reported, "The mole has reached the correct level because the team encountered the granular base materials used as the first course of most major roads. Our next job will be to replace the mole with scaffolding and forms. Then the area excavated by the mole will be surrounded with steel-reinforced concrete walls and a roof. That structure is designed to support the road and provide a haven for the team as they dig laterally toward the cables."

On March 28, Raymond entered my office in the warehouse with a bottle of expensive brandy in hand, "We need to celebrate. An hour ago, one of my men brushed soil off one of the cables. Let's get Brad and tell him that all three cables are located within a foot of where he claimed they would be."

"That is extraordinarily good news!" I shouted joyously.

Although it was the middle of the night back in Washington, I followed orders by making a phone call. In response to the words, "Allen Dulles, here," I reported, "Sir, it's a baby boy. He was born less than an hour ago."

"Congratulations. That is indeed good news. Please keep me informed of any change in the condition of the mother and baby."

*

Sections of the steel-reinforced concrete walls and roof of the tap chamber were slowly added as the British team uncovered space around the cables; this chamber would eventually provide sufficient room for two men to work, tapping different cables at the same time. It was designed to be strong enough to support heavy vehicles such as fully loaded trucks, and even tanks as they traversed the road above. The tap chamber was waterproof by design because even a slight amount of moisture in a communications line could result in an electrical short; that short could be detected by enemy operators and might compromise the entire program. At my request, a microphone was hidden in the tap chamber and another in the amplifier chamber so we could hear what was happening in those two locations after the British technicians left. To provide easy access, a wooden ladder was installed between the base chamber and the tap chamber.

*

In the days that followed, the British replaced most members of the first team with a group of signals experts. They would perform the taps and install all of the equipment required to exploit the information available in the telephone conversations and teletype messages that the Russians and Warsaw Pact nations exchanged with each other daily.

Soon after the new group arrived, they also assumed the guise of American GIs and went to work in several places at once. A concrete floor was poured in the last 68 feet of the tunnel. Unique racks of equipment designed to fit beneath the curved surface of the tunnel were installed in what the British dubbed the equipment chamber. The amplifiers in those racks would ensure that the signals derived from the taps had sufficient strength to be exploited in the operations room over a quarter-mile away. The cables that would carry those signals were laid along the top of the sandbags, through the basement, and into the windowless ground floor of the warehouse; this large open area was called the operations room. There the cables were attached to 165 of the latest technology, AMPEX reel-to-reel tape-recording machines my team had recently installed. To complete the signal path, a cable was installed from the amplifiers back into the tap-room. Extensive tests were performed on all of the individual components and the entire system to ensure that the signal paths worked properly.

Between the base chamber and equipment chamber, the British installed what they called a "torch-proof door." Its purpose was to prevent armed East Germans or Russians who discovered the tap chamber from dropping down into the base chamber and firing automatic weapons at the technicians who would frequently be working in the equipment chamber. Shots from their weapons would also be capable of traveling a long way down that straight tunnel. This door was hoisted into place and surrounded with steel-reinforced concrete. On the East German side of the door, it looked like a solid sheet of steel. I directed that a sign be attached to that side which read in German and Russian: ATTENTION—ATTENTION. TOP SECRET SECURITY ZONE—UNAUTHORIZED ENTRY WILL RESULT IN SEVERE PENALTIES. KEEP OUT. THIS MEANS YOU.

*

On the night of May 11/12, the tap team leader, Clarence Compton, ascended the wooden ladder. Three of his associates stood below in the base chamber to render assistance as required. Brad and I, plus American and British technical experts, were positioned around a recorder rack in the operations room. Russian and German linguist and cryptanalysts were also present at that location. Everything was now ready. Tens of thousands of man-hours and millions of dollars had been invested and it all came down to this one moment!

Those of us tasked with managing this effort could only wait and hope. Earlier in the day, Clarence had explained the tapping process he and his team would follow. "First, we will cut and remove the tenth of an inch-thick lead outer casing and seven layers of paper that are wrapped around the wire bundle. This must be done without cutting into any of the ninety-eight twisted pairs of wires tightly packed inside of the cable; if we do cut a wire it could easily short out. Next, each twisted pair is pulled out of the bundle as far as possible. A bit of insulation is removed without nicking or cutting one of the wires. It is soldered to one of the wires that run to the amplifiers and again protected with insulation.

"The trick is to do this same thing 194 times in the very limited amount of space between each of the wires in the cable bundle. The slightest drop or complete loss of signal strength will be noted by individuals who are continuously monitoring these communications lines. Any misstep on our part could easily result in a maintenance team or even a cadre of Russian soldiers showing up to find out what has happened."

A nearby member of the British team observed, "This is like delicate surgery. One tiny mistake and the patient dies."

"It's always pure hell," Clarence said in closing. "As you can understand, we must take our time. Tonight, we will tap the first line and see what happens."

At this point, I requested that Brad assign two people to the observation room on the second floor so that we could be quickly informed of any unusual activity along the Schönefelder Chasse that night.

Everyone in the warehouse gathered around a loudspeaker which was connected to the microphone in the tap chamber. Whispered updates occurred infrequently—"Starting" —"lead casing removed"—"paper removed"— "pair extracted"—"tea break"—"first splice"—"second splice"—"finished." I looked at my watch—that had taken three hours and twenty-three minutes. The entire group in the operations room had communicated with each other in subdued whispers that entire time; now they stood, cheered, and began slapping each other on the back. Most got a drink of water, a cup of coffee, or something stronger, and went to the restroom. All of us had been unaware of the passage of time while we waited.

Soon people returned to almost the same positions they had maintained through the night. There was nothing on the line we had tapped. Questioning looks and verbal comments expressed concern that the tap had somehow failed. Finally, I stood and said, "We shouldn't be concerned. The middle of the night is usually a slack period for communications use. Let's all give it time."

Another hour passed very slowly. At 04:45 Raymond stood and said, "I'm going down to the tunnel and have my people perform what checks they can on the line we've tapped."

Just to have something to do, I went to the observation room and confirmed that nothing unusual had occurred out on the road. Once there, I noticed that the first light of dawn was just visible.

I rejoined a somber group in the operations room. Raymond soon returned and reported, "there doesn't seem to be any problems with our equipment." The tape recorder, we had been gathered around all night had been equipped with a loudspeaker. As the minutes passed, a few people departed the scene after deciding that something was amiss; they would get breakfast before a meeting was called to figure out what had gone wrong.

At a little after 07:00, I was half asleep when suddenly I heard a click and then—"Buzz"…"Buzz"…"Buzz."

"Da," a Russian said, "Yes" answering the phone.

"Eto ty, Tovarishch Polkovnik?"—"Is it you, Comrade Colonel?"

"Da, eta ya."—Yes, it is I."

Our first tap was successful. Nothing of real value was gleaned from this first conversation, but the team knew that Operation Gold had struck real gold.

CHAPTER 59

Friday, May 13-Friday, August 19, 1955

IT TOOK THE British team another three weeks to tap into the two cables that were in "good shape", but it wasn't until early August that the British team returned to Berlin and the tunnel to complete their task. The third cable was the oldest and its insulation was 'worn.' Employing 'extra care' the tappers were again successful in accessing all of that cable's links. Now the CIA and MI6 had access to the over 1,200 communications lines.

No one at any level of Operation Gold was prepared for the tremendous volume of voice conversations and teletype messages that were available to us in the weeks that followed the first tap. Our initial task was to separate those communications links that carried military and civilian leadership information from those that contained information of little real interest. Our telecommunications operatives in East Germany had provided the alphanumeric designations of the communications lines that served East German government, Stasi, and military organizations; they also identified those used by Russian diplomatic, KGB, GRU, and senior military office buildings with telephone and teletype service. We and the British spent a lot of time trying to figure out which tapped lines carried those designations. Soon it became clear that it was easiest to just monitor a link for a while to determine who was using it. Ultimately, all of the highest priority lines were monitored continuously, while others were only monitored sporadically.

While I was supervising the construction of the tunnel in Berlin,

James Lawrence had a large group at CIA headquarters who were locating, recruiting, and verifying the security clearance of the hundreds of linguists, cryptanalysts, intercept console operators, and support staff needed to make this program a success. A substantial part of that group would be sent to Berlin to provide our agreed-to half of the onsite staff. The rest would work in a temporary building left over from World War II, which occupied the Washington Mall near the Lincoln Memorial. There they would process the teletype messages and produce the detailed intelligence assessment of Soviet capabilities and objectives, which was the primary purpose of the program.

The CIA wanted the prestige and funding this exceedingly important project would entail, and at first refused to contact the NSA. That intelligence rival had a large cadre of trained people with all of the required skills. CIA headquarters consistently failed to provide me with the staff I needed to do my job properly; as a result, for months I ended up spending 16- to 18-hour days at the warehouse. I barely even managed to carve out a few hours a week to be with Gretchen.

Two days after the first successful tap, a Scotsman named Richard James arrived to be the British site manager in Berlin. We got along great. Their knowledgeable, very professional operators and linguists soon arrived and began manning consoles. Our operators arrived a few at a time and weren't as well trained or dedicated as their British counterparts. Staffing often threatened to become a critical issue but didn't because Richard was always willing to help hold up our end of the bargain by 'lending' us staff.

By agreement with the British, all incoming voice communications were evaluated in Berlin for intelligence. The important information that needed to be disseminated to decision-makers in the American and British governments and their respective military establishment was sent out immediately via encrypted teletype messages.

Early on, Richard and I spent days in my office talking about the reports we would be required to generate. "My boss's stated top priority is to detect Soviet preparations for war and the second was military-force deployment or redeployment and size," I told him.

"War preparations are also at the top of our priority list," Richard said. "But our second priority is anything associated with nuclear weapon development and deployment."

"That probably does come ahead of force deployment with us, too," I replied. "Also, I suspect high-level interchanges between and within the East German and Russian government officials are also ahead of force deployment."

"One of our primary responsibilities as leaders of this site is to ensure that only valid reports are ever issued by either of our organizations," Richard stated. "A spurious report could easily have earth-shaking consequences."

"Given that, I would suggest that for now, critical RUSH type messages be reviewed and approved by one of us. Once we're able to generate written guidance on the issuance of such reports, perhaps we can delegate that responsibility to the senior man on duty during a shift."

"I concur. One of us will need to be on-call for the foreseeable future," I said.

I was much more fluent in both Russian and German than most of the linguists the CIA had hired. Almost every day, I was involved in interpreting exactly what two individuals were saying to each other when they either talked around a subject or used slang or curse words to convey meaning. Mostly, I'd prevented our facility from looking inept or foolish to the rest of the world by forestalling the release of blatantly spurious high-priority reports.

Our first RUSH message reported that the East Germans and Russians were preparing to 'smash' anyone who sought to reprise 'the workers rioting of 1953' on its second anniversary. We also issued reports that covered a variety of less important topics: the pin which held the treads of the new T-55 Russian main battle tank in place broke frequently and the tread itself was being redesigned to fix the problem; the Soviet army was short on vital equipment of all forms (and not ready for war as far as I could discern); and, the Il-28 jet bombers stationed in East Germany were designed to drop nuclear weapons and would be provided with MiG-17 jet fighter escort in the event of war.

*

For the past three months, Richard and I had been overwhelmed trying to organize the logistics of processing the voice tapes, generating reports, and boxing the tape reels up for shipment to either London or Washington. During the day, sometimes it seemed like all 165 intercept stations were recording at the same time, putting out the magnetic tape at the rate of 15 inches per second. Reels that ran out of tape in the middle of a conversation had to be replaced quickly—yet the reel-to-reel design required manual threading of the tape through the tape head and empty reel, so we often missed a minute or so of a vital conversation.

Voice-intercept operators made split-second decisions about whether what they were hearing was of sufficient importance to be taken to the adjacent secondary processing room. In that room, transcripts were generated via typewriter. Hardcopies, if generated, had to be packaged with the associated tapes. Reports were being generated and shipped out via the secure teletype links with Washington and London. The word hectic does not adequately describe the scene Richard and I tried to control daily.

On August 19, we got together for our usual, Friday meeting. "I think that with the new men who just arrived from London, we now have sufficient staff to man all 165 intercept positions from 06:00 to 20:00 local time," he said. "That'll ensure we intercept the most important traffic. If and when more manpower becomes available, we could consider 24-hour-a-day operations. Until then, only the most important links can be monitored continuously."

"I appreciate you Brits taking up the slack until we can hold up our part of the bargain," I said. "My leaders in Washington have assured me that at least 22 fully trained analysts, linguists and intercept operators from our NSA will arrive in the next 30 days."

CHAPTER 60

Saturday-Sunday, April 21-22, 1956

I'D TAKEN THIS weekend off, because, for the first time in two months, Erica had asked to accompany Gretchen on her overnight stay at my apartment. Since our vacation in Greece a year and a half ago, our interchanges had mostly involved how I would pick up and drop off Gretchen. Yet my standard peck on the cheek and hug always reminded me that nothing had changed.

Every week, Gretchen consumed several books designed for children a year or two older than her. With my concurrence, in the fall of 1955, Erica had enrolled her in the primary school located right on the campus of Humboldt University. "The faculty prides itself on this advanced educational facility," Erica said, to convince me to not place her in a primary school in West Berlin.

Every time I saw Gretchen, I couldn't get over how much she'd grown and started to build her own character. She always seemed excited to share something new with me. Over supper this evening, she asked me, "How many lives does a German cat have?"

Suspecting the answer, but not wanting to spoil her joke, I replied in English, "I don't know, how many?"

"Nein!" she said uproariously.

I laughed out loud and moved to hug her. *My daughter is very clever and so cute,* I said to myself.

That evening, with my assistance, Erica cooked us a wonderful meal and we watched television until Gretchen went to bed. Erica and I made small talk for the next hour and then went to separate bedrooms. We seemed just like old married folks—except for that one significant difference. I still ached for Erica's touch and feel.

I read Herman Wouk's *Marjorie Morningstar* until I fell asleep alone. If I hadn't had Gretchen in my life, I don't know what I would have done. It had been a long time since I'd heard Erica weep over Stephen, and outwardly she seemed happy. Perhaps it's been long enough for her to start thinking about the future.

*

Several times over the last months, I'd been tempted to save the cost and hassle of maintaining a full-time observation post in the "warehouse." Nothing ever seemed to happen on the rural stretch of Schönefelder Chasse opposite our facility. It's a good thing I desisted. At 01:49 that fateful Sunday morning, the phone beside my bed rang. I picked the receiver up and said, "Altschuler."

"Jones here, sir. You better get over here quickly."

At this point, I was used to getting woken up in the middle of the night to solve some kind of a problem at the warehouse. It had been raining for several days but had now stopped. Once I arrived there, I asked Jones, "What's up?"

"Our guy in the surveillance room was using night-vision goggles to survey the area on the other side of the fence. A little over an hour ago, he observed forty to fifty men arrive in the vicinity of the tap chamber. They appear to be digging up the road."

"What?!" I shook my head, trying to get my mind around what he said.

After that, I went upstairs and knocked on the observation room door. Following a brief delay, while the curtain was closed, I was admitted and immediately said, "Are you sure they're digging in the middle of the road exactly where the taproom is located?"

"See for yourself, sir," the man said, helping me place the strap for the night-vision binoculars over my head. It took me a while to adjust to what I was looking at. Finally, I realized the ghost-like white creatures moving in the distance were men wielding shovels and pickaxes.

"Shit. They'll discover the roof of the taproom soon. Breaking through that concrete structure will take time, but then...we've no way of stopping them."

After perhaps half an hour, someone knocked on the door, the curtains were drawn and I stepped outside. I followed Jones down to the duty officer's room. In reply to my questioning look, Jones pointed to his ear. Immediately, I could hear digging and clanging from the microphone in the taproom.

I called Richard and told him to come in immediately. Once he arrived, each of us dispatched a message to our respective headquarters explaining the situation and requesting "permission to detonate the explosives in the tunnel when we decided it is necessary."

Together, we went up to the surveillance room to assess the latest developments on the surface. Once there, I observed, "That large pile of rubble in the middle of the road indicates they will soon be in the taproom."

"Looks like the party's over," Richard replied, shaking his head. Just after dawn, one of our monitoring positions overheard a conversation between an unidentified individual and a Captain Ivanovich, who said, "Sir, it was raining heavily and several circuits shorted out. So, I dispatched a party to investigate. We have uncovered an American tap into our communications lines. What are your orders?"

The reply from the other individual was "Wait until I can come to the site."

Nearly two hours later, the man in the surveillance room reported the arrival of a convoy of Russian staff cars.

Soon we heard a conversation in the taproom. It was between a Russian colonel, who was addressed as such, and a subordinate. "How did they do that? It is fantastic. This tunnel goes under the highway."

Richard and I dispatched a third message to our respective headquarters indicating that if we didn't receive permission to detonate the tunnel explosives soon, it might be too late. We couldn't risk causing an international incident by injuring or killing Russians. It was now after 02:00 in Washington and just before dawn in London that Sunday morning.

Finally, in frustration, I said to Richard, "I don't think we should risk anyone else's life, but I'd like to go into the tunnel and see if we can determine what's happening."

"I'll join you," Richard said.

We boldly walked the almost quarter mile to the torch-proof door. Drawing nearer, we could hear the deafening sound of a machine cutting metal. As we got closer, it was apparent that they had dug around the fire-proof door and were cutting through the tunnel wall. We continued forward and were standing near the source of the noise when the bottom half of a metal-tunnel section suddenly fell forward. Then someone shouted in Russian, "Out of my way. I'll take care of them."

When a Russian officer with a machine pistol in his hand stuck his whole upper body through the hole, we made a hasty retreat. His first shot hit a sandbag beside me. The second must have hit an overhead light fixture that suddenly went out. The third hit the rubber-wheeled mining cart on rails I had sent flying back toward him. Richard and I ran down the tunnel as fast as we could, but the entire way I expected to hear the report of his next shot at about the same time as the bullet entered my back. I ran near the light switch for this part of the tunnel and ducked down as a fourth shot went over my head. Reaching up, I switched off the lights in the part of the tunnel the Soviets now controlled.

Some way further along, Richard and I paused, listening to determine if we were being followed. When we heard nothing, I hastily went up to the barracks, and shouted, "The Russians have discovered the tunnel. I need volunteers to help seal it."

Eight men who were playing poker in a recreation room and were already dressed shouted, "I'm available!" almost in unison.

"Follow me," I said.

Near the dividing line between East and West Berlin which had been previously marked on the tunnel wall, I said to the group, "Move as many sandbags as possible from behind us to fill the opening to the ceiling."

They were getting in each other's way, so I organized a kind of oblong assembly line—they all followed each other as bags were grabbed, carried, disposed of, and additional bags acquired.

Because we knew our bosses would insist on details, Richard went to the surveillance room and recorded what he could observe from that vantage point. The duty officer was tasked with taking notes on the conversations in the equipment room.

I went to my office, found a large piece of white card stock, and wrote a message to our enemy with a large felt-tipped pen. Before the final few bags were put into place, I put the sign where it could be easily seen. It read in Russian, German, English, and French: YOU ARE NOW ENTERING THE AMERICAN SECTOR.

Mid-afternoon, the last of our tap lines went dead.

The Berlin Tunnel I'd helped build operated for exactly eleven months and eleven days. In a way, I felt like I'd lost an important battle and was forced to make a full retreat. I'd labored unceasingly to make it a success. These efforts weren't in vain—we'd learned a lot and would continue to process the data we'd received, but were denied new information from this vital source.

CHAPTER 61

Friday, April 27-Friday May 4, 1956

IT APPEARED AS if the Russians had discovered the tunnel because heavy, persistent rain had shorted out some communications circuits. A crew that had been sent to repair the circuits had accidentally found our taproom. However, they had only dug in one spot, as if they knew exactly where to dig in advance. These facts, when considered together, made no sense.

All week I had frequent, real-time teletype interchanges with CIA headquarters on the facts surrounding the discovery of the tunnel. Finally, Mr. Dulles sent one of his deputies to Berlin and today we assembled in a Berlin Station conference room. No one was able to shed light on how the tunnel had been discovered. At the end of the meeting, I was given four tasks: (1) write a detailed report containing all known facts about the Russian discovery of the tunnel; (2) complete the first-level processing of all information and tapes generated before April 22; (3) plan and then implement the disassembling and shipment of the intercept equipment out of Berlin; and, (4) turn the "warehouse" over to the U.S. Army. I committed to having all four tasks completed by early August.

After the meeting, I was handed a letter from Mr. Dulles. In it, he congratulated me for a job well done and directed that I report for duty in Washington; my assignment—senior training officer for current and new CIA agents.

Once our guests left, I stared at the walls of the conference room for a long time. I'd been in Berlin for almost ten years. Stephen had been dead for three years. I hadn't found anyone in Berlin except Erica I cared enough about to form a lasting relationship. Gretchen was well adjusted despite her "father's untimely death," and she was doing well in school. She had a winning personality, self-confidence, and a wicked sense of humor for a six-year-old.

Perhaps it was time for me to move on—get a life, as they say. After all, I was forty-one years old. Maybe Erica needs a jolt, such as me leaving Berlin, to make her decide what she wanted in the future for the three of us.

"If you're going to start a real family, you'd better start soon," I murmured aloud. "You don't want someone to mistake you for your children's grandfather. You're already showing a little gray at the temples."

After mulling over everything, I decided to accept the assignment—it meant a big promotion and recognition within the CIA of my contribution. Perhaps I could still have it all—a great job, comfortable home, wife, and kids.

CHAPTER 62

Saturday, May 5, 1956

BY THE TIME I got back to my apartment late on the day the tunnel was discovered, Erica and Gretchen were gone. Last Wednesday, I called Erica to see if they could return indicating I had something important to discuss with her.

Soon after they arrived, we went to the Tiergarten and occupied a park bench while Gretchen played with other children. I was still struggling with how to tell them that I was leaving Berlin. For some time, neither of us said anything; then we turned to face each other, both talked at the same time, and as a result, laughed. She gently placed her hand on top of mine. "Thank you again for having Nora here with Gretchen last summer while I went on my dig. I invited her back to help with Gretchen again." I could feel my whole body sink into the bench beneath me. I hadn't known Erica would be leaving again this summer. This meant that we would only see each other a few times between now and when I left Berlin, perhaps forever.

Erica could see my change in demeanor. "I know it's late," she said, now squeezing my hand, "but I wasn't sure there would be a dig. The communist university chancellor is responsible for signing foreign travel permits for university people, and he's been turning down most requests. He just approved my professor's dig for this year the other day. I need the results of it to complete my dissertation." Her eyes began to water and she sighed. "Can you take Gretchen for the summer?"

"Of course, she and Nora can stay with me." I knew that if I did not take the girls, Erica would not have been able to go on the dig and that it was exceptionally important to her. "If you would like, I can bring the two girls down to Turkey in early August and we can spend another vacation together—looking at ruins, museums and going to the beach."

"That would be lovely. We accept your invitation."

*

After Gretchen was in bed that evening, I decided that I could no longer defer telling Erica my news. She loved my washer and dryer; as a result, she always brought extra clothes to do when she visited. She was sitting on the couch, folding laundry when I entered the living room and sat down in my easy chair. After nervously clearing my throat, I said, "You must have known for a long time that my work would require me to return to the States. When we come back from our vacation in early September, I'll be taking a new assignment in Washington, and be living there full time."

Erica stopped mid-fold. "For how long?" She asked, her voice quivering.

"I don't know…perhaps a year, maybe longer," I said.

"What about Gretchen and me?"

"I'll still help you financially and fully support Gretchen. I may be able to get back here once or twice a year. I want to see Gretchen as often as possible. She can come to visit me when school is out—my family has been wanting to meet her for a long time. She's now old enough to travel by herself. Who knows? She might like the States and want to live there someday. One of my nieces is almost exactly Gretchen's age."

"Yes, but…that's not the same." Her cheeks were flushed and she began shaking her head back and forth repeatedly as if to clear her mind.

"Erica, over the last three years you've made it clear you only want me as a friend. I must move on with my life and so must you. Once you told me to find someone to love and I promised I would. I'll have fewer work-related responsibilities in the States and will earnestly endeavor to find someone. I might be able to work in Berlin again in the future, but for now, it's best that I go."

She stared at me blankly, stood, took the laundry to her bedroom, returned, and sat back down on the couch, silently. I wasn't sure what to think or say so I returned her gaze without saying a word or making a gesture of any form.

After a few minutes—though it felt like years—she formed a half-smile and seemed to compose herself. "Since Stephen was killed, I have been living in a fragile shell—it's strange and lonely in the façade I have formed around myself. I'm just not the same person I was before. You've been the rock that tied me to reality, and for that, I'm eternally grateful. I've been incapable of experiencing any emotion, but especially joy and happiness. My sole focus has been Gretchen and my studies. I'm still both angry and bewildered that my future has been stolen. Kurt, you must understand, I'm still lost in most ways."

I thought of moving over to comfort her but feared she'd resist my touch. "Erica, what has happened to you is horrible. You have bravely gone on with your life, but you're young and have most of your life ahead of you. Have you considered the future—not just academically, but also personally?"

"Getting through the here and now has been so difficult…I haven't allowed myself to think of all my tomorrows."

She stared at me for a long time, it seemed almost like she was somewhere else entirely. Finally, I broke the silence. "We must work together to help Gretchen understand that you want to stay here to complete your education, which is important to you. I must go to Washington so I can advance my career. She's old enough to understand that adults must live their lives."

"You know I can't leave now—I'm so close to getting my degree. Just stay here close to us for another year and then we will see."

I desperately wanted to move to the couch and embrace her; I even ended up chastising myself for several months because I didn't. Instead, I blurted, "I'm sorry, I must leave in September. You must help make this transition as smooth as possible for our daughter and the two of us."

I knew she wanted to cry, but she never did in front of me. Somehow, she kept her composure long enough to rise from the couch. I stood, hoping she would rush into my arms. Instead, she turned and walked down the hall to her bedroom. I stood there transfixed, finally hearing her sobbing from afar. I went to my bedroom, where I spent a restless night wondering what Erica wanted of me.

CHAPTER 63

Thursday, August 2, 1956

THE RUSSIANS USED the discovery of the tunnel I'd helped build to orchestrate a global anti-American propaganda campaign about our violation of the sovereign rights of East Germany and the Four-Power Agreements. But it backfired on them. The CIA was admired around the world for having the guts and fortitude to carry out such an unexpected and successful operation against a totalitarian police state.

Last Friday afternoon, I turned the keys to the "warehouse" and most government-owned equipment and furniture over to a US Army Provosts Marshall. In the last four months, we had sealed the tunnel with cement, processed and/or shipped all of the tape recordings back to London or Washington, crated up all of the equipment for shipment to their point of origin, and destroyed all of the remaining classified material from the safes and file cabinets. My last act was to send a message to CIA headquarters certifying that the "warehouse" no longer contained any classified information.

Today, Gretchen, Nora, and I flew to Rome. I'd arranged for my new Mercedes 180 four-door sedan to be waiting for us at the Rome Airport. We planned to drive to Brindisi on the heel of Italy, take a car ferry over to Greece and then drive to Turkey.

CHAPTER 64

Friday, August 3-Saturday, September 1, 1956

MID-AFTERNOON, THREE WEARY, but happy travelers arrived at the villa I'd rented on the coast of Turkey. That morning, we'd gone to the Bazaar in Izmir to purchase several day's provisions.

The villa was situated on a low bluff with a commanding view of the Aegean. Below it was a broad sandy beach. Nora and Gretchen had separate rooms with a shared bath at one end of the villa. Erica and I would each have larger bedrooms with private baths at the other. An open room that contained the kitchen, dining area, and large living room formed the center of the villa. Outside was an expansive terrace, facing the sea and running the full length of the building.

The girls unpacked and jumped in the Aegean Sea less than an hour after we arrived. I tried to get the kitchen organized and began to wonder what I'd serve them for supper when a car drove up and a smiling Erica emerged. I hugged her and instead of moving away quickly, she embraced me closer, almost intimately. We stood there for several minutes but separated slowly when we heard the laughing girls approach. Gretchen ran to her mother's arms and they spent several minutes bonding with each other.

Soon Erica gave me the smile that always melted my heart. "I need to wash the dust of the dig off, and then we can see about supper together."

We ate on the terrace as the sun set over the Aegean. Erica and I had prepared a delicious meal of lamb shish kabobs with mushrooms, saffron rice, and mashed chickpeas. While we ate, Erica described her dig. "My professor said once I document the dig in my dissertation, he'll recommend I be given my doctorate."

I observed, "So in the future, we will all have to address you as Dame Professor Doctor Schäfer, and show due respect."

"To all of you, I'll remain plain old Erica, if you please."

After supper, we played a game of Scrabble in English so Nora, Gretchen, and even Erica could increase their vocabulary.

The girls went to bed exhausted, leaving Erica and me sitting on the sofa in the living room. She took my hand and held it, then kissed my palm tenderly. I began caressing her neck and ear. She snuggled into my arms. "You're leaving me after protecting me for so long," she said. "I'll miss our time together."

Where is this going? Has she finally decided to let me into her shell? "I'll only be gone in body," I told her, holding her tighter. "But I'll always be with you," I said, pointing to her heart.

She took my head in her hands and kissed me. We began caressing each other. I'd wanted this so badly but was still unsure of Erica's motives. Perhaps she was concerned I'd find another woman in Washington; making her and even Gretchen less important to me. I let her take the lead; I'd been craving to touch and hold her like this for so long. The intensity and passion seemed even better than years earlier when we were young and our relationship new.

As our wonderful month together unfolded, I became convinced that Erica genuinely loved me and wanted us to spend the rest of our lives together. Yet I still didn't know where we stood as a couple. One night, I simply asked her. "So, are we together now? Is this what you want?"

"When you told me you were leaving, I suddenly realized I couldn't live without you," she replied. "I love you. Now I'm never going to let you go."

Each day with Erica was like living a dream come true. The night before we left the villa, we agreed that she would get her doctorate as soon as possible and I would do everything possible to complete my assignment in Washington. We vowed to meet somewhere Christmas time and plan our future.

*

Before I left Berlin, Erica and I decided to finally tell Gretchen about our relationship. "Your Uncle Kurt and I were very close once before you were born," Erica said. "But then we spent time apart and I married Stephen. But dear, we want you to know that Kurt is your real father."

 Gretchen stared at me with wide, beautiful eyes that were just like her mother's. "I do not remember much about Stephen," Gretchen said. "Uncle Kurt has always felt like a father to me. I love you both so much," she said; then in-turn, she hugged us each tightly.

CHAPTER 65

Thursday-Wednesday, October 4-24, 1956

THE FIRST LETTER I received from Erica after arriving at my new assignment indicated that she was scheduled to defend her dissertation in late September. It also described how the new chancellor of her university, Ernst Neumann, was thought to be a Stasi Agent. In her second letter, she indicated that he had called her to his office and ordered her to have "no contact with people from West Berlin and especially those from Western Imperialistic Nations." Per Erica's instructions, my first letter to her had been mailed care of the university. It had been opened by someone. Her reply provided the address of a West Berlin friend that our future correspondence should be routed through. It also included a photograph of Gretchen in her first-day-at-school dress.

*

On October 4, I got another letter from Erica—it resulted in me being vexed for days; unsure what I should or could do.

Dearest Kurt,

My dissertation was approved and yesterday that communist son-of-a-bitch Neumann called me to his office. Instead of congratulating me, he told me he was holding up my new credential because of questions about my loyalty to the state.

He indicated that people "who oppose the proper authorities cannot be allowed to teach our youth."

When I objected, he told me I must assist our leader's efforts to ensure that the Americans are not allowed to make Germany a colony. Then he said if I did agree to help, he'd allow the university to acknowledge my doctorate after only a year or two. I'd have to begin teaching communist doctrine in my classes, go to some conferences in the West and try to influence some people there, and/or go on a dig in a NATO country and transport some documents.

The academic community immediately organized a united position in my support. So, when three days later I was again called to his office, I hoped he had reversed his earlier position. Once I sat before him, he rose to his feet, walked around behind me and grabbed my breast. I was appalled and had to push the chair back hard before I could force him to release me.

He returned to his desk, smiling as if he had just marked his territory on my body. Then, more appalling said, "Sleep with me once or twice a week for the next few months, and I'll approve your degree. Then matter-of-factly he told me that if I didn't agree with one of his two demands, I would be investigated by the Stasi over my loyalty to the regime.

I was speechless, stood and left the room without saying a word.

I cannot believe that any woman in her right mind would have anything to do with that smarmy scheisse kopf (shit head). I talked to several senior *women professors and they said that reporting it to the president of the university or the authorities would only cause more problems and recommended that I forget the incident.*

I will never go to his office again no matter how many times he summons me. I plan to continue teaching my classes and will defer any decision until we talk at Christmas time. Your daughter's first letter is attached.

It is only you that I love. In three months we will be together again.

Erica

Gretchen's letter written in scrawled German read as follows:

Papa,

Visit me soon. I miss when we are together in the park and reading books.
I love you.
Gretchen

*

I was able to access CIA files on Ernst Neumann and determined he was a Stasi Agent who was fluent in German, Russian, and Polish. In 1948, he tried to emigrate to the American Zone using a false birth certificate. His photograph and description taken at the time were a part of the file which also contained the notation: **The birth certificate he provided was that of an individual who died in Cologne in 1946.**

Our files also indicated that from 1950 through late 1954, Neumann had been 'in charge of the Stasi counter-espionage interrogation center in the basement of Stasi Headquarters.' In that role, he was certainly involved in the torture and death of many of the 67 operatives we and the British had lost during that period. After I read that I shuddered, thinking about the probable fate of that affable gentleman, Manfred Mittag, his wife, and three children; all five of them had just disappeared from the face of the earth after being arrested en masse by the Stasi.

Soon after receiving Erica's disturbing letter, I airmailed Andreas a message in a simple substitution code that only he and I knew. It requested his help and gave him explicit instructions: (1) determine where Ernst Neumann's office is on the university campus; (2) follow him every day after he leaves the university and take photos of him; (3) get his fingerprints; (4) send fingerprints and photos to me via Pan Am airline express service; and, (5) determine his daily routine.

Andreas sent me several photographs of Neumann, along with a beer glass with his fingerprints. Those prints were not in the CIA fingerprint database, but MI6 had a set of 1933 Hamburg Police prints and photos in their files. Neumann's real name was Heinrich Fuchs; he was born and raised in Danzig and was arrested as a communist subversive shortly after Hitler took power. Once released from police custody, Fuchs fled to Russia. A notation in the MI6 file said: "**Wanted by the International Court of Justice for crimes against humanity; he was one of the chief perpetrators of the Katyn Forest Massacre in 1940. Several survivors identified a Polish-speaking German named Heinrich Fuchs as one of the senior leaders of this group of murderers.**

I did some research; in 1939 Hitler and Stalin agreed to divide Poland between them. Twenty days after the Germans started World War Two by attacking Poland, Russia began occupying their three-fifths of that country. The Russian army immediately arrested the elite of society, including Polish military officers, political, religious, and business leaders, plus intellectuals including university professors and newspaper editors. All of these people were taken to Western Russia and put in prison camps near each other. In April 1940, the NKVD, predecessor of the KGB, took control of these prisoners with orders from Moscow to execute them. Over 22,000 Poles were shot and buried in mass graves in the Katyn Forest.

The more I discovered about him the more outraged I became. Neumann/Fuchs had repeatedly shown a total disregard for the lives of other human beings. In the name of communism, he became an inhuman killing machine.

During my sleepless nights that followed, his victims including Manfred Mittag, his wife, and three children paraded before me. These apparitions were followed by haunting images of row after row of people in a forest falling into a deep pit as machine guns mowed them down. Soon wounded survivors were wriggling through the bodies of the dead and up into the layers of dirt recently piled on the top of their mass grave; first, a hand would appear, then a blood-soaked head would surface gasping for air. My nightmares accurately reflected the sworn testimony of the few survivors of the Katyn Massacre.

My sense of well-being returned once I decided on a drastic course of action. *Fuchs is a corrupt Stasi agent, dedicated communist, and most importantly, an international criminal who deserves to die. The world will be a better place without him, yet he now thinks himself safe. If I'm successful, his legions of victims can finally rest in peace.*

CHAPTER 66

Wednesday-Friday, November 21-23, 1956

EARLY WEDNESDAY MORNING of Thanksgiving week, I called in sick from the departures lounge at La Guardia Airport in New York. Three years ago, I'd been given a British passport in the name of Jonathan Edwards to ensure that no one noted my travel between Berlin and London while the first tunnel was being built. Nobody asked for it back after the tunnel project ended, so I just kept it. So, as Mr. Edwards, I flew via BOAC through Heathrow to Berlin's Gatow Airport in the British Zone—a 23½-hour trip.

I took a taxi from Gatow to the apartment building on Bernauerstrasse. As anticipated, Helmut was waiting for me inside. He was on the CIA's payroll, and his only job was to maintain the charade that an East German family inhabited each of the four apartments. All of these families had immigrated to the West weeks or months before. He also generated spurious reports for the communist party on their activities. This apartment building was how the CIA personnel got into East Berlin without any official notice by East German authorities. The entire apartment house was in East Berlin, but the front stoop and sidewalk were in West Berlin. It's one of the many anomalies that resulted from the division of an already existing city into four parts after the war. The apartments were filled with the disguises required for our agents and operatives to move freely throughout East Berlin.

I was paying Helmut almost as much as the CIA was to ensure that when I needed his help, it would be available; I trusted him implicitly.

Four weeks after Andreas received my letter, he reported that he had trailed Neumann for 18 days. Although he was married, Neumann visited a prostitute in a run-down section of town every Thursday after work. He usually left the prostitute's apartment at a little before midnight so he could catch a subway train.

When I was in the OSS, they had issued us a long, thin, very sharp-bladed stiletto and trained us on how to use it to silence an enemy quickly. I'd carried it while on duty in France and Germany, but had only been forced to use it once. It had been in my duffel bag when I had been discharged from the hospital after the war. I kept it, knowing that one day it might come in handy.

I donned a bum's outfit—wig, a false beard, slouch hat, and worn hobnail boots. A rope served as the belt for my worn, heavy wool trousers, and I covered my body in a World War Two German private's greatcoat. An empty, battered suitcase topped off my disguise. I looked like thousands of other men who wandered around the worker's paradise of East Berlin every day. Most had severe mental or physical problems which made them outcasts of society and unemployable. The knife was tucked securely inside my shirt in a sheath attached to a lanyard that circled my neck.

I practiced my slouched posture and hesitant, stumbling walk. "What do you think?" I asked Helmut.

"You look like the real thing," he said, shaking my hand. It was a little before 19:00. The prostitute's apartment was in a building south of the city's center and I was north of it. It would have been around an hour-and-a-half walk at a brisk pace—three hours in my guise as a crippled bum. I'd memorized the route I would take and intended to get there early so I could find a proper place for an ambush. Neumann's hated face was seared into my brain.

On the way, however, my resolve to serve as judge, jury, and executioner for the international criminal Heinrich Fuchs, AKA Ernst Neumann wavered. I repeatedly asked myself, "Are you capable of committing cold-blooded murder? My resolve returned when I thought about the terror that his tens-of-thousands of victims must have experienced at his hands. He deserved to die. Unfortunately, I must make it happen quickly and then get away from the scene. He deserved to suffer for minutes if not hours or days like many of his victims had."

When I arrived, I found a gasthaus down the street from the prostitute's apartment. I attempted to buy a beer with a soiled, crumpled five Mark note but was kicked out—while there I noted that the bar's clock read 22:34. According to Andreas, Neumann would be leaving the prostitute's apartment around 23:15. He always came out of the front door of the apartment, turned left, and stayed on the same side of the street en route to the nearest subway station.

I found that there was a dark alley along that route that provided a view of the apartment's front door. The shadow of the alley's mouth was the perfect place for an ambush. I put on tight-fitting leather gloves, removed the knife from its sheath, and never wavering from my resolve as I waited.

Time passed slowly. Few people were out on the street at this time of night. There was a misty fog and the streetlights formed only small islands of light. Suddenly, I heard a door open and was startled as if waking from a daze. A man emerged from the apartment building I was watching, turned up the collar of his overcoat, and headed my way. He entered one of the islands of light. It was Neumann for sure. I took a deep breath as a tight knot formed in the pit of my stomach but stayed perfectly still. His footsteps became louder and louder in the silence of the night. Closer and closer. When he entered my view, I sprung out of the dark, startling him. "Herr comrade, can you spare a poor, unfortunate ex-soldier a pfennig or two?" I asked him, holding my grubby left hand out.

The knife in my right hand was held at my side. Before he could say anything, I brought the blade up and struck. He was a big man and managed to twist in an attempt to escape. I felt resistance as the knife glanced off of a rib or his breastbone, but then quickly went in up to the hilt. I stepped back as he shuddered, went down to his knees, and silently fell forward onto his face.

After sheathing the knife, I grabbed his arms, and with some effort, was able to drag him into the dark alley. I searched for the pulse in his neck—he was dead. I felt a deep satisfaction that I'd been able to remove this awful man from the ranks of the living.

He wore a nice leather trench coat and a suit coat. I was eventually able to remove both by moving him from side to side. Then I removed his shoes and trousers. Undressing a dead man is difficult. The weight of the torso makes each step cumbersome. I was sweating when I finally removed all of his clothes except his underwear. I retrieved the suitcase hidden in the shadows at the back of the alley, folded and then placed each clothing item neatly inside. His watch, billfold, keys, and Stasi identification card went on top of the other things. With some effort, I finally managed to get the straps that held the suitcase together cinched up.

When they found his body, the police and Stasi would assume that he had been mugged by a bum for his clothes and valuables. They would then search East Berlin for someone wearing them. They would never realize that his clothes were in a trash receptacle in West Berlin and his assassin was thousands of miles away. When planning this night, I was tempted to leave my stiletto behind; using it to attach a flag with the White Eagle of Free Poland to his chest, but decided not to implicate the numerous Poles that continued to fight for the freedom of their beleaguered country.

Leaving the scene, I resumed my halting gait. The streets of East Berlin were silent at that hour. About fifteen minutes later, I heard the wail of a police siren, which I assumed was heading toward the scene of my crime. I ducked into the shadows of a nearby alley as the police car passed by. The sound eventually faded and I continued my journey. I had lost all track of time but steadily moved toward safety. As I neared the back of the apartment building on Bernauerstrasse, I paused to ensure that no one was lurking in the shadows. I mentally counted the seconds, surveying the scene. After perhaps ten minutes of total silence, except for an owl's occasional mournful cry, I ambled over to the back door, opened it, and was greeted by Helmut.

The rest of my Thanksgiving holiday round trip was uneventful. However, as I dozed on the plane during the long flight back over the Atlantic, and almost every night after that as I sought sleep, the grimace on Hoffman's face as he died haunted me. On occasion, I even reprised our entire encounter. My guilty conscience refused to allow me to rationalize his killing.

CHAPTER 67

Saturday, December 1, 1956

IN MY LAST letter to Erica, I asked if she could still leave East Berlin for our Christmas vacation, suggesting we rent an apartment in Paris. Today, her reply arrived.

Dearest Kurt,

You'll never believe what happened. Ernst Neumann was found dead in an alley in a bad section of East Berlin! Rumor at the University has it he was mugged and his clothes and valuables were stolen.

The university president and faculty hurriedly appointed my major professor as the new chancellor. They are hoping to present the government here with a fait accompli. They also immediately prepared the paperwork awarding me my doctorate and have scheduled my graduation ceremony for January! That's, however, only a formality. So, fate works in very mysterious ways—I am now a Doctor of Philosophy in Classics Studies.

My major professor, Gerhard Richter, has nominated me to be designated as eligible for a professorship, Berufungsfähigkeit in German. It is the next step after a doctorate. It will require at least two more years of study and teaching. However, if the government doesn't interfere with his appointment as chancellor, I will immediately take over some of his classes and start giving lectures to other students. At 33, I'll be the youngest lecturer the university has ever had. How about that?

That awful man is now gone and will remain nameless from this point on. Hence, I see no reason why Gretchen and I can't fly from West Berlin to Paris for the holidays. We can leave early on 23 December and return on 3 January.

I long to hold you again and am looking forward to Paris. I understand the French know how to celebrate both Christmas and New Year's Eve. Perhaps Nora can join us so we can have some private time to get reacquainted.

Hugs and kisses,

Erica

CHAPTER 68

Sunday, December 23, 1956-Thursday, January 3, 1957

TIME SEEMED TO fly by as my unusual family took in the holiday sites and celebrations in Paris. On New Year's Eve, we let Gretchen and Nora eat out on their own. Erica and I went to a gourmet restaurant called Benoir Paris. After a wonderful meal and champagne, I took Erica's hands across the table. "Now that you have completed your studies, why don't you and Gretchen join me in Washington for a few months? I'm committed to stay there until at least July, and then we can decide where we want to live and what we want to do with our lives."

"I'd be bored just counting the time until summer. Plus, I've started working on my lecturer's certificate. This distinction is very important to me."

"Can't you pursue that certificate in West Germany or even in the States? I worry so about your safety and that of our daughter. Plus, we need to find a way to be together as a family."

"Kurt, you must understand. I have made a personal commitment to my university and people who are important to me."

"—am I not important to you?"

"Yes, of course. Except for Gretchen, you're the most important person in my life, but it's just…"

"—Then marry me and make me the happiest man on this planet."

"I want to marry you, but it's just that I have…

"—then let's go shopping for a ring while we are here in romantic Paris," I said kissing her hand.

"It's just that professor Richter is counting on me. So many of his staff have left for universities in the West...his duties as chancellor will mean that he can teach only a few high-level post-graduate classes...I have agreed to take over most of his classes."

I moved my head back and looked at her askance, but she just continued, "At the age of 33, I'm the youngest professor at the university...you must understand I assured Professor Richter; he's counting on me!"

When I did not respond, she asked, "Can you get a job in West Berlin while I complete my lecturer's degree requirements? I should be finished in about eighteen months."

I'd assumed that she would joyously accept my proposal and we would be discussing our future together. Instead she was asking me to accommodate her by returning to Berlin before we could get married. By eliminating Neumann, I'd mistakenly opened a path for her to stay in East Berlin. Erica and I had been at this juncture once before and I had botched everything so badly that I tried to hide my disappointment, but the glum look on my face conveyed my feeling, and when I did not respond to her proposition, she squeezed my hand and said, "There won't be a dig this year." So, she pleadingly added, "Irrespective of anything else, we can plan to spend a month together this summer. We can defer the decision on when we marry until we determine which direction both of our lives take."

I smiled, kissed the palm of her hand and said, "I'll only agree on two conditions; first, we spend next summer's vacation in the States—you and Gretchen will meet my family for the first time—you might find that you want to live there. Second and most importantly, you actively seek a position in West Berlin or better in West Germany. I cannot share everything I know with you, but you must believe me when I tell you that the three of us are just not safe in Berlin."

"I accept your conditions," Erica said, kissing and fondling my hand.

CHAPTER 69

Thursday, August 1-Sunday, September 1, 1957

TWENTY-TWO HOURS AFTER they left Berlin, Erica and Gretchen landed at New York's LaGuardia Airport. My parents and I met them at the gate. I immediately noticed that Erica was not wearing her wedding ring. In the past, she had only taken it off when we made love. I took that as a visible indication that she was ready to move on with her life. We exchanged letters constantly, but the only commitment I'd gotten out of her was to keep an open mind about her and Gretchen joining me in the states following their visit.

Dad drove his large Lincoln Continental limousine to their penthouse facing Central Park on East 77th Street. Once we were alone, Erica pulled me close to her and kissed me. "I knew your family had money," she laughed, "but I had no idea they were quite so well off."

"I kept saying you and our daughter could have anything you wanted or needed. Tell me you love me for my kindness, patience, and prowess in bed, not my money."

"Of course, but it is just…you know…a bit overwhelming."

"You'll grow to love my parents. They're very down to earth. And they'll try to spoil their granddaughter."

Each of us got our own bedroom, but Erica and I were conveniently forced to share a luxurious, large bath located between our bedrooms, which just happened to be in a secluded area downstairs. My parents insisted on showing us the city—museums, the Empire State Building,

Statue of Liberty, and Broadway plays. We took Gretchen to Jones Beach several times and once to Coney Island, which I admitted was a bit rundown from when I went there in my youth.

On our last evening in New York, Erica and I ate a wonderful meal in the Peacock Alley Restaurant at the Waldorf-Astoria, followed by dancing on the roof in the Starlight Room. At close to midnight, I took Erica to the top of the Empire State Building to see the view. As we stepped out of the elevator on the top floor, I could see a young man in a tuxedo move out of view. I gestured Erica in that direction. My college roommate at Yale was now a musicology professor at Julliard and had arranged for some of his students to help me.

Erica and I took in the view to the south as five young violinists came toward us playing "Fascination," the theme from the movie *Love in the Afternoon*—Erica's favorite movie. She looked around in awe as the observation platform turned into a nighttime concert hall. In the next moment, I went down on one knee.

"Erica Hoffmann, love of my life, will you marry me?" I held out a gold band for her.

"Yes, of course, silly," she said, a smile taking over her face. "I've been expecting you to ask."

I placed a plain gold band on the ring finger of her left hand and said, "Now we're engaged in the European tradition. How about a short engagement—there is no waiting period in several states south of here. We can have a honeymoon in Florida."

"No, we must wait. I want my whole family to be there. Papa won't leave the farm now because it's harvest time. Plus, your family can afford to fly to Berlin."

"Okay, how about a wedding in Berlin in November or December?"

"Both Gretchen and I will be out of school beginning in mid-December, thus just before Christmas would be best. Perhaps your parents can take Gretchen somewhere so we can have a honeymoon alone."

We kissed and I held her tighter than I ever had before. So many lonely years I had waited for this moment. Finally, we were going to be together forever. As the violinists switched to Beethoven's "Moonlight Sonata" we moved slowly around the building, admiring the view. Eventually, someone came up behind us and, in a considerate whisper, said, "The last elevator leaves in fifteen minutes." The music stopped, and we enjoyed one more lingering kiss.

*

As the Cold War deepened and the situation in Berlin became more precarious, I decided to acquire an American passport for Gretchen. The notarized paperwork Erica, Stephen, and I generated when she was born made acquiring that document a simple task; It would ensure that as my daughter, I could extract her from most situations, otherwise, she would be treated as an East German citizen. She used the passport for the first time on this trip. It reflected my last name, Altschuler, as hers for the first time in her life.

CHAPTER 70

Monday-Friday, September 9-20, 1957

AT THE BEGINNING of her visit, Erica had informed me that she had agreed to remain at Humboldt University until June of next year in return for being awarded her lecturer's certificate. The week after she left the States, I informed my superiors that I would resign from the CIA in December. Once we were married, I planned on acceding to my father's request and take over his business—I contemplated moving its headquarters back to Germany—more than half its sales were to European firms, so that made sense.

Those plans were immediately shattered by events in Berlin. In the middle of the night, the telephone in my apartment in Washington rang. An international operator asked if I would accept a collect phone call from Erica Schafer. Intercontinental phone calls were prohibitively expensive so I was concerned that something had happened to her or Gretchen and agreed to pay the charges. Erica was sobbing as she said, "I went into the university today just to find out my teaching schedule... Those communist shit heads... they've done it again. While I was gone, they forced my major professor, Gerhard Richter, to resign as chancellor and got a dedicated communist appointed in his place. His name is Karl Holtzmann. I know of him! He'll make Humboldt into a hell hole! One of his first acts was to fire all of our little grade school teachers and replace them with communists. Now there is no school in East Berlin we can trust to educate Gretchen!"

Hesitating because I did not know exactly what to say, I finally blurted, "Erica dear, how can I help you?"

"Come to Berlin as soon as you can! In addition to everything else, my grandmother is sick and maybe dying. I need your help."

"I'll leave tomorrow morning," I said, then listened as the line went dead and a dial tone followed.

My immediate thought was that Erica would now give up her teaching position and join me for the rest of our lives. In a quick phone call the next morning, I arranged for a leave of absence from the CIA.

Forty-six hours later, my TWA DC-6 landed at Tegel and I took a taxi to Erica's apartment. It was 08:46, Thursday morning when I knocked on Erica's door. There was no answer. A brisk walk to her office in the nearby university was also fruitless. I was worried—not knowing if she and Gretchen were safe was unnerving. After asking directions I found the office of the university's grade school; the school secretary reported that "Gretchen Schafer has not shown up for class the last two days."

In frustration, I walked back to Erica's office and determined that she was not there. I was pacing up and down the hall when a student opened a nearby door. I glanced in and saw Erica. She was directing 15 to 20 students as they were busily packing the contents of the office into suitcases. I rushed in, grabbed Erica and swung her around, "You're safe. I was getting worried."

The questioning look on my face led her to say, "Professor Richter has resigned from Humboldt and is now the head of the classics department at Tübingen University near Stuttgart. He left yesterday, but he and his family could take only one suitcase each with them into West Berlin. We are packing these suitcases," pointing, "with everything from his office—books, notes, artifacts, and even his ancient coin collection. I have the keys to his house and a list of the things his family wants from there. It may take us two trips to get all of his possessions out of his house, but we intend to help him get everything out of East Berlin before the authorities even realize he is gone."

I checked the hall, shut the door to the office, got everyone's attention, and said, "For this to work each of you must be discrete—leave here separately, take a different route, and leave East Berlin through different checkpoints on each of your trips. If you don't someone may report our activities to the authorities."

Erica took over and made sure that each student knew that the contents of the suitcases were being transported to one of the student's grandfather's warehouses in the British sector, and how to get to the Richter's residence. After I determined that Gretchen was safe with her grandparents, I help Erica get the students organized and even made several trips over the border with suitcases myself.

Later that day, I collected Gretchen from her grandparent's farm, determined that Erica's grandmother was better, and rented a suite of rooms at the Hilton. Erica joined us for supper and shared some news: "Professor Richter indicates that he is going to try to get me a lecturer's position at Tübingen."

"If he is successful that would mean the three of us could move there and I could move my father's business to Stuttgart," I observed enthusiastically. "There is convenient air and train service from there to all of Europe."

I was so certain that Erica and I had finally found a way to be together that I went into the Berlin CIA office, filled out the required resignation forms, and shared parting banter with a number of my associates.

A week later, my vision for the future was again crushed. Erica returned to our hotel room in a very emotional state, "Professor Richter told me that Tübingen University had reviewed my academic credentials…and… they refused to admit me to its lecturer program," she said, barely getting the words out. "I must perform post-doctorate work for two more years… or even longer…before I could even hope to enter the lecturer program."

Eventually, she dried her eyes with the handkerchief I provided and continued, "I can't believe what he told me next…Tübingen refuses to have any lecturing professors below the age of 40," she said, holding me tightly. "Plus… he said the academicians in the universities of West Germany look down on their fellows who…like me…have been educated in the East since the war. And…and…" She again cried softly, unable to speak.

"Oh, my love, I'm so sorry."

Tears trickled down her cheeks, but after a few minutes her composure returned and she said, "He informed me that too many of the best professors left Humboldt for the Free University in West Berlin and other institutions in the West in the late 1940s. Adding that the truth is that Humboldt is probably no longer in the top tier of German educational institutions."

For all of the years I'd known Erica, she had strived for one goal—to be a young, female lecturer in a field dominated by older men. All of her hopes and dreams came crashing down with these revelations. All I could do was hold her and hope her spirit was not also crushed.

"Also, Dr. Richter indicates that he can't even offer me a position on his post-doctoral staff until next September at the earliest." Then her smile left, and she began to sniffle again.

I placed my forefinger under Erica's chin, raised her head, and kissing her tenderly. "My love, is something else bothering you?"

She took a deep breath again and now in an angry voice said, "It will be difficult for me to take Gretchen to a good school in West Berlin each day and still meet all of my commitments at the university."

After a long silence and much thought on my part, I said "Perhaps, we have no choice but to get married now and move to America or West Germany. Frankfort would be an excellent location for my business if you don't want to leave Germany."

"I can't just leave my family and students—they all count on me! Can't you get your old job here in Berlin back? We could get married in December, live in West Berlin and I could commute to the East until I get my lecturer's certificate—then we can move—it's just one more year then I'll gladly leave Humboldt and East Berlin forever!"

CHAPTER 71

Friday, September 27, 1957

LAST WEEK, IAN Fleming's fifth best-selling novel about James Bond was published. Many young CIA agents envisioned they would soon be taking out the bad guys, and being seduced by beautiful women. They would be sadly disappointed at the mind-numbing realities and daily slog that were the real spy game—the more senior one got in that organization the further one got from any real danger except the possibility being buried in a mountain of paperwork.

On Monday of this week, I withdrew my resignation and on Friday I was appointed operations officer for all CIA activities in Eastern Germany including Berlin—a purely administrative job with tremendous responsibilities. I'd be replacing an individual who was forced to return to the States immediately because of his wife's medical problems. My cover would be as a part of the US Trade Delegation—I would have diplomatic immunity—whatever good that would do—in the past, the communists had often ignored the protection that such status afforded individuals they suspected of spying on them.

Today I was briefed on the status of our operations by Chief-of-Station, Mike McGregor. I was gratified to learn many of the cells of the spy networks I'd help established in the 1940s were still functioning. Peter and Andreas were still supporting us. Peter was now primarily a sleeper agent, who was only asked to provide information when it was critical.

I also learned that the situation in Berlin and Germany had changed dramatically in the three years since I'd been involved in the daily operations of Berlin Station. Early in the Cold War, we'd prevented many, perhaps even most, Russian and East German spies from performing their assigned espionage tasks by identifying, arresting, and/or expelling them.

Now, thanks to the information provided by a Russian GRU Lieutenant Colonel and double agent named Pytor Popov, we knew how bad the situation had deteriorated.

Popov, whose codename was "Arctic," had been working for us for four years, first in Vienna and then at a military installation eighty miles north of Berlin. His highly classified Limited Distribution file indicated he provided extensive information about spy networks being operated by the GRU (Soviet Military Intelligence). These spies were mostly located in West Germany, but a few were in other parts of Western Europe and even America.

The most recent entries in the Arctic file indicated that in March he'd informed us of a meeting he'd attended with Minister of Defense and Hero of the Soviet Union, Marshall Zhukov. In his speech, Zhukov had urged the assembled generals "to improve combat readiness and discipline because our plan calls for us to strike first in the event of war with the West. We must be at the Rhine River at the end of the first day and the English Channel the next day!"

"As you can imagine," Mike observed, "dissemination of this information was tightly controlled, yet it sent shock waves through the Pentagon and White House. Even the old warhorse President Eisenhower was upset at this revelation."

*

Ten days after I arrived back in Berlin, we rented an apartment near the one I vacated a year earlier. All of my furniture was in storage, and I'd learned today it would be at least two more weeks before I could move in—so I continued to stay in the Hilton with Erica and Gretchen. We found an excellent private school near our new apartment for Gretchen. An administrative group at CIA headquarters took responsibility for packing up my apartment in Washington and shipping everything to me in Berlin.

CHAPTER 72

Friday-Sunday October 18-20, 1957

ONE OF MY primary duties as Operations Chief of Station was to manage covert activities. This meant I would soon be directly responsible for all American assets—agents and operatives—located in our zone of occupation in West Berlin, all of East Berlin, and East Germany. The British MI6 and French DGSC also had spy networks operating in the Russian occupied areas. Our operations were loosely coordinated with theirs and the resulting information shared, especially if it affected the other country directly.

The more I looked at what was happening, the more concerned I became. I made a spreadsheet reflecting the date and circumstances surrounding the compromise of each of our field agents or operatives. Nothing made sense until I realized that everything except the identity of the agent or operative had been provided directly to the British. Now I worried about what I could and should do with this information.

We had known for some time Soviet assets were operating within the British Secret Service, MI6. Only individuals with the right connections and education were asked to join them. Among those recruited was a group of graduates from Cambridge University. Most were students there in the early 1930s and joined MI6 before or during World War Two. All of them soon held responsible positions within that organization. Yet it turned out everything they learned was being fed directly to their Soviet handlers. The first to be exposed were Donald Maclean and George Burgess; in 1951, they fled to the Soviet Union to avoid arrest.

A third member of the group, Kim Philby, was thought to be a double agent, but since his complicity couldn't be proven, he was allowed to leave MI6 under a cloud. In 1955, he was identified in the press and parliament as a spy, but friends in high places saved him from prosecution. He was currently working as a journalist in London, so he couldn't be the direct source of these latest revelations.

Today, I was introduced to a man named George Blake in Mike McGregor's office at Berlin Station. Blake was my MI6 counterpart in Berlin. Together, we would be coordinating the spy activities of the Western Nations against Russia and East Germany.

"The last time we met, your name was Jonathan Edwards," Blake said to me, laughing.

"That's right. I remember you now. I was in charge of Berlin tunnel construction, so your bosses thought I'd best travel under a different identity. And I remember you took notes at the meeting we had about the tunnel in London…in January 1954."

"That's correct."

"You had just returned after spending three years in a North Korean POW camp. Those guys are a rather brutal lot."

"Yes, it wasn't easy, but I survived and was eventually released after more than three years of captivity."

Over coffee, the three of us discussed various ongoing operations. Suddenly, George asked Mike, "Is there anything new from your end on the numbers and type of aircraft at the new Russian airbase between Halle and Leipzig?"

I hesitated. That base was outside of the British sphere of interest, which was northern East Germany—hundreds of miles away. Before I could say anything, Mike replied, "Our man there reports that 64 MIG-17 fighters are now operating out of that base. Last week, he observed seventeen Su-7 fighters land there for the first time. We assume there will be an entire regiment of them deployed there soon. Those are the Russian's latest and most advanced aircraft. They're also building a second runway there."

"Hmm," Blake remarked. I inconspicuously observed him. *Could he be trusted? Could he possibly be a double agent?*

"How long have you been here, George?" I asked as Blake was making his way out once our discussions finished.

"I arrived in August of 1955," he replied.

After he left, I got out my spreadsheets. Our losses increased significantly right after Blake arrived in Berlin. Also, he had been in an early meeting where details of the tunnel which was "accidentally" discovered by the Russians were discussed. Now he wanted the latest information about a specific target that would probably be routinely provided to MI6 sometime in the future. I may be paranoid, but this was too many coincidences to be random.

I was concerned enough to call one of my most trusted subordinates, Harold Keller into my office. "Don't tell anyone else what you're doing," I warned him. "Surreptitiously look into George Blake's background for me.

One couldn't accuse an agent from an allied country of being a double agent without iron-clad proof—which was almost impossible to obtain—so my real objective at this point was to prove to myself that my suspicions about George Blake were unfounded.

*

My furniture and possessions from the States were delivered to our new apartment on Wednesday. Erica, Gretchen and I spent Saturday morning unpacking and getting things organized. Late that afternoon, the three of us went to their apartment in East Berlin to pack up their possessions. As she put Stephen's possessions into charity boxes, Erica paused over some of his things, but ultimately all of it was given away. When she finished, I walked behind her and put my arms around her waist, kissing her neck. Finally, we were going to be a real "we."

Once the suitcases were full, we transported them three at a time to my apartment via the subway. It was only forty minutes away, so we made two trips on Saturday and completed the move on Sunday. Fortunately, the VoPos at the train stations didn't give us a second glance.

*

Erica and I both became exceptionally busy, so I hired a woman named Helga to help us around the apartment. She made breakfast, walked Gretchen to school, cleaned the apartment, walked Gretchen home after school, and cooked dinner.

CHAPTER 73

Monday, October 21, 1957

SINCE THE NIGHT Erica and I became engaged, I muddled over what I should tell the station chief, Mike McGregor, about my personal life. I finally decided that my opening statement would go something like, "Mike, I've never hidden the fact that I have a seven-year-old daughter with an East Berlin resident. They have both moved into my apartment and we're going to be married in December."

Uncertainty led me to contact Brandon via telephone while I was in the States; he told me Mike was a "by-the-book man." I decided to remain silent for now.

*

Soon after I arrived that morning, Harold Keller entered my office. "Well, there is no smoking gun."

I looked up at him, relieved. "I didn't expect one."

"But…well…uh…George Blake isn't British by birth. He was born in Holland. He was a part of the resistance and was arrested by the Gestapo when he was 17. Once released, he hiked through Western Europe to Spain and eventually got to Great Britain. There he joined MI6 and worked in their Dutch section for the duration of the war. Afterward, he received language training, including Russian, for several years at Cambridge. In 1948, he was posted to Seoul, South Korea, captured early in the war, and was treated like a hero by MI6 after he was released. It doesn't appear anyone in that agency ever asked any questions about his time in Korea. As you know, he arrived here in late 1955, and after a short time, began managing British covert operations."

"That's about what I expected."

"There is one more thing," Harold said exhaling loudly. "Most of the UN POWs were thin and emaciated when they were released. They had been subjected to starvation, physical torture, and brainwashing. Blake was in robust health, showing no signs of any kind of abuse. He justified this by saying, 'I was treated as a diplomat and was kept in a special prison.' One must wonder what kind of prison he was in. He might have been in China or Russia for those three years as far as anyone knows."

"Huh. Three years of double-agent training with one who already speaks and reads Russian would allow them to perfect all aspects of his story and avoid detection. Thanks, Harold. I know how to handle Blake."

Today I met with the 31 CIA agents who worked for me in Berlin for the first time. "Gentlemen, you all know my background," I said. "I was an agent like you for years and have spent the time since I arrived back studying what is going on here. You've been doing a great job, but we're losing too many operatives—18 cell leaders and 37 of their sub-operatives have just disappeared since mid-1955. These Germans are patriots who are working with us to free a part of their country from communist domination. We may be wasting their lives needlessly. Each operative has been assigned a cover name. On occasion, I've heard someone refer to their real name or other information like location or area of responsibility. From now on, use only their cover name in all conversations and correspondence. Discussions about these individuals will be limited to those who have been approved as having the need to know!"

I slowly made eye contact with each agent. "As long as I am in charge of Berlin Station's covert operations, the following policy will apply. Provide each operative a set of responsibilities. Direct them to only contact us when they have something new, different, or important to report. This will reduce the number of times they're put at risk contacting us. Having them tell us 'no change' is a waste of their time and ours because we must service their dead drops. Occasionally, you will need to change their tasking. Do so as expeditiously as possible."

I paused, ensuring I had everyone's attention. "Most of you realize there may be another reason we're losing operatives. I won't go into details, but from now on we will implement new procedures to protect our sources from our closest ally, the British, by generating two different kinds of reports. The one detailing who, what, when, where, and how will be sent to Washington and our head office in Frankfort.

"For the reports to the British, most details will be omitted. I sense our British counterparts here in Berlin have a leak—I can't prove it, but I want us all to be cautious about what we share with them. This restriction will not be discussed outside of this facility. Is that clear?"

CHAPTER 74

Tuesday, November 12, 1957

JIM WEBSTER WAS one of our best young agents. Since "Arctic," aka Pyotr Popov, had been transferred to Berlin from northern East Germany, he had been placed in charge "of handling him," in CIA jargon. He asked for an urgent appointment with me.

"What gives, Jim?" I asked.

"Sir, it's Arctic. He's acting erratic and I'm concerned he may be about ready to go off the deep end."

"Tell me what you know."

"His file indicates he's always been willing to take risks when he needed to contact us. When he reestablished contact with us in 1956, he just walked up to someone in one of our trade delegations and handed him a note. It explained he was ready to work for us again and asked for 10,000 West Marks. A Stasi agent who was escorting the Americans around was nearby and it was a miracle he didn't see it happen."

"We were only able to make contact with him a few times while he was up north. The most important thing he told us was that the Russians have a complete set of plans and the requirements specification for the U-2 spy plane."

"He has certainly been an asset we must protect," I observed.

"Now that he has been transferred to GRU headquarters here in Berlin, contact with him has been much easier," Jim said. "Every week or two he gives us something new and valuable, so I haven't applied your new rule to him.

"About three months ago, he appeared very nervous during a brush pass with me. Then a few weeks later, he made a chalk mark on our signal column indicating the dead drop was full, but it was actually empty. Both the dead drop and column are on Museum Island in East Berlin, so there is always a risk for both of us when we use it. I erased the chalk mark immediately, and a week later it was there again. This time, several rolls of film were in the dead drop; they contained very valuable information about GRU operatives in West Germany."

"Do you think it's time to pull him out?" I asked. "He can defect to the West and the Russians will never know exactly what and how much he has provided. If they capture and interrogate him, they'll eventually know everything."

"That's the reason I am here," Jim replied. "I think we should meet him at a safe house and evaluate his competence to continue. Plus, he could use a little training in spycraft. Perhaps he could spend an entire Saturday over here with us."

"That's wise," I said, shaking Jim's hand. "Make it happen and keep me informed. Bold double agents are often more successful, but don't often survive long."

When I arrived home that evening, Erica rushed into my arms and started to choke up, but was eventually able to tell me what the problem was, "That bastard Karl Holtzmann, called me into his office today and indicated they had received complaints from the other faculty members that I was living in West Berlin with an American. He told me it is illegal for GDR employees to have close and continuing contact with westerners. That rule applies to me because the university receives most of its funding from the state.

"Before I could tell him you were part of a group that was trying to promote trade with East Germany, he said, 'You must break off contact with this man immediately and move back to East Berlin. If you do so, you will be allowed to keep your job. If you want to prove your loyalty to your country, you could also join the communist party and begin telling your students of the advantages of the socialist system.'"

I shook my head back and forth fearing the ramifications of her complete revelation as she continued, "What makes me the maddest is the Stasi or someone must be following me. How else would they know about us? I have never shared details of my personal life with anyone at the university."

"In a police state," I sighed, "they have their ways."

Erica began crying inconsolably, "I was going to be the youngest lecturer…and amaze the world with my archeological discoveries…and now…" she said between her tears, "…it's either many more years of study away from the city I love…and my family, or …finish my lecturer's education here in a second-rate university…or get a job doing something else here in West Berlin."

After holding her for some time, I said, "You were going to contact The Free University and see if there is something there for you. Did you?"

"Yes, I never shared what I learned. They have a large number of students studying the classics and have a program similar to ours, but have more qualified candidates for professorships, including people who have completed the lecturer's courses, than openings. I could talk to them again, but I don't hold out much hope," she said again drying her eyes.

"After we're married next month, you can do anything you want," I said, trying to reassure her. "Just tell me your decision and I'll support it."

CHAPTER 75

Monday, November 18, 1957

"IS NOW A good time for a debrief on our meeting with 'Arctic' last Saturday?" Jim Webster asked as he put his head into my office.

"Yes, give me a full rundown."

"It was a nightmare. He forgot the location and address of the safehouse. He was supposed to memorize that information and destroy the piece of paper it was written on. He destroyed the paper but then forgot the information. He had written the emergency phone number we'd given him in a notebook. He telephoned his wife and had her read the emergency number to him. Then he called our switchboard from the same phone booth, revealing his location. They called the safehouse. I had to expose myself and the safehouse while I retrieved him. When I finally got to the street corner, he was nowhere to be seen. Finally, I found him having a beer, looking out a window of a nearby gasthaus for me. It's amazing he's lasted as long as he has."

"How did it go after that?"

"I tried to explain to him that at least 10,000 Stasi, KGB, and GRU agents cross over the dividing line between East and West Berlin every day to spy on us here. Some of them might know him or he might somehow catch their attention while he passed through the checkpoints. He told me without hesitation, 'Most of those people have specific assignments they surveil—they will not be looking for me,' I believe he envisions himself a master double agent who is invulnerable and will continue to be a hero forever."

"He is such a valuable source we must try to get him to be more security conscious," I said.

"How'd the training session go?" I asked.

"He paid attention to most of it, but I got the impression his mind was elsewhere."

"Anything else you'd like to tell me, Jim?"

"Arctic may not remember an address, but from memory, he gave us a complete description of the GRU group that controls all of their military spies in the West, including names on an organization chart and the location of their offices on the Karlshorst military base. He also gave us the names and deployment locations of several new spies the KGB recently dispatched to the West. He's one of a kind, and we can't afford to lose him."

CHAPTER 76

Tuesday, December 3, 1957

MID-AFTERNOON, FIELD AGENT Art Therber walked into my office and shut the door. "I met with Prince (Peter Hoffman) today—the second time in almost three years that he has requested a face-to-face meeting. He wanted me to give you this," he said, holding out a manila envelope. "He insisted I hand it to you personally, unopened. As you know, the first rule for those of us who handle operatives is security. I've certainly never mentioned your name to him."

I was shocked by this revelation but tried to remain calm. "Thanks for the heads-up, Art," I said, taking the envelope. The only way Peter could know about me being in the CIA and my current position was for the Stasi to know about me—that was bad both personally and career-wise.

The envelope was unmarked on the outside. Inside I found several pages of a form printed on gray, light-weight card stock which I recognized immediately. They were copies of handwritten sheets from the files the Stasi kept on every individual who came to their attention. Over the years, Peter had made handwritten duplicates of many of these files either at our request or on his initiative. The form itself was oriented with the short side to the right—a continuation sheet was used for entries made after the first sheet was full. Printed on the top and bottom of the form were the words, "MINISTRY FOR STATE SECURITY SECRET.

A shudder went down my spine as I saw my name: KURT LANGE

ALTSCHULER. Someone had found the records of my birth as I never use my middle name. My file number was 18.293.

I opened the file and there I was: a photo of me walking into the American Mission Building. Underneath that, a form with a detailed description of me. Birthdate, place of birth, parents' names. The address of my apartment. The two pages covered my time as a reporter for the AP. An entry indicating that I had "written stories favorable to the cause" was crossed out. Since the Stasi didn't exist before 1950, some of this information had been taken from earlier records kept by someone else—probably the KGB.

The few sentences about my time with the United States Information Agency were crossed out and a note beside it read, "SEE ENTRIES BELOW."

Someone was keeping an eye on me because Entry 28 reported, 20.08.1956—Subject vacated apartment and apparently departed Berlin.

Entry 29—24.09.1957—Individual, believed to be subject, seen entering the American Mission Building.

The next three pages made my head swim. "Altschuler has possibly been a CIA agent since his arrival in Berlin in 1946 or 1947. He was probably using earlier guises to hide his true profession."

The words jumped off of the page as it detailed how I had been "the site manager for the building of the Imperialist's Tunnel, which invaded Sovereign East German Territory from 1954 to 1956. Recently, he returned from a tour of duty at CIA Headquarters in Washington and assumed the role of CIA Chief-of-Operations Berlin in late September. A new entry further down the card stated, "His primary function is to direct all covert operations in East Germany and enemy-occupied West Berlin." These entries and updates were all made on 04.11.1957—a month after I assumed my current position.

The name at the top of the sixth page jumped up at me—ERICA CHRISTINE SCHAFER. Peter's warning was unmistakable—your true identity is known—you, Erica, and I are in EXTREME DANGER!

The card gave Erica's birthdate and place of birth as Berlin, which was incorrect. Her address was where she lived until she moved in with me in October. It showed her parent's first names, Gunther and Anna, with a note that they were killed during the war, probably in late 1944—

also incorrect. Only relative: daughter, Gretchen, born in January 1950. Married, 03.09.1949. Husband, Stephen Schäfer died of natural causes in 1953.

It was safe to assume that Peter had created this document and placed it into the Stasi files to protect Erica from any ramifications should either his or my association with the CIA ever be discovered. But it was disconcerting to see that she had a Stasi file.

These documents clearly would force Erica and me to modify our plans. Could we marry? Could I even stay with the CIA in Berlin? If someone compared Erica's information with that on file at the university or other public records, they would undoubtedly discover that this card had been intentionally falsified which could lead back to her brother and their true relationship.

Like a flash of light, it hit me—the dossier on me was conclusive proof that George Blake was a double agent. Until we had met again, he thought the CIA agent who had overall control of the building of the Berlin Tunnel was named Jonathan Edwards. When he found out who I was, Blake told his KGB handlers, who told the Stasi soon after I had met Blake.

But if I gave the first five pages to my superiors as proof that Blake was a double agent, Peter Hoffmann would be in immediate danger. He was relying on me to determine what to do with this information. He was also warning me that the Stasi, and certainly the KGB, knew the part I played in the spy game in Berlin.

For one of the few times in my life, I was overwhelmed. I sat at my desk staring into space and rereading each entry for the rest of the day. My first inclination was to get all of Erica's family, including and especially Peter, his wife, and new baby to West Berlin immediately. After much thought, I decided to place these files in a two-drawer safe next to my desk. I was the only one with its combination; this time bomb could wait until I arrived at a calm, rational decision.

CHAPTER 77

Tuesday, December 3, 1957

ERICA WAS FREQUENTLY late getting home, but tonight she hadn't arrived in time for the evening meal, which Helga always had on the table at 19:30. She would usually call if she was going to be this late. Perhaps Chancellor Holtzmann had gone through with his threat and had her arrested for continuing to live with me. What could I do? My stomach knotted as the minutes passed. Even worse, what if the Stasi had managed to pull all of the facts together and had arrested both Erica and Peter?

I tried not to worry Gretchen during dinner. She spent most of the meal expressing how happy she was her cousins from Chicago would be visiting us soon.

"Where's mommy?" she asked when we were nearing the end of dinner. At that moment the telephone rang, and we both rushed over to it. Gretchen answered and after a brief conversation handed me the phone.

"I was beginning to get worried," I said once I knew it was Erica.

"I'm at the gasthaus in Bernau. You remember, the village near Papa's farm."

"Yes, I remember. Why are you there?"

"Several men from the local cooperative farm arrived today and began taking most of the crops Papa had stored in the silo and sheds. They took most of his animals, too. They had an order from the authorities to collectivize Papa's farm. They are allowing him to keep only the 30 hectares around the house, plus one-third of his animals and last season's crops."

Doing a quick conversion, I said, "Leaving him less than 15 American acres. It will be difficult for your parents to make a living on that small amount of land!"

"It does include the house, orchard, and garden," Erica added. "He's expected to work on the collective farm and will get a share of what that produces. But Papa wants to fight this somehow."

"I doubt he'll be successful," I observed. "When are you coming home?"

"I'll stay here tonight but be back tomorrow. Kiss Gretchen for me. I love you," she said, and the line went dead.

I then spent some time explaining to Gretchen what had occurred and eventually managed to assure her that her grandparents and great grandmother would be safe because Erica and I would help them if required.

CHAPTER 78

Wednesday, December 4, 1957

THE INFORMATION IN the files Peter had sent consumed me. First, I needed to know if my apartment was being tapped. I waited for Helga, our maid, to leave then let the "technical specialists" from my office in. They used instruments capable of detecting listening devices of all forms to sweep my apartment. They assured me it was clean and added it to the list of locations that were regularly evaluated.

After Erica arrived that evening, she led me to the study, closed the door and asked, "What are we going to do?"

"Realistically, we have few alternatives. It would seem best for you to take the job at Tübingen, I go into the import/export business, and we purchase a farm for your family nearby. Your parents probably won't accept an outright gift, but they would soon own that farm due to the generous deal we would make with them." I thought about telling her I would hire Peter to be a business partner, but decided not to. Erica would probably not understand why I was including him and I couldn't explain.

"That makes the most sense, but there are some issues. One is Grandmother Hannah. She says she wants to die on the land she's toiled on for fifty-two years. Plus, Papa is now so angry he has vowed to stay on the farm. I think he is adamant. What other options do we have?"

"Your entire family, including Peter's family, could leave Germany for America. We settle wherever and purchase a farm on the same terms."

"None of them speak English, so I can't imagine them doing that.

And I can't abandon my family—not when they need me so much. Papa hates that Peter is working for the communists. They hardly even speak anymore, so I need to be here for them."

Peter was sacrificing everything important, including family, friends, and perhaps even his life to rid his nation of communism. Of course, I could say nothing to anyone about what was happening with him and the danger he was in. I hated keeping things from Erica, but there was no way around this.

"It's still early," Erica said, looking at her watch. "I'll call Professor Richter and see what I can do," she said as she made her way to the living room phone.

Erica returned only a few moments later, looking disappointed. "He just learned today that there isn't sufficient funding in his department for another research assistant in the fall. Maybe he'll have a position for me a year from now," she said, trying to sound hopeful. "I'll retain my current position at Humboldt and get an apartment in the East. We could marry secretly, somewhere out of Berlin. I could visit Gretchen and you frequently, but would have to avoid being seen entering this building. That way, I can stay at Humboldt, get my lecturer's certificate, and make my classics department the best in Germany."

At that moment I thought about telling Erica everything—then got the sinking feeling that she probably couldn't handle the truth. I was having difficulty grasping the ramifications of our current circumstances myself.

CHAPTER 79

Thursday, December 5, 1957

IN THE SPY game, a little paranoia is necessary to succeed. But too much usually results in loss of direction and inability to function. Like a game of chance, you must envision a holding by both friends and opponents that allows you to win.

On the first of December, Ian Simpson became the new Berlin Station Chief. I knew and trusted him. In our first private meeting, I told him most of the truth and concluded by saying, "I want to resign from the CIA or at the very least, be reassigned back to the States."

"Kurt, your experience and knowledge make you the most valuable member of my staff. For that reason, I have to deny your request. Over the years, other members of our staff around the world have been identified by the bad guys. Here in Berlin, there is a tacit agreement between us and them not to kill or kidnap each other's agents or their families—operatives and other minions in the espionage contest are fair game—for now, professionals are off-limits."

"Most compromised agents were soon reassigned and none were as senior as I am. Remember, my job is to know about everything we're doing in our entire area of responsibility."

"As long as you don't enter the East, Kurt, you're probably as safe here as in West Germany or even the States. Let the duty desk know where you are at all times. If you disappear from the streets of West Berlin, we can raise hell with the Russians before the Stasi beat anything of value out of you. Is there anything else?"

"The East German citizen, who is the mother of my daughter, teaches at Humboldt University in East Berlin; she visits my apartment frequently and sometimes spends the night."

"I knew about your unique private life but didn't know you were so close. This does present a security problem. Why doesn't she just immigrate to the West?"

"She is a professor at Humboldt and will have difficulty getting a high-level position in the West. Recently, her bosses at the university began making our relationship an issue."

"This is a difficult decision for me…Perhaps you could…let me think for a moment…" Ian said staring at me and shaking his head back and forth in doubt.

After making a decision, he said, "As long as it doesn't affect your ability to do your job or compromise security, it's yours to work out within your family. Thanks for letting me know. I will modify my earlier dictum about visiting the East. If you need to go there for family matters, make sure to let us know before you leave here."

"Okay, thank you. One more thing—as you know, I have several contacts at fairly high levels in MI6. I believe there is a mole in their organization that compromised my identity. Various sources have reported that a large number of MI6s operatives in East Germany and Eastern Europe have been compromised. We have also suffered losses of a similar nature. Would it be acceptable for me to go to London and see if I can convince them to determine if they have a double agent?"

"It's worth the try. Now get out of my office before I change my mind. What you've revealed today involves a lot of risk for us; for me, it's mostly professional—for you, on the other hand, it'll be mostly personal."

Objective accomplished—the Stasi can't use the exposure of my relationship with Erica to gain some kind of advantage. Erica and I can go forward with our revised wedding plans. I can't accuse George Blake directly, but I can, perhaps create suspicion in a few MI6 officials' minds as to the existence of a double agent. They might also begin looking for where he is in their organization. I made a few calls to close friends in MI6 on the KY-7 scrambler phone and scheduled a trip to London for early next week.

CHAPTER 80

Saturday, December 21, 1957-Saturday, January 4, 1958

BEFORE WE LEFT to be married in Switzerland, Erica rented an apartment between her university and the Friedrichstrasse train station; that subway station was the main train crossing point between East and West Berlin.

Using my contacts in the East, I determined that Karl Holtzmann was a mid-level bureaucrat in the East German Ministry of the Interior and not a Stasi Agent. He had found out about Erica's relationship with me somehow; perhaps she hadn't been as circumspect as she claimed to be, or she'd been followed to our apartment building, and then I was tailed to the American Mission building? At the very least, Erica and I must keep our marriage and daily activities secret from everyone. Despite Ian's approval, one of my associates in Berlin could make it an issue with our superiors back in the States. We would be walking a tight rope—one misstep could be fatal.

The next day, I went to a store that sold detailed maps of Berlin and purchased several that covered the area around Erica's university. I also had one of my office staff go to the building department to acquire top and side views of the Friedrichstrasse Train Station.

*

On the week of our wedding, my entire family flew from New York to London and then on to Zurich. Erica's grandmother was unwell, so her parents declined to attend the wedding.

A three-car convoy took us to the justice of the peace's office in central Lucerne, where we were officially married in a simple fifteen-minute ceremony. My father stood beside me and Gretchen beamed as she stood beside Erica. It was beautiful.

The convoy then motored to the ski resort of Gstaad. My father rented a beautiful five-bedroom chalet near the main lift at the bottom of the hill. He also got a nearby, cozy one-bedroom chalet just for Erica and me.

For the next ten days, we skied, made snowmen, baked in the sauna, ate at some wonderful restaurants, and relaxed from the cares of Berlin.

*

During the nights in the chalet, Erica and I discussed how to keep our marriage a secret.

"You're going to need to act normal at all times," I advised her." If someone sees you nervous or tense, that's a tell that you're up to something. Remember, suspect everyone, trust no one."

"Those things may be easy for you to say, but I'm not an actor."

"Work on them; they'll become second nature. Next, you must become aware of everything around you. Never relax or let your guard down."

The next evening, I spread the plan of the train station out on the dining room table. "As you know, seven different subway lines funnel through Frederichstrasse Train Station. Four go into the British Zone of West Berlin after one or two stops in East Berlin. All four of those have stops near our apartment. Three go north and south; this northern route" pointing to the map "ends up in the French Zone and this one," I said, moving my finger, "goes southwest and has a stop at the Potsdamer Platz subway station, which is in the West."

"Yes, I know all of that," Erica said. "I have a little map of the Berlin subway system in my head and seldom need to look at the maps on the wall."

"Good, but have you ever gone down into all three levels of train tunnels at the Friedrichstrasse station? It is a labyrinth of passages and connecting tunnels. Here are top and side views of them. You need to memorize them."

"Why?" Erica asked.

"Let's say you're planning to come over to our apartment and feel almost certain you're being followed. You will need to mislead them. Act like you've changed your mind, go to a different subway line, and see if they're still following you. Many times, it will be your imagination, not a real tail. If you're being followed, you can take a different subway to a nearby station, stop for an evening meal, and go back to your apartment. Never knowingly lead anyone into the West, and especially not to our apartment building." I paused a moment to let everything sink in, then continued. "Plus, you'll need to vary your daily route as much as possible. Stay around the university as little as possible…"

"—But I have meetings and regular office hours."

"Keep all of those commitments but go to the library or a museum. You're an archeologist after all. Stay home when you don't need to be at the university. When you leave the university for the day, go directly to your new apartment. Sometimes they'll follow you there, assume you're in for the night, and the surveillance will end for the day—the people trailing you have lives, too. Wait at least thirty minutes, then go out to shop, or to eat a meal somewhere. If you're being followed, never try to lose them unless you have to come West."

"So, you're saying I may have to try to evade them."

Affectionately touching her nose with my index finger, I said, "If that becomes necessary, my love, then this situation is much more serious than I think it is. We'll have to talk about that when the time comes."

This conversation felt like a new form of intimacy. Here we were, a few nights after our wedding, planning what was essentially a covert operation. It felt like she was finally coming into my world.

"Part of your act will be to go out with colleagues or friends frequently," I added. "Don't become a recluse. You're a very attractive woman. If a man asks you out, accept. Have fun, but remember you're married to me," I said, smiling.

"You don't have to worry," Erica said, snuggling into my arms.

"Try to come to visit Gretchen and me once or twice a week. Spend the night as often as you can. As we discovered before we left, there are four different ways of getting into our apartment building—the service entrance is accessed via a secluded back alley and the best to use; you have a key to that entrance. Alternately, you can call me from a payphone, let me know where you are, and I will pick you up. You can hide on the floor in the backseat of the car when we near the building."

"Kurt, I know that you must have received some spy training. No one is smart enough to think all of this up."

"You'll just have to keep your suspicions to yourself," I said smiling. After caressing her cheek affectionately, I added, "It will do neither of us any good for you to speculate."

"Yes, yes," she said, tossing the map onto the floor and leading me to bed.

PART 3

1958-1960

"Whether you like it or not, history is on our side. We will bury you."

—Soviet Premier Nikita Khrushchev,
November 18, 1956.

CHAPTER 81

Monday, January 6, 1958

IN EARLY OCTOBER of 1957, the Russians shocked the world by launching the first artificial satellite, Sputnik 1, into orbit. It broadcast a beeping signal for 21 days. Before this, the world viewed the Russians as a bunch of backward peasants, incapable of such sophisticated technical accomplishments. Within a week, headquarters tasked all field offices, especially ours, with finding out from the academic community how much East German scientists contributed to this effort.

Only two of our operatives were experts in technical areas related to aeronautical and electrical engineering. One got back to us quickly with a negative response. The other, Gerhard Huber, made contact with an aeronautical engineer and hit pay dirt. This afternoon, I asked him to meet Ian and me in a safe house for a debriefing.

"My sub-operative, Peter Maier, is a physicist at the Dresden Technical University," Huber told us. "His friend, Deter Bergmann, has been working in Russia and recently returned on home leave. They have had extensive discussions about his time in Russia. He learned Bergmann worked on Sputnik, which in Russian means 'traveling companion.' The program is led by a man named Sergi Kotolev, who is probably in his early fifties. He indicated about forty percent of the staff were German, but the Russians were managing the entire effort. My report provides the names and areas of expertise of three other German and four Russian scientists working on the program. My source was unable to get his friend to tell him where the development and manufacturing facility was located but offered that 'it was a damnable cold and remote hell.'"

Later that day, I read the report describing the latest from Popov; while on home leave back to Kalinin, he'd stopped in to visit friends in GRU Headquarters in Moscow. They were apparently very disturbed by the recent dismissal of their hero and leader, Marshall Zhukov. He reported no threats to his situation despite the recent arrest of a number of GRU agents whose existence he had exposed. We were concerned that the Russians would eventually perceive there was a leak and follow a trail back to him.

CHAPTER 82

Tuesday, February 4, 1958

ALTHOUGH HELGA HAD only been with us for three months, simplifying our lives tremendously, I had to let her go in January. We just couldn't risk her knowing about Erica's infrequent clandestine arrivals at our apartment. Gretchen was in a private school, and she stayed late for an after-school recreation, music, and education program. That way I could drop her off on my way to work and pick her up at the end of the day.

My unusual relationship with Erica settled into a pattern. She'd visit one night a week—mostly on Saturday. Then, Gretchen and I would go over one evening a week and have supper with her.

At first, Erica thought she was being followed every time she came over. I recommended a spy's trick of stopping to window shop or read something on a kiosk and waiting for the follower to pass by. She soon realized these people were going about their business and just happened to be taking the same route she was. Each week she seemed to gain more confidence. Then, one evening, she determined that someone was actually following her. That time and another time the next day, she went shopping and returned to her apartment. After that, they appeared to have lost interest in her.

CHAPTER 83

Friday, March 7, 1958

"WILLIE IS UNDER Stasi surveillance and twice they have subjected him to hours-long interrogation at the local police station," Andreas reported at our meeting in the Bellevuestrasse safe house.

I'd dispatched him to check on Wilhelm Werner, the pub-owning operative who helped him escape from East Germany almost ten years earlier. In January, one of Wilhelm's sub-operatives had been arrested by the Stasi. To protect him, I decided to close down his cell. He destroyed all of the physical evidence of his spy operation, severed contact with his subordinates, and now just tended bar. He wanted to become a sleeper operative, so we left him in place. That would prove to be a mistake.

"They are subjecting Wilhelm to a standard KGB interrogation technique that the Stasi has wholeheartedly adopted," I observed. "They start harassing the subject by having him answer a 'few routine questions,' release him, let him worry over his fate, and repeat the process sometimes for weeks or months until they arrest him to begin more rigorous interrogation."

"For years, he led our best cell," Andreas observed.

"If the Stasi and/or KGB arrest him and begin serious interrogation, he will be forced to reveal details about his extensive operations," I said grimacing, then after a long pause, continued. "Wilhelm's situation will give me an opportunity to implement my new policy—instead of just letting the Stasi or KGB arrest and torture one of our exposed operatives; we will extract him from behind the Iron Curtain."

"That won't be easy," Andreas said, "Three to five Stasi agents watch the gasthaus around the clock. They are anticipating that we will try to free him—so this is going to be a very difficult operation."

"So, they have set the trap and Wilhelm is the bait. Sounds to me like a spectacular diversion might get the Stasi's watchers attention long enough for us to remove Herr and Dame Werner from under their noses. Let's get busy planning just such an operation."

Now that I was responsible for clandestine operations at Berlin Station, I intended for my men and me to take a more active role in the spy war. It had been years since I had experienced the exhilarating adrenalin rush that results from operating on the other side of the border against a clever and dedicated foe.

CHAPTER 84

Natalie
Monday-Tuesday, March 17-18, 1958

WHEN I RETURNED from work this evening, the tall man with the heavy Saxon accent I'd first seen disguised as a workman all those years ago was waiting outside of my apartment in West Berlin. He stopped me and said, "Fraulein Werner. It's been a long time since we first met. Your parents send their regards. Could we have a brief conversation?"

At first, I was startled since I didn't recognize him. Then memories of our two encounters flooded back into my mind. I sputtered, "Uh…Yes…where should we go?"

"I've arranged for us to use a small private room in the manager's office. It's just here," he said, pointing to the building in front of us, and I joined him there.

"I won't spend time talking about all of the good things you and your parents have done for us," he said after settling inside the office. "Your parents are now under constant surveillance and may be arrested by the Stasi any minute. With your help, we are going to bring them to the West."

"Of course. I'll do anything to get them to safety."

"Okay. Here is what you must do. Call into work, tell them you won't be in for the rest of the week. Go upstairs, put a few things into a bag, enough for three days. Write your boyfriend a note that you have been unexpectedly sent to your company's home office in Frankfort for the rest of the week. I'll be waiting in a black sedan parked outside. We'll spend tomorrow going over what you'll need to do."

The next day, in what they called a safe house, I met a distinguished gentleman dressed in an expensive three-piece suit; he spoke high German. The three of us covered details of the extraction, with emphasis on my role. Once the tall man seemed to have slipped and called the other man Kurt. For that, he received a facial expression of strong disapproval. I guessed that must be his real name.

During this meeting, I wanted to ask the tall man about the changes to his face, especially his now intact lower earlobe. I never found an opportune moment to ask.

CHAPTER 85

Wednesday, March 19, 1958

THE BUS THAT went from the subway station at Aldershof in East Berlin to Schönefeld Airport dropped me off in front of my parent's gasthaus just before 09:45 this morning. I glanced over at the fence that separated the little village where I grew up from West Berlin; it was only about 300 meters away. In this area, the fence took its current form about five years ago—chain-link fencing strung along the bottom of three-meter tall concrete posts buried firmly in the ground, spaced about two meters apart, and topped with two strands of barbed wire.

Several VoPos armed with submachine guns were spaced thirty to forty meters apart. They walked back and forth along a path located just this side of the fence. There were several wooded areas in West Berlin near the fences, but all trees and bushes had been removed from a wide swath on this side of the fence, creating a free-fire zone for those troops.

The familiar ring of the bell attached to the front door of the gasthaus welcomed me home. Mama emerged from the kitchen and gasped, rushing over to me. Before she could say anything, I put my index finger to my lips and removed a card from my purse. "SAY ALOUD: What are you doing here, dearest Natalie? You should have called to let us know you were coming," it read.

She understood what was happening and read the card out loud. I replied, "I got some time off from work and decided on the spur of the moment to come for a visit." I held up another card that read, "Are there listening devices everywhere?" Mama nodded.

"Where's Papa?" I asked aloud.

"He went to the government-owned liquor warehouse in Rangsdorf to pick up some cases of vodka, schnapps, and kegs of beer. The only reason your father is allowed to have a truck is he transports liquor for Konsom (East German State-owned Distribution Center) to a number of smaller businesses between here and there. He will be back soon."

I wrote a note: "We are going this evening. Pack two or three suitcases."

Mama immediately sensed what needed to be done, and responded, "Dear, I'm glad you came today. I've been feeling poorly. I'll go upstairs and rest. You can wait on the customers until Papa returns."

I gathered up most of the notes we had written and threw them into the fireplace to burn. Fifteen minutes later, the first customer arrived. He was wearing a suit, so I assumed he was a Stasi agent. "Sit anywhere," I told him with a smile, handing him a menu, though my hands were trembling.

"You're new. Do you live nearby?"

"My parents manage this gasthaus. I have come for a brief visit."

"Oh, really? Where do you live now?" he asked.

A bit nervously and with trepidation, I answered, "West Berlin."

"Can I see your identity papers?"

"Who are you and why would you need to see my papers?"

Flashing an identity card, he said, "I'm Frederick Koch from the State Security Service."

I took my West German passport out of the pocket of my skirt and handed it to him.

"You do not have an entry permit."

"I don't need one to come over for the day. I'll be going back to Berlin this evening or early tomorrow morning."

"See you only stay here for 24 hours, otherwise you will need to register at the local police station. Is that clear, young lady?"

"Yes, I'll leave before then," I said with assurance. "Now, what can I serve you?"

"I'll have a half-liter of beer. Where are your mother and father?"

"Papa went to get some supplies and Mama is upstairs resting before the crowd arrives for lunch."

As I pumped his beer, he stood up, went over to the fire, and picked up a poker. I watched him retrieve a piece of unburnt paper. I brought the beer to his table as he turned the piece of paper over. The word "suitcases" was darkened, but visible.

I quickly turned away from him and disappeared into the kitchen. Once there I took a deep breath and tried to control my trembling hands. *I am not a very good spy.*

After I stirred a few pots, I heard the cellar door open and went down the stairs to let Papa know I was here. I handed him a new note, "SAY ALOUD: Natalie dear! You have come for a visit."

"Mama's not feeling well and is upstairs resting," I replied. "We'll have to take care of the lunch crowd."

He took the pencil from my hand and wrote, "They are listening from the police station."

I shook my head indicating that I was cognizant of the Stasi surveillance.

We quickly moved the cartons and kegs into the cellar from the back of Papa's 1937 Opel Blitz 2.5 truck. I was relieved to see the truck because it was an integral part of our escape plan. Papa prided himself on being allowed to have possession of this state-owned vehicle. To keep it running, he salvaged spare parts from scrapped vehicles in a junkyard located a few kilometers away. There were plenty of spare parts because this vehicle had been the main light truck used by the Wehrmacht during World War II.

I tapped Papa lightly on the shoulder. "We escape tonight. Mama upstairs packing," read the note I handed him.

"This afternoon, I will pack," he wrote back. Then, he said aloud, "We need to go upstairs—the customers will arrive soon."

I wrote, "One of the Stasi guys is already here."

He shook his head and wrote, "Always here. Waiting for us to make a move."

CHAPTER 86

Wednesday, March 19, 1958

BY 15:20, MY parents and I were the only ones left in the gasthaus. We took this opportunity to transport their three suitcases to the basement and hide them in a dark alcove next to the stairs. Once we were back on the top floor in our living area, Papa looked out a window. "Two Stasi cars out front," he wrote on a note. "Usually only one. They are reacting to your presence."

I knew it was time to open the hidden compartment in my suitcase that the tall man had made by slicing the inner lining. I removed a set of instructions for my parents to read. The list started:
1. You will make the usual call for the last round of drinks at exactly 22:30.
2. At precisely 22:45, the lights will go out and local telephone service will be interrupted…

We passed notes back and forth so I could answer their questions. One of Papa's notes said, "The Stasi agents are here 24 hours a day. Sometimes they park their car so it blocks my truck at night. What if that happens tonight?"

"They know and have prepared for that eventuality," I wrote back.

I burned the instructions and notes in the fireplace—making sure they were complete ash—and then placed my suitcase beside the others.

With some difficulty, the three of us acted as normal as possible during the evening meal and bar service. The time dragged by. I had to force myself not to look at my watch every few minutes. At a little before 17:30, two different Stasi Trabants pulled in and parked just outside our front door. After that, the day watchers left.

The first of the new Stasi agents came into the gasthaus and ordered a beer. Over the next four hours, we served three more agents. Eventually, all four ate and slowly drank two or three half liters of beer each. Today, they had decided to keep an eye on us close up.

At 21:34, two additional agents entered and settled into a table near the back door and kitchen. With so many obvious Stasi agents present, several of our regular bar patrons decided they'd be better off going home to their wives.

I was in the kitchen when Papa rang the bell and announced, "Last round. The kitchen is now closed and, in accordance with the law, the bar will be closed in thirty minutes." I was startled, frozen in place for perhaps a minute. Then I could feel the adrenaline rush one reads about when facing a real threat. I exited the kitchen, ensuring everyone was served, then headed back to wash the dishes.

Even though I was prepared, I was still startled when I heard the two dull thuds in rapid succession. Immediately, the lights went out. Several patrons made their way to the nearby windows. I heard someone say, "The electrical substation on the corner has blown up and is on fire! The lights as far as I can see are out, including all of the streetlights."

The only light that remained was from the coals in the fireplace and the small fire outside of the windows. Right on schedule, a customer whom I knew was Andreas said, "That is not at all unusual. The electrical components we are forced to use are made in Romania and are inferior. It is amazing they work at all."

Mama brought a kerosene lamp out of the kitchen and placed it on the bar. It provided just enough light for everyone to move through the long shadows without hitting the tables and chairs that filled the room.

One of the Stasi agents shouted at Papa who stood at the bar, "Proprietor, immediately call the fire company, then the power company to let them know!"

The payphone was a large square wooden box, with slots for payment and a rotary dial; it rested on one end of the polished wooden bar. Papa picked up the receiver of the phone, jiggled the cradle. "It's dead," he said, as per his lines. "The telephone switching box is on the same street corner, perhaps it was also damaged in the explosion."

The Stasi agent I had heard addressed as Herr Klein earlier in the evening started giving orders to his obvious subordinates. "Fuchs, use the two-way radio in your vehicle to notify the fire service, then call the power service; after that, drive over to the police station and set up an incident command post there. Lange and Schmidt, go investigate what's happened. Hahn, go check with the guards along the border; this could be a ruse. Becker stay here and help me keep an eye on these three."

Four of the Stasi agents departed. Most of the patrons in the bar decided to check out the fire or go home. After only five minutes, the man I knew was Andreas and the two Stasi agents were the only patrons left in the gasthaus. After consuming the last of his beer, he rose to his feet, and said, "Good evening all." He acted as if he was a bit unsteady after a few too many, and walked toward the front door. Once he got behind the Stasi leader, he took out a small pistol, put it against Herr Klein's temple, and said, "Slowly unholster your gun and drop it on the floor—slowly, ever so slowly. Tell your subordinate to do the same. Neither of you is to say or do anything, is that clear?"

The Stasi agent named Becker had been nursing his beer. "What the? Uh…I…" He started to reach for his pistol as my father put a gun to the back of his head. Both Stasi agents complied by dropping their weapons.

Both Andreas and my father kept the two men covered while Mama and I picked up their weapons from the floor and placed them on the bar. Our captives were ordered to lie on their stomachs with their hands behind their backs.

Klein said, "You'll never get away with this. You're surrounded by my…"

"—Our weapons have silencers. We will just kill you. If you want to live, comply immediately."

Papa finally had to hit Becker's head hard with his gun barrel. As the dull thud reverberated around the room, Agent Klein obeyed and his bleeding subordinate followed.

Once the men were on the floor, Mama and I handcuffed their hands behind their backs and gagged them with dish towels while Papa and Andreas continued to hold weapons to their heads. Papa ordered, "Stand up, walk behind the bar and down the stairs into the basement." When they failed to cooperate, Andreas hit the senior Stasi agent in the head with his pistol, again and again. Finally, he fired a silenced round into the floor. The dampened sound reverberated around the room. Reluctantly, both Stasi agents awkwardly descended the stairs. Papa unlocked his workroom and the two men were shoved into it. The heavy door was slammed shut and locked.

All four of us relaxed momentarily, knowing this critical phase of our escape plan was successful. We each grabbed a suitcase and went up the basement stairs that led outside. The Stasi had parked one of their Trabants behind Papa's truck. Using a thin metal object with a hook on the end, Andreas unlocked the car's door, took the emergency brake off, and put the transmission into neutral. The four of us easily pushed the tiny Trabant out of the way. Andreas next punctured all four of its tires with a sharp metal object, and cut the cord on the hand-held two-way radio, effectively neutralizing it.

While this was happening, we put our suitcases into the back of the truck and got in. Papa took the wheel and we watched as Andreas also disabled the other two Stasi Trabants in the gasthaus parking lot. He jumped into the back of the truck, hit the cab with his open hand, and we headed west, not north or east as the Stasi would expect.

Unfortunately, the Stasi agent named Hahn, who had been sent to investigate conditions at the fence, saw the truck leaving. He ran along the fence and ordered several VoPos to shoot at us. I could hear bullets hitting the truck. *We are not going to make it,* I said silently to myself, cringing. Then the truck's passenger side window and windshield exploded into a massive spider web pattern as a bullet passed just in front of us.

The windshield was so opaque that Papa could not see out of it. Instead of stopping, he used the pistol resting on his lap to quickly fire three shots into the windshield. Immediately, thousands of pieces of the shattered glass, pushed in by airflow, fell into the cab; they covered all of us. The hail of bullets continued until suddenly, a massive explosion lit the nighttime sky.

I had always admired my father for his calm, cool action under the most difficult circumstances, and this night it certainly saved our lives. I looked at my watch, relieved—the explosion was right on schedule. A group of sappers working from the West Berlin side of the fence managed to place small explosive charges near three of the concrete posts. At 23:10, the explosion created a massive gap in the fence. The Stasi and VoPos would assume we intended to use the hole to reach West Berlin and would concentrate their forces there. Instead, we were taking a different, more circuitous route.

In the dead silence that followed the explosion, Papa drove west two kilometers, and then Andreas signaled for him to turn onto an unpaved back road located in a wooded area. It was bumpy, and we were forced to slow to a crawl, but trees and brush hid us from the main road. We forded a small stream, which was high because of recent rains. After fifteen minutes, we arrived at a metal gate in the chain-link fence that surrounded Schönefeld Airport. Andreas scrambled out, removed a key from his pocket, opened the lock, and removed the chain. We drove through, and he secured the gate again.

Using hand signals, Andreas directed Papa when to turn, and we eventually ended up in a scrapyard that contained pieces of aircraft, rusting trucks, and damaged electrical equipment of all forms—the detritus left behind when this airfield was almost totally destroyed in the last year of World War II.

He signaled for us to stop, and went around to the driver's side door. "You will not need the gun I gave you earlier, or the Stasi's pistols, from this point on," he said. "They could get you in trouble if they were found in your possession." He took all four guns and put them in his haversack. He then removed his hat, wig, false nose, and chin and added them to his bulging pack. "We are a few minutes early, so I will walk from here. A Russian staff car will pick you up in ten to fifteen minutes. "They will never think of looking for your truck here, just park it under that tree next to that junk pile," he said, pointing to a void in the clutter a few meters away. "Good luck." He shook Papa's hand, then hugged Mama and me. With a jaunty gait, he walked up a nearby path into the woods and disappeared.

CHAPTER 87

Kurt
Thursday, March 20, 1958

THE PLAN CALLED for me to enter East Berlin through the Bernauerstrasse apartment house and change into a Russian Colonel's uniform. Then I was to walk three blocks to a rendezvous with one of our operatives; I only knew him as Becker. He would be dressed in his chauffer's uniform and drive the Russian GAZ staff car he used each day as chauffeur for Soviet occupying forces.

I stood on a deserted street corner on that clear, cold night. The cheap brown overcoat I wore covered my uniform, but the two red stripes down the outsides of my trousers were still visible. I carried my round hat with the leather visor in a brown haversack because its red stripe plus a large amount of gold braid and decorations were too conspicuous. As the minutes passed, I looked at my watch, hoping he would arrive soon.

Becker was almost thirty minutes late when he pulled up and I got in the back seat. He explained, "Last minute, I was assigned to pick up a very drunk General Kuznetzov and transport him home. Sorry I am late."

At both the East Berlin/East German border and Schoenfeld Airport checkpoints, we were waved right through without stopping. The whole way, I was concerned that our tardiness would somehow mean the mission would end in disaster. At the previously selected, secluded spot, we hurriedly changed the license plate and ID number on the staff car. Following that, Becker walked back to the airport terminal. He left his chauffer's cap and coat in the car and donned my overcoat. He would take a bus and then a subway back to central Berlin.

I drove down a road parallel to one of the runways, made several turns, and finally managed to arrive at the rendezvous point only 15 minutes late. I became concerned as I approached the junkyard—no one was present. Had the escape plan that Andreas and I had worked out so diligently failed? I pulled up, exited the vehicle, and looked around to assure myself that this was the point described by Andreas. No one was there. I walked back and forth for a minute; then, in frustration, but keeping my voice as normal as possible, I called, "Natalie…Wilhelm…Helga…"

At first, nothing happened and no one responded, then as if by magic, the three of them emerged from their hiding place behind the fuselage and tail of a World War II Junkers aircraft. They were concerned about the delay and had hidden deep in the debris field.

I helped them get their suitcases into the car's trunk and then said to Wilhelm, "I have not shared the details of this part of the extraction with Natalie. You are my German driver. I'm a Russian officer who has just returned from a leave of absence in Moscow. In the back seat, there is a chauffer's leather billed hat and matching dark-blue coat. There is a forged set of identification papers, including a driver's license in the coat pocket. Study them so you at least know all of the details. Also, please remove your eye patch, and if possible, prevent anyone who attempts to see your right eye from realizing that it is opaque."

Turning to Helga, "You are my German-born wife. There is a Russian fur coat on the backseat. Put it on with this cloche hat. Natalie, you are my adopted daughter; put on the blond wig and cloth coat with large buttons in the back. Your coat is the latest fashion from West Berlin."

"We want to thank you for getting us out of that mess," Wilhelm said sincerely. "Those Stasi guys were close to realizing that I was not going to contact other members of my cell. Soon I would have been arrested. If they had tortured me or threatened Helga, I would probably have told them everything. I admit I'm not strong."

"We still have a few hours before we can relax," I said. "The last passenger flight from Moscow arrived thirty minutes ago and the guards at the front gate have recently been changed, so we will probably just be waved through. Wilhelm, slow down as we approach the front gate and try not to be forced to make a complete stop. After that, drive East to the autobahn and turn north. In a few kilometers, there will be another checkpoint at the East Berlin border with East Germany. Again, just slow down. We still have to get into West Berlin."

"We're ready to get out of the hellhole that the communists have created," Papa said.

"Helga and Natalie, get in the back. I will sit in the front and give Wilhelm directions," Kurt said. "Remember to play your parts. If we get stopped for any reason, only Wilhelm and I will speak."

CHAPTER 88

Natalie
Thursday, March 20, 1958

THE CHECKPOINT GUARDS at the airport saluted and waved us through with no fanfare. Fortunately, Russians did not countenance being delayed by a subordinate country's guards. The man in the Russian uniform, the one I'd heard identified as Kurt, began reviewing details in our identity documents, in case we were stopped at some point during the rest of our journey and questioned.

At a little after 02:00, we were stopped at the second checkpoint. This time, the East German transit police stopped us, examined Papa's papers closely, asking questions about where we had been, and where we were going in the middle of the night. Papa answered each question and then several more about the information on the driver's form and route sheet. The guard wrote down the car license plate number and vehicle identification number on a clipboard.

The man who seemed to be in charge of the other two machine-gun-toting guards hesitated and then shined a flashlight in Papa's face. He stepped back and gave the signal for us to proceed.

Before the large round white pole blocking our way could be lifted, a young Russian officer burst out of the guard shack and shouted, "Halten Sie." He approached the passenger side of the vehicle and signaled for the man called Kurt to roll his window down by making a circular motion with his hand. After the young officer spouted several sentences in a foreign language I recognized as Russian—Kurt exited the vehicle and expressed what I decided was disgust as he dug in his uniform coat pocket and handed over several documents. Mama grabbed ahold of my hand and squeezed it tightly. Papa sat rigidly in his seat. All three of us were certain that we would soon be arrested and sent to Stasi hell. Several more minutes passed during a back-and-forth interchange between the two men outside the car.

At this point, the young Russian officer grabbed the handle of the back door and attempted to open it, raising his voice at the same time. After that, harsh words and gestures were exchanged between the two in Russian uniforms. That was eventually followed by a more subdued discussion between them. Then Kurt delivered what appeared to be a telling argument and then a stern rebuke. The contrite young officer returned to the shack and we were allowed to proceed.

After several minutes, Kurt broke the silence by saying in German, "That was close. He wanted us to all get out of the car. They apparently have received descriptions of you three via telephone; that young officer wanted to spend the time required to convince himself that you were not those miscreants. I threatened and cajoled him; then tried to pull rank on him, and finally said, 'I'll make it my primary task in life to make your existence a living hell if you further delay my wife and her daughter's return to our home.'" None of us said anything in response.

Thirty minutes later, we were traversing the familiar streets of central Berlin. "Wilhelm, turn right here and go around Alexanderplatz," Kurt told Papa. "The second turn to your right will be Rosenthaler Strasse. Go straight on it and I'll tell you when to slow down. We will pick up someone who will drive from there. Wilhelm, you will sit in the back with your family until we are at our destination."

Soon we stopped, picking up a bald-headed man dressed in a brown overcoat and carrying a small suitcase. Papa moved to the back. The man took the wheel, handing the bag to Kurt. After a few turns, we stopped in a dark alley. Kurt got out of the car, put the suitcase on the hood of the car, removed the Russian Colonel's uniform, which he folded neatly and placed in the small case, and then put on a pair of black shoes. Underneath the uniform, he had on what I can best describe as a tight-fitting, athlete's black tracksuit. We were driven a kilometer further, made more turns, pulled into a side street, and parked. The street ahead was blocked by a wall. "Wilhelm, leave your hat and coat in the car," Kurt said. "You and I will take the heaviest bags. Helga, you and Natalie can each carry the lightest two. We have about a block and a half to cover."

Kurt then turned and shook the bald-headed man's hand and whispered loud enough for me to hear the name, "Becker."

The four of us walked side by side down one street, up another blocked side street, and through a back garden. Kurt removed a key from a chain around his neck, and we followed him into the central vestibule of a small apartment house and stopped in front of a door. "I must get out of these clothes," he said. "Wait here for a few moments, then we will go through that door into the West."

True to his word, he soon returned in a suit and trench coat. He handed Papa an exceptionally handsome wool topcoat with a silk collar. "All of your coats are gifts from a grateful nation for services rendered."

Kurt opened the apartment house door. A large Mercedes sedan with its motor running was waiting. Once the bags were in the trunk and we were seated in the back, Kurt turned to us and said, "Welcome to West Berlin and freedom. This street is Bernauerstrasse. The apartment houses which line the southeast side of it are in East Berlin, but the street and sidewalks are in the West. Part of the illogical division of an already existing city."

We were taken to a two-bedroom, two-bathroom apartment called a safe house. "If the Stasi know where you are, they will try to kidnap you," Kurt warned. "So, stay here until I return tomorrow morning. Then we will discuss your future. Believe me, we will do everything to ensure your safety. The kitchen is well stocked, there is a TV in the living room. You really have no reason to risk leaving here. Helga, I know you would like to talk to your son and tell him what has happened. Natalie, I know you have a boyfriend. Don't contact anyone until we talk tomorrow. Goodnight, and welcome to a free future."

CHAPTER 89

Friday, March 21, 1958

KURT ARRIVED MID-MORNING with two others. "This is Karen Cramer and George James. They both speak German and are here to assist you with your resettlement in the West. You have a number of options. Natalie, I know you speak and read English. Wilhelm and Helga, do either of you speak English?"

"We both speak and read a little but are not really able to converse," Papa replied.

"Well, that is both good and bad. You two," Kurt said, pointing to Mama and me, "will be on the Stasi's kill-on-sight list. Wilhelm, your name will be near the top of a list of people they want to capture and interrogate before you are executed; they want to know all the details about your spying operation. The Russian KGB and GRU, as well as the East German Stasi, have a large cadre of spies and managed to infiltrate most levels of the West German society, even the federal and state governments. If you are going to live in West Germany, we will need those government entities' help. Few people we have resettled there have been found and either kidnapped or killed, but I must warn you, it has happened."

"What does this mean for us?" Papa asked.

"It would be safest if you all resettled in America. You would not need to change your name. We will provide training in the English language, customs, and history of your new country—you could quickly become citizens. You have all already earned a substantial sum in American dollars.

Wilhelm, you and Helga can afford to purchase a house and a business, if you would want to continue to work. When you reach 65, you can retire and live comfortably for the rest of your lives. Natalie, your stipend may be less substantial, but it's still enough for you to start a new life."

"Many of our relatives live in West Germany and we were looking forward to reconnecting with them," Mama said, smiling in the hope that this would happen.

"Well, the next best alternative is for you to change your names and live in West Germany permanently. The official information about your new identity will reflect that you have lived over here since before the war. The likelihood of the communist agents finding you is small. But contacting friends and relatives who know your real name will add to that risk. The more people who know your real names and your story, the more likely someone in the East will learn who you are and where you live."

"Our son is getting married in two weeks and we must be at the wedding at Freising, just north of Munich," Papa said adamantly. "Is there that much danger if we continue using our real names?"

"Werner is a fairly common last name and there may even be a significant number of Wilhelm and Helga Werner's living in West Germany. Your ages and physical description would potentially allow them to narrow a record search down to you. I'm particularly concerned that Wilhelm here will be easy to identify," Kurt said, looking at Papa. "In fact, last night I was certain that the game was up when the guard shined his flashlight into Wilhelm's face. That would need to be repaired, or they will eventually find you."

"Can that be done?" Papa and Mama asked almost in unison.

"Perhaps. You'll need to consult an expert. But don't forget, you have humiliated the Stasi and they have proven to be a vindictive organization. Although the actual gain to them may be small, they will probably still pursue you."

"Are those all of our alternatives?" Papa asked.

"There is one other you should consider. Since 1956, General Reinhard Gantz has been the head of the German Federal Republic's Foreign Intelligence Service. I talked to him on the KY-7 scrambler telephone this morning to tell him you have been successfully extracted from the East.

Most of your reports have been sanitized to protect you and your operatives as the source, but over the years he has been informed that many of the people he recommended we contact were still active in the field."

"So, I was also working for him?" Papa asked.

"No, his organization was an end-user of the reports we generate. He indicates he would like to meet you and says he has the need for someone with your first-hand knowledge of the East to work with him. His organization's headquarters is in the Pullach District of Munich. Wilhelm, it might be best for you to talk to him before you make any decisions. I can make an arrangement for you and Helga to fly on a private plane from here to Munich tomorrow."

"I think that is best. We appreciate your offer, but I want to talk to the General first. Continuing the fight against the communists appeals to me," Papa said.

"And our son will be close by," Mama added, overjoyed at the prospect.

Kurt turned toward me. "That leaves you, Natalie. What do you want to do?"

"I have a wonderful job here in Berlin. My boyfriend and I have been living together for some time. He is a junior officer in the West Berlin police. We have decided to get married in the fall.

"What would he want?" I asked.

"To stay here, I'm sure. I couldn't imagine changing our lives. We are happy."

"If your father begins working for the Foreign Intelligence Service, it will be best for you two to leave Berlin. We can pull some strings and get him a similar or better job with one of the police forces in West Germany. Spiegel is a big organization with offices all over Germany."

"We both love this city and I know he will want to stay. This is his hometown," I pleaded.

"Natalie, the perimeter of West Berlin is almost 160 kilometers long. The East Germans have eighty-one checkpoints, through which almost half a million people pass each day. There are unmanned gates in the wall/fence they have built around the city, which they use to enter West Berlin at will. Several times, they have brought a cadre of men to kidnap people off the streets—over 100 people a year just disappear. Many of them have eventually been found weeks, months, or even years later in Stasi prisons."

It seemed like he was overly cautious and exaggerating the threat. I decided to remain with my boyfriend in Berlin, the city we both loved.

CHAPTER 90

Friday, April 4, 1958

IN THE 13 years since World War Two ended, nearly 200,000 people a year had left East Germany for the West. At first, the almost 1,400-kilometer (860-mile) long border between East and West Germany, although guarded, was porous and many people escaped that way. By 1953, the inner-German border fence was completed, eliminating that avenue of escape. This left the only easy and relatively safe route to the West—the Berlin subway.

Such a large number of people began arriving in Berlin that the West German government was forced to open a reception center at Marienfield in the American sector of Berlin to house and process them. Virtually all of those individuals and families were flown to West Germany because the infrastructure in Berlin was already overloaded. Five to seven flights a day were used to transport them to the West.

Now that virtually all of the refugees from East Germany were being funneled into one location, the West German government, with our assistance, started interviewing everyone. The interviews were conducted by specially trained agents from the West German Security Service. Ostensibly, those sessions were designed to determine an individual's capabilities, wishes for the future, and where they might want to settle. In reality, one of its main functions was to identify possible East German and Russian spies. Those suspected of being spies were subjected to additional interviews. Their life stories and identity papers were scrutinized very closely. Most suspected spies were forcibly taken back to the East. A few agreed to work for the Security Service and began feeding carefully crafted half-truths and misinformation back to the East. Others were admitted to the West, but local and regional authorities were notified to keep an eye on them.

Another purpose of this camp was for us to gather intelligence on what was happening behind the Iron Curtain. This week we received word from the German Security Agency that they had important intelligence information to give us; they would hold a man named Fritz Lang and his family for a few days while we decided what they should do with him.

Berlin station was the first CIA site to be equipped with the AMPEX VRX-1000 videotape recording system. We kept one camera, monitor, and recorder in our offices, loaned one to the Germans at Marienfield, and one was kept in a safe house for use in covert operations.

Ian Simpson, my boss, was a tall, lanky Texan who always wore cowboy boots and a Stetson hat. He was gregarious, always ready with a joke or quip. He and I gathered in a conference room to review a video tape we'd been told would be of great interest to us and our military intelligence people. The interview was conducted in German.

"Our interview today is being recorded. Please state your name, date, and place of birth," an interviewer requested.

"My name is Fritz Lang. I was born in Leipzig on 19 June 1914."

"Tell us your background."

"I graduated from Dresden Technical University in 1937 with a degree in Aeronautical Engineering. I went to work for Messerschmitt at their design bureau and factory in Magdeburg. One of the main programs I worked on was the ME-262 jet aircraft. After the war, I was working at the Messerschmitt factory in Regensburg, Bavaria, helping to design a car, since my company was forbidden to make aircraft. I made the mistake of returning to Leipzig to help my parents celebrate their 50th wedding anniversary. I was kidnapped by the Russians and taken to their Mikoyan design bureau headquarters near Moscow. For the last twelve years, I have helped them design and build the MiG-17, MiG-19, and MiG-21 aircraft."

"Tell us about your personal life."

"I was not made a prisoner as such, but they made it clear I could not leave the Moscow area without permission, under the threat of imprisonment or death. There was a surprising number of educated Germans who worked at the factory. Soon after I arrived, I met a German girl named Frieda Mueller. She was a mathematician. We fell in love, got married, and now have three children."

"Tell us about your other job."

"The Russians have the plans and specifications for all of the newest American fighter aircraft—the so-called century series jets—the F-100, F-101, F-102, F-104, F-105, and F-106. One of my recent jobs was to determine and write reports in Russian describing what all of the instruments and controls on these aircraft were designed to do."

"Go on."

"The Russian aircraft I helped design are all very simple. They are equipped with only the controls and instruments required to fly the airplane. Even the radars are simple devices. The Russians' design philosophy is 'keep it simple and reliable.' They want as many aircraft as possible; as inexpensively as possible. Their pilots are expendable and should be glad to die for communism. The American aircraft cockpits are crammed with all kinds of devices to help the pilot fight and survive, but many of those instruments are not very reliable. The American designers push technology to the limit and the result is their aircraft work wonderfully when they work."

"How did you escape?"

"My wife and I worked very hard to win the Russians' trust. We even spouted the communist doctrines to our superiors. It was all part of a plan for us to get back to Germany and escape to the West. My father died recently. We were allowed one month's home leave to attend the funeral. Our travel documents allowed us to take the train from Moscow to Leipzig. We arrived there with our children the day before the funeral. It was on Sunday. I immediately purchased tickets for Berlin. Two hours later, we arrived at the East Train Station, then took the subway to the Tempelhof station, which is near here."

At this point, the recorder ran out of tape. As the operator installed the next tape, I told Ian, "I think we need to interview this guy and determine if he is the genuine article. If he is, we should offer him asylum in the States."

Ian agreed. "What he knows could be of exceptional value. Assign Walter Thompson to handle him, including escorting him and his family to the States."

"Let's get Walter in here, start with the first tape again, and then give him his instructions," I said. Ian nodded and I walked out of the conference room.

CHAPTER 91

Tuesday, May 13, 1958

ALTHOUGH ERICA HAD a key to the apartment, she hadn't entered by the front door in months. When I arrived home with Gretchen this evening, Erica was sitting on the couch waiting for us. Gretchen ran to her mother and gave her a hug. They sat on the sofa, talking about school and friends while I went to the bar and made myself a drink. Finally, in a surprisingly grown-up manner, Gretchen said, "I have much homework to do before supper. Please excuse me, mother and father." I chuckled; she was growing up so quickly.

All this time I'd been using questioning looks and hand gestures to silently ask, "What's going on?" Erica had pointed to a bookshelf to my right, her ear and then moved her hand back and forth. So, I decided to play along, "What a pleasant surprise. Are you staying for supper?"

"I had some free time this afternoon and decided to visit my daughter for a change. I want to spend the night here."

"I think we have enough food for three. I planned to serve schnitzel and potato salad."

"Sounds delicious." She took my hand and signaled for me to take my shoes off, which I silently did. She led me to the bedroom and undressed. I stood there dumbfounded as she led me into the bathroom, turned on the shower, and then whispered, "I was given six transmitters to scatter around your apartment. They want to determine what you really do in Berlin."

I felt an immense wave of fear go up my spine.

"Is one of those devices in your bedroom?" I whispered.

She took me into the bedroom and pointed to the top of a tall chest. I led her back into the bathroom. "Finish your shower, join me in the kitchen, and then over the course of the evening show me where you've hidden each listening device."

The two of us acted as normal as possible throughout the evening, but after midnight I crept into Erica's room, and together we managed to get out of the apartment through the servant's entrance without making any noise. "This may only be a test of your loyalty," I said once we were outside. "Or, they may be on to us. It's best we do nothing. We'll leave the devices where they are; don't come back until they tell you to collect them. The transmitters have a limited range and their batteries have a very short life. I suspect you will be told to collect them sometime in the next week."

CHAPTER 92

Thursday-Wednesday, May 22-June 4, 1958

WHEN I GOT home nine days later, a note was waiting for me on the dining room table. It read, "Kurt, I came over today to pick up a few things. Nothing important. I'll get over this weekend if I'm not too busy. Erica." I determined that the microphones were gone and realized that had been the purpose of her visit. I was relieved; this spying effort had certainly failed, but I knew this was probably only the start.

Before noon on Saturday morning, Erica came by asking if we could go for a walk.

I looked at her questioningly. It had been months since we had been seen in public in West Berlin during the day. "Okay, let's have Gretchen join us."

Once we were settled on a park bench, and Gretchen was playing on the swings, I made certain no one could hear us. "What happened on Thursday?"

"Oh. The same Stasi agent showed up at my office and asked me to retrieve the microphones. He waited for over an hour while I made the round trip. I handed them to him, noting he had searched my office from top to bottom. Everything seemed to have changed position slightly. He told me 'I want you to find out what your friend, Mr. Altschuler is really doing in Berlin.'"

"I replied, 'University Chancellor Holtzmann has instructed me that since I'm a quasi-government employee, I must avoid contact with foreigners, especially Americans.' "

"In reaction, he said, 'In your case, we will make an exception. You and Herr Altschuler are 'estranged lovers' and have a daughter together. We will pay you a nice stipend to reestablish a close relationship with him. Seduce him into telling you exactly what he does here in Berlin.'" Erica brushed my hair out of my eyes softly with her fingertips, the first time she had done so in public for a long time and smiled, "He said I should live with you."

At this point, Erica and I were facing each other and both laughed aloud at the ridiculousness of this situation. My wife was being paid to sleep with me in order to find out what I really did in Berlin. This even though, at some level in the Stasi organization, they knew I was a senior CIA agent. Together we would star in our own romantic comedy, except any misstep by either of us could have serious, even deadly consequences.

They were going to expect Erica to find out more about me so, a week later, I left some sensitive trade papers around, which Erica photographed with the little camera they gave her. It hurt nothing to sow the least bit of doubt in their minds. I also concluded that probably only a few Stasi leaders at the top were allowed to know my true role with the Americans in Berlin and that was probably a good thing.

During this time, Professor Richter contacted Erica indicating that the best he could offer her was a research assistantship. She immediately refused and told him she was even more determined "to make my Classics Department the best in Germany."

CHAPTER 93

Friday-Monday, June 6-9, 1958

IT WAS ONE of those cloudless, warm late spring days when the flowers are all blooming and the trees have regained their foliage. Erica and I again sat on a park bench in the Tiergarten, holding hands, watching Gretchen at play. This had become almost a daily ritual. Erica had kept her apartment because neither of us had sufficient free time to move her things.

"Have your friends said anything about the documents you've photographed?" I asked Erica, once I could ensure that no one would hear.

"They've only told me to keep looking."

"Good."

"I need to tell you; I've applied to conduct a dig in Turkey again this summer," Erica said. "The funds mostly come from the government, which means Chancellor Holtzmann will have to approve them. This will be a good test of whether he trusts me or not. He wasn't exactly happy when the Stasi overruled him on the matter of you and I living together. Do you think we could get that wonderful villa we had the year before last?"

"I won't do anything until your dig is approved. I may be able to get three to four weeks off, but no more. We could do August again."

On Monday evening, Erica called. "I'm waiting on a side street, three blocks south of the Potsdammerplatz subway station. Please pick me up," she said, sounding nervous. Once I saw her and pulled up, she got into the back seat, then down on the floor, and said, "We need to talk. Let's go home."

Once Gretchen was in bed, we settled on the couch for a nightcap.

"Today, Holtzmann began our meeting by saying, 'I have decided to approve your dig, but there are two conditions. First, my bosses are insisting that a senior administrator accompany the group to ensure that everyone stays together and comes back.'"

"That's ludicrous; everyone on your dig could walk to the West in a few minutes," I said. "It's only four or five blocks from the University to the Brandenburg Gate!"

"Somehow I realized this might be all about me when he told me the second condition, saying, 'I do not care what the Stasi agent told you, it reflects negatively on this institution when a senior member of our faculty lives in West Berlin with the enemy.'" Her eyes began to well up. "'It must stop,' he told me…I…I just…" Erica turned toward me with a pleading look and put her head on my shoulder.

After a pause, while I brushed her tears away, she continued, "I'm being given conflicting instructions…cannot possibly satisfy both…After much discussion, I told Holtzman, 'I still have my apartment over here and will use it most of the time while also trying to satisfy the State Security agent by finding out what Herr Altschuler's job is. Will that be satisfactory?' He smiled and gave me an affirmative answer."

"Well, I'm a bit sad we won't be living together publicly. I have to admit I got used to it," I said hugging her while trying not to show too much disappointment.

"It's just my discussions with Holtzman went downhill from there when he told me, 'We agree you and your students and the administrator will depart in early June and everyone including you will return to Berlin in early August. This is mandatory!'"

"Surprised at how adamant he was, I replied, 'After the dig, I was planning on spending several days exploring the ancient city of Troy and then a week, maybe more, studying the pots and other artifacts from Troy that Dörpfeld discovered, which are in the Archaeological Museum in Istanbul. The Pergamum Museum, here, also has a large number of artifacts from that same city found by Schliemann. Most of those artifacts have not been properly documented. I'd like to start making that happen. This would be a major accomplishment that would help place this university in the top rank of research institutions in the world.' "

"He replied, 'We can only afford to keep the students in the field for two months, and the administrator will need to accompany them back here at the beginning of August. So as long as you can pay for everything, including your research material, your project is approved. I will expect you to produce that reference work quickly; the politicians always like for our accomplishment as a nation to receive worldwide attention.'"

"So, what's the issue?" I asked, brushing her tears away. "You got what you wanted."

"The problem is that in order to ensure that we had a vacation together, I'm committed to a major research project which will take years and cost a small fortune. Plus, most importantly, it will mean our month together is ruined."

"Not at all. It'll just be different," I said, kissing her cheek. "We'll find a place to stay near Troy. It's only a few kilometers from a beach, right?"

"Yes, that's true."

"There are some resort islands in the Sea of Marmara near Istanbul. We'll have a wonderful time. Make me a list of all of the reference books you need for your study and I'll order them for you. This will give you something to occupy your mind while you're alone in your apartment. Now, how many days do you want to stay in Troy?…"

CHAPTER 94

Friday, July 11, 1958

IN LATE MARCH of this year, Popov told us that a sleeper agent named Andrei Tairova had lived near New York City for several years. Popov had found out about him after his wife, a woman named Margarita, had completed her training and was on her way to join him.

Most of the GRU spies were sent to European countries. Thus, despite their claimed prowess, the FBI had little experience dealing with tradecraft-educated foreign spies. An overzealous, or perhaps just incompetent, FBI agent blew the whole operation. He followed the Tairovas too closely and was spotted. Instead of going to the home Andrei had established for them on Long Island, they disappeared. Their handlers at the UN apparently gave them new identities.

After a high-level altercation between the two agencies at the presidential level, they were both directed that protecting CIA sources was the FBI's most important task. We decided it was time for our agent codenamed Arctic to defect.

When he finally arrived at the safe house almost two hours late for our next meeting, he told Jim Webster that the subway system confused him and he got on a sealed train between the East Train Station and Potsdam. "I was supposed to have orders to travel on that train. When I disembarked at the other end I was detained," Arctic said, "After showing my credentials, I was allowed to go back to East Berlin, but was told my mistake would have to be reported to my commander."

"That's only part of the difficulties you have," Jim said. "We believe your identity has been compromised. It is time for you, your wife, and sons to come to the West. You will receive asylum and compensation."

His response surprised us. "They could not be on to me. Today I was informed by my chief that General P. P. Mielkishev will arrive in Berlin. He will meet the Swedish spy, Stig Wennerstroem, at Karlshorst tomorrow. This is very sensitive information. East Berlin is considered to be a safe place for them to meet because the Swede can pretend to be going to the East to visit Museum Island."

Nothing our agents said would change Popov's mind. This led us to believe his wife and sons didn't even know about his double-agent activities, and he was afraid to tell them.

Sweden was not a member of NATO, so the American government did not usually share secrets with them. The director of the CIA decided we would not inform the Swedes that one of their senior air force officers was a traitor. I agreed with this decision because it might further compromise Arctic.

CHAPTER 95

Saturday, September 20, 1958

CLASSES AT THE university started again, and today was the first opportunity Erica had to spend the night with us since we returned from a vacation in Turkey. We were snuggling on the couch as Gretchen slept in her bed. "The excuse I invented for Chancellor Holtzman last spring continues to rebound on me adversely. On Wednesday, he invited me to his office for lunch, asking me how my book was coming?"

"I explained that 'the artifacts at Troy have been identified as being from nine distinct periods of time starting in 4000 B.C. and extending to Roman times. One could produce several volumes on each of these eras. Honestly, I have determined the task is too monumental for our little department here at Humboldt to undertake,'" Erica said, grabbing her cup of tea on the coffee table before us. "He said the national Minister of Education was informed of my project and wants to fully fund it. After the first volume is published, he will boast to Socialist Party Secretary Ulbricht of this wonderful achievement."

I laughed, unable to resist. Erica turned in my direction with a look of disdain. I smiled. "What happened then?" I asked her, rubbing her back as she sipped her tea.

"I had no choice but to ask him for a full-time photographer to take photos of all the Troy artifacts in the Pergamon Museum. There are hundreds on display and thousands in vaults in the basement. It will take him months to photograph the pots and other objects next to a ruler to show size. Once he's finished, I'll have the students write the descriptions of each object using the museum accession numbers and I'll write an introduction. The first volumes will cover the period from 4000 to 3400 B.C."

"If I didn't know better, I'd think you actually want to undertake this project," I said, kissing her neck lightly.

"Yes, this could be my life's work. Next summer, I'll take the photographer to Istanbul and we'll get images of the objects there."

"Enough about your new project, let's move to the bedroom and see if we can dig up something there," I said, taking her hand.

CHAPTER 96

Monday, November 17, 1958

A WEEK AGO, Nikita Khrushchev used a Warsaw Pact foreign ministers conference as a forum to issue an ultimatum to the other countries occupying Berlin. "The Western powers have violated the demilitarization clause of the Potsdam Agreement of 1945 by rearming West Germany. They have used their privileges in West Berlin to undermine the integrity of the German Democratic Republic. For the sake of peace in Europe, the Warsaw Pact must take action to put an end to the occupying powers' presence in Berlin. To this end, the Western powers need to recognize the German Democratic Republic's sovereignty over all of East Germany, and eliminate their outpost in West Berlin." Later in his speech, the Soviet foreign minister Gromyko demanded, "West Berlin must be demilitarized within six months and declared a free city."

Three days later, a dead-drop message from Popov requested a 15:30 face-to-face meeting at our safehouse. Washington was so concerned over those two speeches that we'd been tasked to make every effort to find what was really going on behind the Iron Curtain. After almost five years, Arctic was still the CIA's best source. Ian and I were in the safe house recording room next door watching and listening to the conversation between Popov and his handlers. I provided a real-time translation from Russian to English for Ian.

"Well, are you ready to leave Berlin?" Popov asked in jest to kick off the meeting. Both of his handlers were startled, then smiled. "Not a nice joke my friend," one said in Russian. The other asked, "Are Khrushchev's moves propaganda, or a real threat?"

"From what I can tell," Popov said, "the threat to abrogate the Potsdam Agreement is genuine; apparently, the politburo has been discussing this for months. Now they appear to have made a decision. They have not increased the alert level of the Russian and East German forces for fear of escalation. All of us in Soviet intelligence have been tasked with measuring official American and British reaction to the threat. Also, they want daily reports on the reaction of occupying forces themselves and West Berlin citizens. That's what I'm doing over here today."

"What is the attitude of your comrades in the intelligence service?"

"They are jubilant, believing this will force the Western Powers to negotiate with our East German allies. It will also reduce the Western Allies' influence in West Berlin. Six months from now, they expect all of the Western Powers will be gone or, at the least, a much different situation will exist here. Much more favorable to the East."

After another hour of questions and answers, Arctic chimed in. "The real reason for this meeting is that I have been recalled to Moscow and will leave in two days."

"Perhaps you should consider defecting. You were not supposed to go back until two months from now," our senior agent in the room with Arctic said. "We were all concerned for your safety; you're our most valuable double agent."

"I cannot; my family has already returned home. I will be safe."

Our team spent hours going over all of the ways Arctic could contact us in Moscow, and how we would stay in contact with him. He left the safe house with a confident smile on his face. *Lamb to slaughter,* I thought at the time.

CHAPTER 97

Thursday, December 18, 1958

OVER THE LAST few weeks, Russian troops and other Soviet officials who had previously performed a number of functions along the border suddenly disappeared from sight. They were replaced by East Germans, VoPos, Transport Police (TroPos), and Grenzpolizei (Border Police). They were supervised on-site by individuals in civilian clothes that everyone knew were Stasi. All interfaces between the Western Powers and West Berlin citizens were ostensibly now in the hands of the East Germans. The Russians had not counted on the truculence of the allies.

A bulletin was distributed to all American government personnel stationed in Berlin. "If you go to East Berlin," it read, "East German officials will attempt to require you to show your identity card or passport. They have no authority in Berlin. Refuse their requests. If they insist, immediately say the following: 'I am a member of the allied occupation force here in Berlin. In accordance with the four powers agreement, I demand free and unlimited passage into all parts of Berlin.' If passage is denied, state, 'I demand a Russian official be summoned immediately.'"

CHAPTER 98

Wednesday, January 7, 1959

ERICA, GRETCHEN, AND I met my family in Miami to celebrate the Christmas holidays. My father rented a large Spanish-style mansion right on Ocean Drive in South Beach. It was a lovely time and the three of us hated returning to dreary Berlin.

When I arrived back at work, Ian welcomed me with bad news. "On Christmas day, Popov requested a quick-brush meeting in Moscow. But he didn't show up to the meeting, which, as you know, is not unusual. If he thought he was being followed, he would automatically abort the handoff. He arranged another meeting for last Sunday where he informed us, he had been dismissed from the GRU, placed in the reserves, and was being sent home to Kalinin. Nothing about why, but we can guess."

"Once he was called back to the Soviet Union after only serving part of his normal tour of duty here, I was concerned," I replied. "If they just suspect him and have no hard proof, perhaps they won't interrogate him too closely."

"You know how the KGB operates. Interrogate a suspect, release him and allow him to relax for a while. Then call him in to 'clear up a few matters, nothing important.' Eventually, they find a way to catch him in a lie. Let him go, to think about it. Call him back and begin a more intense interrogation. Once he starts talking, they explain he will be allowed to confess his transgressions and all will be forgiven. After he prepares a written confession, he will be subjected to mental and physical torture until he is willing to confess to anything," Ian said, sighing. "After he's broken, they'll decide whether to use him against us in some way. Eventually, they will have a show trial, likely followed by an execution."

"We can't do anything but wait. Eventually, he may surface again. Kalinin is only fifty miles northwest of Moscow. A short train ride away from our guys there."

CHAPTER 99

Tuesday, February 10, 1959

TODAY I RECEIVED a verbal invitation to a going-away party for George Blake. When I'd made my trip to MI6 in London over a year ago, I expected he'd be recalled quickly. I couldn't provide the definitive proof of his culpability, because it would have compromised Peter as the source; however, I felt what I'd provided them should have raised sufficient suspicion that they'd investigate him further immediately.

For the last two years, I'd kept a spreadsheet on British and American operative losses in Central Europe. I took it out of the safe next to my desk and wrote at the bottom: "February 11, 1959—George Blake leaves Berlin." It indicated the British had lost thirty-nine operatives in East Germany, Poland, and Czechoslovakia—Blake's area of responsibility. Most telling, the operatives providing the most valuable information had been eliminated first. They had been in positions of responsibility in their individual countries; if allowed to continue, they could have caused severe damage to the communist cause. Someone somewhere had decided who would be exposed, and who would be allowed to continue to function from a list that must have contained all of the MI6 operatives in Central Europe.

As far as I could discern, we'd lost five cells, a total of twenty-seven people to Blake's treachery. There might have been more. Perhaps the measures I'd implemented when I'd assumed responsibility for CIA covert operations in Berlin had saved some of our operative's lives. We'd never know for sure.

What I had in front of me convinced me that Blake had informed the Russians about my tunnel. They'd delayed the discovery of the tunnel until he got his new assignment—which just happened to be Berlin.

CHAPTER 100

Friday, March 20, 1959

LATE LAST YEAR, Arctic had given us information about the number of deployed Soviet nuclear-tipped ballistic missile-carrying submarines and their production rate. Officials in Washington were anxious for more details, so a coded letter was sent to Popov's home in Kalinin in January. The letter was apparently intercepted by the KGB and somehow deciphered. One-time codes are usually unbreakable unless one knows the key. Soon, we concluded that, under duress, Popov must have revealed the key.

In his latest contact, Arctic scheduled a brush pass in central Moscow for March 18. He showed up in the uniform of an army colonel, making it appear that he had received a promotion. He passed a message containing little of military value, although all of his previous correspondence had very important information. This heightened our suspicions. The message was unnumbered and formatted differently from anything else he had ever sent us. We concluded that Arctic had been turned and was cooperating with the KGB—he was trying to save his life and perhaps prevent his family from being disgraced.

CHAPTER 101

Tuesday-Thursday, April 21-23, 1959

ALL OF US working in Berlin and West Germany had been alerted to the possibility the Soviets might locate some of their only operational ballistic missiles in East Germany; this move would allow them to threaten most of Western Europe. The branch of the Russian military that controlled these missiles was known as "The Strategic Rocket Forces."

In early April 1959, a coded message was intercepted and decrypted by an analyst at NSA. It directed two construction crews and their equipment be taken to a railroad embarkation station near Minsk in the USSR on April 19, 1959. American intelligence officials realized these units had just completed construction of the first Russian operational ballistic missile sites near Leningrad. It was fortunate they were using a code we could decrypt; otherwise, we might never have been able to follow the thread that led to the two new ballistic missile bases the Russians built north of Berlin.

On April 21, one of our operatives, who was a conductor, boarded the special train at Frankfurt am Oder on the East Germany-Poland border. He determined the soldiers and equipment aboard were destined for Grünheide, just 25 kilometers east of Berlin. A courier rushed this information via a dead drop in East Berlin to me. I immediately went to Ian's office to share the information. "This is exceedingly important," I said. "I should be on-site to coordinate our efforts in person. What do you think?"

"Kurt, you know the risk, but it's your area of responsibility. I won't overrule your decision. However, I perceive you will be in significant danger."

"I'll take Andreas with me, and together we'll ensure success."

The next day I traveled East in my guise as an East German army major; Andreas served as my driver. Five kilometers from our destination, our Russian GAZ staff car was parked in a barn and we changed into farm laborer's garb. We joined three of our local operatives and a motorcycle in the back of a tarpaulin-covered farm truck for the short ride to Grünheide.

Late in the afternoon of that rainy day, Andreas and I were led to a hill overlooking a rail siding. Through binoculars, I observed specialized construction equipment being unloaded from rail cars. It was almost dark before the entire convoy was unloaded and parked for the night along the road that headed north, out of town. Tents were pitched in a clearing beside the road, and soon the cooks were serving supper to the troops. I followed several of the officers from a distance as they walked to a nearby gasthaus to eat. A minute later, I entered that establishment.

The Russians made the mistake of assuming that the dirty, hunched-over man in soiled clothes sitting next to them could not possibly understand a word of Russian:

"Have you looked at the plans. It's going to take us at least six months to build all of the facilities those primadonna, asshole rocket guys demand."

"They always get everything they want, while the rest of us go begging."

"My salary was cut by 500 rubles a month so they can have their toys to play with."

"The requirement that we locate all of those buildings under the trees will be difficult, if not impossible. You cannot hide such a large complex under trees!"

"I agree; that is crazy. Some say American airplanes can see what we are doing through the trees, so why bother?"

"At least there will be no shortage of alcohol here in Germany. All the best vodka is going to waste, powering those bastards' rockets."

The next day, the Russian convoy took public roads. It moved at only about 15 kilometers per hour over narrow, country lanes. Several of our operatives, plus Andreas and I, both preceded and followed the convoy in farm trucks and on motorcycles using the main road and side roads.

They split into two groups at Zehndenick—one proceeded directly north to the forest near Vögelsang, and the other went almost 20 kilometers to the left and eventually took a dirt road east into the forest several kilometers south of Fürstenburg. We were able to pinpoint the exact location of each of these facilities on a set of topographic maps I'd brought with me.

I couldn't stop yawning as I got into my East German Officer disguise in the backseat of the staff car late that evening. It had been forty hectic hours since I'd slept, and I was more than exhausted. In perhaps two hours, I would be able to crawl into my own bed. I unsuccessfully fought sleep but knew that Andreas would wake me if anything untoward happened during the drive back to East Berlin.

The blue flashing lights and sirens startled me. Suddenly, Andreas and I were dragged from the staff car and forced into waiting cars. I was situated between two beefy individuals in the back seat of a Volga sedan. I protested in my most officious German, "Comrade, I am on a mission, and my superiors will be very unhappy." They remained silent, and repeated efforts to get them to tell me why we had been stopped failed to elicit a response. Somehow Andreas just disappeared from the scene at this point.

Soon they drove me past the new Stasi Headquarters building I had seen in CIA file photographs. My two minders each took one of my arms and effortlessly transported me down a set of stairs into a basement. There, four other Stasi agents, who I recognized from photos of their senior people, escorted me to one of the cells which lined both walls. They opened the metal door and allowed me to look in. Erica and Gretchen were huddled in one corner. Erica had a bloody cut over her right eye and was staring forward in an almost catatonic state. Gretchen sobbed and screamed, "Papa, help us."

One of the men looked at me, saying, "We will release your wife and daughter if you tell us everything you know about CIA operations in Berlin—if not, they will suffer a very unfortunate fate."

I struggled with my captors, intent on returning to that cell and freeing my family. Then for a brief period, I was allowed to wander aimlessly searching for my family and an escape route. Eventually, I'd decided it was best if I could leave now and soon return to rescue Erica and Gretchen.

The three men who grabbed and dragged me to a nearby cell seemed to come out of nowhere. The cell was all tile with a large open drain in the middle, and massive hooks hanging from the ceiling on chains. "Here is where we dispose of people who do not cooperate. They are dispatched with a single bullet to the head, then attached to hooks, hoisted off the floor, their throats are cut, and their blood is allowed to drain from their bodies. Then their bodies are cut up and fed into that shredder in the corner. Firehoses are used to wash the residue down into the sewers. They just disappear from the face of the earth and are never heard from again."

At this point, I thought back to the hand-to-hand combat training I'd received in the war and looked around for something I could use as a weapon. Finding nothing, my will to fight ebbed quickly; my thoughts focused on saving Erica and Gretchen. I loved them so much and the words just tumbled out, "I'll tell you everything I know! Just release my family," and began mumbling every secret I knew. The identity of our numerous operatives…the spies the West Germans had managed to place in high positions within the communist government…the names of my staff and their assignments.

Suddenly, I woke up, startled. Realizing it had all been just a nasty dream. Andreas was pressing my shoulder. "Most of the trip you have been murmuring unintelligible words," he said. "The apartment on Bernauerstrasse is just over there. I must get rid of this car. I'll call you next week so I can collect the beer you promised me."

Making sure the marked-up map was in my pocket, I exited the car and walked to the CIA apartment house. After changing into my suit, I began combing my hair in a mirror. Seeing myself, it suddenly hit me. I'd been foolish to go into East Germany on a mission many of my subordinates or operatives could have handled. At that moment I vowed that was my last trip to the East for the CIA. Bravado is one thing, stupidity is another. It's too much of a risk for that adrenaline high. Maybe I was just getting older, perhaps smarter.

CHAPTER 102

Natalie
Saturday, June 27, 1959

ULTIMATELY, MY PARENTS retained their last name and moved to Munich; Papa went to work in the General's relatively new organization. Mama was happy to just be a hausfrau.

As I had anticipated, my boyfriend Ernst Vogel did not want to leave West Berlin. We immediately moved to the French Sector and left no forwarding address anywhere. On the lease for the new apartment we rented, we used only his last name and our real middle names. We now did all of our shopping near our new home. I continued to work at *Spiegel* but was allowed to move to a different building and use my future husband's last name and my middle name—Emilia Vogel—when introducing myself at this new worksite. We were married in Munich a year ago. I changed my last name legally, dyed my hair blonde, and at first, looked over my shoulder a lot. Eventually, I relaxed and began living the life of a happy and carefree new bride.

CHAPTER 103

Kurt
Monday, May 4, 1959—Friday, December 4, 1959

ONCE MY GROUP'S initial report reached CIA Headquarters, they opened a file titled: *Possible SHYSTER Missile Base in East Germany.*

The entries in that file grew as my team of local German nationals, the British MI6's operatives, and U-2 overflights concentrated on this new threat. SS-3 SHYSTER was the NATO designation for a missile system which the Soviets called the R-5M. It was a single-stage, maximum 1200-kilometer (750-nautical-mile) range, liquid propelled, inertial guided missile. It was designed to carry a 1 megaton nuclear warhead and was capable of reaching virtually all of Great Britain and France from the two bases located north of Berlin. Below is a summary of the reports that those TOP SECRET US/UK EYES ONLY files contained:

1. May 3, 1959. At both Vögelsang and Fürstenburg, heavy equipment has been observed excavating a circular hole estimated to be 30 meters deep and 100 meters across.
2. June 17, 1959. Concrete has been poured to form sides, support columns, and the floor of the hole that will probably be a hardened bunker. The only entrance/exit is 6 meters (19 feet) wide. The position and dimensions are shown in the attached photos/data.
3. July 9, 1959. Steel-reinforced concrete roof estimated to be 3

meters thick was recently poured at both bunkers, and earth was then moved over them.

4. August 19, 1959. Four apparent launch pads have been constructed near the bunkers at both locations. The pads are reinforced concrete with embedded anchor bolts; these support the missile in an upright position prior to launch.

5. September 9, 1959—Eight trailers probably carrying SHYSTER missiles entered East Germany via rail at Frankfurt am Oder. The canvas-covered objects in trailers are described as cylindrical tubes estimated to be 22 meters (72.8 feet) long by 1.5 meters (4.92 feet) wide. Trailers appear to be the same as those observed in the 1958 May Day parade in Moscow.

6. September 10, 1959. Russian troops secured the area around the rail loading ramp at Juterbog, and all roads leading north. Analysis of available photographs taken from the ground indicates eight SHYSTER missiles were being transported. The warheads that are normally transported separately were not apparently part of this convoy. It has been verified that Vogelsang and Fürstenburg bases have each been supplied with four of these missiles.

7. October 18, 1959. A special, heavily armed train transited Frankfurt am Oder on the way to Juterbog.

8. October 19, 1959. Heavily armed truck convoy transported eight trailers north. Trailer size and shape consistent with nuclear-warhead transporter observed by U-2 during missile/warhead mating exercise near Novgorod on October 13 of last year. Photos taken from along the road show a total of eight trucks transporting probable missile warheads. The plutonium detectors positioned beside the road functioned properly and registered positive.

9. November 22, 1959. Missile warhead mating exercise observed at Vogelsang missile base by U-2.

10. December 4, 1959. A vertical, apparently ready-to-launch missile located on launch pad number 4 at Fürstenburg was observed from the ground last week. U-2 overflight today indicates that missile is NO LONGER ON LAUNCHPAD. Assume earlier observation was a training exercise.

American military intelligence reports contain words that reflect the confidence the preparer has in the information. The word "possible" is used to denote a 50% to 75% probability the information is correct. The word "probable" denotes a 90% likelihood the information is valid. The only time these equivocation words aren't used is when three unimpeachable, totally independent sources all provide the same information.

At this point in time, the Western intelligence community declared the SHYSTER missiles in Germany were operational and posed a significant threat to America's NATO allies.

Analysts estimated it would probably take six hours from the time the Soviet Rocket Forces received the command to prepare to launch a missile until it could be ready to fire. The report stated:

"(TOP SECRET) First, the missile must be removed from the hardened bunker; then the warhead must be mated to the missile body and the inertial guidance system must be installed. Then, the missile carrier hoists the missile into a vertical position. It is then fueled with alcohol and liquid oxygen. Last, the on-board test systems verify the missile's operational readiness." A long, arduous process.

Beginning immediately thereafter, British Canberra Bombers were kept on alert 24 hours a day at Royal Air Force Station Gütersloh, West Germany. These aircraft were tasked with destroying the Russian missiles based at Vogelsang and Fürstenburg before the missiles could be launched. At this time, a tactical nuclear bomb was the only weapon with a high probability of destroying these bases and the missiles themselves. Non-nuclear weapons were too inaccurate to destroy most point targets. Britain, France, and NATO faced a tough choice: Start a nuclear exchange or allow the Soviets to destroy Britain and France in a first strike. Cold War intensity deepened dramatically with this deployment by the Soviets.

CHAPTER 104

Sunday, August 9, 1959

THE FIRST OF Erica's planned twenty-seven volumes on Troy's artifacts was published in May. It was well received by the experts on both sides of the Iron Curtain. The communist government awarded her the East German National Prize, Third Class. She was told she was expected to use the 25,000 East Mark prize to complete her important work.

Erica had decided to spend June and July in Istanbul working with the Turkish museum curators and directing the photography of the items for the next volume. Then she would join Gretchen and me for a tour of Athens and the Greek islands. Every other day, she planned on working, while Gretchen and I would relax full time.

CHAPTER 105

Monday, September 28, 1959

OUR THIRD, WHICH would turn out to be our last, contact with Popov was made in the men's room of a restaurant in central Moscow. He managed to surreptitiously pass a note to our agent; it was handwritten on pieces of thin paper rolled into a cylinder, looking much like a crumpled cigarette butt. The note read, "I've been arrested. I am cooperating with my captors. They indicate if I help them, they will take me to Berlin and allow me to become a double agent. I remember my old emergency phone number. If I ever get to Berlin and can defect, I will call. Believe nothing I do or say until I am again safely with you."

CHAPTER 106

Monday-Tuesday, October 12-13, 1959

THE UNEXPECTED SUMMONS to the CIA Headquarters in Washington gave me just enough time to go to the apartment, pack a bag, and make sure Erica could pick Gretchen up from school that day. She agreed to move into our apartment in West Berlin until I could return. I caught a DC-6 out of Tempelhof for Heathrow and a new Pan Am Boeing 707 jet onto LaGuardia. A commuter train out of New York's Penn Station got me into Union Station in Washington at 12:23. After a cab ride, I entered the headquarters building five minutes before my meeting with Mr. Dulles. I left my bag at the front desk and was shown into the CIA Director's Conference Room.

There I met two men. Frank Collins, a tall, broad-shouldered man with sparse hair covering his balding pate. He wore an ill-fitting, three-piece suit that was obviously off the rack, and his shoes were badly scuffed; his handshake was perfunctory. The other man's name was Thomas Lane. He sported an expensive suit, well-trimmed mustache, and short crew cut that all indicated he cared about his appearance, but his dead-fish handshake was off-putting. We'd just taken seats at the conference table when a security man came in. Each of us was in turn taken to another office and asked to sign special security paperwork.

At 13:15, Mr. Dulles entered and took a seat at the head of the conference table. "Gentlemen," he said, "all of you have now been cleared for a new, Top Secret program called Project LUMAR. We will again dig a tunnel into East Berlin and tap into the buried communications cables the Soviets and their allies are using to keep us from knowing what they're doing.

"There are several major differences between this tunnel and the last one. First, this is strictly an American effort. Many of us still suspect someone in MI6 told the Russians about the first tunnel. They seemed to just zero in on the exact location of the taproom in the middle of that road. Another big difference is President Eisenhower has decided that this time, NSA will be the lead organization, not us. This decision was made because they have trained linguists, teletype machine intercept operators, cryptanalysts, and management staff to process the information quickly and efficiently. I agreed with the President that they were better equipped to man the intercept facility after it was built, but I argued that we should build the tunnel. Secretary of Defense, Thomas Gates, argued his Army Corps of Engineers would again build the tunnel and his NSA military operators in the Army and Air Force would man the intercept stations, so the CIA did not need to be involved at all."

Mr. Dulles took a sip from the coffee cup he'd carried into the room and continued. "It was close, but I finally convinced President Eisenhower that we should intercept and process the material from those landlines used by the East German Stasi, Russian KGB, and GRU as well as the other Warsaw Pact intelligence agencies. So, we will have a place at the table and space in the exploitation building for our exclusive use."

"The three of you will be directly involved in managing this program for us," pointing to each of us in turn. "Frank Collins, you will have overall control of the CIA part of the program. Thomas Lane, you will be our sole representative on a committee that will control the project—someone from NSA who will be the overall chair of that committee, and an Air Force general will be the third man on it. The general's people will provide direct supervision of the digging and associated construction activities.

"Oh, and Kurt Altschuler," he said, looking directly at me, "you'll be responsible for keeping this project secret from the thousands of Soviet and East German spies who roam around West Berlin every day. Those DoD guys will not be familiar with the situation on the ground and will make mistakes, which could blow this thing sky high before we even get started."

"What's the time frame for this project?" I asked.

"A highly regarded Air Force civil engineer with the right clearance will arrive in Berlin in about three weeks. His family is coming with him, so he will be just another Air Force officer who's on a tour of duty in Berlin. Kurt, you were in charge of building the last tunnel. Help him in every way you can. Half the money is hidden in the current military budget for improvements to the buildings at Tempelhof. The other half is hidden in our budget under the line items for European operations. Make arrangements to reserve what money we need and then pay for something the military needs to do their job, perhaps the hardware. Get started and complete it as soon as you can."

"Sir, I am Operations Manager for Berlin and Eastern Europe," I said. "You know, I'm pretty busy."

"I want you to try to do both jobs. This job will have priority for your time. Ian will just have to take up the slack. If you two have a problem, let me know. At this point, I don't really have anyone senior enough to take your place."

"We'll do our best, sir," I replied.

"Okay. I want the three of you to read this material," pointing to a stack of classified documents on the nearby table. "Let me know if you need my help. Otherwise, I will assume you three will handle all of the details. I expect monthly status reports until the intercept facility is online and fully functioning."

When Mr. Dulles rose to his feet, so did everyone else. After he left the room, my two companions looked at each other and then at me. I thought at the time they wanted me to leave so they could talk, but instead, I said, "That certainly wasn't what I expected. What about you two?"

Thomas Lane reacted immediately. "I can't believe the old man gave up so easily. This tunnel's construction and the entire output of the exploitation center should be under the direct control of the CIA—this is a covert spy operation."

"You're correct," Frank Collins said. "I'll get an appointment with the Director of Operations—we need his help to reclama this decision."

"Is he cleared for this program?" I asked.

"Probably not, but since I am the program manager, I'll have him cleared. Then we'll get him to take action—he hates the NSA and DoD."

"But the decision was made by President Eisenhower," I said.

"He always favors the military—old generals never change."

"Perhaps we should read the information in these folders before we decide to attempt an end-run around Mr. Dulles," I suggested. They agreed and for the next three hours or so, we read and discussed the new information. It became obvious they still were interested in exploring ways to wrestle more or perhaps all of the program away from the DoD.

I said little during this entire interchange. At 17:20, I stood up, shook both of their hands, and said, "I've been up for twenty-nine hours and am dead on my feet. I've scheduled a flight back to Berlin for tomorrow morning, so I'm going to have some supper and get some sleep. I must tell you both, the Army Corps of Engineers did an outstanding job of building the first tunnel. The CIA struggled to hire enough trained people to man all of the positions in the Intercept and Exploitation Center. Those who proved capable of doing the job were mostly former military men who had worked for NSA either in the military or otherwise. I personally think the President made the right decision, and I intend to follow Mr. Dulles' orders until he tells me differently. I work for him and we have our marching orders." I walked out of the room as my companions stood there, visibly astonished.

CHAPTER 107

Wednesday, November 4, 1959

THE CONSTRUCTION OF the new tunnel would be managed by the American Air Force using Tempelhof AFB Berlin as a center for the operation. So, before I left CIA Headquarters, I had my security clearance forwarded through the Department of Defense to that facility. Today, I made arrangements through the base commander to get a security badge so I could enter and leave the base at will.

Lt. Colonel Mark Powell, who was cleared for the program, met me at the front gate of the base. After a warm greeting, he took me to the base badge and identification office. Once I had a badge hanging from a chain around my neck, Mark showed me the offices that would house the LUMAR program. "In the Air Force, we call it a tank," he said. "Like an army tank, it's made out of metal on all six sides to prevent conversations from being heard outside. Also, there are no telephones in this space."

Inside the metal door, we walked down a short hallway leading to three doors. "This area contains a private office for the program manager, which is just here," Mark explained, pointing to that office. "There's a small conference room, and another room with desks and conference tables for the rest of us to use when necessary. Entry is strictly limited to those cleared for the program. When the door is unlocked, entry is still controlled via a cipher lock. Since you're a guest in this facility, you'll not be given the combination to either lock. When you need entry, just ring the buzzer and someone will admit you."

"That's acceptable. As I understand it, this will be the only place in Berlin where we can discuss any aspect of this program," I said.

"Correct. A package of LUMAR material arrived by a special courier from Washington last week. It's locked in that two-drawer, top-secret Mosler safe over there against the wall. I've been intending to get down here and take a look at what this program is all about."

"I can give you a summary if you'd like."

"That'd be helpful."

For the next hour, Mark and I discussed the background on the first tunnel and what we had to do to get the second one built. In closing, Mark said, "So many aspects of this program will be challenging; I hope Major William Craig is a good engineer and leader. He previously worked in another part of the Air Force, hence no one in Security Service knows anything about him. His personnel folder indicates he has twelve years of experience and successfully completed several major projects. Both you and I have too many other responsibilities to devote much time to solving the numerous problems this program entails."

"I concur, Mark. Hope he's a good man."

CHAPTER 108

Friday, December 5, 1959

MAJOR WILLIAM CRAIG, the tunnels production manager, somehow convinced someone in the States to delay his departure until after Thanksgiving. When Mark received notification of this delay, he phoned me on the KY-7 Scrambler telephone. "This high-priority program is like a broken ship—it's going nowhere."

Mark called me a second time and said, "The good major's family is now staying in the States, so I've arranged a room for him in the Bachelor Officers' quarters here on the base. Can you attend a kick-off meeting in the tank on Monday at 10:00?"

"I'll be there."

Mark admitted me to the tank and while we waited for the major, suggested we exchange backgrounds. I glossed over the details of my thirteen years with the CIA, claiming to have been primarily an administrator except for the three years when I'd been responsible for the original tunnel.

"I entered West Point in 1943 and graduated in 1946," Mark said to begin his description of his life. "I elected to join the Air Force when it was formed in 1947 and was one of the first officers assigned to the AF Security Service when it was formed in 1948. The antennas on the roof of this building allow us to maintain cognizance of many communist military and civilian activities. When the tunnel is complete, the information available from their landlines will be tremendously more valuable—they won't know we're again listening to their telephone conversations and teletype messages."

"I'll warn you now. When the first tunnel was operational, we were overwhelmed by the volume and importance of the information we intercepted. Hopefully, you will be better prepared than we were."

Thirty minutes after the meeting was supposed to start, Major Craig sounded the buzzer and was admitted to the tank. My first impression wasn't favorable. His uniform was obviously old and worn; his shoes were scuffed and unpolished; his hair and mustache were overlong and shaggy compared to most military men; he had cut himself shaving and a bloody piece of toilet paper was pressed against his chin. His limp handshake, bleary eyes, and bent posture reminded me of someone whose life was in shambles. *Is this guy capable of leading this or any effort?*

At Marks's request, I described the original tunnel in detail. Then he and I took turns going over the details of the new tunnel we were going to build.

Throughout this interchange, William remained mute. "This may be an oversimplification," Mark said at the end of the meeting, "but as I see it, we have several tasks. One, determine where and how we can build the new tunnel so its existence can be hidden from the communists, citizens of Berlin, and our closest allies; two, determine the equipment and men required to do the job; three, develop a detailed roadmap of tunnel construction; and, four, get everything over here and make it happen. The people back in the States have made it clear they want the tunnel completed as soon as possible—the end of next year is the goal. They have tasked us with generating a detailed program schedule by December 15—giving us less than two weeks."

We went down to the officer's club for lunch. Mark had iced tea and I had a beer. William had two beers; his hand was shaking as he took his first sip. I gave Mark a questioning look. Because we were in a public place, the conversation centered on Berlin as a military duty station. William had mostly listened as if deep in thought, but blurted, "Building that tunnel will be a very difficult task." I looked up at the ceiling and then at Mark askance. Such information was never supposed to be discussed in a public place.

After lunch, we went back to the tank; I spread a map of the border between the American and Russian sectors on the conference table, anchoring it in place with ashtrays. "The Russians, with East German help, recently rerouted their most important communications links away from the border and enclosed them in a metal pipe. Here's the path of those new communication links," I said, running my finger along a blue line drawn on the map.

The other two men huddled over my shoulders as I pointed to the southern area of the American zone. "As you can see, the new line has been relocated several kilometers east of the border," I said. "It would be difficult for us to construct a tunnel that long—meaning we must search up here in urban areas of central Berlin—among other things, the River Spree will be between us and our objective. It's a deep, wide barrier, which exacerbates the challenges."

"How deep and wide is the river?" William asked.

"Berlin is located here because the river is navigable up to this point. It depends on where we dig, but it's about 400 to 500 feet across and 50 to 60 feet deep," I replied.

William whistled. "Most tunnels under bodies of water start and end several hundred yards before and after the shoreline. How big is the pipe and how deep is it buried?" William asked.

"The pipe is a little less than 3 feet in diameter and is buried about 8 to 9 feet beneath the surface."

Mark interjected, "Our tunnel entrance must be hidden from view at our end, and must come up under the pipe containing the communication lines without disturbing the surface."

"What you're describing is impossible," William said.

"This may be a bit overwhelming, but that's the reason you've been sent to Berlin and assigned to Security Service," Mark said. "Kurt and I will help you, but you're the engineer in charge of this program, and every one up to and including the President expects you to make this happen. If you need help of any form, let us know."

William seemed nervous. "I need to look at the map and read these documents, I'm sure I'll then have a large number of questions. Can we meet again on Wednesday?"

CHAPTER 109

Tuesday, December 15, 1959

ONE OF OUR many permanent surveillance posts in East Berlin was a restaurant in Lichtenberg near Stasi Headquarters. The owner and two of the numerous waiters were our operatives. The light fixtures located above the booths along one wall were equipped with microphones, which were connected to recently developed voice-activated recording devices hidden in the basement. In recognition of their elevated status in a communist society, the highest-ranking Stasi officers were always seated in those booths. Information collected this way were usually tidbits, because the Stasi agents said nothing of interest or talked around a subject; occasionally, sufficient details were imparted to allow us to glean something of real value.

Almost two years ago, one of the senior Stasi officials met a man wearing a nice western-cut suit in this restaurant. The owner went to the basement to hear what the two said to each other: "The car is parked in space 947. Here are the keys and claim ticket. The tank is full. It takes about eight hours to get there; we expect you to be back tomorrow evening. Park the car in the same garage. Our man will meet you in front of the building at 21:00."

One of the waiters followed the man by subway to a parking garage near Kurfstendamm. The courier drove a car with West German plates out of the garage. Since he was obviously going West, we notified the West German Security Service. Two hours later, they were able to attach another recently developed instrument, a tracking device, to the undercarriage of the car while it was stopped at the West German Terminus of the Central Autobahn route out of Berlin. The German agents then followed him to Bonn. He parked outside of the Bonn University Library and proceeded to the fourth floor. There he was seen removing books from a shelf near the top of the bookcase, reaching behind, and retrieving two packages. He placed them in a briefcase, which he opened to show the guard at the exit that he didn't have any books.

Continuous 24/7 video surveillance of that dead drop-location was established. Soon, two individuals were seen placing items in it. When the courier returned a week later to pick up these new items, he was arrested on his way out of the library. His name was Manfred Lehmann—a West Berlin resident who, when he was first interrogated, claimed he was a traveling salesman with customers in Bonn, Cologne, and Berlin.

The two individuals who had been identified when they placed items in the dead drop were immediately arrested. Gunter Kraus was a senior administrator in the German President's office. Clara Sommer was a Senior Deputy Minister for the Defense's secretary. Both were in deep cover, having immigrated from East Germany just after World War II; both began working in Bonn when it became the German capital in 1949. They were arrested for giving West German State secrets to the KGB via the Stasi. Today, all three were convicted of covert espionage and sentenced to twenty years in prison. This incident in the Cold War became known in the German press as Operation Hecke (Hedgerow).

At the time, I thought this coup made up for the ever-increasing manpower losses we were experiencing among our operatives. I was wrong. This series of events ultimately proved to be one step forward and two steps back.

CHAPTER 110

Thursday, December 17, 1959

ALTHOUGH NEITHER MARK nor I had time to spare from our other duties, we spent numerous hours trying to help William complete a plan for the new tunnel.

"So, we've decided that we need to hide the tunnel entrance in an existing structure west of the River Spree. And, since the path of the Russian communications pipe turns east, away from the American zone here," I said, pointing on the map before us. "The building must front on the river in this eight-to-ten block area on the east side of Kopenicker Strasse in the Kreuzberg District."

"We've also agreed that the building must have a large basement, so soil can be stored in it temporarily until dump trucks can haul it away," Mark said.

"The most important thing we've decided," William said, "is we're going to dig a pit perhaps fifty feet deep. A large elevator will be installed in a shaft we'll build, which will allow us to start tunneling at that depth. This way we won't need a long access ramp, which means the building doesn't need to be huge. The distance from the building to the communications pipe will be about 1400 feet."

"The Army Corps of Engineers dug the last tunnel with short-handled shovels. Are we going to do the same thing again?" I asked.

"We're going much deeper and will be tunneling under a body of water, so I'd like for us to use a tunnel-boring machine," William quickly responded. "It is a mechanical device with a round head that has holes in its front surface; when the head rotates, it removes the soil ahead. Behind this machine is a tunnel shield which serves to protect the diggers while support-structure elements are put in place. Automatic soil removal systems are available with some Tunnel Boring Machines, universally referred to as TBMs. This will minimize the amount of hand labor and speed up the overall construction rate."

"Let's estimate how long each of these tasks will take, and then we can tell our bosses when we can be done with the digging," I said.

An hour later, we had produced a schedule that showed construction beginning on June 15, 1960 and finishing on October 17, 1961. Eight months to dig the pit and install the elevator in the shaft; eight months to dig the tunnel and install a terminal room.

At this point, William announced, "I want to go back to the States for the next month or so. While there, I'll do several things: first, go by the Army Corp of Engineers Headquarters in Washington and review my plan with them; two, select the construction equipment we'll need to complete this project; third, contact elevator manufacturers and make sure a heavy-duty elevator is available that will meet our needs; and, lastly, visit my family while on leave for two weeks. I'll return here in mid-to-late January, depending on how things go in the States. Mark, here are my travel orders and leave request. Please sign both."

Mark and I looked at each other, then up at the ceiling, not believing what we were hearing. *Will this guy ever get down to business on this high-priority project?*

William looked at me. "Kurt, while I'm gone you can find us a suitable building. I'll approve your selection when I return."

Mark signed the paperwork and William left for the States the next day.

I included the project schedule in my second monthly report back to CIA headquarters. Since I didn't receive any return correspondence, I decided the schedule must be acceptable to them.

CHAPTER 111

Monday, January 11, 1960

OVER THE HOLIDAYS, Gretchen, Erica, and I spent a week in Switzerland skiing. It took me a week to catch up on what had happened at my CIA and Trade Mission offices in my absence. Today, I had some free time and decided to begin working on my task of finding a building for the terminus of the new tunnel. Despite a cold breeze, the sun was shining and there were only a few clouds in the sky. A taxi dropped me off at Kopenicker Strasse. I then walked down a side street to the River Spree and then north up the sidewalk beside it. A number of large apartment buildings occupied the huge lots that extended several hundred feet from Kopenicker Strasse to the river. The only problem was they all appeared to be occupied. Since I had rented for almost 13 years, I knew that tenants in Germany have very strong rights—they must be given three months' notice, and can easily contest the eviction in the courts. This usually ties the eviction process up for months, even years. So, buying an existing apartment building might not be a good solution.

After walking a few blocks, I sat down on a bench and considered another option. *Purchase a building, leave the tenants in place, and use only the basement for the construction.* This might work, provided we again hand-dug the tunnel. Can a deep pit be hand-dug? Too many machines, making too much noise, and too many people who would know something was going on. That whole line of thought was ridiculous, so I abandoned it and continued on my excursion.

Five blocks south of where I started, I saw a realtor's "For Sale" sign. This meant some of the apartment buildings were privately owned in what was known in the States as a cooperative. Those types of buildings would be even more impossible to buy.

The realtor's office was only a few blocks west, so I walked over there and presented a card with the name Herman Vogelmann, Investment Advisor on it. Soon I was sitting in the office of a personable young man who asked, "How can I help you?"

"I represent a group of Swiss investment bankers who want to purchase apartment buildings here in Berlin. They're particularly interested in properties along the river. They believe people will pay a premium for an apartment with a view of a river—plus that area just east of Kopenicker Strasse and south of the Schilling Bridge is already a prime residential area. Do you know of anything on the river?"

"There are some vacant lots there—even one really large one, but most apartment houses are owned by banks and investment funds, or contain privately owned apartments. The companies that own the buildings are interested in buying similar properties, not selling."

"How about a fully or partially vacant apartment building?"

He paused for a moment as if scrolling through a number of buildings in his mind. Finally, he exclaimed, "Oh! There is one. It was damaged in the war, repaired when there was a shortage of housing after the war, but two years ago the Kreuzberg Town Council declared it to be unsafe for human habitation. The last tenants moved out perhaps three months ago. One whole side of the building must be replaced. It was built in the 1870s and at one time was a real showplace—marble façade and columns, wrought iron railing and balustrades, and a dome-ceilinged restaurant on the top floor."

"What is the address and who owns it?" I said, trying to keep the excitement out of my voice.

"Because it is a local property, I happen to know the owner of the construction company hired to rebuild the property. Let me try to contact him."

I sat quietly in front of the realtor as he spoke through a lengthy phone conversation. When he hung up the phone, he looked at me a bit disappointed. "The basement, ground floor, and some apartments on the south side of the building are scheduled to be gutted over the next few months. It will apparently take them the rest of the year to complete the remodeling efforts."

"Hmm. I'd still love to see it. Can I?"

"Yes, of course."

Soon we were walking around the outside of the building. Signs indicated we were not allowed inside. A metal tube had been affixed to a window on the third floor and extended down to the ground. A dump truck beneath the tube was being filled with the debris from the building.

As we parted, the realtor said, "Would you be interested in making an offer on this building? I would be happy to represent your principals."

"I am not certain this is exactly what my principals had in mind," I said. "But I'll talk to them and let you know. Thanks for your time."

I caught a taxi and was at the Kreuzberg Town Hall in ten minutes. Using public records, I determined who owned the building.

CHAPTER 112

Natalie
Wednesday-Tuesday, February 10-16, 1960

DER SPIEGEL, THE weekly magazine I worked for, was published on Thursday, so it would be available on Friday for people to read over the weekend. Hence, as a head fact-checking editor, my subordinates and I were the last to approve the copy, meaning I always worked late on Wednesday evenings.

It had been almost two years since I had helped my parents escape from the East. Long ago, I had stopped looking over my shoulder, searching for a tail. Berlin's streets were safe, even at night for women, so I'd stopped worrying about my safety.

It was almost midnight as I trudged through drizzle and fog under heavily overcast skies. The streetlights formed small islands of gray in an otherwise bleak world. I looked forward to a quick shower, and then crawling under the warm covers with my husband.

As I passed a dark alley, someone thrust his arm out, grabbed me, and placed something over my mouth. Another person jabbed a needle into my neck. I could smell a sweet alcohol-like odor and feel myself going limp as they dragged me toward the street. I lost consciousness soon after seeing the trunk of a car close—with me inside.

*

I slowly became aware of my surroundings, coming out of the fog of whatever drug I was given. It was dark and cold—very cold. For a long time, I huddled up in a ball trying to keep warm; then suddenly I realized I was completely naked! There was a bare mattress beneath me—I could feel the cheap cover fabric and large tufted buttons! Startled, I sat up, suddenly realizing what had happened—I had been kidnapped by the Stasi and was now in one of their prisons in East Berlin. Where else could I be? Who else would kidnap me?

I began trembling and shaking out of fear. My pulse began pounding in my ears and I felt my throat constrict. Nausea caused me to roll over, lurch forward, and vomit over the top of the bed onto the floor. After lying back down, I began hallucinating; soon, they came in—the Stasi officers I'd helped restrain in Papa's bar became shadows moving around the dark room. I grabbed the mattress on both sides, attempting to wrap it around me. I wanted to cover my nakedness and protect myself from them. "I cannot stand it in here!" I screamed at the shadows. "Let me out! Let me out now! Please!" My screams continued for what seemed like hours, only stopping after my throat began to swell.

My ears continued to ring for what seemed like an eternity. Eventually, deep breathing helped me to calm down. It took much longer to regain rational thought, probably because of the drugs still in my system. *They have undressed you and placed you in this dark room to intimidate you*, I told myself. *You must regain your composure or they will have won. You must not let them overwhelm you.*

Not knowing how long I'd been here and unable to sleep, I stood and felt block walls as I circled the room. Soon I found the metal door. There was a handle, but no latch. The door was locked or bolted from the outside. Bending over, I could feel a solid smooth cement floor. By standing on the bed, I could not touch the ceiling, and the room had no windows or other openings. There was no toilet. After placing the bed in one corner, I leaned against the wall and urinated on the floor. Exhausted, I lay down on the bed and managed to go to sleep.

Later, I awakened slowly from a deep sleep and realized I needed to defecate. Once finished, I wished I'd resisted this bodily demand. The stench was unbearable. Burying my face in the mattress was the only way to avoid the smell.

By putting the bed in the middle of the room and avoiding that corner with the vomit and fecal material, I was eventually able to walk around the room slowly—then was able to increase my pace, by putting my arms out and touching the walls. Eventually, I stepped in my own feces. As best I could, I scraped it off on the rough block wall. The stench increased. Moving the bed to the far corner, I tried to sleep, but could not—counting seconds, then minutes did nothing to help acclimate me to my circumstance. Sleep eventually came and soon I was home safely in bed making love with my husband. I awoke and, despite my surroundings, satisfied myself.

This time when I awoke, I had difficulty swallowing and my eyes were dry. Until this point, I had avoided thinking about how thirsty I was. My body was conserving fluids, and I hadn't peed for a long time. Rolling over on my side in an attempt to get enough saliva to moisten my mouth did no good. Were the Stasi going to kill me by depriving me of water? I remembered an article in the Spiegel about hunger strikers in India; they could last only ten days without water.

I constantly wondered how many days I had been in this cell. I had no time reference, so all I knew was that was more than one and not yet ten.

CHAPTER 113

Kurt
Monday, February 15, 1960

THE WEST GERMAN Federal Intelligence Agency had an office in the Charlottenburg District of Berlin. I had been there many times for meetings with my counterparts in that organization. My urgent summons to a meeting in their office surprised me. When I arrived, I was escorted into a conference room. Wilhelm Werner shook my hand firmly and then turned to another man in the room. "I would like to introduce you to someone you have heard of, but perhaps have never met—Reinhard Gantz, my boss."

"Nice to finally meet you," Herr Gantz said, "We asked you to join us because Herr Werner's daughter disappeared off of the streets of West Berlin at about midnight last Wednesday. We assume she has been kidnapped by the Stasi in retaliation for her parents' extraction from the East. Similar disappearances occur every year, and it is always the Stasi or Russians who are responsible. We were hoping you had someone who could confirm they have her and perhaps even tell us where she is being held."

Since most of the operatives in our East German spy apparatus were recruited based on General Gantz's recommendation, I took his request seriously and immediately thought about Peter and the cards the Stasi maintained on everyone in the East who got their attention. Natalie's card should tell us what had happened to her.

"Wilhelm, you probably remember I was concerned your daughter was not safe here in West Berlin. We'll do our best. I will of course only tell you she is over there—any other information might compromise our sources."

CHAPTER 114

Natalie
Thursday, February 18, 1960

TRYING TO SAY words aloud became difficult. My head pounded. I had given up trying to figure out why they were doing this to me; I no longer cared. I envisioned I must be near the seventh or eighth day—death could not be far off.

I dozed awhile and awoke feeling sad. My life was ruined. *Only twenty-eight years old and I am going to die. We had almost saved enough money to purchase our own apartment. Soon I could have worked part-time and we could have started a family. If a Stasi offers me a drink of water, I will refuse. It would be better to die now than spend years in this prison. I would miss my husband, but why go on? Why struggle? Why live when there is no future?*

Occasionally, I thought I had heard noises outside the door. They were always brief, and I convinced myself I was just imagining them. Hallucinations had been my only companion for a long time. At first, I thought this was just another of those—metal clunking against the door. Then, as I sat up, a blinding light came through the open door. I shielded my eyes with one hand, then instinctively covered my breasts with my other arm, and moved so my crotch was hidden from view.

Two men entered the room—the first I had seen since my capture. Then, a familiar voice said, "Fraulein Werner, our first encounter was very unpleasant for my associate and me," a man spoke. "We wanted you to experience what we experienced at your hands. I'm sure your husband and parents are as worried about you as our families were about us."

After struggling to focus my eyes enough to see the man who was talking, I finally recognized them—Stasi Agents Klein and Becker.

"You handcuffed us and placed us in that sealed room," Klein continued. "It took us several hours to remove the gags. The door was well hidden and our efforts to attract the attention of those investigating your crimes were unsuccessful for six days. When they finally found us, we were so thirsty that we made ourselves sick by drinking more water than our bodies could tolerate. Here is a five-liter container filled with water. Drink as much as you want."

"They even thought we had defected to the West, we were missing for so long," Becker added.

"What of my clothes?" I did not get an answer as they walked out of the door, locked it, plunging the room into total darkness. I rushed over, took the heavy jug in hand, and guzzled down some. Then I poured some over my foot. In the process, I spilled too much, vowing to conserve this vital resource in the future.

CHAPTER 115

Kurt
Tuesday, February 20, 1960

MAJOR CRAIG NEVER returned from his Christmas work trip back to the States. It was mid-January before I heard that he had applied for compassionate reassignment. His wife didn't want to bring their three children to Berlin and threatened to divorce him unless he refused the assignment. He felt this assignment was an important step towards his next promotion, so he decided to come unaccompanied. His wife acted on her threat. Eventually, the military approved his request.

The new engineering manager wasn't scheduled to arrive for several months, so Mark Powell and I got together in the tank to discuss what we should do about the apartment house on Kopenicker Strasse.

"In my limited free time, I've continued to look around for another structure which could serve as the entrance to the tunnel, and the only other viable candidate in that area is a large vacant lot one block further south," I said.

"I don't think we want to have to build a building in the middle of Berlin before we can start to work," Mark said.

"I concur. Here is what I propose: a large insurance company located in Zurich recently purchased our building as a long-term investment. They paid forty million Deutsche Marks. If we offer them a huge profit, they'll probably take it, because it will look good on their profit/loss statement this year. As you know, half of the money for the construction of the tunnel is in the CIA's European operations budget. I'm going to Zurich next week to make them an offer."

*

A dead-drop message Andreas had retrieved from Peter's basement was waiting in my office. Once decoded, it read, "Natalie (Emilia) Vogel (nee, Werner) is currently being held in the basement of Stasi Headquarters in the Lichtenberg District—Her trial for espionage is yet to be scheduled." I notified her father immediately using the KY-7 scrambler phone.

I'd only gotten her involved because her parents were so closely guarded day and night. It was the only way I could figure to contact them in advance of the escape, which was essential for our plan to work.

CHAPTER 116

Natalie
Tuesday, March 20, 1960

NOW THEY WERE giving me as much water in a bucket as I wanted. Still no food or clothing. Endless time passed as I became thinner, but I was no longer hungry.

Suddenly, I was startled awake when two men invaded my cell, removed my mattress, and used a fire hose to wash my naked body and cell. It was the first time this had happened; I had been living in my own filth until now. The force of the water stung as I cowered in a ball in the far corner of the cell. The drain in the middle of the room backed up until water covered the whole floor. The men laughed at me. "This is the way they clean the monkey cages at the zoo," one said. "Frustrated animals in a zoo masturbate. Why don't you show us what you got, bitch?"

"How could you two be so depraved," I screamed at them. "Kill me. Death is preferable to this degradation."

Before they locked me back in the cell, they threw a different mattress at me. It was filthy; soon I realized it was infested with some type of live vermin. I didn't have a choice—the concrete floor in my cell was so cold I had to use the mattress. I passed the time finding the bugs on my body and squashing them. My skin became raw and inflamed.

I was never given food. Over time, my entire body became emaciated, and my belly became distended almost as if I were pregnant; this I knew was impossible because I had experienced my monthly cycle shortly after they kidnapped me. The next time they washed my cell, one of the men said, "Even your husband would probably have a problem getting it up for you, you ugly, skinny broad. You are repulsive!" Somehow, I could not help repeating that insult to myself in my waking hours and again when I dozed.

Then they began turning the lights on for a few seconds or minutes, and then off for hours. I craved the light. "Please leave the light on. I need light!" I screamed.

They eventually added a bucket for me to relieve myself in, two buckets—such luxury—but still no food. I had not defecated in a long time. They took the bucket I relieved myself in but did not clean it before they put a large portion of porridge into it. It was the first food I had been given and I was ravenous—taking giant handfuls in each hand, gulping them down. In minutes, I vomited up most of what I'd consumed. I then resolved to make this meager fare last as long as possible.

CHAPTER 117

Kurt
Monday, April 11, 1960

I FLEW TO Zurich to deal directly with the owners of what ultimately became known as "the building." Modern Switzerland was prosperous, looking like Germany had before the war. All those lives and treasure had been wasted in the madman Hitler's grasp for glory.

The bureaucracy in the insurance company was very easy to deal with, and more efficient than the Soviet officials I'd been working with for the last 13 years. Still, it took almost the whole day before I could present my proposal to the ultimate decision-maker, Herr Liam Leuzinger. His office had a commanding view of the city. His three-piece suit and turned-up collar reminded me of my father on his way to a meeting at the Bundestag thirty years ago.

"I represent a group of people, including my father, who fled Germany at the behest of the Nazis," I said once Leuzinger and I were seated comfortably in his office. "Fortunately, they managed to get their money to America and have lived there since. They want to help their homeland get back on its feet. We learned your company owns the property at 576 Kopenicker Strasse in Berlin. They are willing to offer you forty-five million Deutsche marks for a quick sale."

"So far, we've spent almost one million Deutsche Marks in demolition and restoration costs," he said, acting every bit the hidebound, reserved Swiss banker.

He probably knew I'd determined what his company had paid for the building. Plus, they had waited a year and paid some tenants money to leave their leases—so there had been significant expenses.

"We both know you will have to make a substantial investment before the building is safe for occupancy. My investors want to return that building to its previous glory, including the restaurant on the roof that overlooks the River Spree. It was once the finest in Berlin."

"I'll need to consult my partners before I can tell you if we are interested and what we might want to receive in remuneration. Can my secretary bring you some refreshments—coffee or tea?"

"Coffee with a little sugar would be nice."

Fearing they would reject my offer out of hand, I let out a sigh of relief once he left the room.

Leuzinger reentered the room shortly after, with his young secretary following closely behind him. She quietly placed the coffee on the table before me and smiled kindly before closing the door behind her.

"You, of course, know the south end of the building must be replaced," Luezinger said as I took a small sip from the cup. "I'll be frank with you. The cost estimate we received from a contractor was more than we had originally estimated. We are honest people who don't want to take advantage of your investors. We have over forty-two and a half million Deutsche Marks invested at this point. Give us an eight-million-mark profit and you have a deal. Oh, and we want the deal to be concluded by June 30, 1960. We are a publicly-traded company, and this will allow us to record the profit in this quarter."

I didn't want to appear too eager to conclude the deal, so I said, "That is significantly more than I'm authorized to pay. Can I call my head investor's office in New York?"

"Use the phone in the conference room next door," the banker said as his index finger pointed behind him to a door. "Give my secretary the phone number and she will make the connection."

I called my father, who had been aware I might call him. I spent some time providing details on the deal. In reply, he mouthed his previously agreed lines: "Don't pay more than fifty million Deutsche Marks. Understand?"

"Yes sir," I replied.

We agreed on the escrow company in Zurich that would handle the transaction and the title company in Berlin that would take care of the title transfer. Leuzinger and I shook hands; I left overjoyed that our largest difficulty in building the tunnel had been solved.

The next morning, I flew to Frankfurt and had a CIA staff car transport me to the I. G. Farben Building. The security office verified my identity and issued me a badge. I'd called earlier to make an appointment with Fred Huddlestone, the comptroller of the CIA for all of Europe.

"Line item 314-278 in our budget is for a program I'm working on," I told him after settling in his office. "Details about this program are limited on a need-to-know basis and I'm currently the only one in Europe who knows the details. There will be other disbursements that I will request you make from time to time. At this point in time, Director Dulles, two other individuals in Washington, and I are the only ones who are cleared for the details."

He sifted through a bunch of papers before him. "I see the item number and a large amount of money on that line."

"Okay, here's what I need you to do. Make out a check for 50 million Deutsche Marks from one of your covert accounts and send it to this address, referencing the transaction number on this piece of paper. Select one of our covert-holding companies as the new owner. Send all the details of this transaction via courier to me in the care of our Berlin Office."

"I'd do as you request, except I received instruction directly from my boss in Washington that none of these funds can be disbursed without the express written permission of the Director of Operations."

I was stunned. *Those son-of-a-bitches—Frank Collins and Thomas Lane—they made it clear that no tunnel was preferable to one controlled by the DoD—petty bureaucrats—bastards—as far as they were concerned, the defense of their country and doing the right thing were unimportant—getting ahead politically was all-important to them.*

CHAPTER 118

Natalie
Tuesday, April 5-Monday, April 18, 1960

A LEERING MALE guard entered my cell, handed me a smock, and told me to put it on. He then led me to a room down a long hall and showed me a seat. Bright spotlights shining in my eyes prevented me from seeing who else was in the room. Soon my interrogation began. I refused to answer the two men's questions despite their constant cajoling and threats. Eventually, I was returned to my cell by the same guard. As I went through the door, he grabbed the collar of my smock; its buttons popped as he tore it off of me. I cowered in one corner fearing he would rape me. After he left, I discovered that the bed frame, mattress, and buckets were gone—my only choice was to stand, sit or lie on the bare, cold concrete floor.

After what seemed an interminable period of time, but was probably only a day or two, I began yearning to get back into that interrogation room. This time I was led down the hall naked, but allowed to put on a clean smock which hung over my spotlighted chair. I spent what seemed like hours telling them what I knew: Papa's recruitment, the long period while I took Papa's reports to Berlin, and how Mama and Papa had been rescued. I did not tell them of my brother's involvement, the names of the few of Papa's fellow spies I knew, nor did I tell them about my ex-boyfriend Michael, or when the tall man stayed in our gasthaus. Those secrets I intended to take to my grave. The coffee they gave me must have been drugged.

When I next woke up, I was naked in a different, lighted cell that had obviously been disinfected. I was so weak, I dozed off again. Eventually, I realized that I had been sleeping on a relatively clean mattress, between sheets, and also had a blanket! A washcloth, soap, toothbrush, tooth powder, and a towel were on a small table adjacent to two buckets of water. After cleaning myself as much as possible, I felt better—maybe cooperating with them was my only logical choice.

They began to feed me gruel and water with an occasional piece of bread and sausage. The lights were turned on and off in what seemed like varying periods of time.

For my next interrogation, they kept the spotlights off as they went over my previous statements. One man asked me questions in a polite manner, as another would take over and intimidate me; he even went behind me, threatening to hit me. I still had no concept of time, but this session went on for what must have been seven or eight hours straight. I was exhausted when it was over.

This time they took me back to my cell and I was allowed to keep the smock, and also, the bath slippers I'd been given.

CHAPTER 119

Kurt
Tuesday, May 3, 1960

FOR OVER TWO weeks, I tried to communicate with CIA headquarters to get the funds released. Yesterday, I applied for a ticket to fly to Washington and was told by our local comptroller I needed to talk to Ian, the station chief.

"You remember last fall when I went back to Washington on short notice?" I asked Ian.

"Yes, of course. You never did tell me what that was about," he replied.

"Well, I'm going to walk a fine line here, so you'll have to be patient with me. Director Dulles assigned me to do my normal duties here and also a special, highly classified project. At this point in time, only four people in the CIA know about it. I'll need special permission to get you briefed on it, which I will try to do ASAP. In the interim, it looks like the only way I can do my job is to go to Washington and confront people at the Director of Operations level; these two guys are preventing me from completing the critical first step. I can tell you this—it's primarily a DoD project and certain people in the headquarters want to subvert a presidential decision on this matter. They perceive that if they delay until the new President is elected, they will be able to take over most or all of this highly important project."

Ian sighed, releasing an exhaustive breath. "Politics," he said. "I hate politicians and their hidden agendas; most of those bastards at the headquarters love to cause problems for no good reason. Please, go on."

"You know how Washington hides money for our activities in various places in the budget?"

"Sure."

"Well, half the money for this program is hidden in our budget under a line called Sustaining Operations. The DoD's half of the money is going primarily to pay for the personnel to complete this activity. It makes sense for us to use our money to make a large real estate purchase. We only have until 30 June to complete this transaction. I've been working on it for months. If we don't complete the purchase, it will set the whole program back months."

"I understand," Ian said.

"Our comptroller in Frankfort indicates the Director of Operations in Washington has frozen those funds. I worked for two weeks without success to get them unfrozen from this end. Looks like I'll have to fly to Washington and perhaps even talk to Mr. Dulles himself to get this problem solved. Oh, and now I'm being told by Harry I can't fly there using my usual time charge."

"Who are the two individuals causing the problem?"

"Frank Collins and Thomas Lane," I replied.

"I know both of them and consider them to be as worthless as tits on a boar hog," Ian said, laughing uncomfortably. "Typical ne'er-do-wells and hangers-on found in every large organization. Politicians both; they'd trade their own mother for a small political advantage. If they'd spend as much time doing their assigned jobs as they do stomping on others to get ahead, the whole headquarters would function much more effectively. They're toadies of the bastard, Herbert Zales, who's now our newly appointed acting Director of Operations. I wish our old Chief, Harold Simmons, had stayed until the new administration came into power in January. I guess you can't blame him; he would have been out of a job in seven months."

Ian pulled out a sheet of paper and began scribbling a long number down. "Here's my contingency fund charge number. Take whatever time is required to get this situation fixed. You'll find that Director Dulles is trying to keep the ship afloat until January. You will undoubtedly step on some toes, so be careful."

CHAPTER 120

Natalie
Wednesday, May 4, 1960

TODAY WAS THE worst day so far. The water they gave me must have been drugged again because I awoke to the sound of clanking metal and was again naked, the smock covering my body was nowhere to be found. Two uniformed guards rushed through the door, grabbed me, and took me out into an open area surrounded by cells and interrogation rooms on all four sides. Hundreds of men were being forced out of their cells. The guard who held my arm faced the other cellmates. "Gentlemen!" he screamed. "This prisoner has requested each of you satisfy her in any way you want to or can." He made sure my private parts were fully exposed to the view of each inmate as they slowly and forcibly paraded me around the cavernous room.

The other inmates just stared at me. I was surprised when only a few made lewd comments. Almost all of them were dressed in filthy clothes. All were in need of a shave or haircut. Several had long, ragged beards that did not appear to have been trimmed for months or even years. Many, if not most, were obviously infirmed, and showed external signs of physical and mental abuse and torture. *How long have these poor men been kept in here? They are all men. I must be the only woman here!*

Most of them cowered in silence, but one apparently demented individual dared to lurch forward, trying to grab my exposed breasts. I was horrified, stripped of any dignity I had left. The guard beat the man to the floor with the truncheon he carried in his other hand. After everyone got an eye full, I was escorted to the interview room I'd been in before. The smock again rested on the back of the chair. I hurriedly put it on, along with the bath slippers that were on the floor.

The Stasi agent who always acted friendly said, "Natalie, we really don't want to harm you, but as you can tell, we are the only ones that are protecting you from those savage beasts out there. You probably cannot even imagine what would happen if we were to open your cell door for a few days and let them visit you one by one. You might survive, but would you want to? You would probably be diseased. Would your husband still want you after they are finished?"

His smooth, calm tone of voice had its desired effect. "Ask your questions again and I'll tell you everything I know," I said, my last defenses crumbling. "In return, I only request a few simple facts: How long have I been in here? What day is it? What time is it?"

Now I told them the full name of some of Papa's operatives from ten to twelve years ago. I knew one of them had died and another had immigrated to the West—the third I didn't know about; I hoped that somehow, he was safe.

Recently, an acquaintance from the old days told me Michael had become a communist party member and was now the leader of a large, official East German workers organization. I freely gave them his full name, age, and told how I had photographed documents he had provided. I did not owe Michael anything—in fact, if I could deal him a little grief, all the better.

I was not able to remember the address of the safe house the tall man and I went to before my parents were extracted. I described the outside and approximate location.

They undoubtedly knew where my parents and brother were, so I told them. They even admitted they knew my father was working for General Gantz, saying they wished he and his men "were on the right side." The gruff man added, "We have a tacit agreement with our counterpart in the West that we will leave their families alone and they will reciprocate. You are the one exception we have made—locking our director's brother-in-law in that basement was not acceptable behavior."

I told them everything about the tall man, including his missing right earlobe. If I failed to add that his earlobe seems to have been repaired the last time I saw him, that was for them to figure out. "I don't know his name, never heard it." I looked up at them convincingly. "The first name of the man who drove the staff car we escaped in is Kurt. That is everything I know. Now tell me, what day is it?"

"May 4, 1960."

"So, I've been your captive for three months. What day of the week is it?"

"Wednesday."

"What time is it?"

"A little after 17:00," the man who had always tried to act friendly said, taking his watch out of his pocket and putting it on his wrist.

"Thank you."

"Now that was not so bad, was it?"

Speechless, I just stared at my two interrogators. *You're both bastards.*

"Are you going to give me a trial and convict me so I can experience the wonders of communism for another decade or two?"

"No."

"Then just kill me now. I no longer want to live in this hell hole."

"Young lady, you have a much different fate, believe me," the belligerent interrogator said in a friendly tone. He rose and banged on the door. A guard showed me back to my cell.

CHAPTER 121

Kurt
Wednesday, May 4, 1960

I ARRIVED AT CIA headquarters in Washington before eight this morning, intending on solving my Program LUMAR problem and returning to Berlin as soon as possible. First, I determined that the offices of Frank Collins, Thomas Lane, and Acting Operations Director Zales were all in the headquarters building. Neither of the junior men had a secretary or a big office, so I decided they were probably of equal rank to me.

Since we had spent a lot of time together in Berlin and while I was stationed here three years earlier, Brandon Williams was my closest friend and business associate. I found his office. He immediately jumped to his feet, giving me a huge bear hug and said, "You old-son-of-a-gun, still in Berlin…"

Eventually, I explained my problem to him and we discussed how to best solve it. Soon he called Mr. Dulles' secretary, arranging a meeting with him for 14:00, then invited Frank Collins and Thomas Lane to also attend.

At 13:45 I knocked on Lane's office door. He was shocked when he saw me.

"Has Herbert Zales been cleared for Project LUMAR?" I asked him the moment he opened the door. Obviously flustered, he fumbled for a response. "Well, I…what're you doing here?… You're not supposed to be here…"

"My question requires a simple yes or no answer, Lane. If the Operations Director has been cleared for LUMAR, we need to ensure he attends today's meeting. If not, then everyone in the CIA who's cleared for the LUMAR Program will be in the Director's office so we can solve a pressing problem."

Still trying to regain his composure, Lane sat down at his desk and picked up the phone receiver. I pressed down on the phone cradle, hanging up his call. "Letting your co-conspirator Frank Collins know in advance the subject of our meeting will only create problems. By not answering my question, you've in effect answered in the negative. Get your suit coat and let's start a leisurely walk to the big boss's office."

Once we were in the Director's conference room, I said, "Thomas, relax. All that's going to happen to your little plan is failure. I'm not going to rub your and Frank's nose in it. Wait and see how a professional conducts himself."

Collins entered the conference room, looked at me, then at Thomas and said, "What's he doing here?" Thomas held his arms out and shrugged his shoulders, indicating he didn't know anything. For the next few minutes, the three of us sat in silence, staring daggers at each other.

Dulles entered the room five minutes late. "We are obviously here to discuss LUMAR. How can I help you gentlemen today?" he said, looking each of us in the eye and then taking his normal place at the head of the conference table.

"Ian Simpson sent me here to clear up a few matters that need not concern us here," I said for the group. "The reason I requested this meeting is so I could inform you that we have found an apartment building that is ideal as an entrance for the tunnel. It's a large, old apartment house right on the River Spree. Since it was built in the 1870s, it has a huge basement instead of a parking garage. In conjunction with the Air Force, a definitive plan has been generated; it calls for the construction of a fifty-five foot deep pit, which will house a large freight elevator. The entrance to the tunnel will start at that level and clear the bottom of the River Spree by about 20 feet. We can store the dirt in the basement until it can be hauled off. Once the tunnel's finished, we can turn part of the building into an exploitation center and rent out the rest, or even use it to house the people who work there."

"It sounds like the Air Force team and you have solved all of our problems," Dulles said.

"I was able to negotiate a purchase price of fifty million Deutsche Marks—more than twelve million dollars," I said.

"That sounds like a bargain. I still don't know what the problem is," Dulles said, looking unsure.

"The comptroller of all European CIA funds indicates that Mr. Zales has directed that no funds be distributed from the LUMAR line item without his express written direction. Since he isn't cleared for this program, there must be some mistake. I need to pay for this apartment house ASAP."

Dulles looked straight at Lane and Collins, who had stayed quiet so far. "Do either of you have any idea how this happened?"

Both of them looked like two young boys who had got caught stealing apples from someone's orchard. "I can look into it for you, sir," Collins offered, almost stammering.

Smelling a rat, Dulles said, "Never mind. I'll have my administrative assistant take care of this problem."

"Mr. Dulles, given the urgency of this program, we should do two things," I said. "Have my boss Ian cleared and made responsible for managing this line item to prevent similar problems in the future."

"Good idea," Dulles said, brought his briefcase onto his lap, and pulled out his planning calendar. "I have a free half-hour in the morning—08:30. I'll invite my administrative assistant, and together we'll take care of all the financial and security problems; Agents Collins and Lane, you don't need to attend that meeting."

Once we were out of earshot of the director's office, Collins blocked my way and ran his index finger across his throat. "That's your death warrant, Altschuler. Your career's over. Mr. Allen 'straight shooter' Dulles will only be here for another seven months. When the new administration takes over, those of us in the know will take over this place and run it right."

"I'll continue to do what's really right and hope the likes of you and Lane here eventually get what you've got coming," I said, forcefully shoving him out of my way.

Lane stood there in silence, like a spectator at a prizefight.

CHAPTER 122

Natalie
Friday, May 6, 1960

THIS MORNING, THE first female guard I had seen took me to a modern bathroom. She stood outside the door after giving me instructions to thoroughly clean myself. A variety of products lay on a wooden shelf. I gloried in the warm water and shampoo. After washing myself thoroughly for the third time, I tried to use the razor they had provided to shave my legs, but it was soon very dull. After I cut myself several times, I gave up. The cuts and nicks looked awful, but I did not care. My hair was full of rat tails and needed to be cut. As I tried to brush through it, several teeth in the comb broke off and pulled out some hair. Looking in the mirror, fussing with my hair, I almost felt human again.

Carefully looking around the corner into the next alcove, I saw clean clothes folded on a bench. I put on cheap underwear, a cotton dress that hung on me, and flat slippers. I waited, smiling and occasionally hugging myself. *What have they got in store for me now?*

Eventually, the female guard escorted me back to the central courtyard, and into what I thought of as my interrogation room. My two tormentors sat in their usual places.

"Natalie, as you can see, we can be very reasonable with people who cooperate with us. Would you like fruit juice and perhaps an egg and rolls?"

"Yes, please," I replied.

I refused to exchange pleasantries with them as I consumed my breakfast. I gulped down the large glass of orange juice and began feeling drowsy.

The next thing I remember was waking up, strapped into the same chair. My right bicep hurt. Since my hands were free, I discovered an adhesive bandage attached to the place where my arm ached.

The gruff man was now very friendly when he said, "We used one of our little helpers to ensure you had told us everything. You can now go back to your cell."

Later, it hit me; they had used a truth serum on me. I began to worry about what I'd told them. Perhaps they had learned something they could use against me in my trial. That night I lay awake, worrying about what they now knew. It is one thing to know what they knew; the uncertainty over what they might have learned was extremely disconcerting.

From this point on my treatment improved; I was given a cell with a light switch I could control, books to read, a small desk and chair, plus a bed with a thick mattress, sheets, and a blanket. It was paradise compared to what I'd known to this point.

CHAPTER 123

Kurt
Friday, June 17, 1960

LT. COL. MARK Powell and I met again in the tank. After each of us got a cup of coffee from a carafe on a small table, we began sharing our news. I went first. "We closed escrow on the building on Monday of this week. That took a substantial slice out of the CIA's share of the budget, but we still have almost ten million left—so when you need money, let me know and I'll have it transferred into the appropriate accounts."

"Unfortunately, my organization hasn't been able to produce a civil engineer with the right mix of experience and security clearance," Powell said. "It apparently takes months for the extensive background investigation to be completed. I've asked that they expedite the process and perhaps process more than one candidate at a time. We're out here at the end of a long chain and will just have to learn to be patient."

"I didn't tell you, but the entire southeast end of the building will have to be replaced," I said. "We now own the building; perhaps, we need to get some German contractors to make repairs before our engineer arrives."

"We have finite funding, so I'd prefer we wait. If we do something that must be modified or destroyed later, we'd regret it. The new guy will be here in the next few months, don't worry."

CHAPTER 124

Natalie
Wednesday, June 29, 1960

TODAY I WAS allowed to shower for the fifth time. The razor worked because it was no longer trying to negotiate months of stubble. When I looked in the dressing room this time, I saw everything I'd been wearing when I was kidnapped—including my wristwatch and purse, money, keys, and address book. All seem to be as I remembered them from months earlier. I dressed hurriedly, hoping something would happen to get me out of this awful place. I had lost a lot of weight but must have gained most of it back as my clothes fit, although a little loose in places.

The female guard escorted me up a ramp to a waiting sedan. My two interrogators sat on either side of me in the back seat and tried to make small talk. I answered with silence or one-syllable words.

We drove through unfamiliar parts of Berlin. After almost half an hour, we stopped in front of the barrier that prevented vehicles from crossing a body of water and got out. I soon recognized the River Spree. *That is the border between East and West Berlin in this area. Are they just playing a trick on me, or are they actually going to release me?*

Using hand gestures, my captors directed me around the barrier and part way across before directing me to stop. They stood by me the entire way. The gruff Stasi agent touched my shoulder and said, "We are getting three of our best spies back in return for you. My government is certainly getting the best part of this bargain. Once you arrive over there, ask them about our people captured in your Operation Hedgerow."

After a brief pause, he continued, "Natalie, we have confirmed that they are returning our three. You can continue across the bridge alone now."

I counted my steps as I saw three individuals start in my direction. *One, two, three, four, five.*

I thought about running but realized this was a ritual in which I must perform my part.

Fourteen, fifteen, sixteen, seventeen. This cannot be real. This has to be another dream. I'll wake up soon or someone behind me will rush out and stop me.

Do not look back—you do not care what is back there. Your future is ahead of you. Thirty, thirty-one, thirty-two, thirty-three.

I tried to recognize someone in the crowd waiting for me—was the man standing to the right of the crowd Papa?

Fifty-three, fifty-four, fifty-five.

The end of the bridge was just a short distance. I could finally make out the faces of Papa and my husband, Ernst. I ran into their arms crying. "Safe, I'm finally safe," I whispered. If they had not supported me, I would certainly have fallen to the ground from emotional exhaustion. That man Kurt had certainly been right—Berlin was not a safe place for me. I would never feel safe in this city again.

CHAPTER 125

Kurt
Thursday, June 30, 1960

WILHELM WARNER CALLED me this morning, asking if we could meet somewhere. I suggested a park near my office, and he was waiting on a bench when I arrived.

"I just wanted to personally thank you for helping us get my daughter Natalie out of Stasi hell." He then spent some time describing her ordeal in detail. It was horrifying. "We are taking her to Munich with us today. She will certainly need therapy before she can live a normal life. Those bastards wanted revenge on all of us who helped Germany remain free. I wonder if those cock-suckers will ever be forced to account for their misdeeds."

"I hope so Wilhelm—I truly hope so. If you or yours ever need help of any form from America, let me know."

"General...er...Mr. Gantz has assured me our government will provide the financial and other support we need to get Natalie back to normal, if humanly possible."

He looked at me with deep concern, the kind seen in a father who only wants the best for his children. On occasion, I have also had that look.

"Kurt,' he said as he got up to leave, "if there is ever anything I can do for you, just let me know. My organization also has contacts on both sides of the border, which are increasing in size and effectiveness daily."

CHAPTER 126

Thursday, October 20-Monday October 24, 1960

FOR OVER THREE months, Mark had been assuring me that the civil engineering lead we'd been expecting would arrive any day. Today, I went over to Tempelhof for a kick-off meeting with the new arrival, whose name was Captain Robert Kerr. Mark, and their security guy, Captain Scott Taylor, who I had met months ago when I'd picked up my badge, also attended the meeting.

Although Captain Kerr was very personable, he was also very young. He was a tall Californian with an athletic build, and his light-brown hair was sun-streaked. He was bound to be disappointed with Berlin—we seldom got more than three or four full to partially sunny days a month in the winter.

During the meeting, he readily admitted his experience level was below what was required for the job. Apparently, he was the only one with the right clearance who was available.

We began by discussing the security threat; Robert immediately grasped the ramifications and complexities of the problem, and by the end of the day, he asked questions I'd failed to grasp. Since our cover was remodeling a building in the middle of a residential district, we were going to need a large number of native German-speaking construction workers. Scott indicated German-born American citizens probably couldn't get cleared for the LUMAR program. Mark agreed to tackle that problem.

During our tour of "the building," Robert demonstrated a grasp of its condition and understood the concept of a pit and elevator tunnel.

Overall, I was impressed. This young man would get the job done. He knew his stuff—he just needed some support and encouragement.

The following week, I took care of several pressing problems for my associates, including getting the existing building permit withdrawn by having the military government declare 'the building' U.S. government-owned property.

CHAPTER 127

Thursday, October 27, 1960

AT MI6'S REQUEST, I flew to London and gave a deposition in the matter of the upcoming spy trial of George Blake. The British had finally determined Blake had been working for the KGB for at least seventeen years. His trial in the Old Bailey was set for next year. The proceedings would be in camera, that is, in secret, but I was still concerned the British hadn't sealed all of their leaks.

"For the last three years, you have been Operations Manager of CIA station Berlin," the Crown Court Prosecutor asked me. "Is that correct?

"Yes, and altogether I have spent thirteen years in Berlin since arriving there in 1946," I said.

"Tell us when you first met George Blake."

"I was in charge of the construction of the tunnel that CIA/MI6 jointly built in Berlin; it had the codewords GOLD/STOPWATCH associated with it. George had been asked to take notes at a kick-off meeting we had here in London."

"The tunnel's existence was discovered by the KGB in April of 1956."

"Correct. I have no proof, but I suspected George told the KGB about the tunnel in 1954. To protect him as the source, they waited until 1956 to 'accidentally,' that is "on purpose," discover the tunnel. They only dug in one spot in the middle of a rural road. It was almost as if they already knew where their target was and weren't even interested in trying to hide their source with some type of subterfuge."

"Okay. You met him a second time in August of 1957 when you returned to Berlin to take up your current position."

"Correct. The Operations Chief in the CIA has the job of directing the covert operations in that station's area of responsibility. George had the same position at your MI6 station in Berlin. I became suspicious he might be a double agent. I plotted out the exact dates from 1953 through 1958 when MI6 and we lost operatives. The losses increased substantially shortly after George arrived in Berlin. The ones we lost had been providing the most valuable information from our viewpoint. It looked to me as if someone was selecting their targets from a definitive list of candidates."

"Can you tell us how many individuals were compromised in this way?"

"From what I could tell, your organization lost thirty-nine and we lost about twenty-seven."

Would you be surprised if I told you we have definitive proof that the true number is forty-two MI6 agents and senior operatives? Almost our entire intelligence collection network in central Europe was lost."

"That's entirely possible," I replied.

"On December 14, 1957, you made contact with friends in MI6 to warn they had a double agent at the top level of the MI6 office in Berlin. Why did you do that?"

"I had unequivocal proof George was a double agent."

"Yet you failed to provide MI6 with that proof."

"Correct. The proof was derived from information provided by an operative who was working in deep cover. I could not then nor will I now reveal the nature or source of that information." A picture of a young Peter just after he returned from Russia came to mind. He deserved a lot better than he has ever gotten in life.

"You allowed other people to suffer from George's treachery."

"In my position, one's forced to make life-and-death decisions every day. I selected the best choice from a number of unattractive options."

"Thank you, Mr. Altschuler, that will be all."

CHAPTER 128

Thursday, December 8-Wednesday, December 14, 1960

MY CIA SUBORDINATES and I continued to direct operatives, gather data, and generate reports. Nothing unique or unusual had happened for several months. I liked it that way. The fact that we hadn't suffered any losses for over four months was especially gratifying.

A month ago, young Captain Kerr had informed everyone in Berlin he had convinced the people in Washington to agree that a ramp along the East wall down to a tunnel entrance, and then all the way under the building, was a better solution for building this tunnel. If the Army Corp of Engineers and Robert thought that a good solution, I wasn't going to question that decision. They had to do the work.

After the meeting, Robert handed me a stack of paper. "We need you to acquire all of the construction equipment and supplies on this list from local sources," he said. "I've provided specification sheets or other data to ensure we get what we need. New or used, doesn't make any difference, as long as they're serviceable."

I had business cards in the name of Klaus Wagner, GmbH printed, put on my entrepreneur's outfit—which was actually one of my best suits—and began contacting people in the building trades. "I am new to Berlin and want to establish a new company. I will purchase the equipment first and then add workers when my company is awarded contracts," I told them. I was able to acquire all the equipment from Captain Kerr's list at reasonable prices, and even bought a defunct construction company that owned most of the equipment we needed.

After explaining what I had done, Robert asked, "Where's this facility located?"

"Perhaps three miles southwest of our tunnel building in an area of similar businesses."

After a big sigh of relief, Robert said, "As far as I can tell, we're finally ready to go. The construction crew, including thirteen German-speaking workers, are scheduled to arrive in January and then we can start construction."

*

Six days later, I was in the tank conference room at Tempelhof when Thomas Lane entered. He and the other two members of the management triumvirate—General Harrison and Gerald Scherman—had been tasked with oversight of the tunnel program; they were in Berlin to give final approval of the project before construction began. Thomas' handshake with me was perfunctory, from time to time throughout the meeting he stared at me with obvious hostility.

Robert concluded his briefing by saying, "As you can see, we're ready to start construction, all we need is your approval."

At this point, Thomas stood and banged his fist on the conference table and asked, "Are we just going to rubber-stamp young Captain Kerr's ramp plan? Before he arrived, the tunnel was over 400 feet shorter and required half the workforce! Plus, we'd have reached our objective months earlier!"

John F. Kennedy had been elected President and his new administration would take office in five weeks. Thomas was obviously again trying to delay construction long enough for the CIA to influence the new administration and end up in charge of the program. I was tempted to either physically or verbally throttle him but kept my seat.

After Thomas continued to try to obfuscate his motives with spurious arguments, a copy of a report generated by the senior cleared officer in the Army Corp of Engineers was consulted. It confirmed their support for the ramp tunnel. Lane's proposal was then voted down—two to one.

Robert Kerr's afternoon presentation provided details on the schedule milestones, construction methods, and listed potential difficulties that might be encountered. It was a very well-reasoned briefing.

At its conclusion, Thomas stood, went to the front of the conference room with a smarmy smile on his face, and announced, "The CIA has received numerous reports that young Captain Kerr, here, is living with an East German woman. That's in direct violation of directives on close personal contact with foreign nationals by those with our security clearance."

Captain Kerr was still standing but looked in a state of shock as he returned to his seat.

General Harrison looked at him and asked him if it was true.

The young captain replied, "Anna Fischer was born in East Berlin, but now is a West German citizen. She works in the base bookstore downstairs. And yes, we live together."

I stood, went to the front of the room, and waved my arms to silence everyone. In my command voice, I requested, "Will everyone except Thomas Lane, General Harrison, Gerald Scherman, and, of course, Colonel Morgan, please leave the area."

Halfway out the door, Robert turned around to the rest of the room. "I don't want anyone here to misunderstand my intentions. I vow unequivocally that I'll give up my security clearance and stop working on your god-dammed tunnel before I give up Anna Fischer!"

Once the room was cleared, I said, "General Harrison and Mr. Sherman, this is the first time we have met. You may not know, but I was the site manager of the tunnel we built in the 1953 to 1956 period. The information gleaned in the eleven months that tunnel was operational convinced me a similar project is imperative for the national defense of our country.

"Since the DoD was given control of most aspects of the new tunnel, Thomas and some of his henchmen at CIA headquarters have done everything they can to delay or kill this project. Their current thinking is that when the new administration is installed next month, they will influence events in their favor. If we stop construction on this project at this juncture, it will be difficult, or even impossible, to ever get it started again. Those few wrong-thinking individuals like Lane here," pointing an accusing finger at him, "don't care if they kill this project. We must save it."

General Harrison took center stage, and I sat down satisfied that I had stated my case succinctly. "I wasn't aware there was doubt in anyone's mind that this is and must remain a DoD program. We have the trained manpower and leadership ability to make this a success."

"I concur," Mr. Sherman said. "Thomas, that means you have again been outvoted."

"But what about security and the young captain's girlfriend? Those must be overriding considerations," Thomas protested vehemently.

"Anna Fischer is a very nice young woman, whom I know personally," Colonel Morgan, the commander of Tempelhof Air Force Base, said. "We did a security check on her when she was hired into the bookstore. She's probably no more of a security risk than the myriad of young West Berlin women that Captain Kerr might be dating."

"But her family lives in East Berlin—the communists can use that as leverage to bend Robert Kerr to their will."

"Mr. Lane, your hidden agenda has been exposed for what it is and I'm tired of your efforts to sabotage this project," the General said. "Captain Kerr works for me. I'm the one who will have to explain to my bosses if this project doesn't start on time—I'm also the one who will take the flack if Robert Kerr or Anna Fischer become a security problem. This isn't your decision to make and I've made it. Call the others back in."

"Sir," I said, "before they return, there's one more important point. The Stasi have unfortunately learned something is going on here at Tempelhof that they want to know about. Colonel Powell, Captain Kerr, Captain Taylor, and I have begun a misinformation campaign. Captain Kerr is at the center of that effort—his continued presence in Berlin is essential for that effort to be successful."

The General replied, "That last point just confirms that we are making the right decision. Let's get everyone back into this meeting."

Once the others were back in their places, the General announced that the tunnel building project has been approved as presented. "Isn't that correct, Mr. Sherman?"

"Yes, I agree."

"Also, Captain Kerr may continue his close association with Miss Fischer."

Thomas sat in his chair in glum silence for the rest of the meeting. As we walked out, he called me aside. When we were alone, he shook his finger in front of my face. "You think you've won. I want to make sure you know you will eventually pay for this mistake. Your name now appears at the top of the shit list kept by a number of senior men in the headquarters. Things will change soon. Very, very soon! Mark my words."

I smiled slyly and whispered, "Catch me if you can."

CHAPTER 129

Friday-Sunday, December 23-25, 1960

THE LAST THREE months had seen life-changing events for my family. The seventy-one-year-old head of Erica's Classics Department died in his sleep during the night. At the age of thirty-six, she took his place. She complained that Humboldt's reputation was diminishing each year, and vowed to make her department the best in the world. She published the fourth volume of the artifacts of Troy series and gained international recognition for the effort. She had read papers she had written at conferences throughout Europe, and had even gone to a meeting in Boston.

In rapid succession, her grandmother died and then her father. Erica's mother, Lena, was in robust health and would have tried to continue working the farm, but the local collective council voted to confiscate it. Now homeless, she moved in with Erica, who applied for and was quickly given a large, modern apartment near Alexanderplatz. She had, after all, recently been given the National Prize of East Germany, the top award available in the field of academics.

Gretchen and I usually only saw Erica once a week for an overnight stay. Lena came to West Berlin frequently and was always available to care for Gretchen when I needed to be away for a few days.

Just before I left my office on Friday, I was informed by teletype message that Thomas Lane had been removed from the triumvirate that managed the tunnel. I smiled, hoping I would never have to deal with the son-of-a-bitch again.

Christmas time was spent in West Berlin. Erica had to review the proofs of the fifth volume of her reference work, which ended up being scattered all over my home office.

PART 4

1961

"Khrushchev is losing East Germany. He cannot let that happen. If East Germany goes, so will Poland and all of eastern Europe. He will have to do something to stop the flow of refugees—perhaps a wall. And we won't be able to prevent it. I can hold the Alliance together to defend West Berlin but I cannot act to keep East Berlin open."

—President John F. Kennedy statement made in discussions with National Security Advisor Walt Rostow about the 30,000 East Germans who fled to West Berlin in the month of July 1961

CHAPTER 130

Monday, July 3, 1961

EVERYONE CLEARED FOR LUMAR knew that if our Stasi/KGB/GRU enemies discovered we were building a new tunnel in Berlin, they would make every effort to determine its location.

Before construction even began, one of the arriving workers revealed to our enemies that he was one of thirteen German-speaking people who would be employed on a super-secret construction project. In reaction, communist intelligence agencies invaded West Berlin one day in early January. This incursion concluded with a harrowing car chase through the streets of the American Sector of West Berlin.

From that point on, a cadre of Stasi agents was assigned to find out what this super-secret construction project entailed.

Once it was decided that the tunnel would be dug using a Tunnel Boring Machine (TBM), I warned Robert and Mark that transport of such a device via surface routes would only alert our enemy that a tunnel was being built in Berlin. In late December 1960, our TBM was flown to Tempelhof Air Force Base in a unique propeller-driven USAF aircraft call the Pregnant Guppy; this misshapen aircraft had been designed to transport American Intercontinental Ballistic Missile sections from their factory to launch sites.

Our next problem was moving this massive machine from Tempelhof to "the building." This was solved one night in January when a pea-soup fog descended on Berlin.

I realized that a major cover and deception program was required. So, I devised a plan to help my military associates convince the communists that this newly arrived construction team was building two nuclear-hardened bunkers—one at Tempelhof and a second beneath the American Mission building. Since those involved in the tunnel's construction were constantly followed and harassed by Stasi agents and operatives, I helped provide them with countersurveillance training.

Five months after tunnel construction began, Robert informed me, "The TBM has taken the top off of a large East Berlin storm drain. While exploring the drain complex, my crew determined that it takes rainwater from a large part of the mostly abandoned industrial area of southeast Berlin and dumps it into the River Spree. A storm drain access shaft is located in the yard of a ruined factory about a quarter-mile from where we cut the drain pipe. We're pretty sure that the repair we made to the inside of the drainpipe is almost invisible from the communist side. Although this appeared to be a minor occurrence at the time, it would turn out to have significant ramifications in the future."

Today, looking back at all that had happened since I found and purchased 'the building', I smiled. We had successfully hidden the existence of the tunnel from the enemy. The tunnel itself was less than three-hundred feet from our target, which is a buried pipe; it contains three huge communications cables; each of those cables has thousands of wires that carry all of the high-level conversations and teletype messages between the Warsaw Pact countries, including East Germany, and their overlords in Moscow. Fabrication of the intercept and exploitation facilities inside 'the building' commenced last week. The first intercept station would come online in late September, and the entire site was scheduled to be fully operational sometime between late December and early January. Dedicated spaces were being constructed for four exploitation agencies—US Air Force, US Army, CIA, and NSA.

New Soviet threats to use every means possible to incorporate West Berlin into East Germany were reaching a climax. No one knew exactly what form Russian action would take, but everyone agreed that if we could read their mail and listen to their conversations, we would be able to glean the what, when, and how of that situation; the tunnel was vital to

America's national defense because it would allow our leaders to manage the situation to our advantage.

*

Tomorrow was an American holiday and I was one of the few individuals who hadn't taken a four-day break. Gretchen was enrolled in a summer science program—she loved it and did not want to miss a day. Erica had lectures and normal university business. Reluctantly, she agreed to accompany me to Robert and Anna's wedding tomorrow afternoon.

My musings were suddenly interrupted as Thomas Lane entered my office. He had obviously entered the CIA Berlin offices with security's permission—he was wearing one of our badges. Before I could say anything coherent, he said, "Remember back a year ago when you ambushed me in my office?" He had a smarmy, weasel-like look on his face. "Now is my time to reciprocate. Here are sworn statements of five senior CIA agents attesting to the fact that you ignored security regulations by providing LUMAR information to unauthorized individuals." He dropped a stack of papers onto my desk. "And, here is a reprimand that has been placed into your permanent CIA personnel file. Effective today you are demoted from GS-15 to GS-13. Your pay will be adjusted accordingly—Junior CIA Agent Kurt Altschuler. Here is another thing you'll be interested in. I have been appointed as Deputy Chief of CIA Station Berlin," he laughed sadistically. "So, I'm now your boss!"

His smile reflected pure pleasure and made me want to throttle him. That was exactly what he expected; a physical altercation in front of the few people in the office would allow my enemies to dismiss me for cause. Perhaps the person who had revealed details of Robert's relationship with Anna was in on the conspiracy, and in the office now.

Before I could say anything, Thomas delivered a telling blow. "I want you to be my subordinate. I want to rub your nose in it like a dog that needs to be trained. If you don't accept this reprimand with all of its ramifications, my cohorts and I will provide definitive proof that for years you have been providing your East German wife with secrets. You'll end up behind bars for the rest of your life. Exhibit one—the awards and decorations that your wife has received from the East German government."

"How do you know that Erica and I are married? I never…"

"That's another transgression—you got married to a foreign national without informing the CIA. I'm not telling you how we found that bit of information. Oh, and you're in my office now. Vacate it at your leisure—as long as you're out of it by noon today. You've been assigned that small vacant cubical near the front door that no one wants." I could still feel the smug look on his face as he walked away.

Thoughts raced through my mind. *Check a gun out of the arms locker and finish him off.* Then I took a breath. *Ian and Brandon will be strong allies. Recently inaugurated President Kennedy has retained Allan Dulles as his CIA Director; he knows the truth. It just doesn't make sense that his signature is on both the reprimand and demotion papers. Could his signature be forged?*

I opened my safe, pulled a shredder up next to my desk, and began destroying my personal notes on a number of topics. The first to go were the cards Peter had provided from the Stasi files on Erica and me.

The files on our agent and operative losses over the last three years were next. I had not been asked to attend the trial of George Blake after giving my affidavit. Since it was in camera, attendance was very limited. I was told that my affidavit had been read into the record. The judge had sentenced him to 42 years—one year for each British agent or operative whose death the evidence proved he had caused.

Late that morning, I moved my few personal possessions into the cubical I'd been assigned. After making sure that I had Ian's home phone number, I walked out of the office with a briefcase containing the reprimand and demotion Thomas had given me and into one of the strangest episodes of my life.

CHAPTER 131

Tuesday-Wednesday, July 4-5, 1961

EARLY THE NEXT morning I met Ian in his home, showed him the paperwork, and explained what had happened. We agreed that none of this made any sense. "This may be a case where we must give them enough rope to hang themselves," he said. "Obviously, a number of people back in the headquarters at fairly high levels are involved in this plot, so we must proceed carefully. If you're willing to accept the reprimand in the short term, be assured that I'll have your back until we can get this situation straightened out."

"I agree, that's our best course of action at this time," I said, knowing he would help me ensure that this mess was merely a temporary setback.

*

On the way to the wedding ceremony at the Kaiser Wilhelm Church in West Berlin later that afternoon, I gave Erica a rundown on some of the people she would meet. "The groom is an American Air Force captain named Robert Kerr who is stationed at Tempelhof. He is marrying a West German citizen named Anna Fischer. Her father is a medical doctor named Bernard Fischer and her mother is Emma Fischer, whom you may know; she teaches foreign languages at Humboldt. Their extended family all live in the East, as do most of the guests at the wedding."

"Emma Fischer and I have served on two committees, but I don't know her that well," Erica said.

"The other Americans are Lieutenant Colonel Mark Powell and his wife, Jane. They have three children and live in Clay Compound. Scott Taylor is another Air Force officer, who is dating an East German girl; her first name is Mia. I've never met her."

"How do you know any of these people?"

I told Erica what I had initially cleared with Mark. "Colonel Powell's older brother was my roommate at Yale for two years; we've stayed in touch over the years. He asked me to contact his younger brother shortly after Mark arrived here two years ago. I now meet him and his two colleagues for a pint at the Grossbritannien Pub every few weeks; these three officers and I have become close friends."

At the reception that evening, I introduced Erica to the guests I knew. Eventually, Erica took my hand and led me over to meet the bride's parents. "Doctor Professor Fischer, I would like to introduce my American companion, Herr Kurt Altschuler."

Hesitantly, Emma Fischer said, "Professor Schäfer, I heard that you had…have an American…friend…and together you have a daughter?"

"That is correct. Congratulations on your daughter's marriage."

"This is my husband, Doctor Bernard Fischer…He is one of those medical doctors. He's affiliated with St. Hedwig Hospital in Central Berlin."

Later, we were seated at a table with Mark and his wife, plus Scott and his girlfriend. Scott entertained us with stories of growing up on a cattle ranch in Texas and how his drawl affected his years as a music major at Harvard.

Later the bride and groom came to our table. Robert introduced his new wife to me and in turn, I introduced her to Erica. "Robert tells me you are the head of the Classics Department at Humboldt, yet you are so young," Anna said kindly.

Obviously flattered, Erica said, "A lot of luck and a little talent. Are you two going to live in America after Robert's tour of duty here is over?"

"Nine months from now, we are going to take over management of his grandfather's farms in California and I'm going to continue my education in art history. I went to Heidelberg for two years. I have been accepted as an undergraduate at the University of California at Berkeley. I'll be able to complete my degree in just one year—I start in January of next year.

Robert's tour of duty isn't over until March—so I will have to leave him here by himself for a few weeks early next year."

"It appears you two have your whole life mapped out. Kurt and I wish you both the best," Erica said, smiling warmly.

Later we were introduced to Robert's family from America. After a delicious meal and usual round of toasts, the reception at the Berlin Hilton continued with a combination of German and American traditions: the log sawing ceremony, cake cutting, first dance, throwing of the bouquet and blind-man's bluff to decide which female would be the next to marry, and throwing of the blue garter to decide which male would get married next. Everyone was still dancing when we left a little after midnight.

*

Robert and Anna eventually retired for the night, but were soon disturbed by a phone call. The senior non-commissioned leader of the construction crew, Chief Weber, informed Robert that one of their men had been kidnapped by the Stasi; the individual managed to escape from the trunk of his captor's car, was hiding in East Berlin, and needed someone to rescue him. If recaptured, the communists would force him to reveal there was a tunnel and disclose its location.

Within the hour, Robert, Scott, Mark, the Chief, and I gathered in the tank at Tempelhof to address this new crisis. Without informing Thomas Lane what was happening, I decided to allow Robert and Scott to affect the rescue using the CIA's secret Bernauerstrasse portal into East Berlin; this was the escape route we'd used to extract the Werner family from East Germany.

Robert and Scott spent over seven harrowing hours in East Berlin. Anna was unhappy because he had missed the activities planned for out-of-town guests that day. He couldn't provide a logical explanation for his absence except for the words: "trust me." The same words I'd used frequently with Erica.

CHAPTER 132

Tuesday-Sunday, August 8-13, 1961

THE HORIZONTAL PART of the tunnel had been completed eight days earlier. Now a massive telescoping vertical shaft designed to surround the communist communications pipe was being hoisted into place. It was designed to dig its way up. Robert Kerr was concerned that the noise it made in this process could be discerned on the surface; there was also the danger of a cave-in, so the excavator was only operated in the dead of night. Every time it was digging, Andreas was nearby monitoring what was happening above ground.

Despite several difficulties, including a monumental subterranean cave-in, the shaft dug its way around the pipe, the surface was undisturbed, and Andreas determined that no one had heard the resultant, significant noise.

On Friday afternoon, Robert told me, "Tonight, we'll complete the vertical shaft installation, and construction of the tunnel itself will be finished. The NSA engineers, who will cut the pipe and tap the communications lines, will arrive here on Monday and begin work on Tuesday." Shaking my hand, he continued, "We couldn't have done it without you. Thanks for all your help, Kurt."

I wasn't looking forward to a long weekend alone. Gretchen was spending a month in East Berlin with her mother and grandmother. When they came to pick her up, Erica mentioned that she signed Gretchen up for a girl's summer camp at a lake in Saxony called Seditzer See. "It's run by the Lutheran Church and is very safe," she said. If specific dates were mentioned, I failed to note when Gretchen would be away from Berlin.

*

At midnight on Sunday, August 13, 1961, the East German government closed all border crossings between West Berlin and communist-controlled East Berlin and East Germany. Less than two hours later, I received a call from the office requesting that I come in immediately. Thomas was there demonstrating a total lack of organizational skills. I couldn't help loving every minute as he repeatedly made a fool of himself. He would give orders and then reverse them. Next, he'd mumble something and expect people to start moving. After he made a fool of himself for an hour, I took over and managed to bring order out of his chaos. For a while, some of the phone lines out of the East were still working and we got reports from operatives on the scene. I sent agents to every crossing point between the two Berlins. They began reporting what they were seeing by telephone. I directed the preparation of reports, which I dutifully took to Thomas for his review and approval. Some of his most irresponsible comments I ignored, and sent the messages out as written.

One of our most reliable sources in the East reported that East German leaders, with Russian approval, were in the process of permanently sealing the border to those living in East Germany and East Berlin. "It is their way of preventing young, educated East Germans from fleeing to the West," he informed us. "New travel regulations will be promulgated on Monday, but most of the crossing points between the two Berlins will be permanently closed."

Later in the afternoon, it was clear that little new, or at least as earth-shaking, would be forthcoming. I put on my suit coat and was on my way out the door when Thomas stopped me. He smiled and I stupidly thought he was going to thank me for my help. Instead, he said, "You're thick as thieves with those Air Force guys. You're going to make sure that I'm allowed to address them in the morning at 09:00. I want you to be there and expect you to support everything I say. Is that clear?"

"Yes."

"Yes, what?"

"Yes, sir."

CHAPTER 133

Monday, August 14, 1961

ANDREAS TELEPHONED ME just before I left for Tempelhof. "The East Germans have failed to close Bernauerstrasse."

"Really? Thanks for the heads up. I need to get Erica, Gretchen, and Lena out. But first I must attend a meeting at Tempelhof."

Colonel Glen Morgan, Mark, Scott, and Robert were waiting in the tank when Thomas and I entered.

Thomas adopted his usual superior tone. "In my hand, I have a communique from the Director of the CIA, Mr. Dulles, to the Secretary of Defense, Mr. McNamara, urging him to dissolve the triumvirate and transfer the entire tunnel building program to CIA control."

"What is his justification for this demand?" Mark asked.

"Captain Kerr's slipshod management of the construction of the tunnel and exploitation center. If he had used his resources expeditiously, we'd have had advanced notice of this travesty!"

Mark moved to the front of the room, where a verbal exchange occurred with Thomas over which intelligence group was at fault because America had no advance notice of the closing of the border. Both men stood toe-to-toe. Their voices continued to rise, and I feared they might get physical with one another.

Finally, Colonel Morgan stood and approached the two men, breaking the tension. "Mr. Lane, you are a guest in this DoD facility. Let me make this clear to you...everyone in this room takes his orders from General

Harrison, and not one of us has any intention of following any orders you give us. Now, please leave before I have a security detail do the job for me." He pointed his finger toward the exit door.

Thomas turned and reluctantly walked to the door; he paused to glare in my direction as if to say everything that had happened was my fault.

*

When Scott, Robert, and I were alone, I looked at my watch and said, "It's only a little after 10:00. Bernauerstrasse is still open."

"—That means we have a chance to save our people trapped in the East!" Robert shouted.

"I've got five people I'm desperate to save. Mia is pregnant with my child," Scott revealed. "I'm sure she'll also want her parents, sister, and her sister's husband to come west as well."

"Anna cried almost all night. She won't be happy until her family is here," Robert stated. "That's eleven people."

"Even I have a group I want to save from life under those bastards!" I admitted.

Scott and Robert looked at me in amazement.

"My daughter, her mother, Erica, and grandmother are all over there. Are both of you free now?"

"Give us a few minutes to get out of our uniforms, and we'll join you on an excursion to the East," Scott said.

*

Nothing looked unusual around the apartment house on Bernaurstrasse or on the way to Erica's building several miles away. I viewed the area surrounding her apartment house for perhaps ten minutes. Then I went inside and, avoiding the elevator, took the stairs to the sixth floor. As far as I could tell, no one saw me. I rang the bell and was surprised when Erica answered. I expected her to be at work. I hugged her lovingly. "I'm so glad you are here," I said. "I wasn't sure how we were going to get you out of the university. We must leave immediately." Looking down the hall I saw Lena standing there, curious about my arrival. "Get Gretchen. Take nothing except your identity papers. There is a way across the border, but it may not stay open long!"

Erica's chin started to quiver as she revealed, "Gretchen is not here... she left three days ago for that camp...she will be gone for five more days."

I tried to comfort her, but she seemed inconsolable. "It's my fault that Gretchen's not here...the communists have proven who they really are... we cannot leave without her."

"Calm down, Erica. I have an American Passport in Gretchen's name. I'll come over and get her next Saturday when she returns. But you and Lena need to come with me now."

"No. I cannot go. I must wait for her. She is only eleven years old! She cannot be left on her own."

After twelve years I knew better than to try to change Erica's mind once it was made up, but I decided to make a suggestion. "I will take Lena with me now, come get Gretchen next Saturday, and then you can go to one of your conferences in Europe and defect from there."

"That might work."

"Lena, we must leave now," I said, moving down the hallway. She joined me and we were on our way.

*

Having been in and out of the back entrance to the apartment on Bernaurstrasse a number of times, I was able to avoid the VoPos who now seemed to be everywhere. Workmen were now carrying bricks, blocks, and barbed wire into apartment houses up and down the street in order to eliminate the last easy way to escape East Berlin.

We were forced to hide in a lean-to opposite the back-entrance door for a long time as construction workers moved back and forth. Finally, at a little after 15:00, I couldn't see anyone nearby and whispered to Lena, "We must run to that entrance." I pointed to a door across the back garden of the apartment. "Once there I will open the door, we will run down the hall to the front door; I may have to unlock it. Freedom is just beyond that door."

We rushed forward, I unlocked the door, and surprised two workmen that were placing blocks over the opening where the front door had been.

The new wall was already too high for Lena to vault over, which was my first thought. One of the workmen shouted in German, "Klaus, come here quickly!" Heavy footfalls indicated that someone was coming down the stairs. I crouched behind the banister and waited. When the machine gun-toting VoPo came into view, I grabbed his coat and hurled him against the wall at the bottom of the stairs. He hit his head and slumped unconscious into a pile.

I grabbed Lena's hand and we moved over the man, up the stairs, and past a darkened room where the windows had already been blocked up. The results on the third floor were the same. I decided that since most of these apartment buildings had flat roofs and no space between their sidewalls, perhaps we could move to an adjoining building and make our way back down to the street.

Once on the flat roof, I looked over and could see people were jumping from the building down the street into firemen's nets. Unfortunately, there was a break between that building and the one we were on. I looked at the street, saw Robert, and shouted at him. He saw me, waved, rushed over, and asked the firemen to rescue us. Before they could move, a VoPo rushed onto the roof and tried to bayonet me. I went down on one knee, grabbed him, and used his momentum to hurl him off the roof. He hit the ground with a thud and just lay there.

A few seconds passed before the firemen's net was beneath us. Lena protested that she would not jump, so I picked her up and flung her over the side. Another VoPo stuck his head out of the entrance to the roof. While I was waiting for Robert and Scott to get Lena out of the net, I stood on the edge of the roof, felt a pain in my head from a gunshot wound, and fell, rather than jumped, into the net.

My friends transported Lena, who had broken her wrist and sprained her ankle, and me to the hospital. My superficial head wound was treated and we were both released. That night Lena slept in her usual bedroom in my apartment.

Of the nineteen people we had hoped to bring over via Bernauerstrasse, we'd only extracted four—my mother-in-law, Mia's sister and her husband, and Robert's nephew, Stephen. Robert, Scott, and I now focused our efforts on freeing the others.

CHAPTER 134

Friday, August 18-Thursday, September 7, 1961

ANDREAS CONTINUED TO move over the line that separated East and West Berlin with relative ease. I didn't want or need to know how. Yesterday he couriered Erica a message, indicating that her mother and I had safely passed over the border. Her reply was disturbing.

Dear Kurt,

On Tuesday, I went to the chancellor's office and requested to be allowed to travel to Paris for a conference of Classics Professionals early next month at the Panthéon-Sorbonne. Today, I was called to his office and got my answer from him in person, "Doctor Schafer, you have told us that you are unmarried. Yet the authorities have received a copy of your Swiss marriage certificate. With it, they have determined that you are married to an American official named Kurt Altschuler. Your loyalty to the regime and communist cause has been called into question. For now, I managed to keep the Stasi from taking you to their center for interrogation. You will no longer be allowed to travel outside of the German Democratic Republic. Plus, you will be required to complete a course of reedu-

cation that will start next week—three hours a day, twice a week. The recognition you have received for your brilliant work has saved you for now, but your professorship at this university cannot continue unless you are a loyal citizen. Is that clear?"

As he was escorting me to the door, he whispered, "I had to go all the way to chairman Ulbricht to keep you from being arrested. Don't betray my trust."

Love,

Erica

*

Despite my fall from grace, many agents at the station continued to support me. The following week, Art Therber brought me another Eyes-Only correspondence from Prince—Erica's brother, Peter. I carefully opened the envelope. A note handwritten in German said, *"The following letter was mailed to our office and was postmarked West Berlin. I have handled it with care; please do the same. It may have useful fingerprints."* A document and handwritten envelope were enclosed in a glassine sleeve.

I put on rubber gloves and used a pair of tweezers to determine what was inside the envelope. It was a certified copy of my marriage certificate to Erica, reflecting both her maiden name and former married name.

At my request, Ian sent it in an Eyes-Only envelope to Brandon in Washington. Today, Ian received a response. "Fingerprints on envelope and document inside are definitely those of the two individuals we suspect; other fingerprints unidentifiable. Need handwriting sample of the suspect to confirm who addressed the envelope."

That afternoon, I gave Ian a handwritten note that Thomas had left on my desk. He forwarded it to Washington.

*

Andreas delivered a letter from me to Erica which said:

"I'm looking for a way to bring you two out of there. It would be easier if Gretchen were over here

with Lena and me. One adult can often be brought over safely through a variety of means. Should I come over next Saturday?"

She prepared a written reply while Andreas waited.

"Gretchen arrived back at my apartment safely, right on schedule, Saturday. She is a very intelligent eleven-year-old and understands exactly what is going on. She is concerned for our safety and wants to stay with me until we can both come over together. She's especially worried that you may be arrested trying to rescue her."

*

Within a few days people realized that, unlike the large number of disruptions in travel between East and West Berlin over the years, this closure was going to be permanent. Soon, most people in East Berlin seemed to be looking for an escape route.

Robert, Scott, and I met several days a week in Robert's tank to plan the extradition of fifteen people—Erica and Gretchen; Robert's wife, Anna's parents, siblings, and their children; and, Scott's prospective bride and her parents.

Almost immediately, the East German government announced a process for immigration to the West. Special consideration would be given to hardship cases, it was announced. Andreas looked into it and determined that the officials in charge of reviewing applications were accepting bribes. I asked him to get details, especially to determine how much they wanted.

Today, the two of us got together in my old office in room B327. "Kurt, that entire immigration permit process is a ruse—an effort on the part of the communists to identify people who need reeducation. It's also a way for them to extricate a tremendous amount of money from people they have no intention of allowing to emigrate. Most of those applying to leave worked in the West and lived in the East. They have lots of money in the form of cash or in banks in West Berlin, and now will pay anything to go West."

"Those hundreds of thousands of East Berliners who took the subway to the West each day were obviously doing something over here."

"Now they will try in vain to find good jobs in the East," Andreas said.

"So, what you are saying is that the East German government will allow almost no one to emigrate under the new rules?" I asked. Andreas concurred and I continued, "Have you been able to determine if there are other escape routes people are using?"

"One of the administrators at the Free University is a good friend of mine. Hundreds of that institution's students are now trapped in the East. He and another administrator are leading an informal organization that is using one of three methods to get all of those trapped students out."

"What are they?" I said, hoping one would help us.

"The first is a real passport made out to the individual carrying it."

"Where did they get those?" I asked.

"They're Belgian passports. The real thing. The father of a student is a senior official, and he provided blank passports and the required seals to make them official. The student's ID photos from the university files are being affixed to those documents. A cover story is even provided for trips across the border. A West German or foreign student meets the trapped student in the East, gives them the passport, and travels with them back over the border."

"That is amazing."

"The second is the passport of another individual who looks enough like the person in the photo to pass through."

"That will not work for us. We have a number of children."

"The third is a sewer recently opened with hacksaws and diligent effort."

"I thought all those had been closed when the East Germans made that massive effort to stop black-market smuggling both ways in the late 1940s and early 1950s. Anyway, that probably won't work for us. The adults might stand the stench and filth, but not the five children."

"Also, I have heard that an individual at the Swiss legation is selling real passports for 300,000 West Marks each."

"Seventy-five thousand dollars each! I could easily afford that amount, especially since I only have to pay for one person—you did give Gretchen's American passport to Erica on your last visit, right?"

"Yes, I did."

"As far as I know, my friends Robert and Scott cannot afford anything near that amount," I said. "I have decided that for now, my friends and I will stick together and try to bring our fifteen people over as a group. If we find a safe route, then numbers probably will not matter. Only as a last resort, you and I will extract Erica and Gretchen by themselves."

I imparted everything except the last part to Scott and Robert in our next meeting in the tank.

CHAPTER 135

Friday, September 8-Sunday, September 10, 1961

"THE ORGANIZATION AT the Free University that is getting a lot of the students out has realized that they need money to house and feed them once they are over here," I announced to Robert and Scott on Friday. "They have agreed to sell us fourteen Belgian passports for the very reasonable price of 5000 Deutsche Marks each. That's only $1,250—a real bargain."

Immediately, Scott and Robert went downstairs to the American Express Bank and withdrew the money.

"Now all we need are photographs and descriptions of each individual," I said after they handed me the money. "Robert, you have ten people that need to be photographed. I think it's best for the other five people to gather at Anna's parents' house for a little party this weekend."

"That makes sense," Robert said. "Everyone but Mia's parents met at our wedding."

"They are allowing people with West German passports over the border again. Robert, perhaps Anna could courier the film over, and return with the exposed film plus descriptions of each individual. I've made an arrangement with a photoshop I trust to process the film on Saturday afternoon. The person who controls the passports has agreed to process them Saturday night. My courier could distribute them early Sunday morning. Our loved ones could pass into West Berlin on Sunday via different routes in groups of no more than four people. Too many people crossing at the same location with Belgian passports might catch someone's attention.

Anna was supposed to meet me in the Potsdamer Platz subway station no later than 14:00 on Saturday and hand off the exposed film. By mid-afternoon on Saturday, I knew the plan had failed. A few calls later revealed that a blonde woman fitting Anna's description had tried to pass through at the border. "I have a West German passport and am married to an American military officer," she protested as she was dragged to a waiting police car at the Friedrichstrasse checkpoint. The observer stated, "It was almost as if they were expecting her and knew when she would arrive there."

Early that evening, I went to Robert and Anna's apartment and told him what I had learned. Without hesitation, he rose to his feet and said he was going East to search for her.

"They may have arrested her in part to lure you over to the East; that nasty Stasi Agent, Deter Holburg already suspects that you're in charge of the super-secret construction project," I objected. "Getting details on that effort has been a top priority for them and the KGB since January. You can't risk it."

"I'll use my green civilian passport to enter the East—they won't know who I am," he said assuredly.

"Your name is probably on a list of people who will be detained at the border for questioning. Even if you got into East Berlin, where are you going to go and what are you going to do?"

"I must do something—action is better than waiting here," Robert said, pleading.

"I have resources in the East. If we find a way to rescue her, I'll let you know. Otherwise, you better wait here and hope they release her soon."

That evening, I dispatched Andreas to make face-to-face contact with Prince (Peter) requesting that he determine what was happening to Anna Kerr (nee Fischer). He responded the next morning. "Subject is being interrogated in the basement of Stasi headquarters—purpose: to find out what her husband Robert Kerr is doing in Berlin."

It surprised us all when Anna walked out of the Potsdamer Platz subway station late Sunday afternoon. She had been in Stasi control for thirty hours. They had subjected her to mental torture, including threatening her family—long prison terms on trumped-up charges for the adults—retraining in communist orphanages for her nieces and nephews. After injecting her with the truth serum, they apparently realized that she knew nothing of real value. They offered to release her immediately if she would spy on her husband and Tempelhof Air Force Base, where she worked.

The threats to Anna's family made extracting all of our people a much more urgent necessity. Not only did we not get the photographs we needed for the passports, but for the foreseeable future, we had to help Anna satisfy the Stasi's demand for information about Robert's mission and Tempelhof Air Base.

In the spy game, moves and counter-moves must be made very carefully. Arresting the female Stasi agent who would meet Anna and receive her submittals twice-weekly would tell the Stasi that she had informed us of her situation. We had to make them believe that she was working for them, if not willingly, at least by necessity.

CHAPTER 136

Tuesday, September 19, 1961

EVEN THOUGH THOMAS Lane had never directed the efforts of a double agent or spy, and had little field experience of any form, he insisted on assuming responsibility for Anna Kerr's interface with the Stasi. It was clear to Ian and me from the start that he had a hidden agenda.

During the week following Anna's imprisonment at Stasi Headquarters, Andreas gave two rolls of film to Anna's father at his office in St. Hedwig's Hospital. The escapees reassembled the next Saturday to be photographed. This morning Andreas phoned me at home, and I agreed to meet him outside of Tempelhof. Once we were together, he whispered, "People who tried to use Belgian passports over the weekend were arrested. Now a tourist's visa application has to be filled out by each passport holder when they enter the East. It will be date and time-stamped at the point of entry, and surrendered when that person leaves East Germany or East Berlin. Also, all tourists must now enter East Berlin through the Friedrichstrasse checkpoint."

"Are we sure this policy has been implemented?" I asked, hoping we had time.

"Positive."

Later that morning, Scott, Robert, and I met in the LUMAR tank, where I told them that the fourteen Belgian passports we'd received that morning were worthless.

After much discussion, Scott asked the group if they had any ideas.

I cleared my throat, and said, "A daring young entrepreneur who carried out several excursions into the East for me has proposed digging a tunnel for us. We pay for it. He persuades people to dig it, and our loved ones are the first to be extricated. He then gets as many paying customers out as he can."

"Give us the details of what he's proposing to build," Scott said.

"Here's a map he prepared. The border fence separates this church from its graveyard. The tunnel he wants to dig would start in the basement of an apartment house in the British Sector and end up in a crypt in a graveyard adjacent to the border fence. A length of some 375 feet—size perhaps one-meter square. Just enough space to crawl through."

"How much?" Scott asked.

"$50,000—200,000 Deutsche marks," I replied. "As we all know, Berlin soil must be supported during digging operations, so most of his cost is lumber to support the earth above the tunnel and to pay the workers. This guy's smart. He selected the site because a builder just razed a structure next door to his proposed tunnel entrance. That gives him a convenient place to get rid of the dirt as they excavate."

"Guard towers are being erected all along the wall so VoPos can monitor activity on both sides of the border," Scott said.

"For now, only two fences—one barbed wire and the other chain-link—pass through this area. It is patrolled by VoPos and guard dogs attached to a line that runs down its center," I continued. "From the window of his recently rented apartment, I could see the large crypt that is his target. I would…"

"—Using my theodolite, I can help him establish the distance to his target," Robert said, jumping in. "And I could help him get his tunnel started in precisely the right direction. Then, by using a piece of taut string, he can keep the tunnel straight and accurately determine the distance covered."

"So that only leaves one problem: money," Scott declared. "I'll go downstairs to the American Express bank and get 40,000 West marks. I'll then have the balance transferred this week. Kurt, you manage the business end of this endeavor. I'll provide the money, and Robert will provide the technical expertise."

Shocked, Robert said, "I can't…You may never…"

"My family owns thousands of acres of land and numerous oil fields—I'm Texas wealthy. I want to make our endeavors a success," Scott revealed.

Robert protested again, "But you…

"—It's settled! This will be our joint endeavor, with each of us making a significant contribution."

We shook hands, and that became the basis for our new escape plan. Later, Scott and I agreed that he would accept $14,000 as my fair share of these expenses.

CHAPTER 137

Wednesday, October 11, 1961

MARK, SCOTT, AND I met in the tank for our regular escape planning meeting. This week, I reported that the escape tunnel would be completed in about two weeks.

"In next week's meeting, we can finalize our escape plan," Scott said.

"Let's move on to other matters," I said. "Thomas Lane has been chastised and put on a short leash by our boss, the CIA Chief of Station in Berlin. His responsibilities have been explained to him, and he barely managed to retain his current position. Unfortunately, someone high up in Washington intervened. We'll still have to deal with him, plus he remains my boss."

"That's a shame," Robert lamented. "I thought we finally would be rid of him."

"I've heard rumors about Lane's gaff, but you two were there—what happened?" I requested.

"First, he revealed the extent to which the spy operations of both East and West had been curtailed by the closing of the border," Robert said, smiling. "He then demanded that Anna give her Stasi handler a document which was classified Top Secret and Limited Distribution. It revealed a plan for bringing reinforcements into Berlin in the event of armed conflict."

"Anna refused to take the document shouting, 'Once my Stasi contact is arrested with this document, they will know that I'm working against them, and my entire family will be condemned to Stasi Hell!!'" Scott recalled. "I wanted to stand up and salute Anna for her courage in facing down that bully."

"Then Lane let his true motive slip by revealing 'it's imperative that I...uh...we break up a major communist spy ring,' Robert said."

"That document was apparently a recent version of that plan and was indeed classified Top Secret," I told my friends. "Other CIA agents who committed such a serious security violation would be sent to prison for years. None of you had the need to know most of what Lane said during that entire conversation—perhaps telling you two was excusable, but not Anna, a foreign national. Plus, the mishandling of classified data has always been a hanging offense."

"The Air Force is equally serious about security," Scott said.

"One thing that Lane said, which is true," I said. "It's becoming very difficult for Stasi agents and operatives to enter West Berlin. Anna will need to keep her lunch appointments for the next two weeks, but I suspect no one will ever approach her again at that café. If they do, West German agents will ensure they're on the way back East and told not to return."

"Anna will be happy to have this all behind her. Thank you, Kurt," Robert said.

"Whether it's all behind her is yet to be seen. The old days of Berlin being an open city, where our spies and their spies pass freely back and forth, has ended," I observed.

"What you're saying is the spy game in Berlin has changed from an overt, open collection of intelligence to covert, undercover operations," Scott said. "The number of people involved will of necessity be reduced, and Stasi covert spying activities will be limited to what they perceive to be critical areas."

"That's correct," I said. "Despite Lane's comments last week, they may perceive Anna is a sufficiently valuable source to assign a covert handler to her. Remember, finding out what Robert here is doing in Berlin is a top priority with them."

"I understand what you're saying, but I hope you're wrong," Robert said. "This has been very hard on her."

CHAPTER 138

Monday-Tuesday, October 23-24, 1961

LAST WEDNESDAY, TWO Stasi agents, one of whom was Deter Holburg, accosted Anna in her apartment in West Berlin. During their verbal assault, which was designed to ensure her continued support, they again threatened her and her family with prison. Robert found her that evening totally traumatized.

When we gathered for another escape-planning meeting. I asked how Anna was getting along.

"She's still in the hospital. The military psychiatrist indicates that she is suffering from Gross Stress Reaction. She may be released in a few days. She is so fragile, we must get her family out as soon as possible," Robert explained. "The tunnel being dug for us needs to be finished quickly."

"I understand what you're saying. Mia's letters are sounding more desperate all the time," Scott said, looking distressed.

"Those Stasi thugs insisted that Anna give them new information about my activities every Friday. This means that we'll have to feed that Stasi dead drop with valid information until we can get Anna's family out," Robert said.

"One of my agents is a tall brunette," I offered. "With a blonde wig, she could pass for Anna from a distance."

"So, she can service the dead drop with information we generate," Scott said.

"Exactly. I won't tell Thomas about this latest development. He'll just get involved and screw everything up. I'll take responsibility for generating the material and getting it into the dead drop."

"Thanks Kurt, you're a true friend," Robert said, shaking my hand.

"Did anyone make it to the escape tunnel this weekend?" Scott asked.

"I went over on Saturday," Robert replied. "They won't be finished until the middle of next week. They've had to dig around a huge water main. Then I helped them get back on the correct track."

"Did either of you hear about all the excitement last night at Checkpoint Charlie?" I asked.

"No, what happened?" Scott said.

"One of our senior occupation officials was denied entry to East Berlin. He demanded that a Russian official be summoned. An altercation with the East Germans followed. To reinforce our rights, a whole fleet of staff and civilian cars with allied civilian and military personnel crossed the border for the next several hours. They traversed the area where the East German government resides without showing their identity cards."

Scott smiled. "We're reinforcing our right under the Four Powers Agreement!"

"This morning, the East German News Agency announced that all persons in civilian clothes who enter East Germany will be required to show their identity papers," I said. "I'm assured this isn't the end of the showdown between the East and West."

*

By the time I got back to the office, the events that were called the Berlin Crisis had begun. American tanks were being moved to Checkpoint Charlie to enforce our rights in Berlin. Soon we received word from several operatives that the Russian tanks and troops were moving toward Berlin. Ian knew of the intelligence integration center I'd established during the early days of the Berlin Blockade and asked, "Will you do the same again?"

I called my appropriate counterpart in the military and, before midnight, we were again integrating all-source information about Russian military movements in room B327. At a little after 02:00, a courier brought the new information that had been derived from intercepts made at "the building." Those intercepts confirmed that the orders to deploy the tanks had been given by Khrushchev himself. Our two years of toil in building the new Berlin Tunnel were helping us navigate this new crisis.

CHAPTER 139

Wednesday-Saturday, October 25-28, 1961

THE BERLIN CRISIS was the only time in the Cold War when Russian and American tanks faced each other. The situation was so intense that if one person had accidentally or intentionally fired his weapon, World War Three probably would have started.

Those of us who lived in what was the front lines of this non-shooting war always paid attention to headlines and news reports as the Cold War deepened. At a summit in early June, Soviet Premier Khrushchev told President Kennedy that he would sign a separate peace treaty with East Germany, abrogating the Four-Powers Agreement that guaranteed American, British, and French rights to access West Berlin.

In response, Kennedy called up the reserves, increased the draft, and then sent large numbers of aircraft and troops to Europe. In August, the Berlin Wall was closed. In response, President Kennedy dispatched 1,500 combat troops and all of their equipment to Berlin. This force was a symbol of America's resolve to protect Berlin and our rights there.

Now, over two months later, the East Germans, with Soviet concurrence, were trying to control the movement of officials from the western nations into East Berlin. President Kennedy directed that his commanders in Berlin and Germany refuse to comply with this latest ploy.

First, ten American tanks showed up at Checkpoint Charlie to enforce our rights to enter East Berlin. The Russians responded by bringing thirty-three tanks into that same area—some actually facing the American tanks, as if ready to fire.

Early on, the little group of people in my basement room determined that the Soviet tanks were a show of force. Information derived from landline intercepts via "the tunnel" and exploited by people in "the building" revealed that the Russian tanks and troops at Checkpoint Charlie were given strict orders. "Under no circumstances will any individual fire his weapon without direct authority from me," signed Khrushchev.

Soon, through back-channel communications, Khrushchev and Kennedy agreed to reduce tensions by withdrawing the tanks. Later, I learned that a Soviet tank moved back about five meters and an American tank reciprocated until all of the tanks returned to their bases. The crisis was over just as quickly as it had begun.

CHAPTER 140

Saturday-Sunday, November 4-5, 1961

AFTER OVER A month of planning, Robert, Scott, and I were ready to assist sixteen people to escape to the West. Robert's brother-in-law had been released from prison early and would join his family in their escape to the West; he had accused communist party functionaries of corruption—their answer was a lengthy prison sentence.

Construction of the escape tunnel had been completed on Friday afternoon when my young entrepreneur friend pushed one of the limestone slabs that covered the floor of the crypt out of the way.

I'd arranged with the rector for us to use the church steeple positioned adjacent to the fence. This vantage point gave us a clear view of the cemetery and the surrounding area.

At a little after midnight, the three of us ascended the ladder to the belfry. Through openings in the stone structure, we saw two pairs of armed VoPos with dogs. They patrolled the well-lit, no man's land between the two fences. Lights atop tall poles along the fences illuminated the area. The gravestones and crypts beyond formed long shadows, which would allow the escapees to approach the vault without exposing themselves.

"My task will be to keep an eye on the VoPos below us inside the fence," Scott said. "I'll wave and point if they become interested in anything in the cemetery."

I'd managed to acquire six sets of the two-way communication devices the East Germans had developed for the Stasi, and had Andreas transport five East so that each group of escapees and I had one.

Robert mounted his thirty-power binoculars on a tripod and focused on the area around the crypt. He whispered, "I can see most of the cemetery and part of an adjacent street."

"The workers' girlfriends should arrive soon," Scott whispered after glancing at his watch.

Two of the diggers agreed to work on the tunnel in return for having their girlfriends, who were trapped in the East, come through first.

"There they are," I whispered as I watched two female figures dart between gravestones and then crawl the last few feet before disappearing near the crypt.

Looking at the luminous dial of my watch, I determined that the first of our groups should arrive in about twenty minutes. This arduous and gut-wrenching task could well be completed in a little over an hour. Time passed slowly, and eventually, Scott began signaling minutes remaining by holding up the fingers on his right hand.

Suddenly, I saw Robert tense up. He repositioned his binoculars, and whispered, "They're too smart to expose themselves like that. One of them has a submachine gun in his hand!"

Robert moved away from the opening. "Kurt, use your gadget to tell everyone to go home," he said quietly. "The bad guys have arrived in force."

"Are you sure?" Scott asked.

"I'm certain. Whoever is on the street is armed."

"Crap."

I was crouching down so that my voice wouldn't carry to the VoPos below. In German, I whispered, "Abbrechen! Sofort abbrechen! (Abort immediately!)"

Standing back from the shadows, I watched submachine gun-toting armed men in uniform and civilians carrying pistols swarm into the cemetery. Gunshot fire erupted in the vicinity of the crypt. Soon, men surrounded it.

The three of us looked at each other, defeated by the reality that we'd tried again and failed.

*

The next day, the three of us met.

"We've lost over six weeks and all that money," Robert proclaimed. "And we're no closer than the day we started."

"Don't worry about the money," Scott said. "We are all feeling angry and desperate. In our communications, Mia sounds more distraught each day. I can afford to purchase Swiss passports for everyone."

"That's over $800,000. Anna, her family, and I could never repay you."

"Don't worry about it. I can easily afford it!" Scott said.

"I've enough to afford my share," I offered.

"The Fischer family's share is still over half a million dollars," Robert protested.

"Don't worry about it, Robert. I'm only in the Air Force because I like it. Anna's family is so exceptional, just knowing I was able to help them to freedom will be my reward."

Robert stared at him, speechless.

Hugging Scott like a brother, Robert said, "We'll all be eternally grateful for your generosity. I accept on their behalf. Thank you. "

"Kurt, as soon as you've completed the agreement with the Swiss diplomat, I'll have a letter of credit for the full amount sent to a Swiss bank," Scott said. "Pay me back at your leisure."

I was more emotional than I'd ever been in front of my friends. I hugged Scott deeply. "Thank you on behalf of all of us," was all I managed to say.

The challenge we faced as we tried to rescue our loved ones had fostered a profound sense of brotherhood among the three of us.

CHAPTER 141

Friday, November 10, 1961

"I'VE GOT A foolproof way of getting everyone out of East Berlin," I announced after joining Scott and Robert in the tank today. "As I told you on Wednesday, the man in the Swiss embassy selling passports was recalled to Bern after the East Germans and Russians protested his activities."

"Tell us about your new alternative!" Robert urged.

"One of the senior officials at the Austrian Embassy decided to get rich. He's selling authentic Austrian passports, and we could be his first customers."

"How much?" I asked.

"Eighty thousand West marks—$20,000 for each passport."

"Let's make it happen, my friends," Scott said as we shook hands and discussed the details of money transfers and potential travel dates and routes.

Our next escape plan was finalized.

CHAPTER 142

Wednesday, November 15, 1961

THOMAS LANE HAD avoided me since his reprimand but continued to occupy my old office. Ian assigned me an office of similar size some distance down the opposite corridor.

After lunch this afternoon, I heard a brisk knock on my office door. Thomas stuck his head inside my office with a smug smile on his face. Before I could say or do anything, he opened the door fully, exposing a young man beside him. "This is James Joerger, who's on his first overseas assignment," Thomas told me. "He's going to be your new protégé."

Joerger was thin, under six feet tall. He had unruly, long, blondish hair, and a ruddy complexion. His grip felt weak during our handshake. Throughout this meeting, he only made furtive eye contact with me. He lacked the usual self-confidence of a CIA agent.

Thomas explained that the three of us had been assigned to extract two long-time double agents and their family from East Berlin. He indicated that these agents were a married couple and suggested that we evaluate using Robert's tunnel and the storm drain to get them out. I should have been suspicious of this suggestion. Instead, I immediately focused on the fact that it might provide an avenue for us to bring our now sixteen people West to safety.

Later that afternoon, the three of us met Robert in his tank. I led the conversation. "What I am about to tell you is strictly 'need to know.' For the last nine years, one man and his wife have been at the center of one of the most productive parts of our espionage efforts against the East Germans and Russians. Unfortunately, their identity was recently compromised."

"How can I help you?" Robert asked, apparently confused.

"—Captain, I recall that you severed and repaired the top of an East German storm drain during construction of the tunnel," Thomas interjected.

"Yes, that's true. As far as we know, the storm-drain repair is almost invisible from the communist side."

"Is there any reason we couldn't get eight people out through the tunnel by reopening that hole?" I asked intentionally, leading Robert's response.

"It's certainly feasible."

"At this point in time, we only have permission to assess the feasibility of such an operation," I said. "We've managed to get one or two people across to the West at will, but extracting all eight safely, including three children, will be tough."

Robert's face changed when he realized that I was insinuating that the tunnel could also be used to extract our sixteen.

Thomas added, "The East Germans have eliminated all of the easy ways to get people to the West. This is a potential solution. We haven't much time to improvise another scheme."

Robert went over to a flat storage cabinet, opened the third door down, moved a few drawings around, and withdrew a map of the area, plus a top and side view of the storm drain and tunnel. He spread it out across the conference table. "This is our tunnel," he said. "It hit the storm drain here. The path of that drain goes from the River Spree all the way back to this area, which was once the manufacturing hub of Berlin. Now, it's primarily damaged and abandoned buildings."

Pointing to the street map, Robert continued, "That complex is located here, about a half a kilometer from where the tunnel and drain meet."

"How would you make a hole in the repaired tunnel flooring and storm drain?" I asked.

"Jackhammer is the quickest, but it makes a lot of noise," Robert replied.

"Won't the noise attract attention?" Thomas asked.

"The whole area is covered with ruined and vacant factories and warehouses," Robert stated. "If we scheduled the extraction for Sunday morning when the area is deserted, we'd have to be awfully unlucky for someone to even detect noise emanating from a drain grate on nearby streets."

"In the East, it doesn't pay for an ordinary citizen to become too curious," I said, validating his statement.

"Who'd run the jackhammer?" Thomas asked.

"My senior NCO, Chief Weber. He helped to build the tunnel and knows about the storm drain. We still have an electric jackhammer in our basement storage area at the building."

We thanked Robert, shook his hand and left.

CHAPTER 143

Thursday, November 16, 1961

SCOTT AND ROBERT were shocked when I informed them in disgust, "That son-of-a-bitch at the Austrian Embassy is threatening to give the photos of our sixteen escapees to the Stasi unless we pay him an additional million West marks!"

"That's $250,000 on top of the $230,000 we've already paid him!" Robert exclaimed.

"I'm willing to pay him, but I'm concerned that we'll never see those passports," Scott said with obvious concern. "He may just continue to make demands."

"If he gives the photos to the Stasi, our escapees will be in immediate danger, probably even arrested," I said, as my voice cracked with emotion. "Anna's parents and Erica are sufficiently well known to be identified immediately just from their photographs."

"We must act quickly," Robert said. "Tell Scott about the double-agent extraction."

"This morning we received permission from Washington to use your tunnel to extract the two double agents and their family this Sunday."

"And then we'll use it to extract sixteen additional people," Scott shouted. "Thank God!"

"A dream opportunity that will be entirely under our control," Robert exclaimed joyously, as we all rose to our feet in unison and embraced each other.

I nodded. "It doesn't leave us much time to make our plans and notify our escapees. Here's what I'd suggest…"

CHAPTER 144

Sunday, November 19, 1961
07:00

EARLY ON SUNDAY morning, Robert and his senior NCO, Chief Weber met Thomas, James Joerger, and me at the main entrance to 'the building.' Two electric carts were used to transport us to the site of the original hole, which was surrounded by a variety of construction tools and supplies Robert and the Chief had positioned there.

The five of us stood around the excavation site. Robert handed out gloves and ear protection. "If you think a jackhammer is loud, you should hear it in a confined space like this."

Soon, parts of the tunnel flooring were loose. Working as a team, we removed pieces of concrete and cut the rebar, piling the rubble nearby.

Three hours later, we lowered the step ladder down into the hole.

Thomas looked at his watch. "It's 10:20. Our visitors should arrive at the rendezvous site in about forty-five minutes."

"Are you going to return to ensure that the tunnel is sealed?" Robert asked.

"Kurt, you're in charge after James and I leave. If there's a problem, Captain Kerr can get his subordinates to help fill the hole."

Thirty minutes later I turned to James. "It's time," I said. We both donned rubber boots. I lowered myself down into the drain. James handed down a box of flashlights, a box of rubber boots of various sizes, and then joined me.

We walked in silence carrying the boxes and ascended the built-in ladder to the surface. I pushed aside the manhole cover. We quickly scrambled out, replaced the cover, and hurriedly moved into a nearby building.

After ensuring that everything was quiet, I whispered, "We can now walk casually to the rendezvous point."

A cold drizzle started. We turned up the collars of our overcoats as water dripped from our hats. The blocks of abandoned and burned-out factories and warehouses were deserted. After covering the two blocks down an adjacent street and a couple of turns, we entered an abandoned warehouse. My eyes slowly adjusted to the mottled light. I could see an older couple in their sixties, another couple in their forties (our double agents whom I knew by name and codename, but had never met), a man in his thirties, and three boys who ranged in age from a pre-teen to a preschooler. Joerger led the group and I followed. I retrieved the manhole key from nearby rubble and moved it up and to one side. After returning the key to its hiding place, I followed the others and secured the manhole by pulling it back over the hole. All of our guests found rubber boots in approximately the correct size.

The trip through the storm drain took about fifteen minutes, and eventually, all eight of our escapees were seated on electric carts. They were handed blindfolds. In English, Thomas explained as I translated, "Please put these on for the trip to the West. Once we arrive at the surface, you'll be told when to remove them. Soon, you'll be in a safe house in West Berlin while we arrange transportation for you to the United States, where you'll be given asylum."

Washington had insisted that our visitors be blindfolded to avoid any knowledge about their route to freedom. The convoy of two electric carts departed with Thomas and James driving. My watch said it was 11:47.

CHAPTER 145

Sunday, November 19, 1961
12:35

OUR SIXTEEN ESCAPEES, divided into four groups, were scheduled to arrive at the rendezvous point every 45 minutes. Mark Powell was in a penthouse on the top floor of the building, where the new arrivals would all stay until all escapees arrived in the West safely. Right on time, Scott drove one of the carts up to the storm-drain entrance. He exhaled, the nervous strain evident on his face. "We're scheduled to meet Mia and her parents in twenty-five minutes. Wish us luck."

"Make sure you two aren't followed before you contact them," I said, shaking his hand.

Right on schedule, at 13:20, Scott and the Chief returned with Mia and her parents.

Twenty minutes later, it was time for the Chief and me to leave. When we arrived at the rendezvous point, I became very concerned. We entered the warehouse and at first, I couldn't see Erica or Gretchen. They had heard us approach and decided out of fear to hide in a dark corner behind some debris. Once they saw it was only the Chief and me, they emerged and we hugged. I kissed them both in turn. "I had every confidence that you'd get us out," Erica whispered, smiling. Gretchen clung to me in silence.

"We won't be safe for at least another twenty minutes. Please quietly follow me. Chief Weber will follow behind us."

It was still raining as we exited the warehouse complex. We followed the same route as before and soon entered the relative safety of the storm drain. Each of us donned rubber boots and took a flashlight. The water level was now high enough that Gretchen had to be careful not to splash water into her boots; I helped her walk to the side of the storm drain by taking her hand to ensure she stayed balanced.

As we approached the hole in the tunnel, I heard a conversation between two men and assumed that it was Scott and Robert, but hesitated. Soon, I recognized the voices of Robert and Thomas; they were arguing. I signaled for the others to stay back, took out my pistol, and approached the ladder that led up into the tunnel. A weapon sounded. I moved forward cautiously. Then I heard Robert and Scott talking. I silently ascended the ladder a step at a time. To ensure that I could react to danger quickly, I extended my upper body above the floor of the tunnel slowly and pointed the gun toward the voices. Scott had a pistol in one hand and was handing Robert one with the other. Thomas was sprawled out on the floor, unconscious among stacked building equipment and concrete rubble.

I surveyed the scene and quickly decided that Thomas must have tried to ambush us. To Robert and Scott, I said, "There are handcuffs in the briefcase I brought with me. Cuff him."

Robert complied, then checked his condition. "His pulse is steady. He'll survive and be madder than hell when he wakes up. He threatened to send us all to prison for thirty to forty years and tried to kill me."

"What happened?" I asked.

"Somehow he figured out what we were going to do and decided to take photos as proof—then unwisely decided to interfere with our extraction. He threatened to see that all of us were convicted of conspiracy, security violations, and misuse of government property. I rushed at him, tripping just before he shot at me. I was able to grab the claw hammer lying among the tools over there and took him out—one blow to the arm and another to his temple. He's unconscious, at least for now."

Gretchen had now entered the tunnel and screamed when she saw Thomas. He was bleeding from both his wounds.

"I'll take my family to join the others in the penthouse and then return," I said, directing Erica and Gretchen to one of the carts. "Chief, why don't you join us? Bring your gun. We need to determine if anyone accompanied Thomas. We don't need any more surprises this afternoon."

Returning at 14:39, I said, "That Thomas certainly has balls, or is stupider than I thought he was. He apparently came alone. Perhaps he intended to only take pictures and observe our indiscretions, but then got carried away."

"If we release him, we'll all pay dearly! We need to take care of the bastard," Scott swore.

Shocked, Robert implored, "Are you suggesting…cold-blooded murder?"

"—I have a plan that may solve many problems concurrently," I interjected.

My companions stared at me in disbelief.

"Rest assured, I'll do nothing that will incriminate us," I promised.

"Let's just get our loved ones out of East Berlin, seal the tunnel, and then release him," Robert suggested.

"You're willing to condemn us to life in prison so that Thomas fucking Lane can take his revenge on us and look big in the eyes of his superiors?" Scott shouted. "Well, I don't give a damn what happens to that son-of-a-bitch. Kurt, take care of him any way you see fit."

"This is one of his usual schemes to dispose of some people he views as enemies," I said. "You two don't realize this, but his enmity toward me is monumental. I'm good at what I do, and he's an incompetent politician who will stomp on anyone to get ahead!"

"Do you think he knew that we'd attempt to use the tunnel to get our families out?" Robert asked.

"I'm sure of it," Scott replied. "And Kurt's correct. If we allow him to live, we'll all suffer."

CHAPTER 146

Sunday, November 19, 1961
15:05

DESPITE THE DELAY that was caused by Thomas' efforts to halt the extraction process, Robert and the Chief retrieved Anna's parents, older brother, and older sister's family only ten minutes behind schedule, and without incident. The remaining group was Anna's younger brother and his family.

As Robert, Scott, and I rode in a cart back to the storm drain entrance, I said, "When I was upstairs, I contacted someone in the East. In about an hour, he'll call Stasi Headquarters and report a clandestine meeting between a CIA operative and a double agent at our rendezvous point. My contact will be believed. We'll let the Stasi take care of Mister Thomas Fucking Lane for us."

"That way we aren't committing murder, per se," Robert said.

Scott nodded. "I also like that distinction."

"How are you going to manage that?" Robert asked.

"That sniveling bastard may need a little help from me," I said, "and I may even have to improvise at some point along the way, but my objective is to let the Stasi eliminate him for us!"

Robert explained where Thomas was, and I followed him to the storage locker. Thomas was conscious when we opened the door and, yelled, "You'll all pay for this! My leaders back in Washington made it clear that my primary reason for being sent to Berlin was to take control of the tunnel for the CIA. Your unauthorized use of the tunnel is prima facie evidence of the NSA and DoD's inability to safely manage such an essential national intelligence asset. Besides, Robert, Scott and you have done everything possible to humiliate and belittle me. Your families deserve to suffer under the yoke of a totalitarian regime, and you each deserve to be in federal prison. You'll spend…"

I'd let him talk up to this point to learn his motivation, but finally, in disgust, I grabbed his hair, jerked his head back, and stuffed a gag into his mouth. I secured it with electrical tape. Next, I yanked him to his feet, shook him violently, and warned, "You're going to the East, so you can experience what the real spy game's about. If anything happens, I'll use the first bullet on you. If we all survive this last extraction, then we may release you. You have your official passport in your pocket. If anything happens to me, perhaps you can convince the East German border guards to honor it."

Both of us kept our guns pointed at Thomas as we walked back through the tunnel, down the step ladder, and through the storm drain. I stopped him when we arrived at the storm drain's metal-runged ladder. Seizing Thomas by the throat, I said, "Do you believe if you try anything that I'll kill you and leave your body down in this drain?"

Thomas nodded.

"When I uncuff your wrists, you're going to climb up this ladder. Robert, go first and keep him covered."

I removed Thomas' shackles. As he started to climb, I shoved his gun between his buttocks. "One wrong step and my bullet will travel up your body. It might even make it to your heart, assuming you have one. Now climb!"

After the three of us exited the storm drain, Thomas's hands were shackled behind his back again. We moved hastily and in silence toward the rendezvous point. Halfway there, I handcuffed Thomas to a lamp post inside a fenced area.

A block further on, Robert pushed open the door to the meeting place. Anna's younger brother, his wife, and two children were standing there. Robert hugged them. Our trip back to the tunnel proved uneventful.

Parting from Robert without entering the storm drain, I said, "It's now 15:35. The chief is currently guarding the tunnel/storm-drain entrance.

You need to join him soon so the three of us can seal the tunnel. I'm leaving now. If I don't return by 17:00, seal the tunnel. I'll take care of our little problem and get back here by then, or go over the border using my numerous contacts in the East. Securing the tunnel is the most important thing."

CHAPTER 147

Sunday, November 19, 1961
15:47

EARLIER TODAY, I located a solid concrete, virtually soundproof room with a heavy door still on its hinges near where I'd handcuffed Thomas Lane to the telephone pole. I took him to that room to extract details of his conspiracy against me.

I securely shackled him to an overhead drain pipe. "You have a choice; I can leave you here to starve to death, or you can tell me what you and your henchmen have been doing," I said to him. He looked frightened, so my actions were having the desired effect.

"You must cooperate with me fully; that includes participating in a little confrontation with the Stasi I have planned for this afternoon. If you survive, you'll be allowed to explain to your fellow conspirators how well you performed on your assignment. Perhaps they'll agree with you and seek to send Robert, Scott, even the Chief, and me to prison. Once I take your gag off, you are to speak at a normal conversational level. I know about most of your duplicitous acts, but have some questions on the details. If you fail to answer my questions truthfully, I'll inflict a few non-lethal wounds. It'll take time for you to either bleed to death or die of thirst. Either way, it will be a very slow and painful way to go...but inevitable."

Once I took off his gag, Thomas assaulted me with a string of curse words and invectives at the top of his voice: "You dirty son-of-a bitching bastard—you'll never get away with this, you cocksucker!"

I placed his pistol up against his head and pulled the trigger. A deafening reverberation filled the room. The bullet took off the tip of his ear, which bled profusely. I tied the cloth I'd used as a gag around his head to stop the bleeding. "Bet that hurts like hell. Don't raise your voice again. I don't appreciate your aspersions about me and my family." Sweat filled his face and despite the pain, I could see the hatred in his eyes. At that point, I realized that I would be in danger when I eventually had to release him, so I had to be very careful. "We don't have much time, so let's get to my questions. Did Director Dulles sign my letter of demotion?"

"Yes—you saw his signature," almost spitting the words at me.

"I also have people on my side who know the truth, so let's cut the crap. Dulles does not know anything about my demotion—yet it got into my official personnel file." I moved the gun over to the other side of Thomas's head, and aimed, as he struggled to avoid the next shot. "A little bit off your other ear will remind you to tell me the truth," I said, touching his ear with the gun barrel.

"Okay! Okay. I'll tell you everything," Thomas said, pleading. "Dulles' secretary has a rubber stamp of his signature she uses to sign most of his routine correspondence—his arthritis makes it difficult for him to sign his name hundreds of times a day. We removed it from the secretary's desk and affixed it to your demotion."

"Who is we?"

"Frank Collins, Director of Operations Herbert Zales, Keith Simmons, and me."

"Good answer. There must be others."

He gave me the names of three other individuals—one of whom worked in my Berlin office. "How did you know I was married? And how did you end up with a copy of my marriage certificate?"

"That's easy—Jeremy Irwin broke into your apartment. The certificate was in an unlocked drawer in your home office desk." Blood was beginning to seep through the cloth on his ear and down his neck. "Once we knew when and where, we applied for and received several certified copies from Switzerland."

"And you sent a copy to the Stasi."

"Yes. Yes, I did."

"Didn't you realize that my wife Erica would probably be arrested by the Stasi, put in prison, and possibly tortured?"

"We meant to totally disrupt your personal and professional life for making us look bad to Dulles over the matter of funding the construction of the tunnel. That whole tunnel project would have gone nowhere without those funds."

Shaking my head in disbelief at the destructive actions these individuals had directed against me, I said in frustration, "Let's move on. How did you find out about our intent to use the tunnel in the graveyard to free our loved ones from East Berlin?"

"That was also easy," Thomas said smugly, almost bragging. "Two airmen and an NCO are assigned the task of cleaning Robert's tank. I bribed one of the airmen to place voice-activated listening devices in the conference room, where you three always met for your planning sessions."

"So, you knew in advance about all of our attempts to get our loved ones out, not just the one that was successful today. Is that correct?"

"Yes. The tank was cleaned twice a week, so we usually had your latest plans."

"And what was your first move?"

"I warned the Stasi that spurious Belgian passports were being used to get people into West Berlin."

"What about the tens, perhaps even hundreds of students who might have enjoyed freedom in the West? They are now stuck behind the Iron Curtain."

"Unintended collateral damage. Some innocents must be sacrificed for the greater good!" he replied nonchalantly.

"How did you get this information to them?"

"The German Bundespost is wonderful," Thomas said gleefully. "Drop a letter with the information into any post box in West Berlin and it is in a secret Stasi P.O. Box early the next day."

"Did you also inform them that Anna Kerr was going to courier film to the East so escapees could be photographed and passports generated for a group of people? She was arrested, subjected to mental torture, and turned into a Stasi operative. As a result, her mental health has been severely compromised."

"You cannot blame that one on me. Your conversation with your military buddies about Anna couriering the film occurred on a Friday. Because of the cleaning schedule, I did not learn about that until Tuesday of the following week. By that time, Anna had been released; you and I were discussing information that she could provide to the Stasi, remember?"

"Fine. That's one thing we can't blame on you."

"No. However, after Anna refused my order relative to the classified document and got me a written reprimand, I wished I had."

I looked at him with disgust—I hated this son-of-a-bitch, "What about the Swiss and Austrian passports?"

"The Swiss diplomat was unwilling to share your group's largesse with me, so I reported him to the Stasi. The Austrian consular official was more amenable; he agreed to give me half, once I explained that we could probably get a million dollars cash out of you and Scott."

I'd struggled to stay calm as Thomas revealed one treacherous and/or duplicitous act after another. "At least you didn't compromise the escape tunnel in the churchyard," I said.

"Sure I did. I followed you three to the location of that tunnel and reported it to the Stasi. They took it from there. All I know is that I again screwed up your plans."

"Now let's get to today. Through the listening device in the tank, you learned that we were going to use the tunnel/storm drain route to also extract our loved ones before resealing it."

"That's correct," Thomas said, almost spitting the words at me. "I intended to only take photographs as you brought your people over to the West. I would use those photos to ensure that you three conspirators spent decades in prison for numerous security violations, misuse of government property, dereliction of duty, and failure to follow orders."

"Then why did you jump Robert?" I said calmly.

"You were getting your escapees out," Thomas said, spitting his words back at me. "I especially wanted your wife and daughter to rot in communist hell or even a Stasi prison as further punishment for your transgressions, not live free! Plus revelation of your wrongdoing would certainly ensure that the tunnel and exploitation center became CIA assets!"

"Thomas fucking Lane, I believe that any court in the United States would sentence you to death for what you have just revealed to me. If you are successful in bringing your accusations into a court of law, I hope that Robert, Scott and I get a fair hearing—if we do, I believe that we will be exonerated of any charges that might be made against us. As I told you, I'm letting you live as long as you cooperate from this point on," I said, removing his shackles from the drain pipe and relocking them behind his back.

"We are going to take a short walk," I said. "You must refrain from opening your mouth to utter a word the entire way. Do you believe that I'll kill you if you utter a sound?"

Thomas nodded his head in acknowledgment.

"Once there, your fate will be in your own hands. You'll learn what a confrontation with trained Stasi agents is like. The trophy in your office indicates that you are a sharpshooter with a Browning Special pistol. We'll see how you perform as you save your own life. Is that clear? Now move."

Thomas nodded. Slowly and silently, the two of us walked to the rendezvous point.

On the way, I thought of the German soldiers I'd killed in the war—it was either them or me and my fellow OSS agents or one of our French resistance fighters. The only person I'd ever killed in cold blood was Heinrich Fuchs, AKA Ernst Neumann, a wanted international criminal. But even now, six years later, the grimace on this face as my stiletto found its mark still haunts me at night.

Although Thomas Lane deserves to die, I did not want his dying face added to my nightmares.

Once we were at our destination—the loading dock of a derelict vehicle tire warehouse, I said, "Please stand with your back against this post as I shackle you to it." I then gagged him again. He didn't resist as I explained. "When the Stasi arrive, I'll give your Browning Special back to you. It now has only 12 bullets, so you'll need to conserve them. You'll have a chance to demonstrate your prowess with it in a real life-and-death situation. You'll be right here in the shadows of this doorway, and they will be approaching via the driveway which leads to the loading dock. Study the scene carefully. There are several pieces of discarded junk scattered around, which may provide them with cover as they approach you. The sun will set soon and twilight will last about 45 minutes. Since it is Sunday evening, the Stasi will probably not have more than two or three men available to dispatch to this site."

Now, all we could do was wait for the arrival of our foes. Doubt over the course of action I'd selected gnawed at my resolve. Robert, Scott and I had become a band of brothers during the emotional ordeal we'd experienced in the last few weeks. Erica and I finally had the certainty of a safe and secure future together. If I live up to my promise and ultimately released Thomas fucking Lane, he and his fellow conspirators would attempt and perhaps succeed in ruining the future for all of us. I resolved to let events dictate a solution. Lane's fate was in his hands, not mine—I could only hope for an acceptable result. But as it turned out, my fate was in his hands.

CHAPTER 148

Sunday, November 19, 1961
16:43

THE NOISY TRABANT'S sputtering engine announced the Stasi's arrival on an adjacent street. I kept Thomas covered with one hand as I released his fetters.

First one, then the second, and finally all three Stasi agents, pistols drawn, cautiously entered through the gate that hung partially off of its hinges. At a signal from the Stasi agent in the center, the three spread out and moved slowly in our direction.

I handed Thomas his pistol, while pointing mine at his temple, and whispered, "Take a position just in front and to the side of me in the door. There you will be in a shadow, difficult for the Stasi to discern, but capable of seeing the entire parking area." I was standing behind a steel pillar, hence protected from Stasi gunfire. A slot in the steel pillar provided me a clear view of the driveway.

Silently and slowly Thomas took the firing stance we had been taught in CIA weapons training; he knelt on his right knee, took his weapon in both hands, trigger finger against the front of the guard. Eventually, he would slowly squeeze the trigger when it was time to fire the weapon.

I tensed up and could feel the adrenalin rush that always occurs before an impending encounter with the enemy.

The Stasi took turns scrambling from the protection of one piece of discarded junk to the next. Thomas was a trained professional. He would wait until he could pin all three of them down; then he would fire his first shot. The twilight was beginning to fade as the three Stasi agents moved again and again toward the loading dock. Everyone wanted the confrontation to occur before it got too dark.

Eventually, Thomas took aim where he expected the man on his right to expose himself as he moved forward. I heard Thomas fire his weapon twice. A deafening BANG-BANG occurred, and the barrel of his weapon jerked up slightly each time. Someone cried out the word *scheisse*, followed by an almost imperceptible thud as he hit the ground. The smell of cordite filled the air. My ears rang.

One down, two to go. I was amazed; Thomas is competent in this one area.

Calmly, Thomas repositioned his weapon. It was now pointing toward the place occupied by the Stasi leader. He wanted to make sure they did not rush him now.

Also, he wanted to take out the leader as early as possible—a wise move.

Then something I hadn't anticipated happened. The Stasi used the muzzle flashed from Thomas' weapon to determine where he was; using hand signals, they both fired several rounds at him. One hit my metal post with a reverberating thud; another hit the metal door frame next to Thomas, glanced off, and continued to bounce off surfaces in the warehouse itself. In reaction, Thomas moved to a prone position, crawled forward, and sheltered behind a concrete wall on one side of the loading dock. He now had the two Stasi pinned down because his position was at least 4 feet higher than theirs—they would have to expose themselves to advance or retreat. Again, a very smart move.

Suddenly, the bullets from several Stasi discharges hit the wall in front of Thomas, making a THUDDING sound each time. They were trying to get him to expose himself.

Because he had moved away from the door, Thomas was no longer under my direct control. That could be bad if a confrontation ultimately happened between us. He has 10 bullets left. I had a slight advantage with 13, but he was certainly proficient with a firearm.

When Thomas deliberately took aim and fired two more shots at the man he had taken down, I was surprised; the man had been lying motionless on the ground for some time. Then I remembered our training—"Make sure a dead man is dead—if you don't, you'll be the dead man."

Our foes were probably equipped with standard Stasi arms, the Walther PPK Pistole-38nl; it was the fictional character, James Bond's favorite weapon. The magazine held only 10 rounds; however, our Stasi friends had probably brought at least several extra clips with them. Overall our weapons and theirs were similar and they probably had an advantage in that one area.

Most Stasi vehicles are equipped with two-way radios so it was a good thing the last two were pinned down, otherwise, they could radio for help. But if they did not check-in soon, help would probably be dispatched to determine what had happened to them. Time for this little game I'd orchestrated was running out; nothing was going as I had anticipated. It was probably ill-conceived from the beginning.

The Stasi decided to retreat. So suddenly, both rose in unison. They fired several shots into the wall to keep Thomas from firing his weapon. They ran across an open area that was perhaps 30 feet wide. Thomas rose to a kneeling position and fired rounds so fast that I lost track of the number of shots he expended. Both Stasi agents were almost immediately down.

I moved out of my hiding place and was walking toward Thomas to congratulate him when one of the Stasi agents fired his weapon at Thomas and then at me. His bullets apparently missed Thomas but caught me in the abdomen. I staggered back and managed to sit down on a nearby raised bench. I watched as Thomas allowed the wounded Stasi agent to stagger out of the warehouse complex and down the adjacent street. I mistakenly assumed that he would go after him to ensure that all of them were dead; that was what he was trained to do.

Instead, Thomas turned and walked toward me—his Browning was pointed at my head. My weapon was resting on the bench beside me. As he got nearer, he said, "You dirty son-of-a-bitch. You thought they would kill me. That way you would not have to do it yourself—you are too weak and cowardly to do it yourself. Well, I'm more than willing to finish you off. You and your associates have caused me exceptional grief; now, you at least will get what you deserve."

He positioned his gun near my forehead and pulled the trigger.

CLICK. He tried again several times not believing that the gun was empty. CLICK...CLICK...CLICK. He rushed over to the nearest dead Stasi, grabbed that man's weapon, and was headed back in my direction. I moved to the end of the bench, I raised my gun, rested it on a low wall, took careful aim at his head, and pulled the trigger. The bullet entered his mouth at an upward angle. Brain matter spewed out behind him. He was dead before he hit the ground.

I had eliminated Thomas but was severely wounded. For what seemed like hours, I struggled to stop the bleeding and get enough energy to stagger back to the tunnel. My primary concern was to avoid falling into the hands of the Stasi. By the time I decided to end it all, my gun was out of reach and I was probably too weak to pull the trigger.

The blood flow has slowed—I'm so weak—I've little time now until the end. Thank God the Stasi won't get me. At least my lovely daughter Gretchen and her mother Erica are safe and secure.

As I peacefully drifted off, I recalled what someone had once told me, *"Your life flashes before your eyes just before you die."* Smiling, I remembered another person had added, *"So make sure it's worth watching."* In my mind's eye, I could see Ben, the AP photographer, was again greeting me at the bottom of the metal stairs when I arrived in Berlin in November of 1946—almost exactly fifteen years ago.

For a brief moment, a sharp noise like a pistol shot startled me, almost bringing me back to the present, but soon I faded back to Gatow Airport far in the past...Ben was again negotiating the number of cigarettes with a taxi driver...Then the present returned as faint sounds kept getting louder—someone moved cautiously into the courtyard and toward me. I could no longer raise my arm to view my watch and had no idea how much time had passed. My heart sank. The Stasi had arrived before I could die! They'll rush me to the hospital and save me for special treatment in their famous interrogation rooms and torture chambers. My run of good luck has finally ended.

Slowly turning my head toward the sound, I finally saw Robert crawling toward me. "I need to get you to the hospital," he said, cradling my head in his lap. "Where's Thomas?"

"Dead...perfect angle...look like...he shot himself...coward...

I took…Stasi bullet…bad," I gasped, then coughed up blood and lost consciousness.

The next thing I remember was Robert's face staring down at me as he and someone else were carrying me on a plank of some form. I smiled but fainted again when the Chief lifted and placed me over his shoulder.

Eventually, a ghost-like apparition said, "There is a severely wounded man in the back of this van. Take him to MEDDAC Emergency Room immediately. Then bring the vehicle back here, clean it up, resume your duties and then forget all about this."

"Yes, sir," one of the buildings' guards whose voice I recognized said.

CHAPTER 149

Sunday-Thursday, November 26-30, 1961

SEVERAL TIMES, I was in a tunnel surrounded by a misty, gray ether; there was a light ahead as I floated above an indistinct floor, weightless and calm. Each time I got near the light I felt a slight pinch in my right arm.

This time there was no pain, just a familiar voice that seemed above me, asking in English, "How long will it be before he regains consciousness?"

"A few minutes. His vital signs are good and he is coming out of the induced coma."

"Good. I'll wait."

Groggily, I moved toward the light that was penetrating my eyelids. First, I sensed the strong smell of hospital disinfectants. Then the faint, but constant din of people moving up and down the nearby corridors. Conversations in German reached my consciousness.

I'm in a hospital. I survived. I'm alive. Are Gretchen and Erica okay? Surely, Robert and Scott will take care of them until I'm able. I can go back to sleep.

Startled awake by laughter in the adjacent corridor, I opened my eyes and saw an acoustic ceiling above me. Fearing that movement would hurt, I assessed the tubes and wires that were hanging from my body; my limbs were very heavy, resisting my efforts to move. Still, I didn't feel any pain, just stiffness. My midriff was compressed inside a wide layer of bandages. Pain and brief nausea followed my effort to take a deep breath.

Be cautious! The rescue by Robert and the Chief may have been just a dream. The voices in the background are speaking German. The Stasi may have you and perhaps are working a ruse to get you to compromise yourself or reveal information about the CIA or the tunnel.

From out of my field-of-view, the same familiar voice said in English, "Kurt, old buddy, I was afraid you were a goner." A face I recognized appeared above me. "They put you in a coma so your body could heal. Before you say anything, let's get the doctor in to have a look at you."

I finally recognized the voice: my longtime friend and CIA associate Brandon Williams. "Where am I?" I asked groggily.

"In a hospital in Zurich, Switzerland. We had you medivacked here. I'll explain it all to you as soon as you're strong enough. I flew to Berlin as soon as I heard you'd survived." Bending over me, Brandon whispered, "Someone had to be at your side to ensure that you didn't reveal all of your secrets to your uncleared doctors and nurses at the military hospital in Berlin and then again here; I relieved Ian of that responsibility as soon as I could get to Berlin."

"But..."

"—We'll move you to our clinic outside of the city tomorrow, and I'll be able to explain everything then. For now, just relax and say nothing."

"Erica and Gretchen?"

"They are flying with Anna's entire family to California today. Don't worry, everyone is safe. Now get some rest."

*

Two days later, Brandon and I were seated at a large table in my clinic room. This was the first time we could talk freely about what had happened.

"This is a secure clinic, where the CIA's sick or injured agents from Europe can be brought to recover," he said. "Your injuries were so severe that you had to have several operations in the University of Zurich Hospital before you could be brought here."

"Before I left the hospital, the doctors said that I'd make a full recovery," I informed him. Then I asked, "Why aren't Gretchen and Erica here with me?"

Brandon spent some time explaining exactly what had happened in Berlin after I was incapacitated. "So, you're telling me that Gretchen and

Erica plus all fourteen of Scott and Anna's family escaped safely, but the Stasi sent a death squad to eliminate them at the safehouse Scott rented in Charlottenburg?" I recounted. "And during the exchange of gunfire between the Stasi and West Berlin Police, Robert's Anna—unpretentious, sweet, but actually tough as nails Anna, used a police van to crush three Stasi agents including that rat bastard Deter Holburg! And after that?"

"Everyone was moved to the executive wing of the Hilton, where the West Berlin Police could protect them," Brandon answered.

"And they all ate Thanksgiving dinner in the presidential suite at the hotel."

"American style—turkey with all of the trimmings."

"And then last Friday they all attended your funeral. It was a rousing tribute. Scott and Robert paid for a gravestone that they announced will say:

To Be Born Free is an Accident
To Live Free is a Privilege
To Die Free is a Responsibility"

"That clearly shows how much they all loved and respected you," Brandon said continuing.

"When are you going to explain why you told everyone that I was dead, and had something or someone buried in my grave?"

"We'll get to that soon," Brandon said. "The body of an indigent man from West Germany was made available by our German friends in their Security Service and was placed in your grave."

"You indicated that last Saturday, Erica and Gretchen left Germany in the company of Anna's family."

"That's correct. The Stasi had placed everyone in that safe house on a 'kill on sight list,' and also have offered a ten thousand Deutsche mark reward for each of them. They didn't take kindly to having six agents killed and one arrested in a twenty-four hour period."

"Where are they going?"

"Robert's grandfather has a huge farm and two large ranch houses. They're staying with them until they can get settled into that area north of San Francisco. The package of information you gave Erica will mean that they won't have to worry financially. We believe they'll be untraceable, and hence safe there."

Next, Brandon asked questions about Thomas's death and I told him the truth—exactly what had happened, not my fabricated version, and concluded by saying, "He was a subhuman who deserved to die. If I'd let him live, he'd have made my military friends and my life a misery. I have no regrets—I'd do it again in a heartbeat!" I just wished my conscience was as unfettered as I made it seem to Brandon.

After he said nothing in response, I asked, "Did the communists discover the tunnel?"

"No. Robert and the Chief managed to seal the tunnel, hide the wooden forms, and return to West Berlin without incident, only a few hours after the original plan. All of the intercept stations and exploitation facilities in 'the building' will soon be fully operational. Robert and his crew will finish construction in the next month or so."

"Are Prince and Andreas safe?" I asked.

"I've been told that they are still in the same positions that they held before recent events."

"You still haven't told me why I'm here and not with my family."

"The Stasi have placed a $100,000 bounty on your head—dead or alive. Your billfold and CIA identity card were in your overcoat, plus your blood and fingerprints were everywhere. They believe you are directly responsible for the death of three of their agents. If you set foot on the continent of Europe, your days would probably be numbered. You might not even be safe in the States."

"Can't you provide Erica, Gretchen, and me new identities?"

"We'll ensure they're safe for now. However, we've something else in mind for you. First, you need to know that the agency has been purged of the nine involved in the conspiracy against you."

"That's good news."

"And we have a new overall director, John A. McCone. Dulles was finally forced out as a result of the Bay of Pigs fiasco. We also have a new operations director. I'm now a Senior Deputy Operations Director. Almost everyone above me is a political appointee. I'm one of the senior professional CIA agents. This will allow me to protect you from any fallout over the death of Agent Lane and those Stasi guys. Your action was not approved in any way, shape, or form. You could easily be in big trouble. But I'll protect you."

"From your tone and tenor, I perceive that you want something in return."

"I'd like you to reciprocate by accepting an exceptionally dangerous special assignment. It will be at least one year in duration and involve working undercover within the Soviet Union. Your appearance will be changed via plastic surgery. Your Russian language skills and operational know-how will be put to severe tests every day. It'll be risky, but you might well prevent World War III. Soviet Premier Khrushchev is a bombastic gambler. We have a source high up in their government who is willing to give us advanced information on the premier's actions, motives, and methods."

"So, what you're saying is that an observer to a poker game will be looking over player Khrushchev's shoulder and providing information about what cards he holds. It's easy to win under that set of circumstances."

"Your job will be to serve as a safe conduit for that information. I'll provide details if you're willing to accept the assignment."

"You leave me little choice. And I have only one condition."

"What's that?"

"You must personally inform Erica that I'm alive, on special assignment with an American government agency, and will retire, joining her permanently in less than eighteen months. She can decide if Gretchen should be told or not."

"Done. Now let me give you some background because we don't have much time…"

The third volume of the trilogy, *The Berlin Tunnel—Another Crisis* continues the story. Available in 2021.

AUTHORS POSTSCRIPT

By 1946, when our story begins, Berlin is just starting to rebuild after the devastating damage it suffered during the Second World War. The shooting war was over, but the ideological clash between the communist and free world that became known as the Cold War was just beginning. Berlin was located 110 miles behind what Winston Churchill called the Iron Curtain; it soon became the epicenter of the Cold War. This war was fought in the shadows of side streets and back alleys of Berlin by spies, agents, operatives, and double agents. Their lives were not as exciting as the adventures of Agent 007, James Bond, but they helped preserve our way of life as surely as any other soldier on the front lines of any battle America ever fought.

In 1965, while I was training as a US Air Force Signals Intelligence Officer, I read a report on Operation Gold/Stopwatch at the base classified document technical library. Even though this was almost eight years after the fact, this project was still classified Top Secret codeword. I used the building of this tunnel as the basis for my first novel, *The Berlin Tunnel— A Cold War Thriller*. This is the second volume of what will eventually become The Berlin Tunnel trilogy. One part of this novel recounts how the Operation Gold/Stopwatch tunnel was built by the CIA into East Berlin in the years 1954-1956. That description and much of this novel is based on numerous recently published nonfiction books that recount the battle for Berlin and the world between the KGB, GRU, and Stasi on one side and the CIA and MI6 on the other.

In 1968, I spent five days in West Berlin. I could not go into the East because of my security clearance. I did climb up on a platform located at the wall and looked over into East Berlin. I saw East German troops patrolling a wide strip of no man's land and an expanse of uniformly gray, nondescript buildings. I turned around and looked back at the new shiny high-rise office and apartment buildings of West Berlin—an excellent example of the superiority of capitalism and a free society. For perhaps the first time in history, a country's border defenses were being devoted primarily to keeping its citizens from leaving. It was clear to me that the entire communist block was a giant prison. I knew why I was serving my country.

During the years 1948 through 1961, an average of 200,000 Germans voted against communism with their feet by leaving East Germany and East Berlin for the West. After the Berlin wall/fence was closed on August 13, 1961, the flood of people was reduced to a trickle. In the 28 years from 1961 through 1989, only 30,000 people managed to escape over, under, or around those barriers. Another 120,000 managed to escape by defecting once they were allowed to leave East Germany for sporting, business, or other approved travel. These two groups together amounted to almost five percent of the population of that communist satellite.

The Cold War started in 1946 and did not end until the Soviet Union splintered into thirteen republics in 1991. However, the danger of war diminished year by year after the Cuban Missile crisis in 1962. In the end, the façade of prosperity that the communists had presented to the world collapsed unto itself; thus substantiating the superiority of the free enterprise system and democracy.

ACKNOWLEDGMENTS

I owe a debt of gratitude to a great number of people. To begin, I'd like to recognize my mentor and primary critic, Karen Black. She is a published author, who helped me by reviewing several versions of my first novel and performed that same role for this, the second.

Dale Bardin agreed to read the "finished master" of this novel. Once that review was complete, he willingly devoted untold hours helping me improve what you have read in many different ways.

Sue Compton agreed to be beta readers and found an embarrassingly large number of grammatical and even a few spelling errors. Her efforts were essential to me providing this readable error-free book. She also completely filled in the Beta Readers Checklist making several suggestions I incorporated into the novel. These included the observation that maps would help the reader understand where events were occurring as the novel progressed.

Members of the Scribblers, a North San Diego writer's group heard me read numerous excerpts from the book and provided valuable feedback. Terry Badger, leader of the Scribblers, and also a published author, served as an early proofreader.

Diana Glimm, my ever-patient bridge partner, was an early reader who made numerous suggestions for improving this novel.

Other beta readers include Ann Keeran, Jean Jantz, Paul Pyka, and Raymond Curtis. All of their comments helped me improve the story in a myriad of ways.

www.ingramcontent.com/pod-product-compliance
Lightning Source LLC
Chambersburg PA
CBHW021826090426
42811CB00032B/2034/J